Jules William Press — JWP

THIS BOOK

The *Saga of the People of Weapon's Fjord* (*Vápnfirðinga Saga*) is a masterpiece of saga telling. It recounts blood feud in Iceland during the Viking Age and takes the reader deep into struggles for power and honor in Iceland's East Fjords. Two young chieftains begin as inseparable friends. As they mature, however, they slide into bitter competition for regional dominance. The contest continues into the next generation, entangling the chieftains' two sons and spreading across Iceland's northern and eastern regions. As one learns, honor and friendship have many interpretations but revenge is mostly expected.

This new translation is a bilingual edition. It offers all the tools necessary to read a major Icelandic saga in both English and the original Old Norse. Each Old Norse saga chapter has its own specific vocabulary, so that the reader is freed from dependence on separate dictionaries. Notes and discussions explain language, geography, law, and society. An extensive series of maps, freshly drawn for this edition, offer an accurate picture of the landscape. After completing the *Saga of the People of Weapon's Fjord*, you will be equipped to read any of Iceland's longer sagas.

For more about sagas, Old Norse language, runes, and the Viking Age, visit our website: www.oldnorse.org.

ABOUT THE TRANSLATORS OF
THE *SAGA OF THE PEOPLE OF WEAPON'S FJORD*

Jesse Byock is distinguished research professor of Old Norse and Medieval Scandinavian at the University of California, Los Angeles (UCLA). He specializes in the study of the Viking World, its sagas, history, and archaeology and is a professor at the UCLA Cotsen Institute of Archaeology. He earned his Ph.D. from Harvard University after studying in France, Iceland, and Sweden. In Iceland, he directs the Mosfell Archaeological Project (MAP) and is a professor at the University of Iceland (Háskóli Íslands) in the Department of History and the Programs of Medieval Icelandic and Viking Studies. He is the author of *Viking Age Iceland* and books, articles, and saga translations.

Randall Gordon is a specialist in historical linguistics of Celtic and Germanic Languages, with concentrations on the development and grammar of Old Norse and Old Irish. He received his Ph.D. in Indo-European Studies from UCLA.

Jules William Press publishes a range of books about the Viking Age. Its series of Old Norse primers, grammars, texts, studies, and audio pronunciation albums answer the needs of the modern student, instructor, and self-learner. The books and materials are purposely affordable, and in many instances with free Answer Keys on our website, oldnorse.org. JWP also publishes a series of novels, eBooks, and audio books as well as archaeological reports about the Viking Age.

www.oldnorse.org & www.juleswilliampress.com

SAGA OF THE PEOPLE OF WEAPON'S FJORD
(*VÁPNFIRÐINGA SAGA*)
A NEW ENGLISH TRANSLATION WITH OLD NORSE TEXT, VOCABULARY, AND MAPS

by

Jesse Byock and Randall Gordon

A Volume in the
Viking Language Old Norse Icelandic Series

Jules William Press JWP

oldnorse.org
juleswilliampress.com

Jules William Press
www.juleswilliampress.com
www.oldnorse.org

Saga of the People of Weapon's Fjord (Vápnfirðinga Saga): A New English Translation with Old Norse Text, Vocabulary, and Maps

ISBN-13: 978-1-953947-13-0

Cover design by Basil Arnould Price
Runestone design by Kalle 'Runristare' Dahlberg www.runristare.se

Printed in Cambria

Keywords: Old Norse, Old Icelandic; Icelandic saga, family saga, Icelandic, Viking, Scandinavia, grammar, Viking language, feud, blood feud, Old Norse Vocabulary, Old Norse word, Weapon's Fjord

PREFACE

THIS DUAL LANGUAGE SAGA EDITION

This edition of the *Saga of the People of Weapon's Fjord* provides a new English translation in a bilingual format. It offers all the tools necessary to read a complete saga in both English and the original Old Norse. The rear of the book contains a full vocabulary and a comprehensive glossary of persons and places mentioned in the saga. Referring to this glossary, while reading the saga makes it possible to quickly locate people, groups, places, and objects that are mentioned early in the saga but sometimes only briefly. The combination of English translation, original Old Norse text, and targeted Old Norse vocabulary is supplemented with maps, notes, and cultural sections. The modern reader is invited to explore the subtleties and wonders of an Icelandic saga.

The *Saga of the People of Weapon's Fjord* is written in Old Icelandic, the dialect of Old Norse spoken in Iceland during the Middle Ages. Readers new to the sagas and specialists alike will be pleased to note that the text in this edition has not been simplified or shortened. We have employed the version of the saga that appears in the *Íslenzk fornrit* series edited in Iceland by the noted Icelandic historian Jón Jóhannesson.

THE MOST FREQUENT WORDS IN THE SAGAS

Word frequency is a key to learning Old Norse, and this saga volume in the *Viking Language Old Norse Icelandic Series* is designed around a word-frequency learning strategy. The symbol ❖ in the Vocabulary marks the 246 most frequently used words found in the sagas. The *Saga of the People in Weapon's Fjord* (*Vápnfirðinga saga* is an ideal text for this learning method since it includes almost all of the 246 words. The only words missing are a few numerals and the noun *vísa* 'poetry'. Of importance, these 246 most common words make up one quarter of *Vápnfirðinga saga*'s vocabulary. Learn them and you can almost read this saga.

The importance of these 246 words cannot be over-estimated. When we look beyond this specific saga, these 246 words make up more than 80 percent of all words in the family sagas. For this reason, we recommend concentrating principally on these words. For a full listing of these most common words, see the 'Word Frequency Section' in Chapter 1 of *Viking Language 1: Learn Old Norse, Runes and Icelandic Sagas* (Jules William Press) and Appendix 2 ('Word Frequency') of the same volume.

TABLE OF CONTENTS

TABLE OF CULTURE SECTIONS

TABLE OF FIGURES

TABLE OF MAPS

ACKNOWLEDGMENTS

We heartily thank Gunnlaugur Ingólfsson at the Lexicographical Institute (Stofnun Árna Magnússonar í íslenskum fræðum), Professors Helgi Þorláksson and Gunnar Karlsson at Háskóli Íslands (University of Iceland), and Dr. Ilya Sverdlov at the University of Helsinki. These scholars generously read drafts of the book and offered invaluable suggestions and edits. We also warmly thank our students, friends, and colleagues Kevin Elliott, Jonathan Grove, Magnús Lyngdal Magnússon, Clare Gillis, Meg Morrow, and Basil A. Price. Likewise, we thank Valgeir Sigurðsson, his granddaughter Þórný Perrot, and Guðmundur Ólafur Ingvarsson for their great help and work with the maps.

A NOTE ON THE MAPS

This edition of the *Saga of the People of Weapon's* Fjord comes with a full complement of maps. They display the movements of individuals and groups as the action shifts from coastal lowlands to inland fjord areas and up into the surrounding highlands. Guðmundur Ólafur Ingvarsson, a superb Icelandic cartographer, worked closely with us and drew these accurate maps. Ilya Sverdlov revised the graphic settings.

The ancient mountain paths traveled in the saga are little known today, but by great good fortune Valgeir Sigurðsson and his granddaughter Þórný Perrot were able to provide this knowledge. Valgeir was raised in Vopnafjörður (the modern Icelandic spelling of Old Norse Vápnafjǫrðr). As a boy, Valgeir herded sheep throughout the region and years later when Jesse spoke with him the horse trails across the heaths and through the mountains were still fresh in his mind.

INTRODUCTION
FEUD, FRIENDSHIP, AND HONOR IN ICELAND'S EAST FJORDS

Each of the wise should wield his power in moderation;
He will find that no one is foremost when stout men gather.
— Sayings of the High One (*Hávamál*, 64)

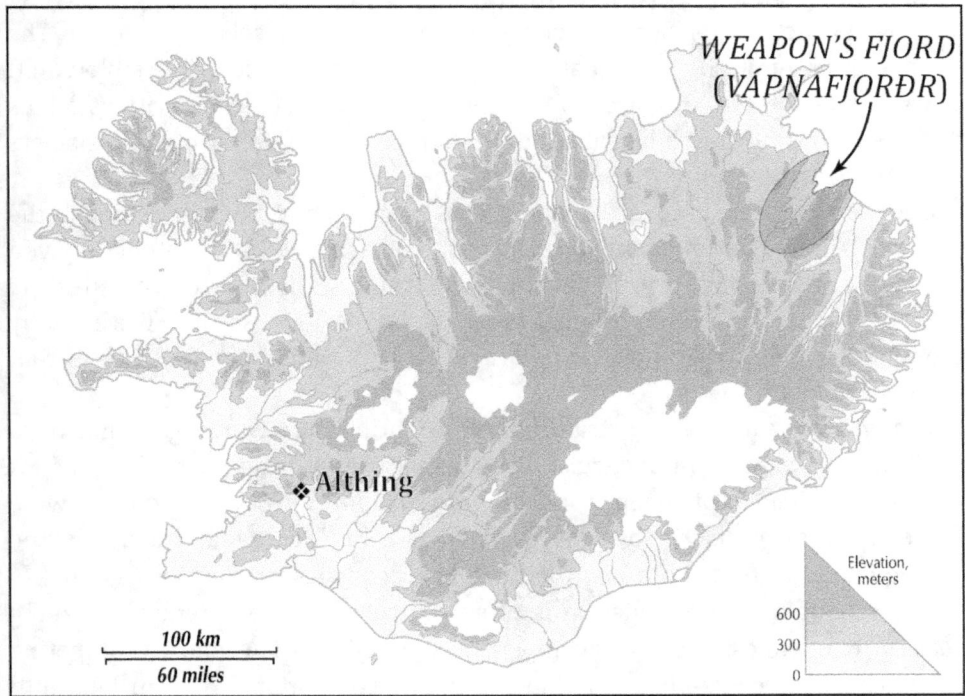

Map 1. The *Saga of the People of Weapon's Fjord* takes place in Iceland's East Fjords. In Old Norse terminology, a fjord (*fjǫrðr*) is the entire region starting with the coastal waters and continuing up into the inland side valleys. These inland fjord 'dales' (*dalir*) are landlocked by the surrounding highlands and mountains. Only a few mostly mountain paths lead out from Weapon's Fjord to nearby fjords and other regions of Iceland

The *Saga of the People of Weapon's Fjord* was likely first written in the 12th or 13th century, but the core story is based on events from the late 10th century. Called *Vápnfirðinga saga* in Icelandic, the saga is set in Weapon's Fjord (Vápnafjǫrðr) a major valley system in Iceland's East Fjords (*Austfirðir*). In particular, *Vápnfirðinga saga* recounts events in the lives of local chieftains called *goðar* (singular *goði*) and free farmers called *bœndr* (singular *bóndi*).

When first thinking of Iceland, people sometimes assume that it is a relatively small island. In fact, Iceland's land mass is roughly two-thirds the size of England

and Scotland together, and the events of the *Saga of the People of Weapon's Fjord* extend over a wide expanse of Iceland's eastern and northern regions. In some ways, *Vápnfirðinga saga* remains a living text since the coastal and inland landscapes of Weapon's Fjord remain today little changed from the saga's Viking Age setting. The saga describes two generations of closely related chieftain families struggling for power and status within Weapon's Fjord and many 21st-century farms and places retain the names that appear in the saga.

In the early 800s, towards the start of the Viking Age, Iceland was an uninhabited island. It lay west of Norway far out in the Atlantic and was largely unknown. Exactly when Scandinavian seamen discovered Iceland is unclear. The discoverers seem to have been a mix of walrus hunters, ships' crews blown off course, and explorers in search of new lands. Iceland's medieval writings tell us that the country came to be called Iceland on account of its forbidding glaciers and long winters.

Once Iceland was discovered, immigrants came mostly from Norway and the overseas Viking Age colonies especially in the British Isles. Most settlers arrived during the mid-9th and early 10th centuries, and among them were a considerable number of people of Celtic origin, especially women. The settlers were led by prominent individuals called *landnámsmenn* ('land-taking-people', a term that includes women).

Vápnfirðinga saga offers extraordinary insight into the workings of northern medieval community. In particular the saga explores loyalties and animosities that drive exchanges of violence and attempts at compromise.[1] It recounts a wide range of choices faced by people involved in bloodfeud, including the consequences of friendship and the need for reconciliation. As the saga makes clear, arriving at a reconciliation is often difficult because it requires making peace with enemies. The saga's competition and hatred between two competing but closely related families continues for two generations and hardens into almost intractable animosity. The final episodes of the saga can be examined as a study, or even a guide, to peacemaking in the face of calls for vengeance.

Vápnfirðinga saga's main characters belong to the second, third, and fourth generations of Iceland's founding families, but the saga itself, as do many sagas, begins with a brief account of the fjord's earliest 9th- and early 10th-century settlers. From other medieval Icelandic writings, including *The Book of Settlements* (*Landnámabók*), we know that Vápnafjǫrðr is named after the early settler Eyvindr vápni. Eyvindr is a common name, but his nickname *vápni* is unusual. It derives from the noun *vápn*, which means 'the weapon' or 'the weapon maker'. In Icelandic and Norwegian sources, the nickname *vápni* refers only to Eyind, a man about whom we know very little.

The initial conflict in *Vápnfirðinga saga* stems from a dispute over the goods of

---

[1] Differences between old and modern Icelandic spellings are slight. For example, Weapon's Fjord is Vápnafjǫrðr in Old Icelandic and Vopnafjörður in Modern Icelandic. This saga edition employs Old Icelandic, that is Old Norse spelling.

a rich Norwegian merchant. Norwegians are frequently mentioned in the family sagas, and their recurrent appearance reflects the bond that Icelanders had with Norway as the mother country. From Iceland's 9th-century settlement into the later Middle Ages, Norway remained Iceland's major trading and cultural partner.

The Norwegian merchant was killed because of greed among Icelanders for his foreign merchandise. As the saga makes clear avarice has numerous sides to it, and as the narrative unfolds, additional questions of honor and ethics frequently come to the fore. Honor and ethics in the sagas are tricky concepts. They are closely tied to banal issues such as maintaining property, insuring wealth, upholding status, and exacting revenge.

In *Vápnfirðinga saga*, issues of honor carry powerful signals. In particular, loss of honor indicates that an individual is incapable of defending his or her property. For a chieftain or *goði*, such a loss, as we see in *Vápnfirðinga saga*, becomes a public announcement that the chieftain is unable to carry out expected responsibilities on behalf of his followers called thingmen. That is the men who follow and support him at the freemen's assemblies called 'things' (*þing* both sing and plural).

Friendship and kinship arrangements play large roles in *Vápnfirðinga saga*. Farmers and chieftains are frequently drawn into conflicts through contractual friendship agreements termed *vinfengi*.[1] Brodd-Helgi and Geitir, the two chieftains who begin the feud, rely on *vinfengi* to augment the support of their followers and thingmen. Through *vinfengi* agreements, chieftains such as Geitir and Brodd-Helgi are seen in the saga expanding their networks of obligations. At times, the survival of chieftains and their thingmen depends on their skills in establishing new ties of friendship as well as maintaining old ones. In particular, leaders employ *vinfengi* in order to create the type of political alliances necessary to influence legal decisions.[2] More so than in many sagas, the disputes in *Vápnfirðinga saga* focus on control of people rather than on acquisition of land. The saga is in many ways a fascinating study of friendship and kinship gone sour.

The Saga of the People of Weapon's Fjord is classed as a family saga. Depending on how one counts them, thirty or so family sagas (often called *Íslendinga sögur* or 'Sagas of the Icelanders') have survived from Iceland's Middle Ages. These mostly realistic-sounding prose stories appeared throughout the different regions of Iceland during the 12th and 13th centuries, that is shortly after the Icelanders mastered reading and writing in a Latin-based alphabet. The family sagas tell how early Icelanders lived and died. They record whether individuals, about whom we would otherwise know almost nothing, were successful or not.

As a large collection of literature, the family sagas lay bare for us the values and norms of Iceland's culture. As in *Vápnfirðinga saga*, choices facing individuals are often described through the lenses of different social strata. The inclusion of

---

[1] *Vinfengi*, meaning 'contractual or political friendship', was different from *vinátta* referring to 'personal, loving friendship'.

[2] Similar issues connected with a somewhat similar feud between two chieftains, Arnkell goði and Snorri goði, in *Eyrbyggja saga* are discussed more fully in a chapter in *Viking Age Iceland*.

varying viewpoints is an aspect of saga telling that distinguishes Iceland's narratives from other medieval literatures. Within Weapon's Fjord, quarrels simmer between the *Krossvíkingar*, the people from the coastal farmstead of

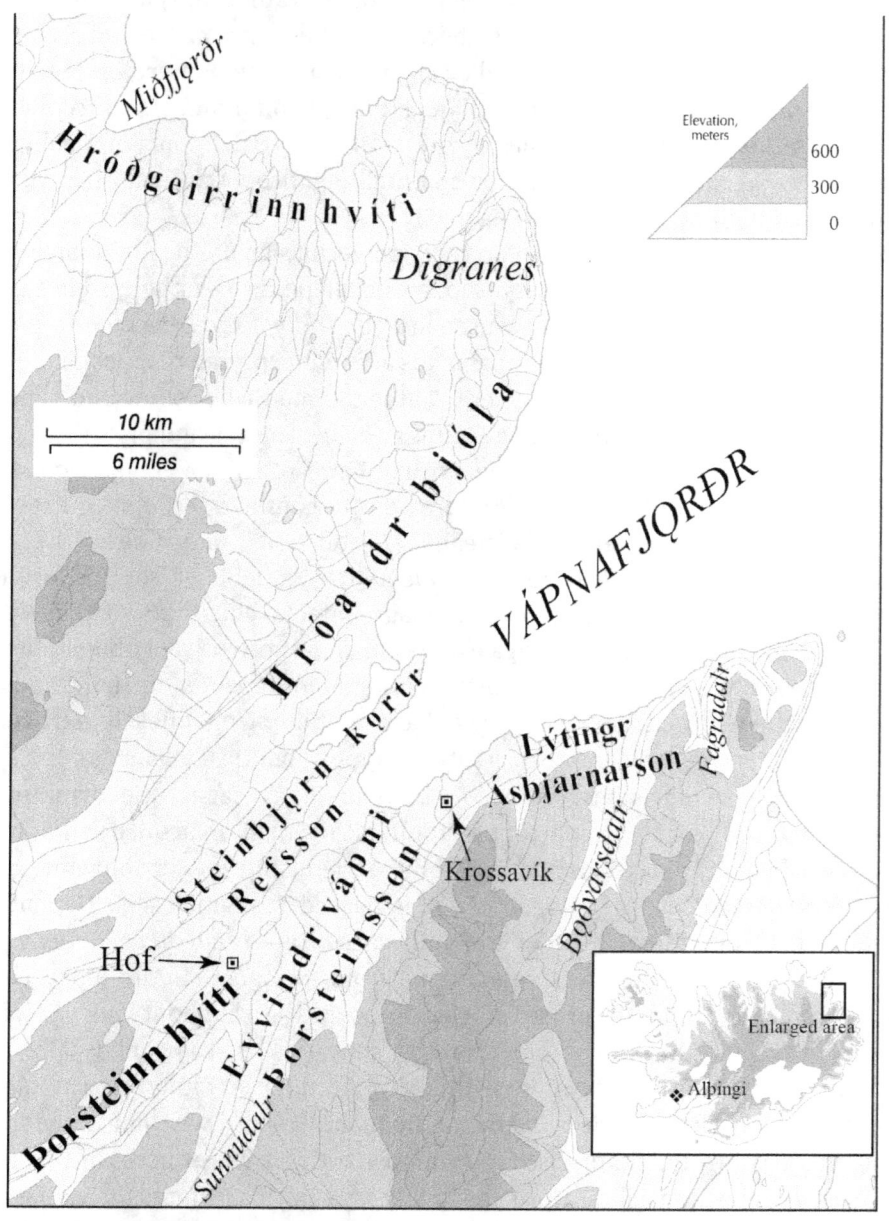

Map 2. Land Claims in Weapon's Fjord (*Vápnafjǫrðr*) from the 9th-Century Settlement of Iceland (the *landnám*). Weapon's Fjord is named after its first settler, Eyvind the Weapon (Eyvindr vápni). The feuding 10th-century chieftains Brodd-Helgi and Geitir are descended from the settlers Thorstein the White (Þorsteinn hvíti) and Lýtingr Ásbjarnarson. Steinbjorn Sturdy (Steinbjǫrn kǫrtr), whose family supports Geitir, lived in Sunnudalr, the South Valley.

Krossavík led by Geitir, and the *Hofsverjar*, the people from the inland farmstead of Hof led by Brodd-Helgi. The two chieftains' establishments employ different subsistence strategies. The *Krossvíkingar* rely principally on marine resources, including offshore fishing. The *Hofsverjar* survive by herding sheep and cattle on the surrounding lowland and highland grasslands. The people at Hof also fish for salmon in the Hof River (Hofsá) that passes their farmstead as it runs down through the valley to the sea. The Hof River remains to this day, among Iceland's richest salmon rivers.

Kross in the place name Krossavík may mean 'cross' or 'crucifix' and *vík* means 'bay'. Krossavík or 'Cross Bay' indicates that this ship's landing site was marked by a cross and perhaps that the earliest settlers were Christians. The word *Hof* can have the meaning of a pagan temple, and this connection is perhaps a factor in the original name of the Hof farmstead. The names of these farmstead date back to the first *landnámsmenn* and may indicate that one of the two rival families, the Krossvíkingar, were originally Christian while the other, the *Hofsverjar*, believed in the Norse gods. The saga, written down in later Christian times, makes nothing of this difference, but the religious distinctions may have been understood as significant to the original saga audience.

BACKGROUND TO THE SAGA

Vápnfirðinga saga is one of a series of family sagas and short stories (*þættir*, sing *þáttr*) about 10th-century families in Weapon's Fjord. By good fortune, two other narratives from this series, the *Saga of Thorstein the White* (*Þorsteins saga hvíta*) and the *Tale of Thorstein Staff Struck* (*Þorsteins þáttr stangarhǫggs*)[1] survive. *Vápnfirðinga saga* picks up the trail of events narrated in the *Saga of Thorstein the White*, and the author of *Vápnfirðinga saga* may have known the *Saga of Thorstein the White*, which describes the settlement of Weapon's Fjord in a way that fills in the back-story of people and families in the *Saga of the People of Weapon's Fjord*.

Thorstein the White's Saga opens with the passage given below describing prominent Norwegian forbearers and then provides information about individuals mentioned at the beginning of *Vápnfirðinga saga*. These *landnámsmenn* include Thorstein the White, Steinbjorn Sturdy, and Steinbjorn's uncle Eyvindr the Weapon.

With the following information from the *Saga of Thorstein the White* and a short explanation of what happened to Thorstein's son Thorgils, the reader has all that is needed to begin reading the *Saga of the People of Weapon's Fjord*, including insight into the hard-nosed financing of Icelandic farming:

> A man was named Olvir the White. He was the son of Asvald, son of
> Gongu-Hrolf, son of Oxen-Thorir. He was a landed man [*lendr maðr*] in
> Norway and lived in Naumadal. He retreated in the face of Earl Hakon

---

[1] The *Tale of Thorstein Staff Struck* portrays a conflict between Killer-Bjarni (the chieftain from Hof who is the son of Brodd-Helgi) and Thorstein Staff-Struck, a local farmer in Weapon's Fjord skilled at weapons. See *The Tale of Thorstein Staff-Struck* (*Þorsteins þáttr stangarhǫggs*): *A New English Translation with Old Norse Text, Vocabulary and Notes*, Jules William Press, 2023.

at Yrjar [a district in Norway, the site of a battle] and died there.

He [Olvir] had only one son, who was named Thorstein and was called Thorstein the White. Thorstein left the country immediately after his father's death. He went out to Iceland with all his goods and landed his ship in Weapon's Fjord. But by then, the *landnám* ['settlement'] was over throughout all Iceland.

That man, who was called Steinbjorn, lived at the farmstead of Hof in Weapon's Fjord. He was called Steinbjorn Sturdy, and his uncle Eyvind [Eyvindr vápni 'Eyvind the Weapon'] had given him all the land between the Weapon's Fjord River [*Vápnafjarðarár*] and the Westdale River [*Vesturdalsár*]. Steinbjorn was a wasteful farmer [*eyzlumaðr mikill*].

When Thorstein learned that all the available land was already taken, he went to Steinbjorn and bought land from him. Thorstein built a farm at Toptavoll [*Toptavellir* 'Topta Plains'] and lived there for several years. He amassed wealth and livestock and became well respected. He had not been living there long before he decided to look for a wife and asked for that woman who was named Ingibjorg, the daughter of Hrogeir Hrafnsson the White. He got her, and with this woman, he had five children. His sons were Onund, Thord, and Thorgils. His daughters were called Thorbjorg and Thora. Thorgils was an especially promising young man.

Thorstein amassed considerable wealth, while Steinbjorn's wealth diminished. Finally, Steinbjorn went to Thorstein and asked him for a loan. Thorstein agreed to lend him money. Steinbjorn continued borrowing and exhausting wealth until Thorstein found Steinbjorn's credit unreliable and the possibility of repayment doubtful. And so, he called in the loan.

The end of their transaction was that Steinbjorn paid Thorstein by assigning to him the estate of Hof. Thorstein now moved to Hof, and he bought himself a chieftaincy (*goðorð*). Thorstein then became one of the most important leaders [*inn mesti sveitarhofðingi*] in the district.

Following the above introduction, the *Saga of Thorstein the White* recounts that Thorstein lived at Hof for many years until his wife Ingibjorg died. He became old, his eyesight failed, and Thorgils, Thorstein's promising son, took over the management of the Hof farmstead. Among Thorgils children was a promising boy named Helgi (later to be called Brodd-Helgi). But Thorgils, while still a young man, was killed in a feud, and Thorstein was forced to once again take on the management of the Hof lands. Now blind and feeble with age, Thorstein, raised Helgi, his strong-willed young grandson. This is how we find Thorstein the White and Brodd-Helgi at the opening of the *Saga of the People of Weapon's Fjord*. We also meet the family of Steinbjorn, who support Geitir against Brodd-Helgi.

MANUSCRIPTS AND THE LACUNA

Vápnfirðinga saga is preserved in several 16th- and 17th-century (and later) handwritten paper copies of a now lost vellum (calfskin) manuscript from the 14th or 15th century. Today, only one page of the older medieval vellum manuscript still exists. Beginning in the late 15th and early 16th century, Icelanders began copying older medieval skin manuscripts onto the pages of inexpensive, manufactured blank paper books imported to Iceland from Northern Europe. By good fortune, the paper copies of *Vápnfirðinga saga* were made when the vellum manuscript was still intact, and the saga is complete apart from a small gap called the 'lacuna' and a section of damaged text at the end of Chapter 13.

The lacuna exists in all paper copies of *Vápnfirðinga saga* where two pages from the medieval vellum manuscript are missing. The presence of this lacuna in all the paper copies implies that before the 16th- and 17th-century paper copyists started their work after the older skin manuscript was already missing these pages. By good fortune, part of the missing lacuna section was found in the 19th century, when a single leaf of the original vellum manuscript was discovered.[1] This current bilingual edition of *Vápnfirðinga saga* follows the saga text in the Icelandic *Íslenzk fornrit, Austfirðinga saga* edition vol. XI (1950), whose editor Jón Jóhannesson drew rom the manuscripts: AM 162 C fol; Stockh. Papp. fol nr. 35;

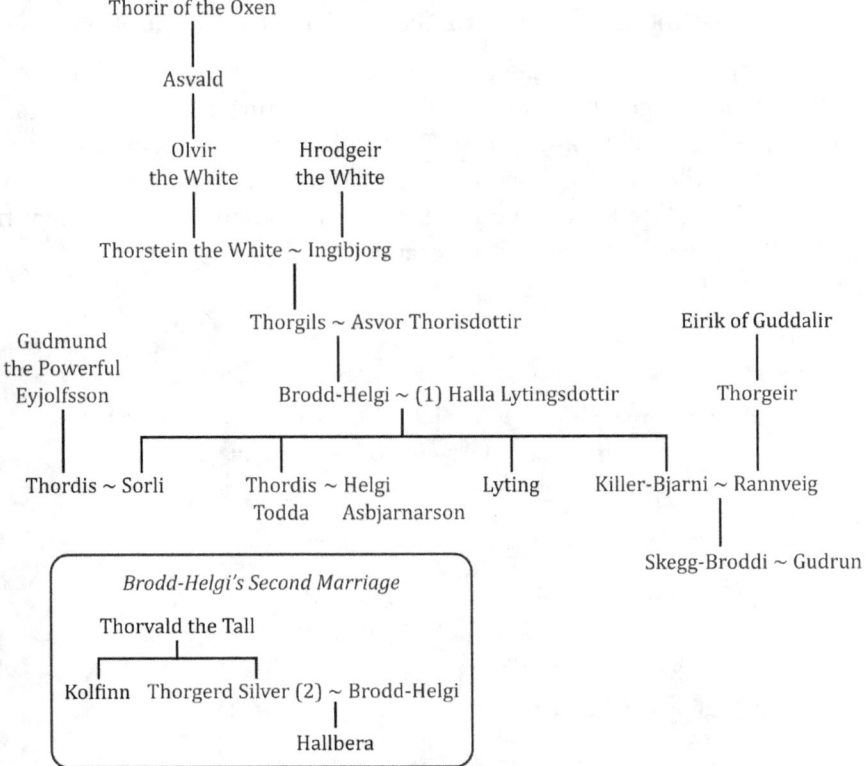

Figure 1. Genealogy 1a. Ancestors and family of Brodd-Helgi.

[1] For more on the lacuna, see Jón Helgason, "Syv sagablade (AM 162 C fol, bl. 1–7)," *Opuscula 5, Bibliotheca Arnamagnæana 31*, Copenhagen: Munksgaard, 1975, pp. 1–42, 62–72; see also Ilya Sverdlov, Randall Gordon, and Jesse Byock, "The Lacuna in *Vápnfirðinga Saga (Saga of the People of Weapon's Fjord)*."

AM 563 b 4to; JS 434 4to; Ny kgl. Sml. 1704 4to; JS 33 4to; and AM 513 4to.

NICKNAMES AND FAMILY TREES

Nicknames, bynames, and epithets in the sagas are often colorful and they frequently convey meaning. The rear of the book contains a 'Glossary of Names and Places in *Vápnfirðinga saga*,' which begins with a list of translated nicknames. For example, Eyjolf the Fat is *Eyjólfr feiti* and *Skíði inn prúði* is Skidi the Elegant.

GENEALOGIES OF THE FAMILIES IN THE *SAGA OF THE PEOPLE OF WEAPON'S FJORD*

The following genealogies give family trees of the people and families in *Vápnfirðinga saga*. Knowledge of kinship ties helps to understand blood relationships and alliances, which were probably well known to the original Icelandic audience. The genealogical information from *Vápnfirðinga saga* agrees for the most part with *Landnámabók* (*The Book of Settlements*).

1A. GENEALOGY OF ANCESTORS AND FAMILY OF BRODD-HELGI THORGILSSON

A crucial connection between the different families that form this kin group is Brodd-Helgi's marriage to Geitir's sister, Halla Lýtingsdóttir.[1] Through this marriage, the saga's major antagonists, Brodd-Helgi and Geitir, are brothers-in-law. Their sons, Killer-Bjarni (Víga-Bjarni) Helgason and Thorkel Geitisson are first cousins. This close kinship between the cousins does not stop them from continuing the feud into the second generation.

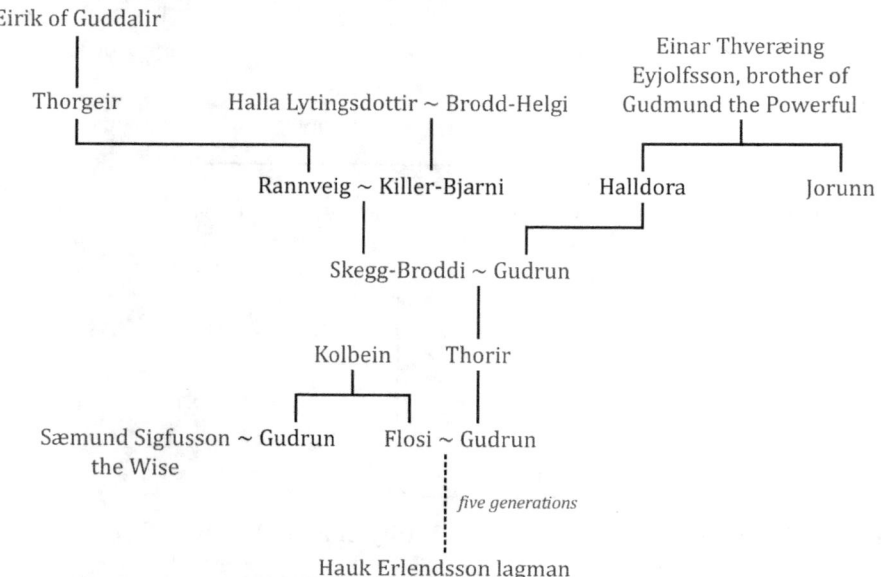

Figure 2. Genealogy 1b. Descendants of Brodd-Helgi.

---

[1] The symbol ~ indicates marriage.

Both families, the Hofsverjar and the Krossvíkingar, are politically connected to Gudmund the Powerful (Guðmundr inn ríki Eyjolfsson), a prominent chieftain and power broker from the Northern Quarter. Gudmund comes forward in several sagas. He plays an important role in *Vápnfirðinga saga*, where he is originally allied with Brodd-Helgi but later switches sides choosing Geitir as an ally. Gudmund also becomes connected by marriage to Geitir's family when his niece Jorunn becomes the second wife of Geitir's son Thorkel (see Genealogies 1a and 1b above, and 2a and 2b below).

As an example of the complications of kinship in Icelandic feud, *Njal's Saga*, *The Book of Settlements*, and *Sorli's Tale* (a short story in *Ljósvetninga saga*) tell that Gudmund is also connected to Brodd-Helgi's family through the marriage of Gudmund's daughter Thordis to Brodd-Helgi's son Sorli. The two feuding families from Weapon's Fjord, the Hofsverjar and the Krossvíkingar, are also connected to opposing factions in the long feud in the *Saga of the Sons of Droplaug* (*Droplaugarsonar saga*), on which see Genealogy 2a.

1B. Genealogy of Brodd-Helgi's Descendants

From the point of view of later history, the most important person on this chart is Brodd-Helgi's distant descendant Hauk Erlendsson (d. 1334). For a time, Hauk was a *lagman* or 'lawman' (*lǫgmaðr* in Icelandic), an important official in the post-independence Norwegian administration of Iceland. One of the key versions of *Landnámabók* is called *Hauksbók* (*Hauk's Book*), named after him.

2A. Genealogy of The Ancestors and Family of Geitir Lytingsson

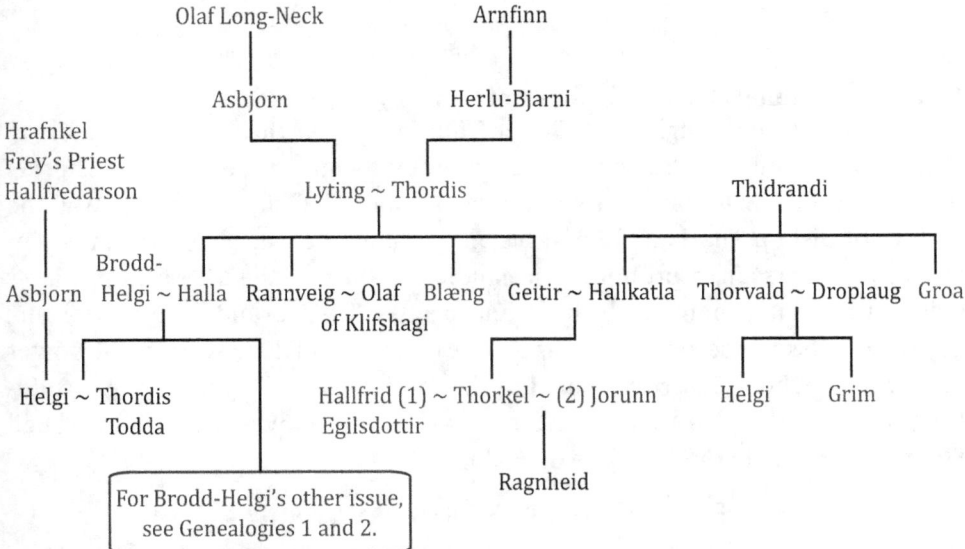

Figure 3. Genealogy 2a. Ancestors of Geitir Lytingsson.

Vápnfirðinga saga traces the family of the settler Lyting and his son, the chieftain Geitir, back through matrilineal and patrilineal lines to famous Viking ancestors in Norway. Geitir's wife Hallkatla is the sister of Droplaug, the mother of Helgi and Grim Droplaugarson of *Droplaugarsona saga*. This connection between Geitir's family and Droplaug's family explains the assistance offered by Droplaug's sons to Thorkel Geitir's son in Chapter 17. As another example of the complications of kinship relationships, Thordis, the daughter of Geitir's enemy Brodd-Helgi and sister of Bjarni Brodd-Helgason, is married to Helgi Asbjarnarson, the enemy of Helgi Droplaugarson, a nephew of Geirir's wife Hallkatla.

2B. GENEALOGY OF GEITIR'S DESCENDANTS

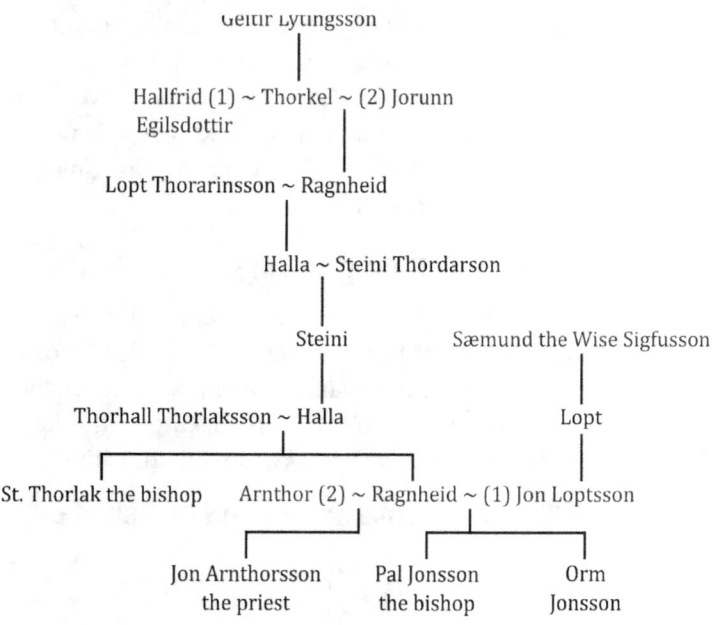

Figure 4. Genealogy 2b. Descendants of Geitir Lytingsson.
Halla Steinadottir (daughter of Steini Thordarson) is the key descendant of Geitir's later family. Halla is the great-great-granddaughter of Geitir's son Thorkel with his second wife Jorunn. Halla married Thorhall Thorlaksson and was the mother of Bishop Thorlak, the first Icelandic saint. She was also the mother-in-law of Jon Loptsson, a prominent Icelandic chieftain of the 12th century. Jon's children became prominent bishops and priests. Their grand-ancestor Jorunn, Thorkel Geitisson's second wife, was a niece of Gudmund the Powerful, the power broker with whom Geitir was allied in the later stages of his feud with Brodd-Helgi (see Genealogy 1A). Thorkel's first wife, Hallfrid, was a daughter of Egil Steinbjarnarson, Geitir's ally (see Genealogy 3).

3. THE FAMILY OF STEINBJORN STURDY

The family of Steinbjorn Sturdy (Steinbjǫrn kǫrtr) plays an important role in *Vápnfirðinga saga*. This family was prominent, but it was not a chieftain family. Eyvind the Weapon, the early settler (*landnámsmaðr*) in the fjord, was Steinbjorn's uncle. As is recounted in the *Saga of Thorstein the White* and the *Saga of the People of Weapon's Fjord*, Steinbjorn originally owned the valuable farmstead of Hof. Steinbjorn, however, lived beyond his means and eventually lost the farm to another *landnámsmaðr*, Thorstein the White (Þorsteinn hvíti), who, as is discussed in the Introduction, was Brodd-Helgi's grandfather (see Genealogy 1A). Thorstein the White had initially lived on a smaller farm, and the acquisition of Hof elevated the fortunes of his family.

The loss of the Hof estate by Steinbjorn and its transfer to Thorstein the White and Thorstein's heirs (Brodd-Helgi and his son Bjarni) underlies the animosity between Steinbjorn's descendants and Brodd-Helgi. Thorstein's descendants at Hof became known as the Hofverjar (the people of Hof), while Steinbjorn's family moved to a smaller farm in Sunnudal, directly across the valley from Hof. We can imagine that on a daily basis the people at Sunnudal would look out across the valley and see the great Hof farmstead standing as a constant reminder of their ancestral loss.

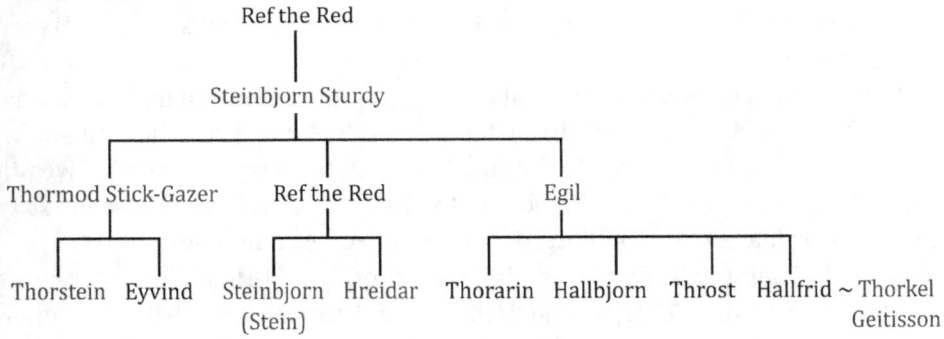

Figure 5. Genealogy 3. Family of Steinbjorn Sturdy.

Steinbjorn had three sons: Thormod Stick-Gazer, Ref the Red, and Egil. Thormod lived at Sunnudal, Ref at Refsstadir, and Egil at Egilsstadir. Steinbjorn's sons are among Geitir's most trusted supporters. Of them, Egil and his several sons come forward most prominently in the saga. In the second generation of the feud, Egil's daughter Hallfrid marries Thorkel Geitisson. This marriage further solidifies the long-standing alliance between Steinbjorn's family and Geitir's family.

Saga of the People of Weapon's Fjord

1. Helgi Earns the Nickname "Spike-Helgi"

We begin this tale at Hof in Weapon's Fjord,[1] where a man named Helgi lived. He was the son of Thorgils Thorsteinsson, son of Olvir, son of Asvald, son of Thorir of the Oxen. Olvir was a landed man[2] in Norway in the days of Earl Hakon Grjotgardsson.[3]

Thorstein the White was the first of that lineage to come out to Iceland, and he lived at Toptavoll[4] out beyond Sireksstadir ('Sirek's Farmstead'). But Steinbjorn the son of Ref the Red lived at Hof. And when Steinbjorn squandered his wealth by being too generous, Thorstein bought the Hof estate and lived there for sixty years. He was married to Ingibjorg, daughter of Hrodgeir the White.

Thorgils, Thorstein's son, was the father of Brodd-Helgi. He took over Thorstein's farm. But Thorkel and Hedin slew Thorgils, Brodd-Helgi's father. Then Thorstein the White took over the farm once again, and he brought up Helgi, his grandson.[5]

Helgi was a big man, strong and early matured. Good-looking and imposing, he was untalkative in his childhood and difficult and headstrong already at a young age. He was cunning and unpredictable.

---

[1] Vápnafjǫrðr ('Weapon's Fjord') was named after Eyvindr vápni, the fjord's first settler. See *Landnámabók, Íslenzk fornrit* I, p. 289. The nickname *vápni* ('the Weapon') is derived from the noun *vápn* 'weapon'.

[2] **landed man:** *lendr maðr*, a Norwegian nobleman whose lands and income were granted by the king in return for enforcement of the king's will. A *lendr maðr* was roughly equivalent to an English baron, with a rank below *jarl* (earl) but above the Norwegian *hauldr* (Icelandic *hǫldr*), a free farmer holding ancestral land.

[3] Earl Hakon Grjotgardsson was the earl of Lade (Old Norse Hlaðir), a rich estate in Norway's Trondelag region, during the time of King Harald Fairhair. Hakon recognized Harald's overlordship of Trondelag and became the king's ally. Hakon's line, which lasted into the 11th century, ruled large sections of northern Norway during the Viking Age, and various descendants of Hakon appear in the sagas.

[4] The precise location of this farm is unclear, but it probably was situated on the tongue of land between the Sunnudalsá (Sunnudal River) and the Hofsá (Hof River).

[5] *Landnámabók* tells that Thorgils had other siblings. The *Saga of Thorstein the White* (*Þorsteins saga hvíta*) relates in more elaborate detail all of the events referred to in this chapter.

VÁPNFIRÐINGA SAGA

1. KAPÍTULI

Summary of Chapter 1. Helgi is a young man descended from prominent Norwegians. His grandfather, the first in his family to come to Iceland, settled in Weapon's Fjord. He took over the farm at Hof from Steinbjorn, another landowner. Helgi's father, Thorgils, was killed, so he was raised by his grandfather. One day, a bull wandered into the pen of their bull and began fighting with it. Seeing that their bull was losing, Helgi attached a spike to its forehead to give it an advantage, and after that their bull won the fight. Helgi was given the nickname 'Spike' (*brodd*) and was called Brodd-Helgi.

Þar hefjum vér þenna þátt, er sá maðr bjó at Hofi í Vápnafirði, er Helgi hét. Hann var sonr Þorgils Þorsteinssonar, Ǫlvis sonar, Ásvalds sonar, Øxna-Þóris sonar. Ǫlvir var lendr maðr í Nóregi um daga Hákonar jarls Grjótgarðssonar.

Þorsteinn hvíti kom fyrst út til Íslands þeira langfeðga[1] ok bjó at Toptavelli fyrir útan Síreksstaði. En Steinbjǫrn bjó at Hofi, sonr Refs ins rauða. Ok er honum eyddisk fé fyrir þegnskapar sakar,[2] þá keypti Þorsteinn Hofsland ok bjó þar sex tigu vetra. Hann átti[3] Ingibjǫrgu Hróðgeirsdóttur ins hvíta.

Þorgils var faðir Brodd-Helga. Hann tók við búi Þorsteins. Þorkell ok Heðinn vágu Þorgils, fǫður Brodd-Helga, en Þorsteinn hvíti tók þá enn[4] við búi ok fœddi upp Helga, sonarson sinn.

Helgi var mikill maðr ok sterkr ok bráðgǫrr, vænn ok stórmannligr, ekki málugr í barnœsku, ódæll ok óvægr þegar á unga aldri. Hann var hugkvæmr ok margbreytinn.

---

[1] **kom fyrst út til Íslands þeira langfeðga:** 'was the first of that lineage to come out to Iceland'.

[2] **honum eyddisk fé fyrir þegnskapar sakar:** 'he squandered his wealth on account of open-handedness'.

[3] **átti:** past tense of *eiga*. The verb literally means 'have' or 'possess', but here it means 'be married to'. This verb was used almost exclusively for the male partner in a marriage, as a woman was seldom said to 'possess' her husband, although either might 'possess' children.

[4] Here *enn* means 'yet again'. After his son Thorgils' death, old Thorstein comes out of retirement and once again takes over the management of the family farm with the added task of raising his grandson, Brodd-Helgi.

It is told that one day at Hof, when the cattle were in the milking-pen, a bull owned by these kinsmen was in the pen when another bull entered the pen. The bulls began to butt each other. The lad Helgi was outside and saw that their bull was getting the worse of it and was backing off. He took a spike and bound it to the bull's forehead, and from then on things went better for their bull.[1] From this incident, he was called Brodd-Helgi ('Spike-Helgi').

He was the most outstanding in physical ability of all the men who grew up in the district.[2]

CHAPTER 1 VOCABULARY

af *prep* [*w dat*] of, by; off (of), out of, from

afbragð <-brǫgð> *n* outstanding example, paragon; **afbragð þeira manna allra** the most outstanding of all those men

afbragðsmaðr *m* outstanding man, a person of great ability

afbrigði *n* deviation, transgression, offense

aldr <-rs; -rar> *m* age

allr <ǫll, allt> *adj/indef pron* all, entire

annarr <ǫnnur, annat; *acc m* annan, *f* aðra, *dat m* ǫðrum, *n* ǫðru; *pl nom m* aðrir> *adj* other, another; one of two; *ord* second

at *prep* [*w dat*] at, in; as to, with respect to

at *conj* that

atburðr <-ar; -ir> *m* occurrence, event; **af þessum atburði** because of this incident

atgǫrvi *f & n* ability, talent, accomplishment; **at atgǫrvi** in ability (*esp* physical)

á *prep* [*w acc*] onto, on, towards (*motion*); with respect to; [*w dat*] on; upon; at; in (*location*)

Ásvaldr <-s> *m* Asvald (*personal name*)

átti *3sg past of* **eiga**

áttu *3pl past of* **eiga**

barnœska *f* childhood

betr *comp adv* better (*see* **vel**)

binda <bindr; batt, bundu; bundinn> *vb* bind, tie, fasten; **binda í [e-u]** bind to [sth], bind on [sth]

bjó *1/3sg past of* **búa**

bráðgǫrr *adj* matured early in life, precocious

Brodd-Helgi *m* Brodd-Helgi ('Spike-Helgi') (*personal name*)

broddr <-s; -ar> *m* spike

bú <*pl dat* búm> *n* home, house, household; farm; estate

búa <býr; bjó, bjoggu~bjuggu; búinn> *vb* live (in a place), dwell

dagr <*dat* degi, *gen* dags; *pl* dagar> *m* day; **einnhvern dag** one day

duga <-ð-; *n ppart* dugat> *vb* do, show prowess; **duga verr** come off badly, do worse (in a contest)

eiga <á, eigu; átti; áttr> *pret-pres vb* own, have, possess; be married or related to

einn <ein, eitt> *num* one; *adj/indef pron* a, an, a certain one

einnhverr *adj/indef pron* some, someone, a certain one; **einnhvern dag** one day

ekki *adv* not

en *conj* but

enn *adv* yet, still; yet again

enni *n* forehead

er *rel particle* who, which, that; *conj* when; where

er *1/3sg pres of* **vera**

eyða <-dd-> *vb* waste; spend; do away with, destroy; make empty; *refl* **eyðask** be squandered, come to naught

faðir <*acc* fǫður, *dat* fǫður~feðr, *gen* fǫður; *pl* feðr, *dat* feðrum, *gen* feðra> *m* father

fara <ferr; fór, fóru; farinn> *vb* go, travel; move; **fara frá** leave, back off, back away

ferr *2/3sg pres of* **fara**

fé <*gen* fjár; *pl gen* fjá> *n* cattle, sheep; wealth, money

---

[1] A similar story is told in the Icelandic *Saga of the Trojans* (*Trójumanna saga*). See also the *Saga of Thorstein the White* (*Þorsteins saga hvíta*).

[2] **district:** *herað* (or *hérað*). In mainland Scandinavia this term nearly always referred to an administrative district with its own assembly, but in Iceland it described a naturally demarcated area such as a valley or a fjord. In this saga, the "district" usually refers to the valley of Weapon's Fjord. It is helpful to keep the geography in mind as the saga proceeds.

Frá því er sagt[1] einnhvern dag at Hofi, er naut váru á stǫðli, at graðungr var á stǫðlinum,[2] er þeir frændr áttu, en annarr graðungr kom á stǫðulinn,[1] ok stǫnguðusk graðungarnir. En sveinninn Helgi var úti ok sér,[3] at þeira graðungr dugir verr ok ferr frá.[4] Hann tekr mannbrodd einn ok bindr í enni graðunginum, ok gengr þaðan frá þeira graðungi betr. Af þessum atburði var hann kallaðr Brodd-Helgi.

Var hann afbragð[5] þeira manna allra, er þar fœddusk upp í heraðinu, at atgǫrvi.

frá *prep* [*w dat*] from; about; *adv* away; **þaðan frá** from that point onward
frændi <*pl* frændr> *m* kinsman
fyrir *prep* [*w acc or dat*] before, in front of; for, because of; **fyrir útan** [*w acc*] outside; out beyond
fyrst *superl adv* first
fœða <-dd-> *vb* feed; rear, bring up; **fœða upp** bring up; *refl* **fœðask** grow up, be brought up; be fed; **fœðask upp** grow up, be brought up
ganga <gengr; gekk, gengu; genginn> *vb* walk; go; **ganga [e-m] betr** go better for [sb]
graðungr <-s; -ar> *m* bull
hann <*acc* hann, *dat* honum, *gen* hans> *pron 3sg m* he
Hákon <-ar> *m* Hakon (*personal name*); **Hákon jarl Grjótgarðsson** *m* Earl Hakon, son of Grjotgard ('Stone-Fence')
Heðinn <*dat* Heðni, *gen* Heðins> *m* Hedin (*personal name*)
hefja <hefr; hóf, hófu; hafinn> *vb* begin
heita <heitr; hét, hétu; heitinn> *vb* call, give a name to; [*intrans*, 2/3sg *pres* heitir] be called, be named
Helgi *m* Helgi (*personal name*); **Brodd-Helgi** *m* Brodd-Helgi ('Spike-Helgi')
herað <heruð~herǫð> *n* district; county; (*in Iceland*) a valley region
hét *1/3sg past of* **heita**

hof *n* temple (*freq a name for a farm*)
Hof *n* Hof ('Temple') (*place name*)
Hofsland *n* the Hof estate
honum *dat of* **hann**
Hróðgeirr <-s> *m* Hrodgeir (*personal name*); **Hróðgeirr inn hvíti** *m* Hrodgeir the White
hugkvæmr *adj* clever, cunning
hvítr *adj* white
illa <*comp* verr, *superl* verst> *adv* badly, ill
Ingibjǫrg <*acc/dat* -bjǫrgu, *gen* -bjargar> *f* Ingiborg (*personal name*); **Ingibjǫrg Hróðgeirsdóttir ins hvíta** *m* Ingibjorg, daughter of Hrodgeir the White
inn <in, it> *art* the
í *prep* [*w acc*] into (*motion*); during (*time*); [*w dat*] in, within; at (*location*)
Ísland *n* Iceland
jarl <-s; -ar> *m* earl
kalla <-að-> *vb* call
kallaðr *ppart of* **kalla**
kaupa <keypt-> *vb* buy
keypti *3sg past of* **kaupa**
kom *1/3sg past of* **koma**
koma <kemr~kømr; kom, kómu~kvámu; kominn> *vb* come; **koma út til Íslands** come out to Iceland (*usu* from Norway)
land <lǫnd> *n* land; country; estate
langfeðgar *m pl* forefathers, ancestors (through the father's line)
lendr *adj* 'landed', describing one who has

---

[1] **Frá því er sagt:** 'It is told', literally 'from that it is said'.
[2] **graðungr var á stǫðlinum ... en annarr graðungr kom á stǫðulinn.** These phrases illustrate the contrast in meaning between the use of a dative and the use of an accusative after the preposition *á*: 'a bull was **in the pen**' (dative indicating location) '... and another bull came **into the pen**' (accusative indicating motion).
[3] **var ... sér:** It is characteristic of the Icelandic storytellers to switch back and forth between past and present tense, even within the same sentence
[4] **þeira graðungr dugir verr ok ferr frá:** 'their bull is getting the worse of it and is backing off'.
[5] **afbragð ... at atgǫrvi:** 'the most talented'.

received a grant of land from a king

maðr <acc mann, dat manni, gen manns; pl nom/acc menn, dat mǫnnum, gen manna> m man; person

manna gen pl of **maðr**

mannbroddr <-s; -ar> m spike

margbreytinn <-in, -it> adj fickle, capricious, unpredictable

málugr adj talkative

mikill <mikil, mikit; acc m mikinn, dat n miklu; pl nom m miklir> adj big, tall, great

Nóregr <-s> m Norway

naut n ox; pl cattle, oxen

ok conj and

ódæll adj difficult, quarrelsome, stubborn

óvægr adj harsh, unmerciful

Refr <-s> m Ref ('Fox') (personal name); **Refr inn rauði** m Ref the Red

rauðr <rauð, rautt> adj red

sagt n ppart of **segja**

sakar gen sg of **sǫk**

sá <sú, þat> dem pron that (one), pl those

segja <sagð-> vb say, tell; **segja frá [e-u]** reveal, tell about [sth]

sex num six

sér 2/3sg pres of **sjá**

sinn <sín, sitt> refl poss pron his, her, its, their (own)

Síreksstaðir m pl Síreksstadir ('Sirek's Farmstead') (place name)

sjá <sér; sá, sá(u); sénn> vb see, look

sonarsonr m grandson

sonr <dat syni, gen sonar; pl synir, acc sonu> m son

staðr <dat stað(i), gen -ar; pl -ir> m stead, parcel of land; place, spot; abode, dwelling; pl (in place names) farmstead

stanga <-að-> vb ram, butt with the head, gore (of cattle); refl **stangask** butt each other

Steinbjǫrn m Steinbjorn ('Stone-Bear') (personal name)

sterkr adj strong

stórmannligr adj magnificent, grand, imposing

stǫðull <dat stǫðli, gen stǫðuls; pl stǫðlar> m milking pen (for cows)

stǫnguðusk 3pl past refl of **stanga**

sveinn m boy, lad

sǫk <gen sakar; pl sakar~sakir> f cause, reason, sake; **fyrir [e-s] sakar** on account of, because of [sth]

taka <tekr; tók, tóku; tekinn> vb take; **taka við [e-u]** receive, take possession of, acquire, inherit [sth]

tigr <gen tiger; pl tigir, acc tigu> m ten; a decade; **sex tigir** num sixty

til prep [w gen] to

Toptavǫllr m Toptavoll ('Field of Ruined Walls') (place name)

tók 1/3sg past of **taka**

um prep [w acc] about; during, in (time)

ungr adj young

upp adv up, upward (motion)

út adv out, outward (motion)

útan adv from without, from outside

úti adv out (location), outside, outdoors

var 1/3sg past of **vera**

Vápnafjǫrðr <dat -firði, gen -fjarðar> m Vapnafjord ('Weapon's Fjord') (place name)

vágu 3pl past of **vega**

váru 3pl past of **vera**

vega <vegr; vá, vágu; veginn> vb kill, slay

vel <comp betr, superl bezt> adv well

vera <er; var, váru; verit> vb be

verr comp adv worse (see **illa**)

vetr <gen vetrar; pl vetr, gen vetra> m winter

vér <acc/dat oss, gen vár> pron 1pl we

við prep [w acc] at, by, close to; with; according to, after; [w dat] against; toward; with

vænn adj beautiful, fine, handsome

vǫllr <dat velli, gen vallar; pl vellir, acc vǫllu, gen valla> m field, plain

þaðan adv from there, thence; **þaðan frá** from that point onward

þar adv there

þat <acc þat, dat því, gen þess> pron 3sg n it

þá adv then

þáttr <dat þætti, gen þáttar; pl þættir, acc þáttu> m tale, short saga

þegar adv at once, immediately; already; **þegar á unga aldri** already by a young age

þegnskapr <-ar> m generosity, open-handedness

þeir <acc þá, dat þeim, gen þeira~þeirra> pron 3pl m they

þeir m nom pl of dem pron **sá**

þeira poss pron 3pl indecl their, theirs

þeira dem pron (of) those (m gen pl of **sá**)

þenna m acc sg of **þessi**

þessi <þessi, þetta> dem pron this, pl these

Þorgils <*gen* Þorgils> *m* Thorgils (*personal name*); **Þorgils Þorsteinsson** *m* Thorgils, son of Thorstein

Þorkell <-s> *m* Thorkel (*personal name*)

Þorsteinn <-s> *m* Thorstein (*personal name*); **Þorsteinn hvíti** *m* Thorstein the White

því *dat of* þat

Qlvir <*gen* Qlvis> *m* Olvir (*personal name*)

Øxna-Þórir *m* Thorir 'of the Oxen' (*personal name*)

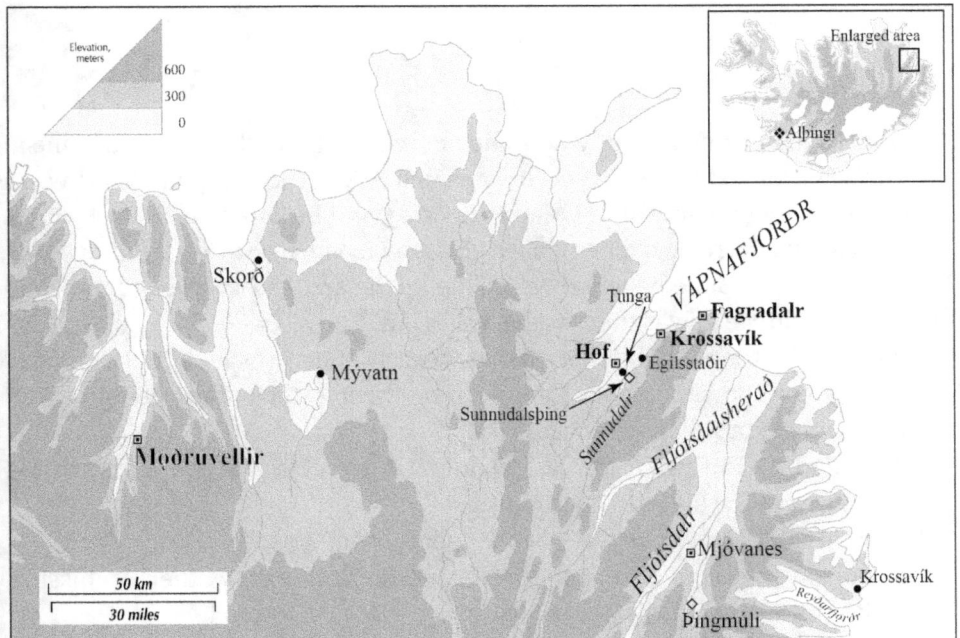

Map 3. The Action of the *Saga of the People of Weapon's Fjord* spreads across Northern and Eastern Iceland as chieftains (marked by squares ▣) and farmers (marked by dots ●) are drawn into the conflict. Within Vápnafjǫrðr's inland region, a diamond (◇) marks the site of the local freemen's *þing* ('thing' or 'assembly'). Called the *Sunnudalsþing* ('South Dale's Thing'), this yearly meeting of the chieftains and farmers in Weapon's Fjord took place in Sunndalr, a narrow side valley hemmed in by the fjord's confining mountains. The family of Steinbjorn Sturdy, who support the chieftain Greitir from Krossavík, lived in Sunnudalr.

2. THE OUTLAW'S CURSE

There was a man named Svart, who came out here to Iceland and built a home in Weapon's Fjord. Next to him lived a man named Skidi, who was poor. Svart was a big man, extremely strong and skilled in fighting, and he was a most unruly man. Svart and Skidi quarreled over grazing rights, and it ended with Svart killing Skidi. Brodd-Helgi took up the prosecution for the killing and had Svart condemned to outlawry. Brodd-Helgi was then twelve years old.

After that Svart set out to the heath that we call Smjorvatnsheid ('Butter-Water Heath'), not far from Sunnudal.[1] He preyed on the livestock of the people of Hof and stole much more than was necessary.

A shepherd at Hof came in one evening. He went to the bed-closet of old Thorstein, where the old man lay sightless.

Thorstein said, "How have things gone today, friend?"

"As badly as they could," replied the shepherd. "Your best wether[2] is missing, along with three others."

---

[1] A peak on the highlands of Smjorvatnsheid to the southeast of Sunnudal is today called Svartfell. According to local traditions, Svart had his den there.

[2] **wether:** *geldingr*, a castrated (or gelded) male sheep.

2. KAPÍTULI

Summary of Chapter 2. Two local farmers, Svart and Skidi, disagree over grazing rights, and the conflict results in Skidi's death. Brodd-Helgi prosecutes Svart at the assembly and has him outlawed. Svart hides in the mountains, stealing sheep by night. One night Brodd-Helgi sets out to find him. He arms himself with a long axe and places a flat stone under his tunic for armor. He tracks Svart through the snow to his hiding place. Svart strikes first but hits the stone and loses his footing, exposing himself to Brodd-Helgi's attack. Before Brodd-Helgi has time to deliver the death blow, Svart places a curse on Brodd-Helgi and his family.

Maðr hét Svartr, er kom út hingat ok gerði bú í Vápnafirði. It næsta honum bjó sá maðr, er Skíði hét. Hann var félítill. Svartr var mikill maðr ok rammr at afli[1] ok vel vígr ok óeirðarmaðr inn mesti. Þá Svart ok Skíða[2] skilði á um beitingar,[3] ok lauk því svá,[4] at Svartr vá Skíða. En Brodd-Helgi mælti eptir vígit ok gerði Svart sekan. Þá var Brodd-Helgi tólf vetra gamall.

Eptir þat lagðisk Svartr út á heiði þá, er vér kǫllum Smjǫrvatnsheiði, skammt frá Sunnudal, ok leggsk á fé Hofsverja[5] ok gerði miklu meira at en honum var nauðsyn til.[6]

Sauðamaðr at Hofi kom inn einn aptan ok gekk inn í lokrekkjugólf[7] Þorsteins karls, þar sem hann lá sjónlauss.

Ok mælti Þorsteinn: "Hversu hefir at farit í dag, félagi?"[8] segir hann.

"Sem verst," segir hinn; "horfinn er geldingrinn þinn inn bezti," segir sauðamaðr, "ok þrír aðrir."

---

[1] **rammr at afli:** 'powerful in strength', meaning 'extremely strong'. Such expressions are frequently used in the sagas. Other examples are *ungr at aldri* 'young in age' and *auðigr at fé* 'rich in wealth'.

[2] **Þá Svart ok Skíða:** '(them) Svart and Skidi'; the accusative personal pronoun *þá* is in apposition to the following names.

[3] **Þá ... skilði á um beitingar:** lit. '[it] divided them over grazing', i.e., Svart and Skidi disagreed over grazing rights. Impersonal expressions are frequent in Icelandic. Here, the logical subject (they) is expressed in the accusative case (*þá*).

[4] **lauk því svá:** 'it ended in such a way'.

[5] **leggsk á fé Hofsverja:** 'began to prey upon the livestock of the people of Hof'.

[6] **en honum var nauðsyn til:** 'than was necessary for him'.

[7] **lokrekkjugólf:** 'locked bed-closet', a private sleeping compartment in the hall, located behind a partition. It is also called a *lokrekkja* or *lokhvíla*. The heads of households usually slept in a *lokrekkja*. Other people slept in the hall on wooden platforms lining the walls on either side of the hearth. By day, the platforms served as benches.

[8] **hversu hefir at farit í dag, félagi?:** 'how have things gone today, friend?' *Félagi* 'partner' is cognate with English 'fellow'. The word literally means 'fee-layer', i.e., one who shares in a farming, ship-owning, or trading venture.

"They have likely joined other people's sheep," he said, "and will come back."

"No, no," said the shepherd, "they will never come back."

"Speak of this to me as you please," said Thorstein, "but don't tell it to Brodd-Helgi."

The day after, Brodd-Helgi asked the shepherd how things were going, and the shepherd gave all the same answers to him as to Thorstein. Brodd-Helgi let on as if he had not heard and went to bed in the evening. But when the others were asleep, he got up, took his shield, and went out.

It is told that Helgi picked up a large, thin flagstone. He set one end in his breeches and the other in front of his chest.[1] He had in his hand a large pole-axe[2] with a long haft. He went on until he came to the sheep-pen, from where he was able to follow the tracks, since there was snow on the ground.

He came up onto Smjorvatnsheid from Sunnudal. Svart went out and saw a hardy-looking man approaching. He asked who was there. Brodd-Helgi gave his name.

"You must be intending to meet me, and not without reason," said Svart.

Svart leapt at Helgi, thrusting at him with a great broad-bladed spear.[3] But Brodd-Helgi warded it off with his shield. The spear hit the edge of the shield and then the flagstone. It glanced off the flagstone so forcefully that Svart fell forward with the thrust. Brodd-Helgi struck at his foot and cut it off.

Then Svart spoke: "Now has been settled the difference in our fates," he said, "and you will become my slayer. But such family misfortune will henceforth arise among your kin, that for all ages it shall last, while the land is inhabited."[4]

After that Helgi struck him his death-blow.

Now old Thorstein awoke at home at Hof. He got up from from his bed and touched Brodd-Helgi's bed. It had grown cold.

---

[1] There is at least one other example in the sagas of the use of a flagstone for protection (*Egils saga*, Ch. 75)

[2] **pole-axe:** *boløx*, a strong, long-shafted axe, often used for felling trees.

[3] **broad-bladed spear:** *hǫggspjót*, literally 'hacking spear'. The *hǫggspjót* of the Viking Age was a kind of spear with a broad blade. Although it could be thrown, it was used mainly in hand-to-hand combat for both thrusting and slashing. Such weapons were favored by the Vikings of western Norway. The *kesja* and *atgeirr* were weapons comparable in design to the *hǫggspjót*.

[4] Svart's curse provides a metaphysical explanation for the two generations of strife described in the saga. In the sagas, curses worked as literary devices of anticipation, usually preceding a profound tragedy. The realization of the curse, however, is explained in social rather than metaphysical terms. Brodd-Helgi's greed and unreasonable behavior lead to his downfall, and other characters behave in such a way as to bring about their own deaths. The curse provided a supernatural thread for the saga author to weave into an already well-known tale.

"Komnir munu til sauða annarra manna,"[1] segir hann, "ok munu aptr koma."

"Nei, nei," segir sauðamaðr, "þeir munu aldri aptr koma."

"Mæl[2] við mik slíkt, er þér líkar,"[3] segir Þorsteinn, "en tala ekki slíkt við Brodd-Helga," segir hann.

Brodd-Helgi spurði sauðamanninn, hversu flakkat hefði,[4] um daginn eptir. En hann hafði ǫll in sǫmu svǫr við hann[5] sem við Þorstein. Brodd-Helgi lét sem hann heyrði eigi ok fór í rekkju um kveldit. Ok er aðrir menn váru sofnaðir, reis hann upp ok tók skjǫld sinn, ok gekk hann síðan út.

Þess er getit, at hann tók upp einn hellustein, mikinn ok þunnan, ok lét annan enda í brœkr sínar, en annan fyrir brjóst. Hann hafði í hendi bolǫxi mikla á hávu skapti. Hann ferr, unz hann kemr í sauðahús, ok rekr þaðan spor, því at snjór var á jǫrðu.

Hann kemr á Smjǫrvatnsheiði upp frá Sunnudal. Svartr gekk út ok sá mann knáligan kominn ok spurði, hverr þar væri.[6] Brodd-Helgi sagði til sín.[7]

"Þú munt ætla at fara á fund minn ok eigi ørendislaust," segir hann.

Svartr hljóp at honum ok leggr til hans með hǫggspjóti miklu, en Brodd-Helgi brá við skildinum, ok kom á útanverðan skjǫldinn ok kemr í helluna, ok sneiddi[8] af hellunni svá hart, at hann fell eptir laginu.[9] En Brodd-Helgi hǫggr á fótinn, svá at af tók.

Þá mælti Svartr: "Nú gerði gæfumun okkar,"[10] segir hann, "ok muntu verða banamaðr minn, en sá ættangr mun verða í kyni yðru heðan af, at alla ævi mun uppi vera,[11] meðan landit er byggt."

Eptir þetta hjó Helgi hann banahǫgg.

Nú vaknar[12] Þorsteinn karl heima á Hofi ok gengr af rekkju sinni ok tekr í rúm Brodd-Helga. Var þat kalt orðit.

---

[1] **Komnir munu til sauða annarra manna**: 'they will (no doubt) have joined with some other people's sheep'. The future auxiliary *munu* 'will' often expresses probability, likelihood, or supposition.

[2] **Mæl**: the simple imperative form of the verb *mæla* 'speak'. It lacks the 2sg enclitic pronoun *-tu* (also *-ðu* or *-du*, depending on the last consonant of the stem), which more often appears in such constructions.

[3] **slíkt, er þér líkar**: 'such as it pleases you'.

[4] **hversu flakkat hefði**: 'how it (the shepherding) had gone'.

[5] **hann hafði ǫll in sǫmu svǫr við hann**: 'he had all the same answers for him'.

[6] **hverr þar væri**: 'who might be there' (*væri*, 3sg past subjunct. of *vera* 'be').

[7] **sagði til sín**: 'gave his name'.

[8] *Sneiða* usually means 'to slice' but here it is synonymous with *sveðja* 'glance off'.

[9] **hann fell eptir laginu**: 'he [i.e., Svart] fell forward with the thrust'.

[10] **nú gerði gæfumun okkar**: 'now has been settled the difference in our fortunes'.

[11] **at alla ævi mun uppi vera**: 'for all ages shall it last'.

[12] **Nú *vaknar* Þorsteinn karl ... Hann *vekr* upp húskarla sína**. Unlike English, Icelandic maintains a distinction between the intransitive *vakna* 'waken' (oneself), and the transitive *vekja* 'wake' (somebody else).

He woke up his farmhands and told them to go look for Brodd-Helgi. When they went out, they followed his tracks all the way and found him where Svart lay dead.

Afterwards they buried Svart's body and took everything of value away with them. Brodd-Helgi became widely renowned. He was greatly praised by all people for this feat of courage that he had performed at such a young age.[1]

CHAPTER 2 VOCABULARY

aðrir *m nom pl of* **annarr**

afl *n* physical strength, might, power; **rammr at afli** extremely strong

aldri *adv* never

alþýða *f* all the people, the majority of the people, the public, the common people

annarr <ǫnnur, annat; *acc m* annan, *f* aðra, *dat m* ǫðrum, *n* ǫðru; *pl nom m* aðrir> *adj* one of two, other, another; second

aptann <*dat* aptni, *gen* aptans; *pl* aptnar> *m* evening

aptr *adv* back

at *conj* that

at *inf marker* to

banahǫgg *n* death-blow

banamaðr *m* killer, slayer

beiting <-ar> *f* grazing, pasturage

beztr *superl adj* best (*see* **góðr**)

biðja <biðr; bað, báðu; beðinn> *vb* ask, beg; command, tell

boløx <*acc/dat* -i, *gen* -ar; *pl* -ar> *f* pole-axe, wood-axe

brá *1/3sg past of* **bregða**

bregða <bregðr; brá, brugðu; brugðinn> *vb* [*w dat*] move quickly; to draw, brandish (a weapon); **bregða við** [e-u] ward off with, parry with [sth]

brjóst *n* chest, breast

brœkr *f pl* breeches

byggja <-ð-> *vb* inhabit

dagr <*dat* degi, *gen* dags; *pl* dagar> *m* day; **í dag** today; **um daginn eptir** (on) the day after, the next day

dauðr *adj* dead

eigi *adv* not

ek <*acc* mik, *dat* mér, *gen* mín> *pron 1sg* I

en *conj* but; and (on the other hand); [*w comp*] than

endi *m* end

eptir *prep* [*w acc*] after (*time*); [*w dat*] after, along; **eptir þetta** after that, afterward

falla <fellr; fell, fellu; fallinn> *vb* fall

fara <ferr; fór, fóru; farinn> *vb* go, travel; move; **fara at** go, proceed

fell *1/3sg past of* **falla**

félagi *m* partner, comrade, companion, friend, 'fellow'

félítill *adj* short of money, poor

fémætr <-mæt, -mætt> *adj* valuable

finna <finnr; fann, fundu; fundinn> *vb* find

flakka <-að-> *vb* roam, wander about (*as a shepherd with sheep*)

fór *1/3sg past of* **fara**

fótr <*dat* fœti, *gen* fótar; *pl* fœtr, *acc* fœtr> *m* foot, foot and leg

fundr <-ar; -ir> *m* meeting; **fara á fund** [e-s] go see, meet [sb]

fundu *3pl past of* **finna**

gamall *adj* old

ganga <gengr; gekk, gengu; genginn> *vb* walk; go; **ganga inn** go indoors

gekk *1/3sg past of* **ganga**

geldingr <-s; -ar> *m* wether, gelded sheep

gengr *2/3sg pres of* **ganga**

gera <-ð-; *ppart* gerðr~gerr> *vb* make, build; do, act; **gera ... at** do ...; **gera** [e-n] **sekan** (*leg*) condemn [sb] to outlawry, make [sb] an outlaw

---

[1] The accomplishment of an outstanding deed at the age of twelve is a folktale convention. Twelve was also the age of legal majority (maturity) in Iceland (*GG* Ia 6, 166, 168, 194). Helgi's successful prosecution of Svart and his subsequent act of vengeance are both accomplishments worthy of praise.

Hann vekr upp húskarla sína ok biðr þá fara at leita Brodd-Helga. Ok er þeir kómu út, rǫkðu þeir spor hans alla leið ok fundu hann þar, sem Svartr lá dauðr.

Síðan hulðu þeir hræ Svarts ok hǫfðu með sér allt þat, sem fémætt var. Varð Brodd-Helgi víðfrægr ok lofaðr mjǫk af alþýðu fyrir þetta þrekvirki, er hann hafði unnit, jafnungr sem hann var enn at aldri.

geta <getr; gat, gátu; getinn> *vb* get; [*w gen*] speak of, mention; **þess er getit** it is told

góðr <góð, gott; *comp* betri, *superl* beztr> *adj* good

gæfumunr <-ar; -ir> *m* difference in fortune, turn or shift of luck

hafa <hef(i)r, -ð-> *vb* have; **hafa [e-t] í hendi** hold [sth] in one's hand; **hafa [e-t] með sér** take, bring [sth] with one

hans *poss pron 3sg m indecl* his

hart *adv* hard

hár <há, hátt; *acc m* hávan; *pl dat* hávum> *adj* high, tall, long

hávu *n dat sg of* **hár**

heðan *adv* from here, hence; **heðan af** from now on, henceforth

hefði *3sg/pl past subjunct of* **hafa**

hefir *2/3sg pres of* **hafa**

heiðr <*acc/dat* heiði, *gen* heiðar; *pl* heiðar> *f* heath, moor

heima *adv* home, at home (*location*)

hellusteinn *m* flat slab of rock, flagstone

hendi *dat of* **hǫnd**

heyra <-ð-> *vb* hear

hingat *adv* to here, hither

hinn <hin, hitt> *dem pron* the other one

hjó *1/3sg past of* **hǫggva**

hlaupa <hleypr; hljóp, hljópu; hlaupinn> *vb* leap, spring; run; **hlaupa at [e-m]** leap at, assault [sb]

hljóp *1/3sg past of* **hlaupa**

Hofsverjar *m pl* the people of Hof

horfinn *ppart* lost, missing, nowhere to be found (*see* **hverfa**)

hræ <*pl gen* hræva> *n* dead body, corpse, carrion

hulðu *3pl past of* **hylja**

húskarl <-s; -ar> *m* farmhand

hverfa <hverfr; hvarf, hurfu; horfinn> *vb* be lost, be missing; disappear

hverr <hver, hvat> *interrog pron* who, which? (*n*) what?

hversu *interrog adv* how, just how?

hylja <hulð~huld-; *ppart* huliðr~huldr> *vb* bury, cover over, conceal, hide

hǫggspjót *n* broad-bladed spear

hǫggva <hǫggr; hjó, hjoggu; hǫgg(v)inn> *vb* strike (a blow), chop, hack, hew

hǫnd <*acc* hǫnd, *dat* hendi, *gen* handar; *pl* hendr, *dat* hǫndum, *gen* handa> *f* hand; **hafa [e-t] í hendi** hold [sth] in one's hand

illa <*comp* verr, *superl* verst> *adv* badly, ill

inn *adv* in, into (*motion*)

jafnungr *adj* as young

jǫrð <*dat* jǫrðu, *gen* jarðar; *pl* jarðir> *f* earth; ground

kaldr <kǫld, kalt> *adj* cold

karl <-s; -ar> *m* man; old man; **Þorsteinn karl** old Thorstein, old man Thorstein

kemr *2/3sg pres of* **koma**

knáligr *adj* hardy, vigorous

koma <kemr~kømr; kom, kómu~kvámu; kominn> *vb* come; **koma aptr** come back, return

kominn *ppart of* **koma**

komnir *m nom pl of* **kominn**, *ppart of* **koma**

kómu *3pl past of* **koma**

kveld *n* evening; **um kveldit** in the evening

kyn <*pl dat* kynjum, *gen* kynja> *n* kin; kindred

lag <lǫg> *n* thrust, stab

lagðisk *2/3sg past of* **leggjask**

lauk *1/3sg past of* **lúka**

lá *1/3sg pret of* **liggja**

láta <lætr; lét, létu; látinn> *vb* let, allow, permit; put, place, set; behave; **láta sem** 'let on as if', pretend, make or behave as if

leggja <lagð-; *ppart* lag(i)ðr~laginn> *vb*

lay, place, put; stab, thrust; **leggja til**
[e-s] með [e-u] attack [sb] with [sth];
refl **leggjask** lay, set oneself; **leggjask**
á [e-t] prey upon (*of robbers, beasts of
prey, etc.*), fall upon, attack [sth];
leggjask út set out (into the
wilderness to live as an outlaw)

leggsk *2/3sg pres of* **leggjask**

leið <-ir> *f* road, path; way

leita <-að-> *vb* [*w gen*] seek, search for

lét *1/3sg past of* **láta**

liggja <liggr; lá, lágu; leginn> *vb* lie

líka <-að-> *vb impers* [*dat subj*] like, be
pleasing (to one)

lofa <-að-> *vb* praise

lokrekkjugólf *n* locking bed-closet

lúka <lýkr; lauk, luku; lokinn> *vb* [*w dat*]
close; end, conclude; shut

maðr <*acc* mann, *dat* manni, *gen* manns;
pl nom/acc menn, *dat* mǫnnum, *gen*
manna> *m* man; person

mann *acc sg of* **maðr**

menn *nom/acc pl of* **maðr**

með *prep* [*w acc*] with (*in the sense of
bringing, carrying, or forcing*); [*w dat*]
with (*in the sense of accompanying or
togetherness*)

meðan *conj* while, as long as

meiri *comp adj* more (*see* **mikill**)

menn *nom/acc pl of* **maðr**

mestr *superl adj* greatest, biggest (*see*
mikill)

mik *1sg pron* me (*acc of* **ek**)

mikill <mikil, mikit; *acc m* mikinn, *dat n*
miklu; *pl nom m* miklir; *comp* meiri,
superl mestr> *adj* big, tall, great

mikill *m acc sg of* **mikill**

miklu *adv* much [*w comp*] (*see* **mikill**)

minn <mín, mitt> *poss pron 1sg* my

mjǫk <*comp* meir(r), *superl* mest> *adv*
much, very

muntu = **munt þú** will you (*sg*) (*2sg
pres of* **munu** *w encl pron*)

munu <mun, munu; mundi; *pret inf*
mundu> *pret-pres vb* will, shall
(*futurity*); be sure to, must
(*probability*); (*past tense*) would, must

mæla <-t-> *vb* say, speak; **mæla eptir**
[e-t]/[e-n] (*leg*) take up the prosecution for [sth]/[sb] (who was
murdered or wronged); **mæla við**
[e-n] speak to or with [sb], say to [sb]

nauðsyn <-jar> *f* necessity

nei *adv* no

nú *adv* now

næstr *superl adj* next; nearest

okkarr <okkur, okkart> *poss pron 1dual*
our (two)

orðit *n ppart of* **verða**

óeirðarmaðr *m* unruly man

rammr <rǫmm, rammt> *adj* strong;
mighty, powerful; **rammr at afli** extremely strong

reis *1/3sg past of* **rísa**

rekja <rakð~rakt-; *ppart* rak(i)ðr~
raktr> *vb* track, trace

rekkja *f* bed; **fara í rekkju** go to bed

rísa <ríss; reis, risu; risinn> *vb* arise,
rise, stand up; **rísa upp** rise up, get up

rúm *n* bed; space, seat

sagði *1/3sg past of* **segja**

samr <sǫm, samt> *adj* same

sauðahús *n* sheep-pen, sheep-fold

sauðamaðr <*acc* -mann> *m* shepherd

sauðr <-ar; -ir> *m* sheep

sá <sú; þat> *dem pron* that (one)

sá *1/3sg past of* **sjá**

segja <sagð-> *vb* say, tell; **segja til sín**
give one's name

sekr <*acc m* sekan~sekjan> *adj* guilty;
convicted, condemned to outlawry;
gera [e-n] sekan condemn [sb] to
outlawry, make [sb] an outlaw

sem *rel particle* who, which, that; *conj*
as; [*w superl*] as ... as possible; where

sér *refl dat pron* him-/her-/it-/one-self,
themselves

síðan *adv* then, later, afterwards

sjá <sér; sá, sá(u); sénn> *vb* see, look

sjónlauss *adj* blind, sightless

skammr <skǫmm, skam(m)t> *adj* short,
brief

skammt *n adj as adv* a short distance,
not far

skapt <skǫpt> *n* handle, shaft; **á hávu**
skapti on a long shaft

skildi *dat sg of* **skjǫldr**

skilði *3sg past of* **skilja**

skilja <-d~ð-; *ppart* skiliðr~skildr~
skilinn> *vb* part, separate, divide;
discern, understand; **þá skilr á um**
[e-t] *impers* they fall out over, differ,
disagree about [sth]

Skíði *m* Skidi (*personal name*)

slíkr <slík, slíkt> *adj* such

slíkt *n adj as adv* in such a way

skjǫldr <*dat* skildi, *gen* skjaldar; *pl* skildir, *acc* skjǫldu> *m* shield

sneiða <-dd-> *vb* slice; glance off

snjór <*gen* snjóvar~snjófar> *m* snow

sofna <-að-> *vb* fall asleep; **vera sofnaðr** be asleep

Smjǫrvatnsheiðr *f* Smjorvatnsheid ('Butter-Water Heath') (*place name*)

spor *n* track, trail, footprint

spurði *3sg past of* **spyrja**

spyrja <spurð-> *vb* ask; hear, hear of, learn, be informed of, find out

Sunnudalr <*dat* -dal, *gen* -dals> *m* Sunnudal ('South Dale', 'South Valley', *or perh* 'Sun Dale') (*place name*),

svar <svǫr> *n* answer, reply

Svartr <-s> *m* Svart ('Black') (*personal name*)

svá *adv* so, thus; such; then; so (*denoting degree*); **svá at** such that, with the result that

svǫr *nom/acc pl of* **svar**

sǫmu *wk n acc pl of* **samr**

taka <tekr; tók, tóku; tekinn> *vb* take, catch, seize; take hold of, grasp; reach, touch; **taka upp [e-t]** pick up [sth]; **[e-t] tekr af** *impers* [sth] comes loose, comes off

tala <-að-> *vb* talk, speak; **tala við [e-n]** speak to [sb]

tekr *3sg pres of* **taka**

tólf *num* twelve

um *prep* [*w acc*] about; around; across; for, because of; beyond; during, for, in, by (*time*)

ungr <ung, ungt> *adj* young; **ungr at aldri** young, at a young age, 'young in age'

unnit *n ppart of* **vinna**

unz *conj* until

uppi *adv* up (*location*); **vera uppi** live, last

útanverðr *adj* the outward, outside, outer part of

vakna <-að-> *vb* awaken (*intrans*), get up

varð *1/3sg past of* **verða**

vá *1/3sg past of* **vega**

vega <vegr; vá, vágu; veginn> *vb* kill, slay

vekja <vakð~vakt-; *ppart* vakiðr~vaktr~vakinn> *vb* wake, awake (*trans*); **vekja [e-n] upp** wake [sb] up

vel *adv* well; very

vera <er; var, váru; verit> *vb* be

verða <verðr; varð, urðu; orðinn> *vb* become

verst *superl adv* worst (*see* **illa**); **sem verst** as bad as it can be, as bad as possible

vinna <vinnr; vann, unnu; unninn> *vb* work; perform, accomplish

víðfrægr *adj* widely renowned, famous

víg *n* (*leg*) homicide, manslaughter, killing

vígr *adj* able to fight; **vel vígr** skilled at fighting

væri *3sg/pl past subjunct of* **vera**

yðarr <yður, yðart; *dat n* yǫru> *poss pron 2pl* your (*pl*)

þar *adv* there; **þar sem** *conj* where

þat <*acc* þat, *dat* því, *gen* þess> *pron 3sg n* it

þá *adv* then

þá *acc of* **þeir**

þá *f acc sg of dem pron* **sá**

þeir <*acc* þá, *dat* þeim, *gen* þeira~þeirra> *pron 3pl m* they

þess *pron* (of) it (*gen of* **þat**)

þér *dat of* **þú**

þinn <þín, þitt> *poss pron 2sg* your (*sg*)

þrekvirki *n* courageous a deed, feat of strength

þrír <þrjár, þrjú; *acc m* þrjá, *dat* þrim(r), *gen* þriggja> *num* three

þunnr *adj* thin

þú <*acc* þik, *dat* þér, *gen* þín> *pron 2sg* you (*sg*)

því *dat of* **þat**; **því at** *conj* because

ætla <-að-> *vb* intend, purpose, mean

ættangr <*gen* -rs> *m* family calamity, family misfortune

ævi *f indecl* age, time; **alla ævi** for all time, forever

ǫll *f nom sg & n nom/acc pl of* **allr**

ørendislaust *adv* without purpose, in vain, for nothing; **fara ørendislaust** go in vain, without a purpose or reason

øx <*acc/dat* -i, *gen* -ar; *pl* -ar> *f* axe

3. FAST FRIENDS

At that time, when Thorstein lived at Hof and Brodd-Helgi was growing up with him, a man named Lyting lived at Outer Krossavik.[1] He was the son of Asbjorn, the son of Olaf Long-Neck, and was a wise and very wealthy man.

Lyting was married to a woman named Thordis, the daughter of Herlu-Bjarni Arnfinsson. They had two sons who come into this story, one named Geitir and the other Blaeng. One of Lyting's daughters was named Halla, and the other Rannveig, who was married to a man named Olaf at Klifshagi in Oxarfjord.

The brothers and Brodd-Helgi were very close in age, and there was great friendship between them. Brodd-Helgi married Halla Lytingsdottir,[2] the sister of those brothers.[3] Their daughter was Thordis Todda,[4] whom Helgi Asbjarnarson[5] married. Bjarni was the name of their younger son, and Lyting the elder. Bjarni was fostered at Krossavik by Geitir.[6]

---

[1] A folk etymology in *Brandkrossa þáttr* derives the name of Krossavik from a bull called Brandkrossi. The name may come from the practice of using crosses as harbor marks or it may signal a Christian connection.

[2] Icelandic names follow a patronymic naming convention in which a child's last name is composed of the name of his or her father with the addition of -*son* or -*dóttir*. Thus the children of Lýtingr Ásbjarnarson (Lyting the son of Asbjorn) are named Geitir Lýtingsson, Blængr Lýtingsson, Halla Lýtingsdóttir, and Rannveig Lýtingsdóttir. This custom of naming is still followed in Iceland today.

[3] A crucial connection in the story is Brodd-Helgi's marriage to Halla, Geitir's sister. The major antagonists Brodd-Helgi and Geitir are brothers-in-law, and their feuding sons, Bjarni and Thorkel, are first cousins. (See the genealogical tables.)

[4] *Todda* is a nickname, a shortening of *Þórdís*. It is also the feminine form of the masculine noun *toddi* 'bit, piece, morsel'. Thordis' nickname is explained as an ironic designation in *Fljótsdæla saga*. "[Thordis] had a nickname and was called Todda because she was so open-handed that when she was giving food to people, she gave nothing less than big portions."

[5] Helgi Asbjarnarson was a chieftain in the adjacent district of Fljotsdal to the south of Weapon's Fjord. He appears in several sagas, most notably *Droplaugarsona saga* and *Fljótsdæla saga*. Note also the reference a few sentences later to his enemies Helgi and Grim, the sons of Droplaug (footnote 2, page 36). The saga writer probably expected his audience to be familiar with these individuals and provided no genealogy.

[6] In medieval Iceland, children were often brought up by foster-parents, either at home or in other households. Children raised at home often had foster-parents appointed from among the servants. Outside the home, foster-parents could be of lower, equal, or higher status than the child's parents. Sometimes (as here) they were also relatives by blood or marriage. Usually these arrangements promoted alliances between different households in addition to ties of kinship and marriage.

3. KAPÍTULI

Summary of Chapter 3. Lyting, another important man in the district, is introduced. His sons, Geitir and Blaeng, are close in age to Brodd-Helgi, and the three are fast friends. Brodd-Helgi and Geitir become chieftains and have an especially strong friendship. They play sports together, consult each other in all matters, and meet nearly every day. Brodd-Helgi is married to Geitir's sister, Halla, and everything goes well between them.

Í þann tíma, er Þorsteinn bjó at Hofi ok Brodd-Helgi óx upp með honum, þá bjó sá maðr í Krossavík inni ýtri, er Lýtingr hét ok var Ásbjarnarson, Óláfs sonar langháls. Hann var vitr maðr ok vel auðugr at fé.[1]

Hann átti konu, er Þórdís hét, dóttur Herlu-Bjarna Arnfinnssonar. Þau áttu tvá sonu, þá er við þessa sǫgu koma.[2] Hét annarr Geitir, en annarr Blængr. Halla hét dóttir Lýtings, en ǫnnur Rannveig, ok var hon gipt í Klifshaga í Øxarfjǫrð þeim manni, er Óláfr hét.

Þeir váru mjǫk jafngamlir, brœðr ok Brodd-Helgi, ok var með þeim vinfengi mikit. Brodd-Helgi fekk Hǫllu Lýtingsdóttur, systur þeira brœðra. Þeira dóttir var Þórdís todda, er átti Helgi Ásbjarnarson. Bjarni hét son þeira[3] inn yngri, en Lýtingr inn ellri. Bjarni var at fóstri í Krossavík með Geiti.

---

[1] **auðugr:** an older spelling of *auðigr* 'rich, wealthy'.

[2] **þá er við þessa sǫgu koma:** '(those) who come into this saga'.

[3] **þeira:** that is, of Brodd-Helgi and Halla Lytingsdottir.

Blaeng was extremely strong and was somewhat stooped when he walked.

Geitir was married to Hallkatla Thidrandadottir, the aunt[1] of the sons of Droplaug.[2]

So good was the friendship between Brodd-Helgi and Geitir that they shared all games and plans together, and they met almost every day. People noticed and remarked how great a friendship there was between them.

At that time, a man lived in Sunnudal named Thormod, who was called Stick-Gazer.[3] He was the son of Steinbjorn Sturdy[4] and his brothers were Ref the Red[5] of Refsstadir ('Ref's Farmstead') and Egil of Egilsstadir ('Egil's Farmstead'). The children of Egil were Thorarin, Hallbjorn, Throst, and Hallfrid, whom Thorkel Geitisson married.[6] Thormod's sons were Thorstein and Eyvind. The sons of Ref were Stein and Hreidar. All of them were thingmen of Geitir,[7] a man of great wisdom.

The relationship of Halla and Brodd-Helgi was good. Their son Lyting was fostered in Oxarfjord with Thorgils Skin. Brodd-Helgi was very wealthy.

CHAPTER 3 VOCABULARY

annarr <ǫnnur, annat; *acc m* annan, *f* aðra, *dat m* ǫðrum, *n* ǫðru; *pl nom m* aðrir> *adj/indef pron* one of two, other, another; second; **annarr ... annarr** one ... the other

Arnfinnr <-s> *m* Arnfinn (*personal name*)

auðigr (*older* **auðugr**) *adj* rich, wealthy; **auðigr at fé** very wealthy, 'rich in wealth'

auðugr *var of* **auðigr**

Ásbjǫrn <*gen* Ásbjarnar> *m* Asbjorn (*personal name*)

barn <bǫrn> *n* child

Bjarni *m* Bjarni (*personal name*); **Herlu-Bjarni** *m* Herlu-Bjarni ('Hood-Bjarni')

Blængr <-s> *m* Blaeng (*personal name*)

bróðir <*acc/dat/gen* bróður; *pl* brœðr, *dat* brœðrum, *gen* brœðra> *m* brother

bǫrn *nom/acc pl of* **barn**

dóttir <*acc/dat/gen* dóttur; *pl* dœtr, *dat* dœtrum, *gen* dœtra> *f* daughter

Droplaugarsynir *m pl* the sons of Droplaug

Egill <*dat* Agli, *gen* Egils> *m* Egil (*personal name*)

Egilsstaðir *m pl* Egilsstadir ('Egil's Farmstead') (*place name*)

ellri *comp adj* older, elder (*see* **gamall**)

Eyvindr <-ar> *m* Eyvind (*personal name*)

fannsk *1/3sg past of* **finnask**

fá <fær; fekk, fengu; fenginn> *vb* get, take, procure; grasp; marry

---

[1] **aunt:** *fǫðursystir* 'father's sister, paternal aunt'.

[2] Here the people of Krossavik are shown to be related by Geitir's marriage to the sons of Droplaug, Helgi and Grim. These sons of the woman Droplaug were the mortal enemies of Helgi Asbjarnarson (footnote 5, page 34).

[3] **Stick-Gazer:** *stikublígr*. The meaning of this nickname is unclear, but it may refer to a stingy person, 'one who stares at a measuring stick'.

[4] **Steinbjorn Sturdy:** Steinbjǫrn kǫrtr. The common nickname *kǫrtr* implies a short, stocky, barrel-chested man. Alan Boucher (*Tales from the Eastfirths*, Reykjavík: Iceland Review, 1981, p. 80n) notes that the name may also mean 'one who is hard to deal with'.

[5] Ref the Red Steinbjarnarson was the grandson of Ref the Red mentioned in Ch. 1.

[6] Thorkel Geitisson's second wife plays an important role at the end of the saga.

[7] The reference to Geitir's thingmen is the first indication to modern readers that he was a chieftain, a fact that would have been known to a medieval audience. Although neither Geitir nor Helgi, nor either of their respective sons Bjarni and Thorkel, is referred to directly as a *goði*, both families are supposed to have held chieftaincies.

Blængr var rammr at afli ok hallr nǫkkut í gǫngu.

Geitir átti Hallkǫtlu Þiðrandadóttur, fǫðursystur Droplaugarsona.

Svá var vingott með þeim Brodd-Helga ok Geiti,[1] at þeir áttu hvern leik saman ok ǫll ráð ok hittusk nær hvern dag, ok fannsk mǫnnum orð um,[2] hversu mikil vinátta með þeim var.[3]

Í þann tíma bjó sá maðr í Sunnudal, er Þormóðr hét ok var kallaðr stikublígr. Hann var sonr Steinbjarnar kǫrts[4] ok bróðir Refs ins rauða á Refsstǫðum ok Egils á Egilsstǫðum. Bǫrn Egils váru Þórarinn, Hallbjǫrn, Þrǫstr ok Hallfríðr, er átti Þorkell Geitisson. Synir Þormóðar váru þeir Þorsteinn ok Eyvindr, en þeir synir Refs Steinn ok Hreiðarr. Allir váru þeir þingmenn Geitis. Hann var spekingr mikill.

Samfarar þeira Hǫllu ok Brodd-Helga váru góðar. Lýtingr var at fóstri í Øxarfirði með Þorgilsi skinna. Brodd-Helgi var vel auðigr at fé.

---

fekk *1/3sg past of* **fá**

finna <finnr; fann, fundu; fundinn> *vb* find; *refl* **finnask** *impers* [*dat subj*] be found, perceived, noticed (by one)

fóstr <*gen* fóstrs> *n* fostering of a child; **vera at fóstri** to be a foster-child, be in a fostering relationship

fǫðursystir <*acc/dat/gen* -systur; *pl* -systr> *f* aunt, father's sister

gamall <*comp* ellri~eldri, *superl* ellztr~ elztr~ellstr~eldstr> *adj* old

ganga <*acc/dat/gen* gǫngu> *f* walking, going; **hallr í gǫngu** stooped, walking with a stoop

Geitir <-is> *m* Geitir (*personal name*)

gipta <-t-> *vb* give away in marriage

góðr <góð, gott> *adj* good

Halla <*acc/dat/gen* Hǫllu> *f* Halla (*personal name*)

Hallbjǫrn <-bjarnar> *m* Hallbjorn (*personal name*)

Hallfríðr *f* Hallfrid (*personal name*)

Hallkatla *f* Hallkatla (*personal name*)

hallr *adj* leaning, sloping; **hallr í gǫngu** stooped, walking with a stoop

háls <háls; hálsar> *m* neck

hitta <-tt-> *vb* meet with, hit upon; hit; *refl* **hittask** meet one another

hon <*acc* hana, *dat* henni, *gen* hennar> *pron 3sg f* she

Hreiðarr <-s> *m* Hreidar (*personal name*)

hverr <hver, hvert> *adj/indef pron* each, every, all; **hvern dag** every day

jafngamall <*pl m* -gamlir> *adj* as old, of the same age

Klifshagi *m* Klifshagi ('Cliff Meadow') (*place name*)

koma <kemr~kømr; kom, kómu~ kvámu; kominn> *vb* come; **koma við þessa sǫgu** appear in this saga

kona <*pl gen* kvenna> *f* woman; wife

Krossavík *f* Krossavik ('Cross Bay' or 'Cross Inlet', presumably an inlet where a cross was erected) (*place name*); **Krossavík in ýtri** Outer Krossavik

kǫrtr <*gen* kartar~kǫrts > *m* short, stocky, sturdy man (*nickname*)

langháls <-ls> *m* long-neck (*nickname*)

langr <lǫng, langt> *adj* long

leikr <-s; -ar> *m* game, play, sport

Lýtingr <-s> *m* Lyting (*personal name*)

maðr <*acc* mann, *dat* manni, *gen* manns; *pl nom/acc* menn, *dat* mǫnnum, *gen* manna> *m* man; person

manni *dat sg of* **maðr**

mjǫk *adv* almost, very nearly; very

---

[1] **Svá var vingott með þeim Brodd-Helga ok Geiti:** 'So good was the friendship between (them) Brodd-Helgi and Geitir'.

[2] **fannsk mǫnnum orð um:** 'people noticed and remarked about'. In this impersonal expression, the logical subject ('men, people') is in the dative (*mǫnnum*).

[3] **hversu mikil vinátta með þeim var:** 'how great a friendship there was between them'.

[4] **kǫrts:** genitive of *kǫrtr* 'short, stocky man', an alternative of the usual form *kartar*.

mǫnnum *dat pl of* **maðr**

nær *adv* nearly

nǫkkurr <nǫkkur, nǫkkut; *acc m* nǫkkurn> *adj/indef pron* any, anybody; some, a certain

nǫkkut *n adj as adv* somewhat

orð *n* word; repute, fame, report

Óláfr <-s> *m* Olaf (*personal name*); **Ólafr langháls** *m* Olaf Long-Neck

óx *1/3sg past of* **vaxa**

ráð *n* advice, counsel; plan

Rannveig *f* Rannveig (*personal name*)

Refsstaðir *m pl* Refsstadir ('Ref's Farmstead') (*place name*)

saga <*acc/dat/gen* sǫgu> *f* story, saga

saman *adv* together

samfǫr <-farar> *f* (*usu in pl*) relationship, marriage

sá <sú, þat> *dem pron* that (one)

skinni *m* skin, skinner (*nickname*)

sonr <*dat* syni, *gen* sonar, *pl* synir, *acc* sonu> *m* son

spekingr <-s; -ar> *m* wise person, sage

Steinn <-s> *m* Stein ('Stone') (*personal name*)

stikublígr *m* 'stick-gazer', miser (*nickname*)

synir *nom pl of* **sonr**

systir <*acc/dat/gen* systur; *pl* systr> *f* sister

tími *m* time; **í þann tíma** at that time

toddi *m* bit, piece, morsel

todda *f* Todda (*abbreviation for* **Þórdís** *and a nickname; see also* **toddi**)

tvá *m acc of* **tveir**

tveir <tvær, tvau; *acc m* tvá, *dat* tveim(r), *gen* tveggja> *num* two

ungr <ung, ungt; *comp* yngri, *superl* yngstr> *adj* young

vaxa <vex; óx, óxu; vaxinn> *vb* grow; **vaxa upp** grow up

vinátta *f* friendship (*esp* a sincere, personal friendship)

vinfengi *n* friendship (*esp* a contractual alliance)

vingóðr <-góð, -gott> *adj* good towards one's friends, friendly

vitr *adj* wise

yngri *comp adj* younger (*see* **ungr**)

ýtri <*superl* ýztr> *comp adj* outer

þann *m acc sg of dem pron* **sá**

þeim *m dat sg of dem pron* **sá**

þau <*acc* þau, *dat* þeim, *gen* þeira~ þeirra> *pron 3pl n* they

Þiðrandi *m* Thidrandi (*personal name*)

þingmaðr <*pl* -menn> *m* 'thingman', the follower of an Icelandic chieftain

Þormóðr <-ar> *m* Thormod (*personal name*); **Þormóðr stikublígr** *m* Thormod Stick-Gazer

Þórarinn <-s> *m* Thorarin (*personal name*)

Þórdís *f* Thordis (*personal name*)

Þrǫstr <-s> *m* Throst (*personal name*)

ǫnnur *f nom sg of* **annarr**

Øxarfjǫrðr <*dat* -firði, *gen* -fjarðar> *m* Oxarfjord ('Axe Fjord') (*place name*)

CULTURE SECTION – OUTLAWRY

Dependence on outlawry simplified the responsibility of Icelandic leaders. It exempted both them and the society from the need to maintain a policing body to oversee the imposition of corporal punishment, execution or incarceration. Outlawry (*útlegð* 'lying outside') meant banishment from human society. It provided Icelandic society with an efficient and cost-effective means of dispensing with troublemakers and legalized blood-taking. Svart had no legal right to kill Skidi because he had not prosecuted him first. The saga does not specify the terms of Svart's sentence, but the words *gerði Svart sekan* 'made Svart an outlaw' (had Svart condemned to outlawry) makes it clear that Brodd-Helgi had the right to kill Svart because he outlawed him first.

    The laws name two types of outlawry: *fjǫrbaugsgarðr*, lesser outlawry, and *skóggangr*, full outlawry (literally 'forest-going'). Both punishments included the confiscation of property. Lesser outlawry brought a sentence of a three-year exile abroad. If a person adjudged a *fjǫrbaugsmaðr* did not leave the country, he became a *skógarmaðr*. A full outlaw was denied all assistance in Iceland. He was not to be harbored by anyone, nor could he be helped to leave the country. This punishment was tantamount to a death sentence. A *skógarmaðr* could be killed with impunity.

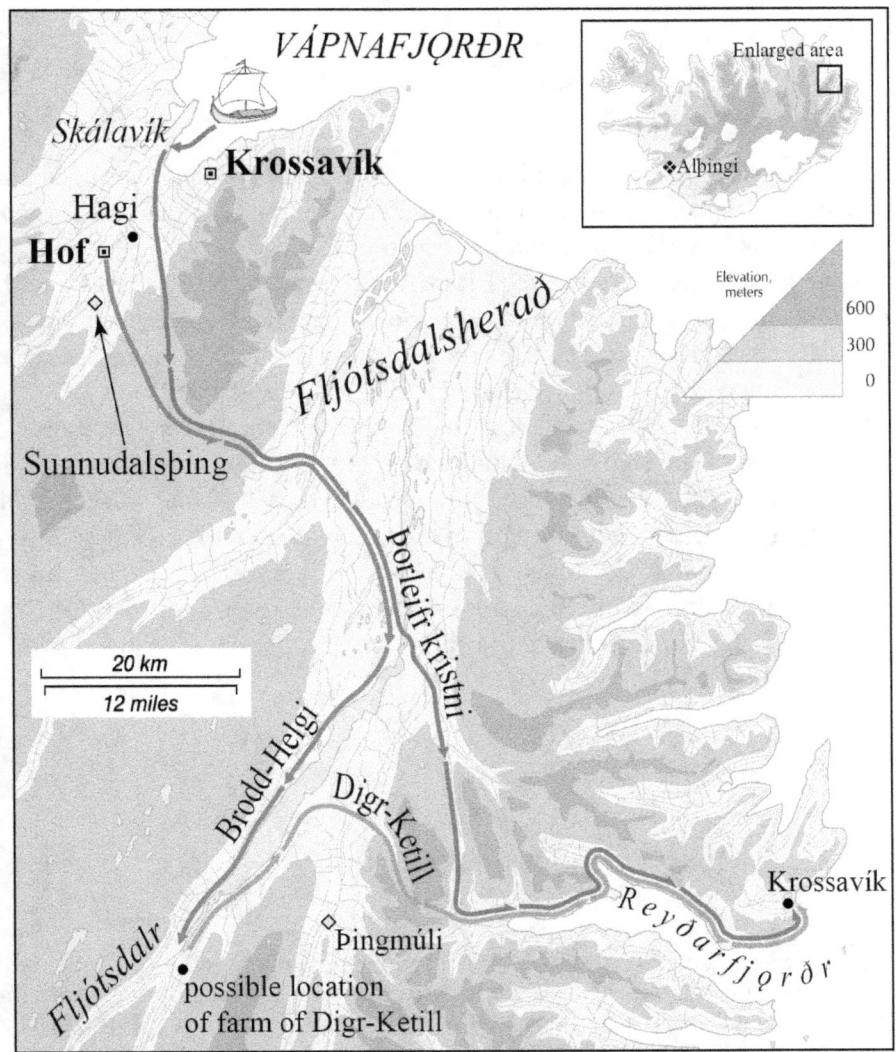

Map 4. A Ship Sails into Weapon's Fjord with Valuable Goods from Abroad. After the ship lands, Hrafn a Norwegian merchant lodges with Geitir at Krossavik in Weapon's Fjord. Hrafn's Icelandic partner, Thorleif the Christian, rides south to his own farm (also called Krossavik) in Reydarfjord, a fjord named after a type of whale. In Ch. 5, Brodd-Helgi visits Digr-Ketill ('Stout-Ketil'), who then rides to Thorleif's farm to legally summon Thorleif.

4. THE NORWEGIAN'S GOODS

It is told that one summer a ship came out from Norway to Weapon's Fjord. The ship was captained by a man named Thorleif who was called the Christian.[1] He owned a farm at Krossavik in Reydarfjord[2] and was the stepson of Asbjorn Shaggy-Head.

The other ship's captain was named Hrafn. A Norwegian by birth, he was wealthy and renowned for his riches. He was an avaricious man, silent and self-contained. It is told that he owned a gold ring, which he always wore on his hand, and a little chest that he often kept with him. People believed it to be full of gold and silver.

Thorleif went home to his farm, and the Easterners[3] got themselves lodgings. Brodd-Helgi rode to the ship and invited the captain to lodge with him.

The Easterner said he would not go there to lodge. "I am told that you are proud and greedy," he said, "but I am simple and moderate, and that is incompatible."

Brodd-Helgi offered to buy some valuables from him, because he was a very showy man, but Hrafn said he would not sell any valuables on credit. Brodd-Helgi answered, "You have made my trip a humiliation, rejecting my lodgings and refusing my trade."

---

[1] Christianity was accepted formally in Iceland at a meeting of the Althing in 1000. Prior to the conversion a number of Icelanders became Christians, mostly those traveling abroad as merchants or warriors and aligning with Christian lords. Non-Christian merchants were usually required to consent at least to preliminary baptism before they were permitted to trade at Christian centers. Early converts like Thorleif were probably vital in facilitating the first stages of the Christianization of Iceland.

[2] This Krossavik (today called Vöðlavík) lies approximately 60 miles south of Vapnafjord, just north of Reydarfjord. It is not Geitir's farm at Krossavik in Vapnafjord

[3] **Easterners:** *austmenn*, literally 'Eastmen' (singular *austmaðr* 'Eastman'). This was a standard term in Iceland for visitors from Scandinavia, most of whom were Norwegian merchants. The terms *kaupmaðr* ('trader') and *austmaðr* are nearly synonymously in medieval Icelandic sources.

4. Kapítuli

Summary of Chapter 4. Two merchants arrive, Hrafn the Norwegian and the Icelander Thorleif the Christian. Hrafn needs lodgings for the winter. He humiliates Brodd-Helgi by refusing his offer and instead stays with Geitir. At the harvest feast, Brodd-Helgi and Geitir are seen talking alone and arouse the suspicions of others. Later, Geitir urges Hrafn to attend the public games, after which Hrafn is found dead. No one confesses to the murder. Brodd-Helgi and Geitir legally claim Hrafn's inheritance at the assembly, but Thorleif loads Hrafn's goods on his ship and sets sail for Norway, intending to give his partner's belongs to their rightful heirs. Brodd-Helgi and Geitir catch him in the act, but they are disadvantaged and Hrafn escapes.

Eitthvert sumar er frá því sagt, at skip kom út í Vápnafirði.[1] Því skipi stýrði sá maðr, er Þorleifr hét ok var kallaðr inn kristni. Hann átti bú í Reyðarfirði í Krossavík ok var stjúpsonr Ásbjarnar loðinhǫfða.

Annarr stýrimaðr er nefndr Hrafn, norrœnn at kyni, auðugr ok fjǫlkunnugr at gersemum,[2] sínkr maðr ok fálátr ok vel stilltr. Þess er getit, at hann átti gullhring, þann er hann hafði ávallt á hendi sér, ok kistil, er hann hafði opt undir sér, ok hugðu menn hann fullan af gulli ok silfri.

Þorleifr fór heim til bús síns, en Austmenn vistuðusk. Brodd-Helgi reið til skips ok býðr stýrimanni til vistar með sér.

Austmaðr kvazk eigi þangat mundu fara[3] til vistar. "Mér ertu sagðr stórlátr ok fégjarn," segir hann, "en ek em smálátr ok lítilhæfr, ok er þat ósamfœrt."

Brodd-Helgi falaði af honum góða gripi, því at hann var skrautmaðr mikill, en Hrafn kvazk enga gripi vildu[4] á frest selja. Brodd-Helgi svarar: "Smæliga hefir þú gǫrt ferð mína,[5] neitat vistinni, en synjat kaupsins."

---

[1] *Skip* denotes a large ocean-going vessel. The merchant ships (*kaupskip*) that made the crossing to Iceland, primarily from Scandinavia, were of the type referred to as a *knǫrr*.

[2] **fjǫlkunnugr at gersemum**: 'well-known for his wealth'. *Fjǫlkunnugr* (or *fjǫlkunnigr*) usually means 'skilled in magic' and is a term most frequently used for sorcerers. Here the word is taken to be synonymous with *fjǫlkunnr* 'well-known, renowned'.

[3] **Austmaðr kvazk eigi þangat mundu fara**: 'The Easterner said he would not go there'. *Mundu* is the past, or preterite, infinitive of *munu*, and is best translated as 'would'.

[4] **vildu:** past, or preterite, infinitive of *vilja* 'want, wish', used in certain constructions where the infinitive follows a reflexive verb in the past tense (*kvazk* [past tense] ... *vildu* [pret. inf.]). Where the main verb is in the present tense, a regular infinitive follows, as for example in Ch. 10: *Guðmundr lézk* [pres. tense] **eigi vilja** [regular inf.] *hafa fé hans* 'Gudmund says that he **does not want** to have his money'. The only preterite infinitives common in prose are *mundu* (from *munu*; see footnote 3 just above) and *skyldu* (from *skulu*). The latter is seen in Ch. 18: *kvazk* [past tense] **skyldu** [pret. inf.] *vera honum í sona stað* 'said that he **would** be for him in place of sons', footnote 1, page 139.

[5] **smæliga hefir þú gǫrt ferð mína:** 'you have made my trip a humiliation'. The adjective *smæligr* does not occur anywhere else in Icelandic. Derived from the common adjective *smár* 'small', its meaning is 'humiliating' or at least 'belittling'. German *schmählich* has a similar meaning.

Geitir also came to the ship, found the captain and said to him that he had acted unwisely, having fallen out with the noblest man in the district.

The Easterner answered, "I had intended to lodge at some farmer's place. Or would you now like to take me in, Geitir?"

Geitir did not give in quickly to that, but it came about nonetheless that he took Hrafn with him. The crew got their lodgings, and the ship was dragged ashore.[1] A storehouse was procured for the Easterner to store his wares in. He sold the wares piece by piece.[2]

When the Winter Nights[3] arrived, the sons of Egil held a harvest feast,[4] and Brodd-Helgi and Geitir were both there. Helgi went in first and sat further in, because he was a very showy man. It was a matter of comment that Helgi and Geitir seemed to be so engrossed in conversation at that feast that no one got either either word or amusement from them.[5] Then the feast was ended and everyone went home to his own household.

During the winter there was a well attended sporting event[6] at a farmstead named Hagi, a short distance from Hof. Brodd-Helgi was there. Geitir strongly urged the Easterner to go to that meeting, stating that he would meet many who owed him money there. Afterwards they went, and Hrafn carried on about the debts owed him.

---

[1] The saga does not reveal precisely where in Weapon's Fjord the ship landed and was beached for the winter. There are two possibilities. Krossavik has a small inlet where boats could have landed, and even into the 20th century sizable fishing boats were beached there during the winter. The best landing site in the fjord, however, is at Skalavik across the fjord from Krossavik on a spit of land called Tangi, close to the present town of Vopnafjörður. *Fljótsdæla saga* (Ch. 14) says that when Geitir's other son, Thidrandi, returned from a journey to Norway, he landed at Skalavik, where he later pulled the ship onto land for the winter.

[2] Most likely this means that the Norwegian retailed his goods instead of selling them wholesale or in bulk.

[3] **Winter Nights:** *vetrnætr*. The Winter Nights were the first three nights of the winter season. It was a particularly important time in the social calendar, when animals were slaughtered for provision over the winter. Food was plentiful and people engaged in social gatherings. During Iceland's pagan period, various religious celebrations were likely observed, including sacrifices to the *dísir*, powerful female guardian spirits. The activities of the Winter Nights were observed into Christian times.

[4] The harvest feast held in the autumn, called *haustboð* (*haust* is cognate with harvest), was one of the main religious festivals from pagan times. Others included a midwinter feast (*miðsvetrarblót*) and a feast at the beginning of summer (*sumarmál*).

[5] The seating arrangements at large social gatherings were the most visible external indication of relative status. The most favored positions were the innermost seats in the hall, situated farthest from the door. Such gatherings provided an opportunity to see and be seen by everyone who mattered. Appearance and behavior at such public events were noted, and Geitir and Helgi's reclusiveness was apparently unwelcome. Engrossing private conversations on such public occasions are often ominous in saga narrative.

[6] Sporting events were popular in this competitive society. Medieval Icelanders engaged in various sports from wrestling and ball games to horse fights. Games were frequently organized as part of the Winter Nights, but they were also played at other social gatherings, such as feasts, local assemblies and the Althing.

Geitir kom ok til skips ok fann stýrimann ok kvað honum óvitrliga hafa til tekizk, ginntan at sér inn gǫfgasta mann í því heraði.[1]

Austmaðrinn svarar: "Þat hefða ek ætlat at vistask hjá einhverjum bónda, eða viltu nú taka við mér, Geitir?" segir stýrimaðr.

Geitir lét ekki skjótt við því,[2] en þó kom þar, at hann tók við honum. Vistuðusk hásetar, ok var skipi til hlunns ráðit. Gǫrvibúr[3] var Austmanni fengit at geyma í varning sinn. Seldi hann smátt varninginn.[4]

Þá er komit var at vetrnóttum, hǫfðu þeir Egilssynir haustboð, ok váru þeir Brodd-Helgi ok Geitir þar báðir, ok gekk Helgi fyrri ok sat innri, því at hann var skrautmenni mikit. Orð var á því, at þeim Helga ok Geiti þœtti svá tíðrœtt vera[5] at því boði, at menn fengi hvárki af þeim tal né gaman. Var nú slitit boðinu, ok fór hverr heim til síns heimilis.

Um vetrinn var leikr fjǫlmennr á bœ þeim, er á Haga[6] heitir, skammt frá Hofi. Brodd-Helgi var þar. Geitir fýsti Austmanninn mjǫk til þessa fundar ok kvað hann þar hitta mundu marga sína skuldunauta. Ok fóru þeir síðan, ok varð honum hjaldrjúgt um skuldir sínar.

---

[1] **kvað honum óvitrliga hafa til tekizk, ginntan at sér inn gǫfgasta mann í því heraði:** 'said he had acted unwisely and had fallen out with the noblest man in the district'.

[2] **Geitir lét ekki skjótt við því:** 'Geitir did not give in quickly to that'.

[3] **Gǫrvibúr:** 'storehouse', an outside storehouse used specifically for storing gear (*gǫrvi*).

[4] **Seldi hann smátt varningin:** 'he sold the wares piece by piece'.

[5] **orð var á því, at þeim Helga ok Geiti þœtti svá tíðrœtt vera:** 'it was a matter of comment that Helgi and Geitir seemed to be so engrossed in conversation'.

[6] **á Haga:** 'Hagi'. A preposition often preceded an Old Icelandic place name and became part of the place name.

And when the games were ended and people were preparing to depart, Helgi was sitting in the stove-room and speaking with his liegemen. (A man came into the room)[1] and told them that Hrafn the Easterner had been killed, and no one knew who the killer was.[2] Helgi went out immediately and condemned what had been done.

Hrafn was given an honorable burial according to the custom of the time.

A man named Tjorvi lived at Gudmundarstadir ('Gudmund's Farmstead'). He was a big man, and very strong.[3] Tjorvi was a friend of Brodd-Helgi and Geitir, and he was absent the whole day when the Norwegian was killed. The account some people gave of Hrafn's death was that he had been directed to a steep cliff and perished there.

Words passed between Brodd-Helgi and Geitir that each should keep half of Hrafn's wealth, but it should not be divided until after the spring assembly. Geitir took possession of the wares in the spring and locked them in his outside storehouse.

Thorleif the Christian prepared his ship in the spring for the outward journey and was fully prepared by the spring assembly. And when the time came, men traveled to the spring assembly in Sunnudal, among them both Brodd-Helgi and Geitir, and in many places few people were left at home.

When the assembly was drawing toward the end, Thorleif awakened early and woke up his crew. They boarded the boat and rowed to Krossavik, where they went up to Geitir's outside storehouse and broke into it. They took out all of Hrafn's share of the wealth and carried it to their ship. Halla Lytingsdottir was there but took no notice.

Now Brodd-Helgi traveled home from the assembly with Geitir. But before they reached home, they were told that Thorleif had taken all Hrafn's share of the wealth and was intending to carry it away. Helgi took the position that Thorleif must be mistaken in the law about that matter, and would immediately hand it over when he was called on.

Then they went out to the ship in many small boats, and when they had greeted each other, Brodd-Helgi declared that Thorleif was required to hand over the property. Thorleif said that he knew little about the law, but he believed that a partner would be obliged to deliver the other's property to the heirs.[4]

---

[1] This phrase is supplied from one of the paper manuscripts. The text is clearly deficient here although there are no gaps in the manuscripts.

[2] A perpetrator was required by law to announce a killing. It was supposed to take place at the dwelling nearest to the scene of the killing, as long as that dwelling did not endanger the life of the killer. An undeclared killing was defined as *morð* 'murder'. A man guilty of murder had no defense in the law (*Grágás* Ia, 153–54).

[3] Tjorvi is unknown in other sources.

[4] It is not known what rights Norwegians had in Iceland at this time. In 1025, Icelanders made a treaty with the Norwegian king Olaf Haraldsson, which stated, "Kin and partner shall take inheritances in Iceland, but if there are none, then inheritances shall wait there for the heirs" (*Grágás* Ib, 195; III, 103). (See Alan Berger, "Lawyers in the Old Icelandic Family Sagas: Heroes, Villains, and Authors," *Saga-Book* 20, 1978–1979, pp. 70–79, esp. 72–75.)

Ok er leiknum var lokit ok menn váru í brottbúningi, sat Helgi í stofu ok talaði við þingmenn sína — — —[1] ok sagði þeim, at Hrafn Austmaðr væri veginn, ok urðu menn ekki varir við vegandann. Helgi gekk út þegar ok mælti illa fyrir verki því, er þar var unnit.

Útferð Hrafns var gǫr sœmilig at þeiri siðvenju, sem þá var.

Maðr hét Tjǫrvi ok bjó á Guðmundarstǫðum. Hann var mikill maðr ok rammr at afli. Tjǫrvi var vinr þeira Brodd-Helga ok Geitis, en hann var horfinn þann dag allan, er Austmaðrinn var veginn. Þat var sumra manna frásǫgn um líflát Hrafns, at honum hafi vísat verit á forað ok týnzk þar.

Þau orð fóru á milli Brodd-Helga ok Geitis, at hálft fé Hrafns myndi[2] hvárr hafa ok skipta eigi fyrr en eptir várþing, ok tók Geitir við vǫrunni um várit ok læsti í útibúri sínu.

Þorleifr inn kristni bjó skip sitt um várit til útanferðar ok varð albúinn at várþingi. En er svá var komit, þá fóru menn til várþings í Sunnudal, bæði Brodd-Helgi ok Geitir, ok var þá í mǫrgum stǫðum fátt heima.

Ok er á leið mjǫk þingit,[3] vaknar Þorleifr snimma ok vekr upp skipverja sína. Stigu þeir á bátinn ok reru síðan í Krossavík ok gengu þar upp ok til útibúrs Geitis ok luku því upp[4] ok báru út allan fjárhlut þann, er Hrafn hafði átt, ok fluttu til skips síns. Halla var þar Lýtingsdóttir ok skipti sér engu af.

Nú ferr Brodd-Helgi heim af þinginu með Geiti. En áðr þeir kómu heim, var þeim sagt, at Þorleifr hefði allan fjárhlut upp tekit ok ætlaði í brott at flytja. Helgi tók svá upp, at Þorleifr mundi lǫgvillr orðinn um þetta mál ok þegar mundi hann laust láta, er vitjat væri.

Fara þeir síðan út til skips ok hǫfðu mǫrg skip ok smá, ok er þeir kvǫddusk, þá mælti Brodd-Helgi, at Þorleifr skyldi laust láta féit. Þorleifr kvazk lítit vita til laga, en kvazk ætla, at félagi mundi eiga at fœra fé erfingjum.

---

[1] Something seems missing from the text, although there are no gaps in the manuscripts. One of the paper manuscripts inserts *Maðr kom í stofu* 'a man came into the room'.

[2] *Myndi* and *mundi* are subjunctive forms of *munu* and appear interchangeably throughout the saga.

[3] **er á leið mjǫk þingit:** 'when the assembly was drawing toward the end'.

[4] By itself, *lúka* means 'to close' (either literally or figuratively), but it is mostly accompanied by a preposition. Whereas *lúka aptr* means 'to close', *lúka upp* is 'to open'.

Brodd-Helgi answered, "We do not intend to have come for nothing."

Thorleif answered, "We shall all sooner fight than you receive a single penny."

"You hear," said Helgi, "what this worthless man says. We shall for sure raise such a storm that some will feel its sting."[1]

Then Geitir spoke up and said, "This does not seem advisable to me, to launch an attack with small boats, when we don't know but that a headwind may come up and drive them ashore. Then we may yet accomplish what we think fit."

This was spoken well of by all, and the advice was taken. The men put to shore, and Brodd-Helgi went home with Geitir and was there several nights.

Thorleif got a fair wind at once, and had a very swift journey. He brought the property that Hrafn had owned to his heirs, and they were very grateful to him for it. They gave Thorleif their share of the ship, and they parted good friends afterwards.

CHAPTER 4 VOCABULARY

albúa <albýr; albjó, albjoggu; albúinn> *vb* fit out, furnish or equip fully

albúinn *ppart* fully equipped (*see* **albúa**)

andviðri *n* headwind

atsókn <-ir> *f* onslaught, attack

Austmaðr <*acc* -mann, *dat* -manni, etc.> *m* Easterner, person from the east (*esp* a Norwegian)

áðr *adv* before

átt *n* *ppart of* **eiga**

ávallt *adv* always

báðir <báðar, bæði, *gen* beggja> *adj/indef dual pron* both

báru *3pl past of* **bera**

bátr <-s; -ar> *m* boat

bera <berr; bar, báru; borinn> *vb* carry, bear

berja <barð-; *ppart* bar(i)ðr> *vb* strike; *refl* **berjask** fight

bjóða <býðr; bauð, buðu; boðinn> *vb* [*w acc*] offer; [*w dat*] invite; **bjóða [e-m] til vistar** invite [sb] to stay at one's house

boð *n* feast

bóndi <*gen* bónda; *pl* bœndr> *m* farmer; husband; head of a household

brott (*also* **í brott**) *adv* away, off

brottbúningr *m* preparation for departure

búa <býr; bjó, bjoggu~bjuggu; búinn> *vb* live (in a place), dwell; prepare, make ready; **búa [e-t] til [e-s]** to prepare [sth] for [sth]

byrr <-jar; -ir> *m* fair wind; **[e-m] gefr vel byr** *impers* [sb] gets a fair wind

býðr *2/3sg pres of* **bjóða**

bæði *adv* both; **bæði ... ok** *conj* both ... and

bæði *n of* **báðir**

bœr <*gen* bœjar; *pl* bœir> *m* farm, farmhouse, farmstead

eða *conj* or

eiga <á, eigu; átti; áttr> *pret-pres vb* own, have, possess; to be married or related to; [*aux*] must, owe, be obligated, have to

einkis *gen of* **engi**

ek <*acc* mik, *dat* mér, *gen* mín> *pron 1sg* I

em *1sg pres vb* am (*see* **vera**)

engi <engi, ekki> *adj/indef pron* no one, none, no

erfingi <*pl* erfingjar> *m* heir

ertu = ert þú are you (*sg*) (*2sg pres of* **vera** *w encl pron*)

fala <-að-> *vb* demand for purchase; **fala [e-t] af [e-m]** offer to buy [sth] from [sb]

fann *1/3sg past of* **finna**

fara <ferr; fór, fóru; farinn> *vb* go, travel; move

fá <fær; fekk, fengu; fenginn> *vb* get, take, procure

fálátr *adj* silent, reserved

fár <fá, fátt> *adj/pron* few

fengi *3sg/pl past subjunct of* **fá**

---

[1] Brodd-Helgi's threat to attack Thorleif has a proverbial sense. See the skald Nefari's lines (ca. 1186) composed as a war cry: *Látum skipta goð giptu, gerum hríð, er þeim svíði*, "Let us deal out the luck of the gods, raising such a storm that they feel the sting." Finnur Jónsson, *Den norsk-islandske skjaldedigtning*, B 2, p. 518.

Brodd-Helgi svarar: "Eigi ætlum vér ørendislaust at fara."

Þorleifr svarar: "Fyrr skulum vér berjask allir en þér fáið nǫkkurn penning."[1]

"Heyri þér," kvað Helgi, "hvat sá maðr mælir, er einkis góðs er verðr.[2] Skulum vér at vísu gera þá hríð, at nǫkkurum svíði."[3]

Þá tók Geitir til orða ok mælti: "Ekki at ráði þykki mér þetta at veita þeim atsókn á smáskipum, en vér vitum eigi, nema komi á andviðri ok reki þá upp, ok má þá enn þat af gera, sem sýnisk."[4]

Þetta var vel fyrir mælt af ǫllum, ok var þetta ráð tekit. Ok létu menn at landi, ok fór Brodd-Helgi heim með Geiti ok var þar nǫkkurar nætr.

Þorleifi gaf þegar byr, ok varð hann vel hraðfara ok fœrði erfingjum fé þat, er Hrafn hafði átt, en þeir kunnu honum þǫkk fyrir. Þeir gáfu Þorleifi sinn hlut skips, ok skilðu þeir góðir vinir síðan.

---

fégjarn *adj* greedy, avaricious

finna <finnr; fann, fundu; fundinn> *vb* find; notice, perceive

fjárhlutr <-ar; -ir> *m* property, valuables

fjǫlkunnugr *adj* well known, renowned; (*usu*) skilled in magic

fjǫlmennr *adj* numerous, with many people, well attended

fluttu *3pl past of* **flytja**

flytja <flutt-> *vb* convey, move, carry, bring, deliver

forað <foruð~forǫð> *n* dangerous place; precipice; pit

fóru *3pl past of* **fara**

frásǫgn <*gen* -sagnar; *pl* -sagnir> *f* story, narrative, account

frest *n pl* delay; **selja á frest** sell on credit

fullr *adj* full

fyrr *comp adv* before, previously, sooner; **fyrr en** *conj* before, sooner than, until

fyrri *comp adj* former, previous; *comp adv* (= **fyrr**) before, previously, sooner

fýsa <-t-> *vb* urge

fœra <-ð-> *vb* bring, present, convey, send, give; **fœra [e-m] [e-t]** bring [sb] [sth]

gaf *1/3sg past of* **gefa**

gaman *n* fun, amusement

ganga <gengr; gekk, gengu; genginn> *vb* go, walk

gáfu *3pl past of* **gefa**

gefa <gefr; gaf, gáfu; gefinn> *vb* give, grant

gengu *3pl past of* **ganga**

gera <-ð-; *ppart* gerðr~gerr> *vb* make, build; do, act; **gera af** accomplish, do; **gera hríð** attack, 'do battle'

gersemi *f* costly thing, jewel, treasure; **auðugr at gersemum** rich in treasures; **fjǫlkunnugr at gersemum** well known for one's riches

geyma <-d-> *vb* keep, store

ginna <-t-> *vb* dupe, fool; **ginna [e-n] at sér** to fall out with [sb]

gripr <-ar; -ir> *m* costly thing

gull *n* gold

gullhringr <-s; -ar> *m* gold ring

Guðmundarstaðir *m pl* Gudmundarstadir ('Gudmund's Farmstead') (*place name*)

gǫfgastr *superl of* **gǫfugr**

gǫfugr <*acc m* gǫfgan> *adj* noble

gǫrt *var of* **gert**, *n ppart of* **gera**

gørvibúr *n* storehouse

hafa <hef(i)r, -ð-> *vb* have; hold, keep

hafi *3sg/pl pres subjunct of* **hafa**

Hagi *m* Hagi ('Meadow') (*place name*)

---

[1] **en þér fáið nǫkkurn penning:** 'than you should get a single penny'.

[2] **er einkis góðs er verðr:** 'who is worth nothing'.

[3] **skulum vér at vísu gera þá hríð, at nǫkkurum svíði:** 'we shall for sure raise such a storm, that it will sting (*or* burn) some', i.e., 'we shall for sure make such an attack that some of them will feel its sting'.

[4] **má þá enn þat af gera, sem sýnisk:** 'then that may yet be accomplished which seems fitting', i.e., 'then we may yet accomplish what we think fit'.

haustboð *n* autumn feast, harvest feast

hálfr <hálf, hálft> *adj* half

hásetar *m pl* crew (of a ship) (*see* **háseti**)

háseti *m* oarsman

hefða *1sg past subjunct of* **hafa**

heim *adv* home, homeward (*motion*)

heimili *n* home, house, homestead

hjaldrjúgr *adj* talkative; aggressively demanding; **[e-m] verðr hjaldrjúgt um [e-t]** *impers* [sb] talks much or at length about [sth]

hjá *prep* [w dat] by, near; at one's place

hlunnr <-s; -ar> *m* piece of wood put under the keel of a ship when ashore; **ráða skipi til hlunns** to drag a ship ashore (during winter)

hlutr <-ar; -ir> *m* lot; thing

Hrafn <-s> *m* Hrafn ('Raven') (*personal name*)

hraðfara *adj indecl* swift, speedy, 'quick-faring'; **verða vel hraðfara** be very swift in travelling, have a speedy journey

hríð <-ir> *f* a time, while; storm; attack, battle; **gera hríð** attack, 'do battle'

hugðu *3pl past of* **hyggja**

hvat *rel pron* what, that which

hvárgi <*n* hvárki~hvártki> *adj/indef pron* neither (of two); *conj* **hvárki ... né** neither ... nor

hvárki *n of* **hvárgi**

hvárr *indef pron* each (of two)

hyggja <hugð-, hug(a)ðr> *vb* think, believe

illa *adv* badly, ill

innri *comp adj* inner, inmost, farther in

kaup *n* bargain, trade

kistill <*dat* kistli, *gen* kistils, *pl* kistlar> *m* little chest, small box

koma <kemr~kømr; kom, kómu~kvámu; kominn> *vb* come; **koma á** hit

kristinn <*wk m* kristni> *adj* Christian

kunna <kann, kunnu; kunni; kunnat> *pret-pres vb* can, know how to; feel (an emotion); **kunna [e-m] þǫkk fyrir [e-t]** be thankful to [sb] for [sth]

kvazk *2/3sg past of* **kveðask**

kveða <kveðr; kvað, kváðu; kveðinn> *vb* speak, say; *refl* **kveðask** say of oneself, declare

kveðja <kvadd-> *vb* greet; *refl* **kveðjask** greet one another

kvǫddusk *3pl past of* **kveðjask**

kyn <*pl dat* kynjum, *gen* kynja> *n* kin; kindred; **at kyni** by extraction or birth

laga *gen of* **lǫg**

lauss <laus, laust> *adj* loose; free, unimpeded

láta <lætr, lét, létu; látinn> *vb* let, allow, permit; put, place, set; behave; **láta at landi** put back to land; **láta laust** 'let loose', yield, give up, hand over; **láta við [e-u]** agree, yield, give in to [sth]

leið *1/3sg past of* **líða**

létu *3pl past of* **láta**

líða <líðr; leið, liðu; liðinn> *vb* pass (*usu of time*); **líða á** pass, draw to a close

líflát *n* loss of life, death (*esp violent*)

lítilhæfr *adj* humble, moderate

lítill <lítil, lítit> *adj* little

lítit *n indef pron* little (*from* **lítill**)

loðinhǫfði *m* shaggy head (*nickname*)

lokit *n ppart of* **lúka**

luku *3pl past of* **lúka**

lúka <lýkr; lauk, luku; lokinn> *vb* [w dat] close; end, conclude; shut; **lúka [e-t/e-u] upp** open [sth]

læsa <-t-> *vb* [w dat] lock, shut

lǫg <*gen* laga> *n pl* laws, law

lǫgvillr *adj* mistaken in point of law, confused about the law

margr <mǫrg, mar(g)t> *adj* [w sg] many a (*in collective sense*); [w pl] many

má *1/3sg pres of* **mega**

mál *n* (leg) suit, action, case

mega <má, megu; mátti; mátt> *pret-pres vb* can, may; be able

mér *dat of* **ek**

milli (*also* **á milli**, **í milli**) *prep* [w gen] between

mundi (*var of* **myndi**) *3sg/pl past subjunct of* **munu**

mundu *vb* would (*pret inf of* **munu**)

munu <mun, munu; mundi; *pret inf* mundu> *pret-pres vb* will, shall (*futurity*); to be sure to, must (*probability*); (*past tense*) would, must

myndi (*also* **mundi**) *3sg/pl past subjunct of* **munu**

mæla <-t-> *vb* say, speak; **mæla fyrir [e-u]** declare [sth]; **mæla illa fyrir [e-u]** speak ill of, condemn [sth]

mǫrg *n nom/acc pl of* **margr**

nefna <-d-> *vb* name, call

neita <-að-> *vb* [w dat] deny, refuse, reject

nema *conj* except, save, but; [w subjunct]

unless

né *conj* nor

norrœnn *adj* Norse, Norwegian

nótt <*gen* nætr; *pl* nætr> *f* night

nætr *gen sg & nom/acc pl of* **nótt**

nǫkkurn *m acc sg of* **nǫkkurr**

nǫkkurr <nǫkkur, nǫkkut; *acc m* nǫkkurn> *adj* any

ok *conj* and; *adv* also

opt *adv* often

orð *n* word; **orð var á því** it was said

ósamfœrr <-fœr, -fœrt> *adj* incompatible, unable to be mixed together

óvitrliga *adv* foolishly, unwisely

penningr <-s; -ar> *m* coin, penny; piece of property, article

ráð *n* advice, counsel; plan; **at ráði** wise, advisable

ráða <ræðr; réð, réðu; ráðinn> *vb* [*w dat*] advise, counsel; rule, govern, manage; undertake; **ráða skipi til hlunns** to drag a ship ashore (during winter)

reið *1/3sg past of* **ríða**

reka <rekr; rak, ráku; rekinn> *vb* drive, herd; drive onto shore, wreck; **rekr [e-n/ e-t] upp** *impers* [sb/sth] is driven ashore

reru *3pl past of* **róa**

Reyðarfjǫrðr <*dat* -firði, *gen* -fjarðar> *m* Reydarfjord (*place name*)

ríða <ríðr; reið, riðu; riðinn> *vb* ride

róa <rær; reri, reru; róinn> *vb* row

rœða <-dd-> *vb* speak; **rœða um [e-t]** discuss [sth]

rœtt *n ppart of* **rœða**

sat *1/3sg past of* **sitja**

selja <-d-> *vb* hand over to another; sell; **selja á frest** sell on credit; **selja smátt** sell piece by piece, bit by bit

siðvenja *f* custom, practice; **at siðvenju** according to custom

silfr *n* silver

sitja <sitr; sat, sátu; setinn> *vb* sit

sínkr *adj* avaricious, covetous

skip *n* ship

skipta <-t-> *vb* [*w dat*] divide, share in; shift, change; happen; **skipta sér engu af [e-u]** take no part in [sth], take no notice of [sth]

skipverjar *m pl* ship's crew

skjótr <skjót, skjótt> *adj* swift, quick

skjótt *n adj as adv* swiftly, quickly; soon

skrautmaðr *m* showy person, show-off, one who loves fine clothes and adorn-

ments

skrautmenni *n* showy person (= **skraut-maðr**)

skuld <-ir> *f* debt

skuldunautr <-s; -ar> *m* debtor

skulu <skal, skulu; skyldi; *pret inf* skyldu> *pret-pres vb* shall (*obligation, purpose, necessity, fate*); (*past tense*) should

skyldi *3sg past indic & 3sg/pl past subjunct of* **skulu**

slitit *n ppart of* **slíta**

stigu *3pl past of* **stíga**

slíta <slítr; sleit, slitu; slitinn> *vb* [*w dat*] break up, dissolve (a meeting or confrontation)

smálátr *adj* content with little

smár <smá, smátt> *adj* small

smáskip *n* small ship

smátt *adv* in small quantities; **selja smátt** sell piece by piece, bit by bit

smæligr *adj* humiliating, dishonorable

snimma *adv* early

stilltr *adj* calm, composed, self-contained

stíga <stígr; steig, stigu; stiginn> *vb* step, walk; **stíga á (skip, bát)** board (a ship, a boat)

stjúpsonr <*dat* -syni, *gen* -sonar, *pl* -synir, *acc* -sonu> *m* stepson

stofa *f* 'stove room', a room in a long house, secondary to the **eldaskáli** and warmed by a stove of flat stones, which served as a living room where women worked the looms, families sat in the evenings, and feasts were held

stórlátr *adj* proud, haughty; munificent; not content with little

stýra <-ð-> *vb* [*w dat*] steer, command

stýrimaðr <<*acc* mann, *dat* manni, etc.> *m* captain of a ship, skipper

sumar *n* summer

sumr <sum, sumt> *adj/indef pron* some; **sumra manna** of some people

svara <-að-> *vb* [*w dat*] answer, reply

svíða <svíðr; sveið, sviðu; sviðinn> *vb impers* [*dat subj*] be hurt

synja <-að-> *vb* [*w gen*] deny, refuse

sýna <-d-> *vb* show; *refl* **sýnask** seem, appear; seem fitting

sœmiligr *adj* honorable, becoming

taka <tekr; tók, tóku; tekinn> *vb* take; **taka [e-t] til** begin, take to [sth]; **taka til orða** speak up; **taka upp** interpret, think, take a position (on a question); **taka upp [e-t]** take, pick up [sth]; **taka við [e-m]** take in, receive, or welcome [sb] into one's house; *refl* **takask** begin, happen

tal <tǫl> *n* conversation, talk

tekinn *ppart of* **taka**

tekizk *n ppart of* **takask**

tíðr *adj* frequent; usual

tíðrœtt *ppart* discussed much (*see* **rœða**, **tíðr**); **þeim var tíðrœtt** *impers* they spoke much together

Tjǫrvi *m* Tjorvi (*personal name*)

týna <-d-> *vb* lose; *refl* **týnask** perish

týnzk *n ppart of* **týnask**

undir *prep* [*w dat*] under; **undir sér** with him

urðu *3pl past of* **verða**

útanferð <-ir> *f* journey abroad

útferð <-ir> *f* journey to a remote place; funeral, burial

útibúr *n* outside storehouse

vara <*pl* vǫrur, *gen* varna> *f* wares

varningr <*gen* -s> *m* wares, goods, cargo

varr <vǫr, vart> *adj* aware; **verða varr við [e-t]** become aware of, learn of [sth]

vár *n* spring (season); **um várit** in the spring

várþing *n* spring assembly

vegandi *m* killer

veita <-tt-> *vb* grant, give, offer; assist; **veita [e-m] [e-t]** grant [sb] [sth]; **veita [e-m] atsókn** attack [sb]

vera <er; var, váru; verit> *vb* be

verða <verðr; varð, urðu; orðinn> *vb* become, happen

verðr *adj* [*w gen*] worth, of value; worthy, deserving; **vera [e-s] verðr** be worthy, deserving of [sth]

verk *n* work, a deed, business

vetr <*gen* vetrar; *pl* vetr> *m* winter; **um vetrinn** in, during the winter

vetrnætr *f pl* Winter Nights (the three days which begin the winter season)

vildu *vb* would, wanted to (*pret inf of* **vilja**)

vilja <2/3sg *pres* vill; vildi; viljat; *pret inf* vildu > *vb* wish, want

viltu = **vill þú**, do you (*sg*) want (*2sg pres of* **vilja** *w encl pron*)

vinr <-ar; -ir> *m* friend

vist <-ir> *f* stay; lodging; **til vistar** to lodge, stay (at one's house)

vista <-að-> *vb* (*trans*) lodge (someone), find lodging for; furnish with food and provisions; *refl* **vistask** lodge (*intrans*), stay, take up lodging

vita <veit, vitu; vissi; vitaðr> *pret-pres vb* know; **vita til [e-s]** know of [sth]

vitja <-að-> *vb* [*w gen*] call on, visit; claim the fulfillment of an agreement or promise

vísa <-að-> *vb* show, point out, indicate; **vísa [e-m] á [e-t]** direct or lead [sb] into [sth]

víss *adj* certain, sure; **at vísu** surely

þangat *adv* to there, thither (*motion*)

þá er *conj* when

þér <*acc/dat* yðr, *gen* yðarr~yðvarr> *pron 2pl* you (*pl*)

þing *n* assembly, meeting

þó *adv* yet, though, nevertheless

Þórleifr <-s> *m* Thorleif (*personal name*); **Þórleifr inn kristni** *m* Thorleif the Christian

þykkja <þykkir, þótt-> *vb impers* seem to be; [*dat subj*] think, seem (to one)

þœtti *3sg/pl past subjunct of* **þykkja**

þǫkk <*gen* þakkar; *pl* þakkir> *f* thanks

ætla <-að-> *vb* intend, purpose, mean; think, consider

CULTURE SECTION – PRICE-SETTING

Trade in Iceland had a seasonal nature. Travel between Norway and Iceland was dangerous during the winter due to storms and the perils of sea-ice. Merchants arriving in summer and fall had to stay almost a year. They sold their goods on credit throughout the winter and collected their debts before being able to leave Iceland in early summer. There were no permanent marketplaces in Iceland where merchants could spend the winter, so they came to agreement with local farmers and chieftains who had the capacity to house and feed them. Merchants traded their goods for Icelandic products, primarily raw wool and woolen cloth of various grades.

Chieftains had the right to set prices on wares that foreign merchants brought into Iceland. Ostensibly the purpose of this practice was to control the greed of foreign merchants. The laws of Free State Iceland called *Grágás* (the '*Grey Goose*' Law) offer a pertinent entry: "It is said in our laws that men shall not buy expensive Norwegian goods from merchants at their ships until the three men who set the rate within each district boundary have done so" (*Grágás* Ib, 72, Ch. 167). Neither the date nor the enforceability of the clause is known.

Although some windfall profits might have accrued from price setting, it was not as lucrative as one might expect because, in most instances, the Norwegian merchant retained the advantage. If dissatisfied with a chieftain in a particular region, the merchant could try to find a more compliant host, as the Norwegian Hrafn does in this chapter. Merchants could take their trade to other regions, and they were free to lodge with either chieftains or farmers. As foreigners without kin to protect them, merchants were dependent upon the support of their hosts to collect debts and to ensure their personal safety. Where possible they entered into arrangements with local "big men," but as Hrafn found, prospering from such arrangements could be a tricky business.

If a host, such as Brodd-Helgi, pressed the merchants too hard for a price advantage or demanded more than a small share of the profits, he could acquire a bad reputation. For a *goði*, the value of the privilege probably was that it gave him first choice of high-status imported goods and validated his rank among the local elite. This advantage was significant in a society in which gift-giving, loans of precious items, and displays of hospitality increased their stature. At expensive feasts and displays of hospitality, the quality of relationships was judged by noting whether the host sent his guest off with "good gifts." These expenses were incurred on special occasions, and they purchased political ties and reinforced pre-existing networks of obligation.

From the saga, it seems that Brodd-Helgi had already acquired a bad reputation among merchants before Hrafn's arrival. Hrafn tells Brodd-Helgi at their first meeting, *Mér ertu sagðr stórlátr ok fégjarn* 'I am told that you are proud and greedy'. In spite of this insult, Brodd-Helgi still wants the first choice of the newly arrived high-status goods. Hrafn's refusal to stay with him dishonors Brodd-Helgi, not least because the merchant rejects the chieftain as a partner in the trade. We can guess that Hrafn rejects Helgi because he wants to find a less avaricious first customer in order to maximize his profits. In a society where public acts contributed directly to an individual's honor and social status, journeys and transactions were particularly significant. Hrafn's refusal to do business was a public humiliation for Brodd-Helgi, whose journey from Hof to the coast would be known to everybody in the district.

5. THORLEIF THE CHRISTIAN AND THE TEMPLE TAX

Brodd-Helgi was rather gloomy over the summer and longed greatly for Thorleif's return. At every gathering, Brodd-Helgi and Geitir met and discussed the loss of their money.

Brodd-Helgi asked Geitir what had become of the little chest that Hrafn had owned. Geitir said he didn't know whether Thorleif had taken it away along with the other property, or if the Easterner had had it with him.

"I don't think anything more likely," said Helgi, "than that you have it in your possession."

"And where is that ring that he had on his hand when he was killed?"

"I don't know," said Helgi, "but I do know that he did not have it with him in his grave."

At every gathering when they met, Helgi would ask about the little chest and Geitir in return about the gold ring, and they disagreed openly about the matter. It progressed to the point that each of them felt he had a claim in the other's property, and their relationship began to grow cold.

The summer after, a ship came out to Reydarfjord owned by Thorleif and two Southerners[1] in partnership with him. Thorleif sold his share of the ship and went to his farm afterwards.

Brodd-Helgi was pleased by this news. But when he learned that Thorleif had turned over all the property to Hrafn's heirs, he thought it would be fruitless to bring the suit against Thorleif. Nonetheless he still intended to get a hold on him.

There was a woman named Steinvor, a priestess who took care of the chief temple,[2] to which all landowners were obligated to pay a temple tax.[3]

---

[1] Southerners: Germans.

[2] This temple's location is not mentioned, and the identity of Steinvor the priestess is otherwise unknown.

[3] According to late sources, the temple toll or tax (*hoftollr*) was levied on all inhabitants for the upkeep of the local place of worship, which might be a shrine, a temple, or simply a farmhouse where people could gather. These sources suggest that the *hoftollr* was intended to defray the costs of travel, building repairs, and sacrifices that the priest or priestess performed as part of his or her duties. In Iceland the income from such taxes rarely seems to have exceeded the costs incurred.

5. KAPÍTULI

Summary of Chapter 5. Brodd-Helgi and Geitir wait for Thorleif to return with Hrafn's possessions, and each begins to suspect the other of secretly hiding Hrafn's gold. Their friendship deteriorates throughout the winter. When Thorleif returns the next summer, Brodd-Helgi learns that Hrafn's goods were distributed to his next of kin, and Brodd-Helgi continues to plot against Thorleif. Thorleif, a Christian, has not been paying his dues to the pagan temple, and Brodd-Helgi convinces a farmer named Ketil to charge him with the offense and summon him to the assembly. Ketil does this but becomes trapped by bad weather and accepts Thorleif's offer of hospitality. Moved by Thorleif's generosity, Ketil pledges his friendship and drops the case. At the assembly, Brodd-Helgi learns of the failure of his scheme. He wrongly suspects that Geitir had a hand in the matter.

Brodd-Helgi var heldr ókátr um sumarit ok langaði mjǫk til kvámu Þorleifs. Á hverjum mannfundi hittusk þeir Brodd-Helgi ok Geitir ok rœddu um fjárlát sitt.

Brodd-Helgi spurði Geiti, hvat af kistli þeim væri orðit, sem Hrafn hefði átt. En Geitir kvazk eigi vita, hvárt Þorleifr myndi hafa haft hann útan með ǫðru fé eða mun Austmaðrinn haft hafa með sér.

"Eigi ætla ek annat heldr,"[1] kvað Helgi, "en þú hafir í vitum þínum."

"Eða hvar er hringr sá, er hann hafði á hendi sér, þá er hann var veginn?"

"Eigi veit ek þat," segir Helgi, "en þat veit ek, at eigi hafði hann hann í grǫf með sér."

Á hverjum fundi, er þeir hittusk, spurði Helgi at kistlinum, en Geitir í mót at gullhringinum, ok greindi þá sýnt um,[2] ok verðr nú svá, at hvárr þeira þóttisk eiga marknað[3] í annars garði, ok tók at fækkask með þeim.

Um sumarit eptir kom skip út í Reyðarfirði, ok átti Þorleifr inn kristni ok tveir Suðrmenn.[4] Þorleifr seldi sinn hlut skips ok fór síðan til bús síns eptir þat.

Brodd-Helgi varð feginn þessum tíðendum. En er hann spurði, at Þorleifr hefði allt fé af hǫndum greitt erfingjum Hrafns, þá þótti honum ógreiðlig sú sǫk Þorleifi at gefa ok ætlaði þó at fá á honum fangstað.[5]

Kona hét Steinvǫr ok var hofgyðja ok varðveitti hǫfuðhofit. Skyldu þangat allir bœndr gjalda hoftoll.

---

[1] **eigi ætla ek annat heldr en ...:** 'I don't consider anything more likely than that ...', literally 'I don't consider any other thing more than ...'.

[2] **greindi þá sýnt um:** 'they disagreed openly about the matter', literally '[it] divided them plainly about [it]'.

[3] **hvárr þeira þóttisk eiga marknað í annars garði:** 'each of them felt himself to have a monetary claim over the other'. *Marknaðr* (= *markaðr*), literally 'market', here probably means a 'monetary claim', and *garðr*, literally 'yard, enclosed space', means that which was in the other man's keeping or possession. The idiom *eiga marknað í annars garði* does not appear in any other text.

[4] **Suðrmenn:** 'Southerners', a term usually referring to Germans.

[5] This is a metaphor alluding to Icelandic wrestling, *glíma*, by the other name *fang*. Helgi strives to get a 'wrestling grip'.

Steinvor went to see Brodd-Helgi because she was related to him, and told him about the problem she had, that Thorleif the Christian did not pay the temple tax like other men. Brodd-Helgi stated that he would take up this case and pay her what they[1] owed, and he took up the case for her against Thorleif the Christian.[2]

There was a man named Ketil living in Fljotsdal who was called Stout Ketil. He was a good and courageous man and a great warrior. It is said that Helgi made a journey and came to lodge with Ketil, and Ketil gave him a warm welcome. They entered into a bond of friendship.[3]

Helgi said, "There is this one matter I wish to request of you, that you would go on my behalf and prosecute Thorleif the Christian about the temple tax. Summon him first, then I will come to the assembly, and we will join forces."

"I would not have entered into a bond of friendship with you had I known that this was at the bottom of it," said Ketil, "because Thorleif is a popular man. Nevertheless I will not refuse you the first time." They parted then, and Helgi went his way.

Ketil prepared to leave home when he thought the time was right. He set off with nine other men, and they arrived at Krossavik[4] early in the day. Thorleif was standing outside. He welcomed Ketil and his men and offered lodgings to them all. But Ketil said it was too early to take up lodgings, as the weather was so good.

Ketil asked whether Thorleif had paid the temple tax, but Thorleif said he considered it as good as paid. "It is my errand here to collect the temple tax," said Ketil, "and it is not advisable for you to withhold what amounts to nothing."

Thorleif answered, "My reason is more than stinginess, for I think that whatever is contributed there is completely wasted."

---

[1] Referring, presumably, to Thorleif and others who had followed his example.

[2] A principal party to a lawsuit could transfer the handling of the prosecution or defense to another party.

[3] Chieftains and farmers sometimes allied themselves through contractual political friendships called *vinfengi* and *vinátta*. The latter term was used more frequently than the former to describe genuine affection, but it is the former term, *vinfengi*, that is used here. These alliances put individuals in a position to expect assistance. Such agreements might be kept secret, especially if, as often happened, those who entered into them shared nothing but a mutual need for support. (See *Viking Age Iceland*, Ch. 13.)

[4] That is, Krossavik in Reydarfjord.

Steinvǫr fór á fund Brodd-Helga, því at hon var honum skyld, ok sagði honum til sinna vandræða, at Þorleifr inn kristni gyldi ekki hoftoll sem aðrir menn. Brodd-Helgi kvazk mundu taka þetta mál ok gjalda henni þat, er þeir eigu,[1] ok tók mál af henni á hendr Þorleifi inum kristna.

Maðr hét Ketill, er bjó í Fljótsdal ok var kallaðr Digr-Ketill, góðr drengr[2] ok garpr mikill. Þat er at segja[3] um fǫr Helga, at hann kom at gisting til Ketils, ok tók hann vel við honum. Þeir binda vel vinfengi sitt.

Helgi mælti: "Einn er sá hlutr, er ek vil biðja þik, at þú gerir fyrir mik, at sœkja Þorleif inn kristna um hoftoll, ok stefnir honum fyrst, en ek mun koma til þings, ok sém vit þá báðir saman."

"Eigi munda ek bundit hafa vinfengi við þik, hefða ek vitat, at þetta mundi undir búa," segir Ketill, "því at Þorleifr er maðr vinsæll, en þó mun ek eigi neita þér í fyrsta sinni." Skilðusk þeir síðan, ok ferr Helgi leiðar sinnar.

Ketill bjósk heiman,[4] þá er honum þótti tími til, ok fara saman tíu karlar[5] ok koma í Krossavík[6] snimma dags. Þorleifr stóð úti ok kvaddi þá vel Ketil ok bauð þeim ǫllum gisting, en Ketill kvað snimmt at taka gisting,[7] svá gott veðr sem væri.

Ketill spurði, hvárt Þorleifr hefði goldit hoftoll, en hann kvezk ætla, at goldinn mundi.[8] "Þat er mitt ørendi hingat at heimta hoftollinn," segir Ketill, "ok er þér ekki ráð at halda því, er engan mun ferr í."[9]

Þorleifr svarar: "Meir gengr mér þat til en smálæti,[10] at mér þykkir þat allt illa komit, er þar leggsk til."[11]

---

[1] That is, probably, *þat, er þeir eigu* [*at gjalda*], meaning 'the tax that Thorleif and others had to pay'. It may be that others followed Thorleif's refusal to pay the tax.

[2] **góðr drengr**: The phrase could be translated 'honest and courageous lad', a high compliment in Old Icelandic. The idea is also found in compounds such as *drenglyndr* 'noble-minded' and *drengskapr* 'courage'. It is used to describe women as well as men.

[3] **þat er at segja**: 'there is this to say'.

[4] **Ketill bjósk [at fara] heiman**: When movement is implied by an adverb or preposition, the infinitive verb of motion (f.ex., *fara*) in a compound construction may be left out. (Compare Shakespeare's "Faith, I'll home to-morrow" [*Twelfth Night*, Act 1, Scene 3].) This is particularly frequent following *vilja, skulu,* or *munu,* but examples can also be found after other verbs, such as the one here, *búa* 'prepare'.

[5] **fara saman tíu karlar**: 'ten men travel together', i.e., Ketil and nine others, ten men in all.

[6] That is, the Krossavik near Reydarfjord.

[7] **Ketill kvað [þat vera] snimmt at taka gisting**: 'Ketil said it was too early to take lodgings for the night'. As with the verb *fara*, the infinitive *vera* is sometimes omitted in compound constructions.

[8] **en hann kvezk ætla, at goldinn mundi [vera]**: 'but he [i.e., Thorleif] said he thought it would be [as good as] paid'.

[9] **er þér ekki ráð at halda því, er engan mun ferr í**: 'it is not advisable for you to withhold what amounts to nothing'.

[10] **meir gengr mér þat til en smálæti**: 'my reason is more than stinginess'.

[11] **mér þykkir þat allt illa komit, er þar leggsk til**: 'it seems to me that whatever is contributed there is utterly wasted'.

Ketil answered, "It is great arrogance to think that you know better than all other men and refuse to fulfill such a legal obligation."

Thorleif answered: "I do not care what you say about this matter."

Then Ketil named to himself witnesses and summoned Thorleif the Christian. And when the summons was finished, Thorleif invited them to stay there, as he thought the weather was becoming unpredictable. Ketil stated that he would leave. Thorleif invited them to come back if the weather started to get bad.

The party went away, but soon they encountered bad weather and were forced to turn back. They arrived at Thorleif's very late, and were very weary. Thorleif gave them a warm welcome. They stayed there stormbound for three nights, and the hospitality was the better the longer they stayed.

When Ketil was ready to leave, he said, "We have had good hospitality here, and Thorleif has shown himself to be the best and most courageous man – and I will give you this reward, that your case will be dropped, and I will be your friend from now on."

Thorleif answered, "I consider your friendship of great worth, but it does not matter to me whether the case fails or not. I call upon that Partner who will not let me incur such penalty." They parted then, and so matters stood until the assembly.

It is said that Brodd-Helgi brought a large following to the assembly and prepared himself to make a move. And when the assembly was well underway, Brodd-Helgi asked what had become of the matter of Thorleif the Christian. He was told the truth.

Helgi answered, "You have deceived me greatly in this matter, Ketil, and our friendship will now be ended." He got no hold on Thorleif, who is now out of this story.[1]

Brodd-Helgi and Geitir met soon after the assembly. Helgi laid much of the blame on Geitir. He said it was on Geitir's account that he had suffered this humiliation, just when he had nearly succeeded in setting things right. With this their friendship began to deteriorate even more.

CHAPTER 5 VOCABULARY

allsíð *adv* very late

allr <ǫll, allt> *adj/indef pron* all, entire

allt *n adj as adv* all, entirely, altogether, completely

annarr <ǫnnur, annat; *acc m* annan, *f*

aðra, *dat m* ǫðrum, *n* ǫðru; *pl nom m* aðrir> *adj/indef pron* other

bað *1/3sg past of* **biðja**

bauð *1/3sg past of* **bjóða**

beini *m* hospitality

---

[1] See the accounts of this episode in *Kristni þáttr* and *Kristni saga*. A notable analogue for this episode occurs in *Bjarnar saga Hítdælakappa*, Ch. 27. There, Bjorn's enemy Thord convinces a man named Thorstein to mount an attack on Bjorn's farm. When the weather turns bad, Thorstein gets lost on the way to make his raid. In an incident that has similarities to Ketil's change of heart due of Thorleif's hospitality, Thorstein and his men are given shelter from the storm at a farm, and their host turns out to be none other than their intended victim. Bjorn shows Thorstein's party such generous hospitality that Thorstein agrees to mediate between him and Thord.

Ketill svarar: "Þat er mikil dul, at þú þykkisk betr kunna en allir aðrir menn, enda viltu eigi gjalda slíkar lǫgskyldur."

Þorleifr svarar: "Eigi hirði ek, hvat þú segir um þetta mál."

Síðan nefndi Ketill sér vátta ok stefndi Þorleifi inum kristna, ok er lokit var stefnunni, þá bauð Þorleifr þeim þar at vera ok talði veðrit ótrúligt gerask. Ketill kvazk fara mundu. Hann bað þá aptr hverfa, ef veðrit tœki at harðna.

Þeir fara á brott, ok var skammt at bíða illviðris,[1] ok urðu þeir aptr at hverfa, ok kómu þeir allsíð til Þorleifs ok váru mjǫk dasaðir. Þorleifr tók vel við þeim, ok sátu þeir þar tvær nætr veðrfastir, ok var því betri beini sem þeir sátu lengr.[2]

En er þeir Ketill[3] váru brott búnir, þá mælti hann: "Vér hǫfum hér haft góðan beina, ok hefir Þorleifr reynzk inn bezti drengr, – ok mun ek því launa þér, at niðr skal falla sǫk þín, ok vera vinr þinn heðan í frá."

Þorleifr svarar: "Mikils þykki mér vert vinfengi þitt, en ekki þykki mér undir, hvárr sekr fellr eða eigi.[4] Heit ek á þann félaga,[5] er mik lætr ekki slíkt varða." Skilja þeir síðan, ok er nú svá búit til þingsins.[6]

Þat er sagt, at Brodd-Helgi fjǫlmennir mjǫk til þingsins ok hyggr sér til hreyfings.[7] Ok er á leið þingit, spurði Brodd-Helgi, hvar komit var um málit Þorleifs ins kristna. Honum var sagt it sanna.

Helgi svarar: "Mjǫk hefir þú, Ketill, brugðizk um þetta mál, enda mun nú lokit vinfengi okkru." Ok fæsk nú ekki fang á Þorleifi, ok er hann ór þessari sǫgu.

Þeir Brodd-Helgi ok Geitir hittusk skjótt eptir þingit, ok talði Helgi mjǫk á hendr Geiti ok kvazk af honum þessa svívirðing hlotit hafa, nær sem hann gæti leiðrétt.[8] Tók þeira vinfengi þá heldr at minnkask.

---

betri *comp adj* better (*see* **góðr**)

biðja <biðr; bað, báðu; beðinn> *vb* ask, beg; command, tell

binda <bindr; batt, bundu; bundinn> *vb* bind, tie, fasten; **binda vinfengi** pledge friendship

bíða <bíðr; beið, biðu; beðinn> *vb* wait; [*w gen*] wait for

bjóða <býðr; bauð, buðu; boðinn> *vb* [*w acc*] offer; [*w dat*] invite; **bjóða [e-m]**

---

[1] **var skammt at bíða illviðris:** 'it was not long to wait for bad weather'.

[2] **var því betri beini sem þeir sátu lengr:** 'hospitality got better the longer they stayed'.

[3] **þeir Ketill:** 'they Ketil', i.e., 'Ketil and his companions'.

[4] **en ekki þykki mér undir, hvárr sekr fellr eða eigi:** 'but it does not matter to me whether the case fails or not'.

[5] The *félagi* referred to here is Christ himself.

[6] **er nú svá búit til þingsins:** 'so matters now stood until the assembly'.

[7] **hyggr sér til hreyfings:** 'prepares himself to make a move'.

[8] **nær sem hann gæti leiðrétt:** 'just when he nearly succeeded in setting things right'.

at vera invite [sb] to stay

bjósk *1/3sg past of* **búask**

bóndi <*pl* bœndr, *dat* bóndum~bœndum, *gen* bónda~bœnda> *m* farmer; head of a household

bregða <bregðr; brá, brugðu; brugðinn> *vb* [*w dat*] move quickly; break (faith or an oath); turn, alter, change; break off, leave off, give up; *refl* **bregðask** fail, come to nothing; **bregðask [e-m]** deceive, disappoint [sb]

brott (*also* **á brott, í brott**) *adv* away, off; **brott búinn** ready to start, prepared to depart

brugðizk *n ppart of* **bregðask**

bundit *n ppart of* **binda**

búa <býr; bjó, bjoggu~bjuggu; búinn> *vb* live (in a place), dwell; **búa undir [e-u]** be the (hidden) reason behind [sth], be at the bottom of [sth]; *refl* **búask** make oneself ready, equip oneself

búit *n ppart* ready, set; finished, done (*see* **búa**); **er svá búit** it was thus set, matters so stood

bœndr *nom/acc pl of* **bóndi**

dasa <-að-> *vb* exhaust

digr <digr, digrt> *adj* big, stout

drengr <-s; -ir, *pl gen* drengja> *m* courageous person; **góðr drengr** honest and courageous person

dul *f* self-conceit, arrogance

ef *conj* if

eiga <á, eigu; átti; áttr> *pret-pres vb* own, have, possess; [*aux*] must, be obligated, have to

eigu *3pl pres of* **eiga**

enda *conj* and (etc.); and if; even; even if; and also, and so; and yet

falla <fellr; fell, fellu; fallinn> *vb* fall; fail, be foiled; **falla niðr** fall, drop, be forgotten; (*leg*) be dropped

fang <fong> *n* grasp, grip, hold; wrestling **fá fang á [e-m]** get hold of [sb]

fangstaðr <*gen* -ar> *m* something to grasp or lay hold of; **fá fangstað á [e-m]** catch hold of [sb]

fá <fær; fekk, fengu; fenginn> *vb* get, take, procure; grasp; marry; *refl* **fásk** get (for) oneself; **fá(sk) fang á [e-m]** get hold of [sb]

feginn *adj* glad, happy, pleased

fellr *2/3 pres of* **falla**

fjárlát *n* loss of money

fjolmenna <-t-> *vb* assemble a following

Fljótsdalr <*dat* -dal, *gen* -dals> *m* Fljotsdal ('River Dale') (*place name*)

fyrstr *superl adj* first

fækka <-að-> *vb* make few, reduce in number; *refl* **fækkask** grow cold, become unfriendly

fæsk *1/3sg pres of* **fásk**

for <*gen* farar; *pl* farar~farir, *gen* fara> *f* journey, trip

ganga <gengr; gekk, gengu; genginn> *vb* go; **[e-m] gengr [e-t] til [e-s]** *impers* [sth] is [sb's] reason for [sth]

garðr <-s; -ar> *m* enclosed space, yard; fence, wall; **í garði [e-s]** in [sb's] keeping, hands

garpr <-s; -ar> *m* a bold, daring, courageous, or warlike man or woman

gera <-ð-; *ppart* gerðr~gerr> *vb* make, build; do, act; *refl* **gerask** become, grow

geta <getr; gat, gátu; getinn> *vb* get; [*w ppart of another vb*] be able to

gisting *f* lodging for the night; **at gisting** to stay overnight

gjalda <geldr; galt, guldu; goldinn> *vb* pay

goldit *n ppart of* **gjalda**

góðr <góð, gott > *adj* good

greiða <-dd-> *vb* pay; **greiða af hondum** pay out, discharge, turn over

greina <-d-> *vb* divide; *impers* [*acc subj*] fall out, disagree

grof <*gen* grafar; *pl* grafir~grafar> *f* grave

gyldi *3sg/pl past subjunct of* **gjalda**

gæti *3sg/pl past subjunct of* **geta**

halda <heldr; hélt, héldu; haldinn> *vb* [*w dat*] hold; keep, retain

harðna <-að-> *vb* harden; become severe (*of weather*); grow worse

heðan *adv* from here, hence; **heðan í frá** hereafter, henceforth

heiman *adv* from home

heimta <-t-> *vb* recover; claim, collect

heita <heitr; hét, hétu; heitinn> *vb* call, give a name to; call, call on; (*intrans, 2/3sg pres* heitir) be named, be called; **heita á [e-n]** call upon, pray to, invoke [sb]

heldr *comp adv* more, rather

hendr *nom/acc pl of* **hond**

henni *dat of* **hon**

hér *adv* here (*location*)

hirða <-ð-> *vb* mind, care for; **hirða eigi**

(um) [e-t] to not care about [sth]

hljóta <hlýtr; hlaut, hlutu; hlotinn> *vb* get, be allotted; undergo, suffer; **hljóta [e-t] af [e-m]** get, suffer [sth] on account of [sb]

hlotit *n ppart of* **hljóta**

hofgyðja *f* priestess

hoftollr <-s; -ar> *m* temple tax, temple 'toll'

hon <*acc* hana, *dat* henni, *gen* hennar> *pron 3sg f* she

hreyfing *f* movement, motion

hringr <-s; -ar> *m* ring

hvar *interrog adv* where?; **hvar er komit um [e-t]** what has become of [sth]

hvárr *interrog pron* who, which (of two)?; *indef pron* each (of two)

hvárt *interrog adv* whether

hverfa <hverfr; hvarf, hurfu; horfinn> *vb intrans* turn (in a circular motion), rotate; be lost, be missing; disappear; **hverfa aptr** return, turn around, turn back

hyggja <hugð-, hug(a)ðr> vb think; **hyggja (sér) til [e-s]** anticipate, prepare (oneself) for [sth]

hofuðhof *n* chief temple

hond <*acc* hond, *dat* hendi, *gen* handar; *pl* hendr, *dat* hondum, *gen* handa> *f* hand; **á hendr [e-m]** against [sb]; **telja á hendr [e-m]** lay the blame on [sb]

illviðri *n* bad weather

Ketill <-ils> *m* Ketil (*personal name*); **Digr-Ketill** *m* Stout-Ketil

koma <kemr~kømr; kom, kómu~kvámu; kominn> *vb* come; **vel (illa) komit** well (poorly) placed, in good (bad) hands

kváma *f* coming, approach, arrival

kveða <kveðr; kvað, kváðu; kveðinn> *vb* speak, say; *refl* **kveðask** say of oneself

kveðja <kvadd-> *vb* greet; **kveðja [e-n] vel** to greet [sb] well, welcome [sb]

kvezk *2/3sg pres of* **kveðask**

langa <-að-> *vb* long (for) (*usu impers* [*acc subj*]); **langa til [e-s]** long for [sth]

launa <-að-> *vb* [*w dat*] reward; **launa [e-m] [e-u]** reward [sb] with [sth]

láta <lætr; lét, létu; látinn> *vb* let, allow, permit

leggja <lagð-; *ppart* lag(i)ðr~laginn> *vb* lay, place, put; **leggjask til** contribute

leið <-ir> *f* road, path; way; **fara leiðar sinnar** go (on) one's way

leiðrétta <-tt-> *vb* correct, put right, redress; **geta leiðrétt** be able to put right,

succeed in correcting

lengr *comp adv* longer (*time*)

lætr *2/3sg pres of* **láta**

logskyld <-ir> *f* legal dues

mannfundr <-ar; -ir> *m* meeting, gathering

markaðr (*also* **marknaðr**) <*gen* -ar> *m* market; monetary claim; **eiga marknað í annars garði** have a claim against another

marknaðr *var of* **markaðr**

meir *comp adv* more (*see* **mjok**)

minnka <-að-> *vb* lessen, diminish; *refl* **minnkask** grow less, decrease

mjok <*comp* meir(r), *superl* mest> *adv* much

mót *n* manner, way; **í mót** in return

munr <-ar; -ir> *m* difference, importance; **fara í engan mun** amount to no importance

niðr *adv* down (*motion or direction*); **falla niðr** fall, drop, be forgotten; (*leg*) be dropped

ógreiðligr *adj* unpayable, uncollectible; difficult; unclear

ókátr *adj* morose, gloomy

ór *prep* [*w dat*] out of

ótrúligr *adj* undependable, unsafe, not to be relied upon

ráð *n* advice, counsel; plan; **vera [e-m] ráð** *impers* be advisable for [sb]

reyna <-d-> *vb* try, prove; experience; *refl* **reynask** prove to be

reynzk *n ppart of* **reynask**

sannr <sonn, satt> *adj* true; **it sanna** the truth

sá <sú, þat> *dem pron* that (one)

sátu *3pl past of* **sitja**

segja <sagð-> *vb* say, tell; **segja it sanna** tell the truth; **segja [e-m] til [e-s]** tell, inform [sb] of [sth]

sém *1pl pres subjunct of* **vera**

sinn *n* time (*instance or repetition*); **í fyrsta sinni** the first time

sitja <sitr; sat, sátu; setinn> *vb* sit; reside; stay

skal *1/3sg pres of* **skulu**

skammt *adv* a short while, not long (*time*)

skilja <-d~ð-; *ppart* skiliðr~skildr~skilinn> *vb* part, separate, divide; discern, understand; *refl* **skiljask** part company

skulu <skal, skulu; skyldi; *pret inf* skyldu> *pret-pres vb* shall (*obligation, purpose, necessity, fate*); (*past tense*) should

skyldr <skyld, skylt> *adj* related by kinship

skyldu *3pl past indic of* **skulu**

smálæti *n* stinginess

snimma *adv* early; **snimma dags** early in the day

snimmt *adv* early (= **snimma**)

standa <stendr; stóð, stóðu; staðinn> *vb* stand

stefna <-d-> *vb* aim at, go in a certain direction; call, call together, summon; (*leg*) summon, serve notice to; **stefna leið** head toward, head for

stefna *f* (*leg*) summons, citation

Steinvǫr <*acc/dat* Steinvǫru, *gen* Steinvarar> *f* Steinvor (*personal name*)

stóð *1/3sg past of* **standa**

Suðrmaðr <*pl* -menn> *m* Southerner, person from the south (*esp* a German or a Saxon)

sumar *n* summer; **um sumarit** in, during the summer; **um sumarit eptir** the following summer

sú *f nom sg of dem pron* **sá**

svívirðing *f* disgrace, humiliation

sýnn <sýn, sýnt> *adj* clear, evident, certain

sýnt *n adj as adv* evidently, clearly

sœkja <sótt-> *vb* seek; pursue; (*leg*) prosecute

sǫk <*gen* sakar; *pl* sakar~sakir> *f* cause, reason, sake; (*leg*) charge, the offence charged; (*leg*) case, lawsuit, prosecution; **gefa [e-m] sǫk** prosecute, make a charge against [sb]

taka <tekr; tók, tóku; tekinn> *vb* take; **taka at** [*w inf*] begin to [do sth]; **taka mál** (*leg*) take up a case; **taka vel við [e-m]** give [sb] a warm welcome

talði *3sg past of* **telja**

telja <talð~tald-; *ppart* taliðr~taldr~talinn> *vb* count; reckon, consider; **telja á hendr [e-m]** lay the blame on [sb]

tíðendi *var of* **tíðindi**

tíðindi (*also* **tíðendi**) *n pl* news, tidings

tími *m* time; the right time; **þykkja [e-m] tími til** *impers* [sb] thinks the time is right

tíu *num* ten

tveir <tvær, tvau; *acc m* tvá, *dat* tveim(r), *gen* tveggja> *num* two

tvær *f nom/acc of* **tveir**

tœki *3sg/pl past subjunct of* **taka**

undir *prep* [*w acc*] under, underneath; [*w dat*] under, depending upon

útan *adv* abroad, away from Iceland (*usu* to Norway)

vandræði *n* trouble, difficulty

varða <-að-> *vb* warrant, guarantee, answer for; (*leg*) be liable, punishable, incur a penalty

varðveita <-tt-> vb keep, take care of

váttr <-s; -ar> *m* witness

veðr *n* weather

veðrfastr *adj* weatherbound

veit *1/3sg pres of* **vita**

vera <er; var, váru; verit> *vb* be

vinsæll *adj* much liked, popular

vit *n pl* place where a thing is kept, case; (*fig*) possession

vit <*acc/dat* okkr, *gen* okkar> *pron 1dual* we (two)

vita <veit, vitu; vissi; vitaðr> *pret-pres vb* know

þik *acc of* **þú**

þótti *1/3sg past of* **þykkja**

þóttisk *2/3sg past of* **þykkjask**

þú <*acc* þik, *dat* þér, *gen* þín> *pron 2sg* you (*sg*)

þykkja <þykkir, þótt-> *vb impers* seem to be; [*dat subj*] think, seem (to one); **[e-m] þykkir undir** *impers* it seems important to [sb]; *refl* **þykkjask** seem to oneself, think, consider oneself

ǫðru *n dat sg of* **annarr**

ørendi *n* errand, mission, purpose

CULTURE SECTION – DUE PROCESS OF LAW

Vápnfirðinga saga is set within the historical and legal framework of early Icelandic society, where significant action takes place in legal courts and assemblies. In Iceland, thirteen local spring assemblies (*várþing*) were held every year, about six weeks before the national Althing, which was held in June. The spring assemblies were intended to deal with regional matters.

The law required three local *goðar* to preside over each meeting and appoint judges to hear cases. Any matter that was not resolved locally was referred to the Althing. Autumn assemblies (*leiðarþing*) met early in the season, two weeks after the Althing. They dealt with business arising from court findings at the Althing. The *goðar* were obliged to attend all such meetings or forfeit their chieftaincies.

The local Sunnudal assembly in Vapnafjord is not mentioned in other medieval Icelandic writings, which seems to accord with the statement in the saga (Ch. 14) that the site was abandoned early. It would have been one of the three spring assemblies in the Eastern Quarter. The tidy system mentioned in the lawbooks was probably not so regular in actual practice, and the saga mentions only two *goðar* presiding over the spring assembly. The third chieftain may not have been named, or there may have been just two. It is also possible that the closely related chieftains at Hof and at Krossavík shared a single chieftaincy or *goðorð*.

As with Ketil and Thorleif in this chapter, the initiation of legal actions often required summoning the defendant at his or her home. The alternative mode of initiation involved publishing the case at the law assembly for prosecution. Witnesses, who had to be free farmers of a certain degree of wealth, were called upon to observe every aspect of the Icelandic legal process, including the initial summons. Witnesses to a summons were appointed by the party making the summons.

Court cases in early Iceland were not always settled in an orderly manner. Success or failure in prosecuting a suit depended largely upon one's ability to appear in court with a strong backing of followers. *Goðar* would attempt to gather as many followers and allies as necessary to bar their opponents from entering the court, or, failing in this effort, to overwhelm their opponents in the court. If one party found it had a clear advantage in strength, legal proceedings frequently gave way to confrontation.

Brodd-Helgi uses Ketil to summon Thorleif so that Thorleif will think that he is only facing a farmer. Such tactics were a recipe for violence and are sometimes recorded in the sagas when describing court cases.[1] Social restraints on such behavior, including the well developed mechanisms of third-party intervention – arbitration and advocacy – kept the system from breaking down. The saga now turns to a series of court confrontations between Geitir and Brodd-Helgi in which Brodd-Helgi employs the same overbearing tactic.

---

[1] The sagas contain accounts of outbreaks of violence during summons, at local assemblies, and at the Althing (*Ljósvetninga saga*, Ch. 11, *Víga-Glúms saga*, Ch. 24, *Njáls saga*, Ch. 145). For background, see *Viking Age Iceland*, pp. 118–41 and 170–95.

6. HALLA LEAVES BRODD-HELGI

It is said that Halla Lytingsdottir spoke to Brodd-Helgi and told him, "Our relation-ship has been good for a long time, but I am feeling very ill, and my management of your household will not continue long."

Helgi answered, "I consider myself well married, and I intend to enjoy this as long as our life lasts." But it was the custom at that time to request separation from the household in such circumstances.[1]

There was a woman named Thorgerd who was called Silver, the daughter of Thorvald the Tall. She was young, yet also a widow, and lived in Fljotsdal at the place now called Thorgerdarstadir ('Thorgerd's Farmstead'). Her brother, who was named Kolfinn, managed the farm with her.

Thorgerd invited Brodd-Helgi to her place with two other men, and he went. She welcomed him extremely warmly and sat him in the seat of honor.[2] She sat down by him and they talked at great length. And before Helgi went home, it is to be said that he betrothed Thorgerd Silver to himself.[3]

Nothing more is said about Helgi until he came home to Hof and was asked for news. He said that a woman was betrothed to a man.

Halla asked, "Is that Thorgerd Silver?" "Yes," he said.

She asked to whom she was betrothed. He told her.

"You do not think that too sudden," she said.

Helgi said that he would go and meet Geitir. He requested that she should stay there in the meantime, and she allowed herself to be persuaded not to leave before Thorgerd came.

This news was quickly reported throughout the district and was spoken badly of, because Halla was popular with everyone.

They sent men after Halla. She went away when Helgi came home, taking her possessions with her.

---

[1] The 'custom' (*siðvenja*) of a terminally ill wife who is no longer able to fulfill her duties offering to leave the household is not known in any other source.

[2] **seat of honor:** *ǫndvegi*, lit. 'opposite seat'. In the traditional Scandinavian long house, the benches were set lengthways along the side walls of the main hall with a fireplace between them. The women sat at one end of the hall. The central section of one of the long benches was the rightful high seat of the farm's owner. The principal guest sat immediately opposite the owner in the seat of honor.

[3] Thorgerd and her family are otherwise unknown, but *Landnámabók* states that Halla was Helgi's first wife, indicating that he was married twice.

6. KAPÍTULI

Summary of Chapter 6. Halla, Brodd Helgi's wife, becomes terminally ill. Brodd-Helgi engages himself to the widow Thorgerd Silver while Halla is still alive, but wishes for Halla to remain by his side. This insults Halla's family, and Geitir has her brought to live at his home. Geitir attempts to collect Halla's share of the property, but Brodd-Helgi refuses. Geitir takes Brodd-Helgi to court, but Brodd-Helgi comes to the assembly with more men than Geitir and prevents Geitir from successfully prosecuting him. Geitir appeals the case to the national assembly, with the same result.

Þat er sagt, at Halla Lýtingsdóttir tók til orða ok mælti við Brodd-Helga: "Samfarar okkrar hafa lengi góðar verit, en ek kenni mjǫk vanheilsu, ok mun þér verða skǫmm forvista fyrir búi þínu."[1]

Helgi svarar: "Ek þykkjumk vel kvángaðr,[2] ok ætla ek at una þessu, meðan okkart líf vinnsk." En þat var þá siðvenja at biðjask ór búi í þær mundir.

Kona hét Þorgerðr ok var kǫlluð silfra. Hon var dóttir Þorvalds ins háva, ung at aldri, ok var hon þó ekkja ok bjó í Fljótsdal, þar sem nú heitir at Þorgerðarstǫðum, ok var at umsýslu með henni bróðir hennar, er Kolfinnr hét.

Þorgerðr bauð Brodd-Helga til sín við þriðja mann, ok fór hann þangat, ok tók hon við honum ágætavel ok setti hann í ǫndvegi[3] ok settisk niðr hjá honum, ok varð þeim allhjaldrjúgt. Ok áðr Helgi fór heim, er þat at segja, at hann fastnaði sér Þorgerði silfru.

Er þá ekki frá Helga sagt, fyrr en hann kom heim til Hofs, ok var hann spurðr at tíðendum. Hann segir, at kona væri fǫstnuð manni.

Halla spurði: "Er þat Þorgerðr silfra?" segir hon. "Já," segir hann.

Hon spurði, hverjum hon væri fǫstnuð. Hann segir henni þat.

"Þat þykki þér eigi of brátt," segir hon.

Helgi kvazk mundu fara ok hitta Geiti. Hann bað, at hon skyldi þar vera á meðan, ok þat lét hon leiðask,[4] at hon fór eigi fyrr en Þorgerðr kom.

Þegar spurðusk þessi tíðendi um heraðit, ok lagðisk illr rómr á, því at Halla var vinsæl af ǫllum mǫnnum.

Þeir sendu menn eptir Hǫllu. Fór hon þá í brott, er Helgi kom heim, ok hafði með sér gripi sína.

---

[1] **mun þér verða skǫmm forvista fyrir búi þínu:** 'my managing of your household will not continue long'.

[2] *Kvángaðr* 'married' was used only for men. *Kvánga* 'cause (a man) to marry' contrasts with *gipta* 'give (a woman) in marriage'. In older writings the man *kvángask* ('takes a wife') and the woman is *gipt* ('given in marriage'), but later on, *giptask* came to carry the general sense of 'marry', applying equally to men and women.

[3] **ǫndvegi:** 'seat of honor', lit. 'opposite seat', the seat immediately opposite the owner, where the guest of honor sat.

[4] **þat lét hon leiðask:** 'she let herself be persuaded'.

Helgi stood out in the doorway and acted as if he did not know that Halla was going away.[1] Halla had hardly mounted on horseback.[2]

Then the messenger announced that they should ride ahead, while Geitir turned to negotiate with Helgi about when he would turn over the property "which Halla has in your keeping."

"It will be fine with me," Helgi answered, "if Halla is not happy at Krossavik once she has come home. She will yet come back here to Hof." With that Geitir rode for home, and to both of them the situation seemed no better than before.

When Geitir came back, Halla asked what Helgi and he had discussed. He told her how things stood.

She answered, "You have been hasty in this matter. It may be that Helgi feels bereft, even before you have deprived him of everything. It is a safe investment with Helgi, and my wealth will not decrease in his house if it gathers interest."

"I see," said Geitir, "where this matter is heading. To me it seems the greatest dishonor is intended if you ride away from his house penniless."

Now the winter passed, and Geitir went to Hof in the spring to collect Halla's valuables a second time. But Helgi would not turn them over.

Then Geitir summoned Brodd-Helgi to the Sunnudal assembly over Halla's property. Both brought a large following to the assembly, and while Helgi had more men, Geitir had a more select group. But when the case should have gone to court, Geitir was overpowered, and Helgi won the case.

Then Geitir presented the case to the Althing, and again Brodd-Helgi nullified the suit, mostly with the support of Gudmund the Powerful.[3] And now the greatest animosity developed between Brodd-Helgi and Geitir.

Helgi stóð úti í durum ok lét sem hann vissi eigi, at Halla fœri í brottu. Halla var

---

[1] It is tempting to understand this part of the story as an account of Geitir's taking Halla away from Helgi before Helgi is ready. In other words, the reader might surmise that Halla does not wait for Thorgerd Silver to come but leaves with the her brother's men. Geitir sends these men to accompany Helgi back from his visit to Krossavik and bring Halla back with them. Helgi appears disappointed or offended that Halla is leaving him and does not even say goodbye to her as she leaves. A difficulty with this interpretation, however, is the form of the verbs that occur in the sentence describing how long she planned to stay. If this were recounting something that did not happen, one might expect the verbs in the subordinate clause to be subjunctives: *þat lét hon leiðask, at hon* **fœri eigi** *fyrr en Þorgerðr* **kœmi** 'she let herself be persuaded, that she **should not leave** before Thergerd **should come**'. In fact, however, the verbs are in the indicative, implying that the actions actually took place: *þat lét hon leiðask, at hon* **fór eigi** *fyrr en Þorgerðr* **kom** 'she let herself be persuaded, that she **did not leave** before Thorgerd **came**'.

[2] At this point in the text, some manuscripts are partly illegible and something is missing. One manuscript has *áðr Geitir, bróðir hennar, kom þangat riðandi* 'before Geitir, her brother, came riding up', but this line may be a scribe's later attempt to resolve the gap. The missing portion probably describes this stage of Helgi and Geitir's hostility.

[3] *Landámabók* and several sagas, including *Njáls saga* and *Ljósvetninga saga*, speak of the marriage between Gudmund's daughter Thordis and Brodd-Helgi's son Sorli. Curiously, *Vápnfirðinga saga* does not mention this well-known marriage, and neither Thordis nor Sorli is even mentioned in the saga.

varla á bak komin [áðr Geitir, bróðir hennar, kom þangat ríðandi].[1]

Þá mælti sendimaðr, at þau skyldu ríða fyrr, en hann[2] sneri til málaleitunar við Helga ok mælti, hvé nær hann skyldi greiða af hǫndum fé þat, – "er Halla á í þinn garð."

Helgi svarar: "Gott þykki mér," segir hann, "ef Halla unir eigi í Krossavík, þá er hon er heim komin. Mun hon enn hingat koma til Hofs." Geitir reið nú heim við svá búit, ok þótti hvárutveggjum eigi betr en áðr.

En er Geitir kom eptir, spurði Halla, hvat þeir Helgi hefði við talazk,[3] en hann sagði slíkt, sem til var.

Hon svarar: "Þú hefir verit bráðr í þessu máli, ok má vera, at Helga þykki sviptir at, áðr en firrðir hann ǫllu saman,[4] ok er fjárstaðr greiðr at Helga,[5] ok mun ekki mitt fé þverra í hans garði, ef þat stendr með leigum."[6]

"Sé ek," kvað Geitir, "hversu þetta mál horfir. Þykki mér svá fremst allrar svívirðingar leitat, ef þú ríðr félaus ór hans garði."

Nú líðr vetrinn, ok fór Geitir um várit til Hofs at heimta penninga Hǫllu í annat sinn, en Helgi vildi eigi út gjalda.

Þá stefndi Geitir Brodd-Helga um fé Hǫllu til Sunnudalsþings, ok fjǫlmennti hvárutveggi mjǫk til þingsins, ok varð Helgi fjǫlmennari, en Geitir hafði mannval betra. En er at dómi skyldi ganga, þá varð Geitir ofrliði borinn, ok kom Helgi málinu fram.[7]

Ok bauð Geitir málinu til alþingis, ok eyddi Brodd-Helgi þá enn málit ok mest af liðveizlu Guðmundar ins ríka, ok gerðisk nú in mesta óþykkja með þeim Brodd-Helga ok Geiti.

CHAPTER 6 VOCABULARY

allhjaldrjúgr *adj* very talkative; **[e-m] verðr allhjaldrjúgt** *impers* [sb] talks at very great length

allt *n adj as adv* all, entirely, altogether, completely; **allt saman** wholly, entirely, altogether

alþingi *n* national assembly

á *1/3sg pres of* **eiga**

áðr *adv* before; **áðr en** *conj* before

ágætavel *adv* excellently

bak <bǫk> *n* back; horseback; **koma á bak** mount on horseback

bera <berr; bar, báru; borinn> *vb* carry, bear

biðja <biðr; bað, báðu; beðinn> *vb* ask, beg; command, tell; *refl* **biðjask** request for oneself; **biðjask ór búi** request separation from the household

---

[1] Something is missing in the original manuscript at this point. The words in brackets are supplied from one manuscript, but this may be a scribe's attempt to rectify the gap.

[2] **hann:** i.e., Geitir.

[3] **hvat þeir Helgi hefði við talazk:** 'what Helgi and he had talked to each other about'.

[4] **má vera, at Helga þykki sviptir at, áðr en firrðir hann ǫllu saman:** 'it may be that Helgi feels bereft, even before you have deprived him of everything'.

[5] **er fjárstaðr greiðr at Helga:** 'it is a safe investment with Helgi'.

[6] **ef þat stendr með leigum:** 'if it gathers interest'.

[7] **kom Helgi málinu fram:** lit. 'Helgi brought the case forward', i.e., he prosecuted the case. This is rather strange phrasing, given that Helgi was the defendant. Because Helgi is unopposed in court, another way of translating this phrase could be: 'Helgi won the case'.

bjóða <býðr; bauð, buðu; boðinn> *vb* [*w acc*] offer; [*w dat*] invite; **bjóða mál** (*leg*) appeal a case; **bjóða [e-m] til sín** invite [sb] to one's house

borinn *ppart of* **bera**

bráðr <bráð, brátt> *adj* sudden, quick; hasty, rash

brott (*also* **í brott, í brottu**) *adv* away, off

brottu *var of* **brott**

búit *n ppart* ready, set (*from* **búa** 'prepare, make ready'); **við svá búit** with matters thus, with that

dómr <-s; -ar> *m* (*leg*) court, court of judgment

durum *dat pl of* **dyrr**

dyrr <*pl dat* durum, *gen* dura> *f pl* door, doorway

eiga <á, eigu; átti; áttr> *pret-pres vb* own, have, possess

ekki *n nom/acc sg of* **engi**

ekkja *f* widow

engi <engi, ekki> *adj/indef pron* no one, none, no

eyða <-dd-> *vb* waste; spend; do away with, destroy; make empty; (*leg*) render void, annul; **eyða mál** nullify a lawsuit

fara <ferr; fór, fóru; farinn> *vb* go, travel; move

fastna <-að-> *vb* pledge, betroth

félauss *adj* penniless

firra <-ð-> *vb* deprive; **firra [e-n] [e-u]** deprive [sb] of [sth]

fjárstaðr <-ar; -ir> *m* investment

fjǫlmennari *comp adj* with more men (see **fjǫlmennr**)

fjǫlmennr *adj* numerous, with many people

forvista *f* leadership, management, authority

fram *adv* forward; **koma [e-u] fram** bring [sth] about, bring [sth] to a successful conclusion; **koma máli fram** (*leg*) prosecute (a case)

fremst *superl adv* foremost, most, greatest (*see* **fram**)

fyrir *prep* [*w dat*] at the head of (leading)

fœri *3sg/pl past subjunct of* **fara**

greiðr <greið, greitt> *adj* clear, unencumbered, free from obstacles

Guðmundr <-ar> *m* Gudmund (*personal name*); **Guðmundr inn ríki** *m* Gudmund the Powerful

hár <há, hátt; *acc m* hávan; *pl dat* hávum> *adj* high, tall

hávi *wk m nom sg of* **hár**

hennar *poss pron 3sg f indecl* her

horfa <-ð-> *vb* turn (in a certain direction); look (a certain way), have a certain appearance

hvárrtveggi *indef pron* each of the two

hvé *interrog adv* how?; **hvé nær** *conj* when

illr *adj* bad, evil

já *adv* yes

kenna <-d-> *vb* feel

koma <kemr~kømr; kom, kómu~kvámu; kominn> *vb* come; **koma á bak** mount on horseback; **koma [e-u] fram** bring [sth] about, bring [sth] to a successful conclusion; **koma máli fram** (*leg*) prosecute (a case)

Kolfinnr <-s> *m* Kolfinn (*personal name*)

kvánga <-að-> *vb* cause (a man) to marry; *refl* **kvángask** marry (*of a man*), take a wife

kvángaðr *ppart* married (*of a man*) (*see* **kvánga**)

leggja <lagð-; *ppart* lag(i)ðr~laginn> *vb* lay, place, put; *refl* **leggjask** lay, set oneself; **leggjask á** arise

leiða <-dd-> *vb* lead; *refl* **leiðask** be led, be persuaded

leiga *f* rent, pay; interest; **með leigum** with interest

leita <-að-> *vb* [*w gen*] seek, search for

leitat *n ppart* sought for, intended (*see* **leita**)

lengi <*comp* lengr (*time*), lengra (*distance*)> *adv* long, for a long time

liðveizla *f* support

líf *n* life

mannval *n* choice people, select body of men

málaleitan (*also* **málaleitun**) *f* negotiation

málaleitun *var of* **málaleitan**

meðan *adv* meanwhile; *conj* while, as long as; **á meðan** in the mean time, meanwhile

mun *1/3sg pres of* **munu**

mund *n* (*in sg*) *or f* (*in pl*) moment; situation, circumstance; **í þær mundir in** those times; in those circumstances

munu <mun, munu; mundi; *pret inf* mundu> *pret-pres* *vb* will, shall (*futurity*); to be sure to, must (*probability*); (*past tense*) would, must

of *adv* too

ofrlið *n* superior force; **bera [e-n] ofrliði** overpower [sb]

óþykkja *f* discord, dislike, ill-will

ríkr *adj* powerful

rómr *m* voice; cheering, acclamation; **illr rómr** criticism, voiced disapproval

saman *adv* together; **allt saman** wholly, entirely, altogether

senda <-d-> *vb* send

sendimaðr <*pl* -menn> *m* messenger

setja <-tt-> *vb* set, seat, place; *refl* **setjask** seat oneself, sit

sé *1sg pres of* **sjá**

silfra *f* Silver (*nickname*)

sinn *n* time (*instance or repetition*); **annat sinn** the second time

sjá <sér; sá, sá(u); sénn> *vb* see, look; understand

skammr <skǫmm, skam(m)t> *adj* short, brief

sneri *1/3sg past of* **snúa**

snúa <snýr; snøri~sneri; snúinn> *vb* turn, go

spurðr *ppart of* **spyrja**

spurðusk *3pl past of* **spyrjask**

spyrja <spurð-> *vb* ask; hear, hear of, learn, be informed of, find out; **spyrja at [e-m/e-u]** ask after, inquire about [sb/sth]; *refl* **spyrjask** be heard of, be reported

standa <stendr; stóð, stóðu; staðinn> *vb* stand

stendr *2/3sg pres of* **standa**

sviptir *m* loss

tala <-að-> *vb* talk, speak; *refl* **talask** speak to one another

talazk *n ppart of* **talask**

umsýsla *f* management; **vera at umsýsla** manage, oversee

una <-ð-, *n ppart* unat> *vb* [*w dat*] enjoy, be happy in, be content with

vanheilsa *f* poor health, illness

varla *adv* hardly, scarcely

vera <er; var, váru; verit> *vb* be; last; stay; **vera til** exist, stand

vinna <vinnr, vann, unnu, unninn> *vb* gain, win; work; perform, accomplish; *refl* **vinnask** last

vissi *3sg past indic & 3sg/pl past subjunct of* **vita**

vita <veit, vitu; vissi; vitaðr> *pret-pres vb* know

Þorgerðr <*acc/dat* Þorgerði, *gen* Þorgerðar> *f* Thorgerd (*personal name*); **Þorgerðr silfra** *f* Thorgerd Silver

Þorgerðarstaðir *m pl* Thorgerdarstadir ('Thorgerd's Farmstead') (*place name*)

Þorvaldr <-s> *m* Thorvald (*personal name*); **Þorvaldr inn hávi** *m* Thorvald the Tall

þriði <-ja, -ju> *ord num* third; **við þriðja mann** 'with a third person', being three altogether

þverra <þverr; þvarr, þurru; þorrinn> *vb* decrease

þykkja <þykkir, þótt-> *vb impers* seem to be; [*dat subj*] think, seem (to one); **[e-m] þykkir sviptir** *impers* [sb] feels bereft

ǫndvegi *n* high-seat

CULTURE SECTION – HALLA'S DOWRY

To a degree unusual in continental medieval Europe, Icelandic women maintained a measure of independence and control over their own lives, including the right to own property. Both as individual and members of their kin group, women had legal rights and responsibilities, which were in some respects comparable to those of men. Nevertheless, women did not enjoy full legal or social equality with men. For example, although women often played substantial roles in feuding, they did not serve as advocates at the local and national assemblies and courts. While a woman could inherit a chieftaincy (*goðorð*), she was ineligible to act as a *goði* and had to appoint a man to act on her behalf.

As in the case of Halla, dowries were often an essential part of a woman's property. The dowry (*heimanfylgja*) was paid to the bride by her family at her wedding. It was managed by her new husband, but because it was her property, it could be reclaimed, along with a share of the profit that had accrued from its use in the estate during the union, in case of a divorce. The bride-price (*mundr*) paid to the bride's family by the bridegroom also remained the personal property of the wife. Dowries consisted of heirlooms, farm implements, livestock, land, and perhaps a portion of a family's known monetary wealth.

In the social context of a family's control over its destiny, the dowry had a value higher than its monetary worth. Brodd-Helgi's refusal to pay back Halla's dowry is a serious insult which humiliates Geitir and his family. Seizing on the importance of the issue, Brodd-Helgi has chosen to make the retention of Halla's dowry a test of his ability to injure the dignity of his opponent and to dominate Geitir in a court case. In the eyes of the community, Brodd-Helgi's refusal to compromise and settle the dispute is a public signal that reveals his intention to strip Geitir of his authority and gain control over the local region for himself. This contention further escalates the feud between Brodd-Helgi and Geitir.

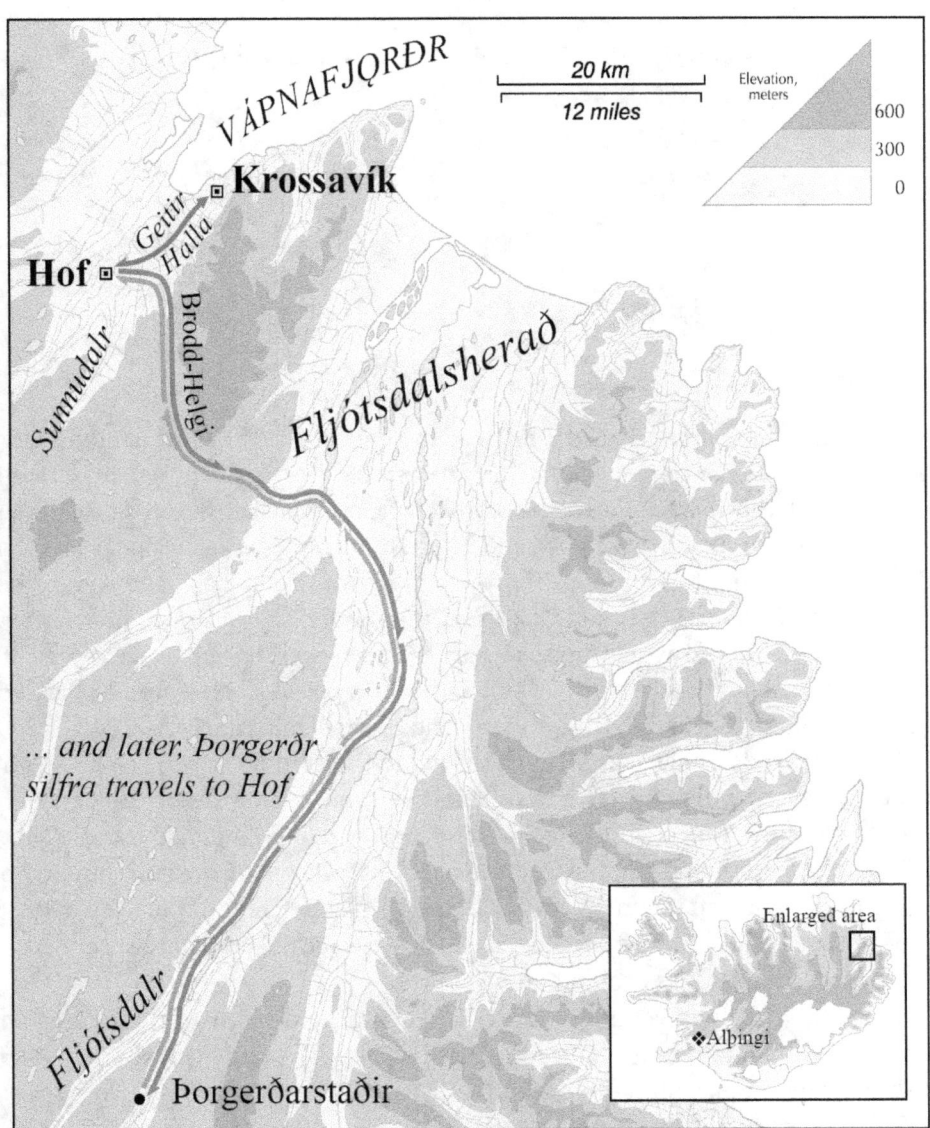

Map 5. Brodd-Helgi Remarries. Brodd-Helgi travels to Thorgerdarstadir (Thorgerd's Stead) in Fljotsdal (River Dale) and engages himself in marriage to Thorgerd Silver. Geitir returns his current sick wife Halla, the sister of the chieftain Geitir, home to her family at Krossavík. Then Thorgerd Silver moves into Brodd-Helgi's estate at Hof.

7. FARMERS, CHIEFTAINS, AND A CONTESTED WOODLAND

There was a man named Thord who lived in Sunnudal at the farm named Tunga, on the same side of river where the Hof farm stood.[1] He was a thingman of Helgi.[2]

Thord and Thormod[3] owned a wood together, but they came to a disagreement over tree-felling and grazing rights, and Thord thought he was getting far less than his share compared to Thormod. Thord went to visit Brodd-Helgi and complained about Thormod's excess. Brodd-Helgi said that he had no desire to quarrel over Thord's property and would take no part in it, unless Thord transferred all the property to him and came to live at Hof with all his possessions. Thord chose to do this and handed over to Helgi his property and rights of inheritance.[4]

One day, Brodd-Helgi asked Thord to ride to the common pasture and see his gelded livestock which were there. When they came to the pasture, Brodd-Helgi said, "We have now accounted for the stock that you and Thormod owned."

Then Helgi went and rounded up the oxen that Thormod owned, chopped off their heads, and left them lying there. He then went home and sent men to Thormod to tell him that he should have his oxen checked on. That was done, and the butchered meat was brought home.

After that Thormod rode to Krossavik. He informed Geitir of the matter and asked Geitir to obtain redress for him. Geitir said that he had no desire to quarrel with Helgi over this situation.

Thormod said, "You are acting unworthily if you refuse to support our case."

"Don't use me to back your quarrels," said Geitir. "Bring the ox-meat here, and I will buy it so that you suffer no loss."

---

[1] The location of this farm at Tunga is uncertain. Most probably it lay on the tongue (*tunga*) of land where the Sunnudal River (Sunnudalsá) and the Hof River (Hofsá) meet, in front of the entrance to Sunnudal (Sunnudalr). (See the accompanying map.)

[2] The statement that Thord is Helgi's thingman is an affirmation that Helgi is a *goði*.

[3] Thormod Stick-Gazer, introduced in Ch. 3, who is a thingman of Geitir.

[4] **property and rights of inheritance:** *arfsal*, a legal term meaning 'sale or cession of one's right of inheritance'. In times of feud or personal crisis in the lives of freemen, *goðar* offered needed assistance and advocacy. Here Thord gives up his property and independence in exchange for the chieftain's support. It was possible, although extremely difficult, for a natural heir to reclaim his inheritance once it had been transferred in this way (*Grágás* Ia, 247–49, II, 85–87).

7. KAPÍTULI

Summary of Chapter 7. Thord, one of Brodd-Helgi's thingmen, quarrels with Thormod, one of Geitir's supporters, over grazing and timber rights. Thord submits himself and all his wealth to Brodd-Helgi in exchange for the chieftain's help. Brodd-Helgi slaughters Thormod's oxen. Thormod seeks Geitir's help, but Geitir does not want any part in the dispute. After Brodd-Helgi cuts down all of Thormod's trees, Geitir advises Thormod to summon Thord to the assembly. Brodd-Helgi finds out and ambushes Thormod, killing him and many of his companions. Brodd-Helgi buries the bodies in a humiliating manner, and Geitir and his men dare not collect the bodies.

Maðr hét Þórðr, er bjó í Sunnudal á bœ þeim, er í Tungu heitir, þeim megin ár, sem Hofsbœr stendr. Þingmaðr var hann Helga.

Þeir Þormóðr áttu skóg saman, ok skildi þá á um skógarhǫggit ok svá um beitingar, ok þóttisk Þórðr mjǫk vanhaldinn fyrir Þormóði. Ok fór Þórðr á fund Brodd-Helga ok sagði honum ofgang Þormóðar. Brodd-Helgi kvazk eigi nenna at deila um fé hans ok engan hlut mundu í eiga, nema hann handsalaði honum féit allt ok fœri til Hofs með allt sitt. Hann kaus þat ok seldisk Helga arfsali.

Einnhvern dag kvaddi Brodd-Helgi Þórð at ríða á afrétt ok sjá geldfé sitt, er þar var. Fóru þeir síðan ok kómu í afréttinn. Þá mælti Brodd-Helgi: "Nú hǫfum vit sét yfir fénað þann, er þit Þormóðr hafið áttan."[1]

Nú ferr Helgi ok safnar saman uxum þeim, er Þormóðr átti, ok hǫggr af hǫfuðin ok lætr þar liggja, ferr síðan heim ok sendir menn til Þormóðar ok biðr, at hann láti forvitnask um yxn sín.[2] Ok svá var gǫrt, ok var slátr þar heim fœrt.

Eptir þat ríðr Þormóðr í Krossavík ok sagði Geiti til ok bað hann rétta hluta sinn. Geitir kvazk eigi nenna at deila við Helga um þenna hlut.

Þormóðr segir: "Illa er þér varit,[3] er þú vilt eigi styðja mál vár."

"Ekki stoða jagmál þín við mik,"[4] segir Geitir. "Ber hingat uxaslátrit, ok mun ek kaupa, svá at þér sé skaðlaust."

---

[1] **áttan:** masc. acc. sing. ppart. of *eiga* 'own', modifying *fénað þann*.

[2] **at hann láti forvitnask um yxn sín:** 'that he should have his oxen checked on'. In the singular, *uxi* 'ox' (also spelled *oxi*) is masculine, but the plural *yxn* is often neuter, as here.

[3] **illa er þér varit:** 'you are acting unworthily', where *varit* means 'of a certain disposition'. In this instance *varit*, the past participle of *verja* (which means either 'defend' or 'wrap, enclose'), has become confused with *farit*, the past participle of *fara* 'go', used in the impersonal expression [e-m] *er svá farit* '[one] is thus disposed'. Compare *illa er þér varit* here with *þat er þér illa farit* 'it is ill-done by you, you are acting unworthily' (Ch. 10).

[4] **Ekki stoða jagmál þín við mik:** 'Don't use me to back your quarrels'. The compound *jagmál* 'quarrel' is otherwise unknown in Icelandic, but *jag* has the same meaning, and the verb *jaga* means 'move to and fro'.

Thormod went home no better off than he had come, and it was reported to Helgi that he had gone to tell Geitir of his troubles.

"I would rather," said Helgi, "that he need go on no more such errands." A little later Helgi summoned his tenants and ordered them to make a journey with him along with his farmhands and guests.[1] He went to the wood that he and Thormod both owned together,[2] and they chopped down the entire wood and dragged every tree home to Hof.

When Thormod found out the injury that had been done to him, he went a second time to Geitir and reported the injustice done to him.

Then Geitir answered, "I think you have a much better excuse for thinking this injury worse than the previous one, because I considered that one of little significance. I also do not wish to assist Helgi in these matters, so I will give you some advice. Look up your kinsmen Stein and Hreidar, the sons of Ref the Red, and ask them to go with you to serve a summons at Hof. Also go to Gudmundar-stadir and ask Tjorvi[3] to go with you. And be sure there are not more than eight all together in your party. You must summon Thord for the tree-felling. But make sure Brodd-Helgi is not at home, otherwise it will do you no good."

With that Thormod went and met with the men that Geitir had named. They all promised to go and appointed a time when they should leave. Thormod rode home and told Geitir where matters stood.

But it is true what is said: "Word travels when it leaves the mouth." Report of this came to Helgi, and he did not leave as had been planned. That morning, when they were expected, Helgi told his farmhands that they should by no means leave the farm buildings that day. "You must cut for yourselves large wooden switches and many long sticks.[4] Men are expected here today, and you should use the sticks to beat the horses they are riding on and drive the lot of them out of the homefield."[5]

---

[1] The author's use of the word "guests" here may have a special connotation. Kings and jarls in Norway often kept a *gestasveit*, a separate group of men who formed a distinct, but less prestigious, part of the *hirð*, the court retinue. The *gestir*, as the members of such groups were known, were used as spies and enforcers for dangerous missions. Toward the end of the Sturlung Age in the mid-13th century, Icelandic chieftains such as Þórðr kakali and Gizurr jarl employed such men. Perhaps the author sought to make a connection between them and Brodd-Helgi, whose aggressive attempts to win power for himself would have struck a chord with the 13th-century audience.

[2] Since Thord had transferred his property to Helgi, the wood that he and Thormod had owned together is now jointly owned by Brodd-Helgi and Thormod, placing Thormod in an uneven power struggle with a much stronger opponent. (See Culture Section below.)

[3] Ch. 4 hints that Tjorvi may have been the killer of Hrafn, the Norwegian merchant.

[4] **long sticks:** *stafir* 'staves' or 'staffs'.

[5] **homefield:** *tún* 'hayfield' or 'homefield'. A *tún* was an enclosed and often well-drained field adjacent to the farmhouse that produced the finest hay because it was manured from the nearby livestock barn or stable. Other hayfields were not so well-maintained and therefore less productive.

Þormóðr fór heim þvílíkr ok hann kom þar, ok var sagt Helga, at hann muni hafa farit at segja Geiti til vandræða sinna.

"Ok vilda ek gjarna," segir hann, "at hann þyrfti eigi optar[1] slíkra ørenda at fara." Litlu síðar boðar Helgi til sín landsetum sínum, ok ákveðr hann þessa til ferðar með sér ok húskarla sína ok gesti ok fór í skóg þann, er þeir Þormóðr áttu báðir saman, ok hjuggu upp allan skóginn ok drógu hvert tré heim til Hofs.

Ok er Þormóðr frétti þetta, hverr skaði honum er gǫrr, þá ferr hann í annat sinn á fund Geitis ok sagði, hverr ójǫfnuðr honum var gǫrr.

Þá svarar Geitir: "Miklu þykki mér meiri várkunn á, at þér þykki sá skaðinn illr heldr en hinn, er fyrr var, því at sá þótti mér lítils verðr. Vil ek ok ekki veita Helga til þessara mála, en þó mun ek leggja ráð til með þér. Finn þú frændr þína, sonu Refs ins rauða, Stein ok Hreiðar, ok bið þá fara með þér stefnufǫr til Hofs. Kom þú ok á Guðmundarstaði ok bið Tjǫrva at fara með þér, ok verið eigi fleiri saman en átta. Ok skaltu stefna Þórði um skógarhǫgg, ok stilltu svá til, at Brodd-Helgi sé eigi heima. Eigi mun yðr elligar duga."

Þormóðr ferr við svá búit ok hittir þá menn, er Geitir hefir til nefnda, ok hétu þeir allir at fara ok ákveða, hvé nær þeir fara skyldu. Ríðr Þormóðr heim ok segir Geiti, hvar komit var.[2]

En svá er satt, sem mælt er: "Ferr orð, er munn líðr,"[3] – ok kemr þetta til Helga, ok ferr hann eigi, sem ætlat var. Þann morgun,[4] er þeira var ván,[5] þá mælti Helgi við húskarla sína, at þeir skyldi hvergi fara frá húsum um daginn. "Þér skuluð hǫggva yðr sviga stóra ór viði ok stafi marga. Er manna hingat ván í dag, ok skulu þér þá neyta stafanna ok berja hrossin[6] undir þeim ok reka svá ór túni allt saman."

---

[1] **optar:** 'oftener, more often', compar. of *opt* 'often'. Its use is frequently idiomatic: *eigi optar* (lit. 'not oftener' or 'no more often') means simply 'no more' or 'not again'.

[2] **hvar komit var:** 'where matters stood'.

[3] **Ferr orð, er munn líðr:** lit. 'Word travels when it passes [the] mouth', meaning word spreads once spoken. The modern Icelandic proverb is *orðin fara, þegar munninn líður*. Several scribal variants appear in manuscripts at this point. The phrase *er munn líðr* appears as *ef um líðr* in two instances, but as *ef um munn líður* in another. (For references, see *Íslenzk fornrit* XI, p. 40, n. 4.) These variations seem to indicate that the scribes were familiar with slightly different versions of the saying.

[4] **Þann morgun:** 'That morning'. The accusative case is often used to denote time.

[5] **er þeira var ván:** 'when they were expected'.

[6] *Hross* (neut.) 'horse' usually means either a gelding or any horse in general. When contrasted with *hestr* (masc.) 'horse, stallion', *hross* specifically refers to a female horse and is the same as a *merr* (fem.) 'mare'.

Thormod and his companions left from home as planned and came to Hof. Seeing no one outside, they rode at once onto the courtyard,[1] where Thormod named witnesses and summoned Thord for the tree-felling.

Helgi was inside and heard the summons. He ran out and thrust Thormod through, and then cried, "Let's drive away these worthless men and give them a reason for coming here to Hof today!"

Now the farmhands ran out and struck the riders' horses, so that they all retreated from the courtyard. That was the end of the lawsuit, and nothing better came of it. Geitir's men only narrowly escaped.[2] People held it to be true that Helgi was the one who had killed the men who died. Helgi had the bodies carried to the ruins of an abandoned house[3] and covered them with brushwood.[4]

Geitir's men were very ill-pleased with their lot, and the worst of it was that they were unable to bury their kinsmen and dear friends.

They came often to talk with Geitir about this matter. He urged them to wait and answered, "It is said that he who has a short sword[5] must seek his opportunity later,[6] and so will it be with us concerning Brodd-Helgi."

CHAPTER 7 VOCABULARY

afréttr *m* common pasture (in the mountains or wilderness)

allr <ǫll, allt> *adj/indef pron* all, entire, whole; **með allt sitt** with all one's possessions

arfsal *n* (*leg*) transfer of one's right of inheritance; **seljask arfsali** (*leg*) cede one's right of inheritance

á <*gen* ár; *pl* ár, *dat* ám, *gen* á> *f* river

ákveða <ákveðr; ákvað, ákváðu; ákveðinn> *vb* fix, decide, appoint

ár *gen sg & nom/acc pl of* **á**

---

[1] **courtyard:** *hlað*, the pavement or courtyard in front of a homestead. It was located within the *tún*, or homefield.

[2] One manuscript adds *bæði sárir ok barðir, en sumir fellu þar dauðir* 'both wounded and beaten, and some fell there dead'. Evidently the scribe felt that the narrative was missing something and needed clarification. Later we learn that Thormod and some of his companions were killed in this incident.

[3] **the ruins of an abandoned house:** *topt*, the walls or foundations of an abandoned building, usually made of turf and stone. *Topt* is found in many place names, for example *Toptavǫllr* (Toptavoll), the name of Thorstein the White's early farmsite (Ch. 1).

[4] Covering of the dead after a battle was required by law so as to protect the corpse from birds and animals. Failure to do so made the killer liable to lesser outlawry (*Grágás* Ia, 154, II, 358). Helgi fulfilled the letter of the law but still succeeded in humiliating the slain and provoking those associated with them by preventing a decent burial.

[5] **a short sword:** *sax*, a short, single-edged sword distinct from a *sverð*, which was larger and double-edged. The term *sax* later came to refer to a large, heavy knife and was not reserved for use as a weapon.

[6] In Jón Jóhannesson's text in the *Íslenzk fornrit* edition, the word *síðar* 'later' in this proverbial phrase is emended to *liðar* (the genitive of *liðr* 'joint of a limb'). This change produces a satisfyingly alliterative construction: *liðar verðr sá at leita, er lítit sax hefir* 'he who has a small knife must seek out a joint' (a truth every butcher knows). This proverb appears in some manuscripts containing the Riddles of Gestumblindi, an episode in *Heiðreks saga* (see *Hervarar saga ok Heiðreks konungs*, ed. Jón Helgason, p. 70). Nevertheless, such emendation, while attractive, is not required by any failure in the sense of the original text.

Nú fara Þormóðr ok þeir heiman, sem ætlat var, ok koma til Hofs ok sjá ekki manna úti ok ríða þegar á hlaðit, ok nefnir Þormóðr sér vátta ok stefnir Þórði um skógarhǫgg.

Helgi var inni ok heyrir stefnuna ok hleypr út síðan ok leggr í gegnum Þormóð ok mælti síðan: "Rekum í brott þessi vanmenni ok látum þá hafa hingat ørendi til Hofs í dag."[1]

Nú hlaupa út húskarlarnir ok berja hrossin undir þeim, ok hǫrfar nú allt saman ofan fyrir hlaðit,[2] ok urðu þau málalok, en ekki betri. Kómusk menn Geitis undan með illan leik. Þat hǫfðu menn fyrir satt,[3] at Helgi mundi verit hafa banamaðr þeira manna, er líflátnir váru. Helgi lét bera líkin í topt eina ok bera ofan á hrís.

Geitis menn unðu stórilla sínum hlut ok við ekki annat verr en þat, at[4] þeir náðu eigi at jarða frændr sína ok ástmenn.

Ok kómu þeir opt á tal við Geiti um þetta mál. Hann svarar ok bað þá bíða: "Þat er mælt, at síðar verðr sá at leita, er lítit sax hefir,[5] ok mun svá oss verða við Brodd-Helga."

ástmaðr <pl -menn> m dear friend

átta num eight

áttan m acc sg ppart of **eiga**

bera <berr; bar, báru; borinn> vb carry, bear; **bera ofan á [e-t]** place [sth] on top

boða <-að-> vb [w dat] order

deila <-d-> vb divide; quarrel; **deila um [e-t]** quarrel over [sth], take up a lawsuit over [sth]

draga <dregr; dró, drógu; dreginn> vb drag, draw

drógu 3pl past of **draga**

eiga <á, eigu; átti; áttr> vb own, have, possess

elligar adv otherwise, else

fénaðr <gen -ar> m sheep, cattle, livestock

fleiri comp adj more (see **margr**)

forvitna <-að-> vb pry into, inquire about; refl **forvitnask** inquire, find out

frétta <-tt-> vb hear, find out about

gegnum (also **í gegnum**) prep through

geldfé n castrated sheep, goats, or cattle

gera <-ð-; ppart gerðr~gerr> vb make, build; do, act

gerr adj & ppart done (see **gera**)

gestr <-s; -ir> m guest

gjarna adv willingly, rather

gǫrr var of **gerr**

handsala <-að-> vb (leg) transfer one's rights to something (by shaking hands)

heita <heitr; hét, hétu; heitinn> vb [w dat] promise

hétu 3pl past of **heita**

hjuggu var of **hjoggu**, 3pl past of **hǫggva**

hlað <hlǫð> n courtyard, the paved area in front of a farmhouse

hlaupa <hleypr; hljóp, hljópu; hlaupinn> vb leap, spring; run

hleypr 2/3 pres of **hlaupa**

hlutr <-ar; -ir> m lot; thing; **eiga hlut í [e-u]** take part in, interfere in [sth]

hrís n shrubbery, brushwood

hross n horse

hús n house, building; pl the group of

---

[1] **látum þá hafa hingat ørendi til Hofs í dag:** 'let us give them a reason for coming here to Hof today'.

[2] **hǫrfar nú allt saman ofan fyrir hlaðit:** 'now everyone retreats together from the courtyard'.

[3] **þat hǫfðu menn fyrir satt:** 'men held this to be true'.

[4] **við ekki annat verr en þat, at…:** 'the worst part of it being that'.

[5] **þat er mælt … er lítit sax hefir:** 'it is said that he who has a short sword must seek his opportunity later'.

buildings on a farm

hvergi *adv* by no means, not at all

hǫfuð <*dat* hǫfði; *pl dat* hǫfðum, *gen* hǫfða> *n* head

hǫggva <hǫggr; hjó, hjoggu; hǫgg(v)inn> *vb* strike (a blow), chop, hack, hew; **hǫggva af** chop off; **hǫggva upp** cut down (trees)

horfa <-að-> *vb* give way, retreat, withdraw

inni *adv* in (*location*), inside, indoors

jagmál *n* (petty) quarrel

jarða <-að-> *vb* bury

kaus *1/3sg past of* **kjósa**

kjósa <kýss; kaus~kǫri, kusu~kuru; kosinn~kjǫrinn> *vb* choose

koma <kemr~kømr; kom, kómu~kvámu; kominn> *vb* come; *refl* **komask** get through, arrive at an end, reach; **komask undan** escape, get away

kómusk *3pl past of* **komask**

kvaddi *3sg past of* **kveðja**

kveðja <kvadd-> *vb* call on, summon

landseti *m* tenant

láta <lætr; lét, létu; látinn> *vb* let, allow, permit; [*w inf*] have something done

leggja <lagð-; *ppart* lag(i)ðr~laginn> *vb* lay, place, put; stab, thrust; **leggja í gegnum [e-n]** impale [sb], run [sb] through; **leggja ráð til** offer advice

leikr <-s; -ar> *m* game, play, sport; **með illan leik** narrowly, by a narrow escape; in poor condition

litlu *adv* little, a little; shortly (*time*); **litlu síðar** shortly afterward, a little while later

lífláta <líflætr; líflét, líflétu; líflátinn> *vb* put to death, kill

lík *n* body, corpse

lítill <lítil, lítit; *dat n* litlu> *adj* little; short, brief (*time*); **litlu síðar** shortly afterward, a little while later

margr <mǫrg, mar(g)t; *comp* fleiri, *superl* flestr> *adj* many

málalok *n pl* end, conclusion of a case or matter

megin *adv* on the side; **þeim megin** on that side

morginn (*also* **morgunn**) <*gen* morgins; *pl* mor(g)nar> *m* morning

morgunn *var of* **morginn**

munnr <-s; -ar> *m* mouth

ná <-ð-> *vb* [*w dat*] reach, catch, overtake; get, obtain; [*w inf*] be able to [do sth]

nenna <-t-> *vb* [*w dat or inf*] have a desire

to, be disposed to

neyta <-tt-> *vb* [*w gen*] use, make use of

ofan *adv* down, downwards; from above

ofgangr *m* excess, abuse

opt *adv* often

optar *comp adv* more often, oftener (*see* **opt**); **eigi optar** no more, not again

oss *acc/dat of* **vér**

ójafnaðr (*also* **ójǫfnuðr**) <*gen* -ar> *m* injustice, unfairness

ójǫfnuðr *var of* **ójafnaðr**

reka <rekr; rak, ráku; rekinn> *vb* drive, herd

rétta <-tt-> *vb* make right; (*leg*) right (a wrong); **rétta hluta [e-s]** obtain redress for [sb]

safna <-að-> *vb* [*w dat*] gather, collect

sannr <sǫnn, satt> *adj* true; **hafa [e-t] fyrir satt** believe [sth] to be true, be convinced of [sth]

satt *n sg of* **sannr**

sax <sǫx> *n* short sword

seljask *refl vb* give oneself up, submit oneself; **seljask arfsali** (*leg*) cede one's right of inheritance (i.e., perform an **arfsal**)

sé *1/3sg pres subjunct of* **vera**

sét *n ppart of* **sjá**

síð *adv* late

síðar *comp adv* later, afterward (*see* **síð**); **litlu síðar** shortly afterward, a little while later

sjá <sér; sá, sá(u); sénn> *vb* see, look; **sjá yfir** look over, survey, look after

skaði *m* harm, damage

skaðlauss *adj* without loss, unscathed

skógarhǫgg *n* tree felling, wood cutting

skógr <-ar; -ar> *m* forest, woods

slátr *n* butchered meat

stafr <-s; -ar~ir> *m* staff, stick

stefnufǫr <*gen* -farar; *pl* -farar~farir> *f* journey to serve a legal summons

stilla <-t-> *vb* arrange, settle; **stilla til** arrange

stoða <-að-> *vb* support

stórr *adj* big

stórilla *adv* very badly

styðja <studd-> *vb* support

svigi *m* switch

tal <tǫl> *n* conversation, talk; **koma á tal við [e-n]** come to speak with [sb]

topt <-ir> *f* 'toft', site of a house; foundation or bare walls, *esp* the ruins of a house

tré <*dat* tré; *pl* tré, *dat* trjám, *gen* trjá> *n* tree

tunga *f* tongue; language; tongue of land at the meeting of two rivers

Tunga *f* Tunga ('Tongue') (*place name*)

tún *n* enclosure; hayfield, homefield

una <-ð-, *n ppart* unat> *vb* dwell, stay, abide; [*w dat*] enjoy, be happy in, be content with; **una við [e-t]** to be content with [sth]

undan *prep* [*w dat*] from under; away from; *adv* away

unðu *3pl past of* **una**

uxaslátr *n* meat of oxen, beef

uxi <*pl* (*often irregularly n*) yxn> *m* ox

vanhaldinn *ppart* wronged, getting less than one's due

vanmenni *n* worthless person

varit *n ppart* of a certain disposition (*see* verja); **[e-m] er illa varit** *impers* [sb] has an ill disposition, is acting unworthily

ván *f* hope; expectation; **er ván [e-s]** *impers* [sb]/[sth] is expected

várr *poss pron 1pl* our

várkunn *f* that which is excusable

vera <er; var, váru; verit> *vb* be

verja <varð-; *ppart* var(i)ðr~varinn> *vb* defend; wrap, enclose; **[e-m] er illa varit** *impers* [sb] has an ill disposition, is acting unworthily

vér <*acc/dat* oss, *gen* vár> *pron 1pl* we

viðr <*gen* viðar; *pl* viðir, *acc* viðu> *m* tree; forest, wood; timber

yðr *acc/dat of* **þér**

yfir *prep* [*w acc/dat*] over, above, across

yxn *pl* (*often irregularly n*) *of* **uxi**

þér <*acc/dat* yðr, *gen* yðarr~yðvarr> *pron 2pl* you (*pl*)

þit <*acc/dat* ykkr, *gen* ykkarr> *pron 2dual* you (two)

Þórðr <-ar> *m* Thord (*personal name*)

þurfa <þarf, þurfu; þurfti; þurft> *pret-pres vb* [*aux*] need; [*w gen*] need, have need of

þvílíkr *adj* such; **þvílíkr ok** the same as

þyrfti *3sg/pl past subjunct of* **þurfa**

CULTURE SECTION – HONOR AND CONFLICT

Here, in the bargain between *goði* and *bóndi*, honor plays a crucial background role, invigorating the issue of choices. The medieval audience would surely have noted, and probably commented upon, Thord's small victory. Thord gets the last bitter laugh in his dealings with his neighbor Thormod, because even though Thord, a poor farmer, has lost his land, he nevertheless has done so in a manner that partly assuages his honor. In choosing to transfer his land to Brodd-Helgi, Thord, for a brief instant, takes control of the direction of the action. He exits from the quarrel with the knowledge – shared by the community – that his opponent Thormod is now embroiled in contention with a powerful antagonist, Brodd-Helgi. Thormod, in return for his determination to bully a neighbor, will now have to defend his person and property against Brodd-Helgi, a dangerous and motivated *goði*.

Thord had few options. Faced with a humiliating situation, he would have been scorned if he had taken no action. Others in the surrounding community would have probably goaded and shamed Thord into challenging and perhaps even attempting to kill Thormod – a risky venture. Instead, Thord turns to an advocate, proving himself a difficult man to humiliate. Once Thord has transferred his land, he cannot be intimidated into dropping his claim. On the contrary, he is relieved of responsibility. The rights of prosecution that come with ownership have been assumed by Brodd-Helgi. With the *Schadenfreude*, or joy in another's discomfort, that we so often see in the Icelandic texts, Thord can enjoy, from a distance, the dangers (and death) that await Thormod in the escalating feud between the *goðar*, Brodd-Helgi and Geitir.

As a *goði*, Brodd-Helgi wants to increase his wealth, power, and influence, but he must weigh those advantages against the costs of taking the farmer's case. The chieftain has no valid right to the land. He does, however, have the power to assert a claim because of his role as the advocate of his thingman, Thord. The *goði* and his *þingmaðr* each have something of value with which to bargain. The thingman receives a service, and the chieftain receives a payment that benefits him financially and politically. Integral to the exchange is the fact that the chieftain Brodd-Helgi is in the right place at the right time, and he has the power to act both in his own and in Thord's interest.

Decisions like the one facing Brodd-Helgi have much to do with a *goði*'s ultimate success or failure. If a chieftain abuses his position and presses his thingmen too hard, he risks losing vital support. His thingmen will seek other means of protecting their families and property. On the other hand, if the *goði* is not aggressive enough in supporting his thingmen, he may similarly lose crucial backing.

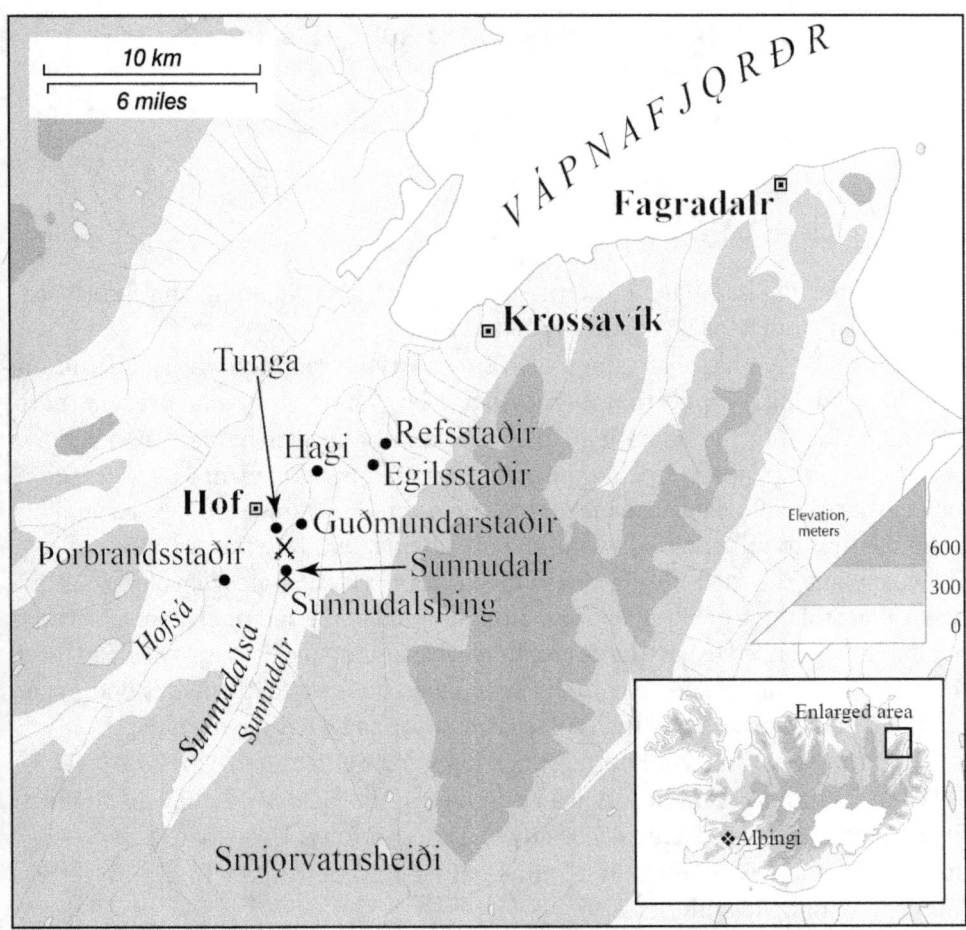

Map 6. A Feud Begins. Two farmers, Thord at Tunga and Thormod at Sunnudal, quarrel over property rights. The dispute escalates, engaging their neighbors, kinsmen, and chieftains. The map shows the probable location of the Sunnudal Assembly and the site (marked by cross swords) of a later battle (Ch. 14) between the chieftains.

8. Geitir Outsmarts Brodd-Helgi

When some time had passed, Geitir sent word to his thingmen, and afterwards they set out from Krossavik and headed to Hof.

Geitir said, "We have not assembled this party so secretly that Helgi will not have learned of it. I expect that there will be a large number of men present there. We must ride into the homefield, dismount and tie up our horses, then remove our cloaks and proceed briskly. I expect that Helgi will confront us, but I don't expect that he will make an armed attack on our men. And we must be careful not to be the first to inflict bloody wounds[1] on anyone, but drag the struggle out.

"Meanwhile, the sons of Egil along with Big Tjorvi will separate from our group and go up along this side of the river around Gudmundarstadir and then enter the woods behind Hof. You need to have large empty coal baskets on the horses. When you reach the homefield wall,[2] go secretly to the abandoned house, take the men's bodies and put them in the baskets, and then come back by the same path to meet me."[3]

They now separated, and both groups followed Geitir's instructions.

When Geitir and his men had nearly arrived at the farmstead, they dismounted from their horses and advanced slowly and carefully. Helgi had a very large number of men with him, and immediately he confronted Geitir. Greetings followed with no friendliness.

Helgi asked where Geitir intended to go. Geitir replied that he had little more to add, but said that he intended to make his purpose clear to all. "We will not offer violence now at this time, although there is sufficient cause for it. We want to make one more attempt before we give up altogether."

---

[1] **bloody wound:** *áverki*, a legal term defining a visible open wound. Such wounds could entail prosecution and demands for compensation and also warrant vengeance-taking (see *Grágás* 1992, 221–22).

[2] **homefield wall:** This was the *túngarðr*, the wall or fence enclosing the *tún*. It was designed to protect the grass inside the *tún*, which was intended for the best hay, from being grazed and trampled by sheep or cows.

[3] Compare *Ljósvetninga saga*, Ch. 20, where Hlenni the Wise conceals two men who had just committed a killing and were being pursued by Gudmund the Powerful by hiding them in pack baskets covered with grass, each one having a calf lying on top.

8. KAPÍTULI

Summary of Chapter 8. Geitir rallies his men with a plan to recover the bodies. He sends a few men, disguised as charcoal makers, through the woods. They come to Hof and load the bodies in charcoal baskets, while Geitir leads a band of men to Brodd-Helgi's front yard to distract him. The plan works, and Geitir is proven to be the craftier of the two.

En er á leið,[1] þá sendir Geitir orð þingmǫnnum sínum, ok fara þeir síðan ór Krossavík ok stefndu leið til Hofs.

Geitir mælti: "Vér hǫfum ekki lið þetta svá leyniliga saman dregit, at eigi muni Helgi spurt hafa, ok get ek, at þar muni fjǫlmennt fyrir vera.[2] Vér skulum ríða í tún ok stíga af baki ok binda hesta[3] vára ok leggja af oss skikkjur ok ganga síðan snúðugt. En ek get, at þá ráði Helgi í mót, en eigi get ek, at hann beri vápn á menn vára. En þat skulu þér varask at sæta áverkum við engan mann fyrri, ok þœfizk svá við.

"Nú skulu fara af liði váru Egilssynir ok Tjǫrvi inn mikli með þeim upp þessum megin[4] um Guðmundarstaði ok svá í skógana bak Hofi, ok skulu þér hafa kollaupa stóra, tóma af dreggjunum, á hrossunum, ok farið, þegar er þér komið at túngarðinum, heim til hússins[5] leyniliga, takið líkamana ok látið í laupana ok farið aptr ina sǫmu leið til móts við mik."

Nú skiljask þeir, ok fara hvárutveggju eptir fyrirsǫgn Geitis.

Ok er þeir Geitir koma mjǫk at bœnum, stíga þeir af baki ok fara at ǫllu tómliga. Helgi var fjǫlmennr mjǫk ok rézk þegar á móti Geiti, ok verða þar kvaðningar með engri[6] blíðu.

Spurði Helgi, hvert Geitir ætlaði at fara, en hann kvazk litlu mundu við auka,[7] lézk þat ætla,[8] at ǫllum mundi þykkja auðsýnt ørendit. "Vér munum nú ok eigi ófrið bjóða at sinni, þótt til þess sé œrin sǫk, ok viljum vér reyna enn framar, áðr en vér ráðum frá með ǫllu."

---

[1] **en er á leið:** 'and when some time had passed'.

[2] **get ek, at þar muni fjǫlmennt fyrir vera:** 'I expect that there will be a large number of men present there'.

[3] The masculine noun *hestr* may refer specifically to a 'stallion' when there is an implied contrast with *merr* (fem.) 'mare'. Often, however, as in this chapter, *hestr* is used as a general word for 'horse' and is more or less interchangeable with *hross* (neut.) 'horse'. (Compare the discussion of *hross* in Ch. 7, footnote 6 on page 73.)

[4] **þessum megin:** 'this side', i.e., on the eastern side of the Sunnudal River.

[5] **heim til hússins:** lit. 'home to the house', here speaking of the *topt*, which seems to be the walls and foundation of a former house.

[6] **engri:** dat. fem. sing. of the negative adj. *engr* 'no, not any'. This adjective is based on the negative indef. pron. *engi* 'no one, none'.

[7] **hann kvazk litlu mundu við auka:** 'he said he would add little', i.e., he would not say any more.

[8] **lézk þat ætla, at...:** 'said he intended that...'.

In this manner they dragged out the struggle through the day, and the crowd drifted this way and that across the fields.

Then a man spoke up from Helgi's company: "There are men over there, and not just a few of them, traveling with packhorses."

Another answered, "Those are nothing but charcoal makers coming out of the woods with baskets on the horses. I saw them today when they went into the woods." Then the subject was dropped.

Then Geitir said, "Now again it is going to end as it so often has. We will come out the worse since we have not succeeded in carrying away the bodies of our kinsmen."

"Why are you carrying on so?" said Helgi. "It is always more fitting that the one who is lower has to bow down. Nevertheless it is most likely that neither of us will receive dishonor from the other at this meeting. We are willing to break off this tedious struggle now, if you see fit, but we are not willing for you to come any nearer to the house than you are now."

After that the crowd broke up. Geitir and his men went to their horses, while Helgi and his men stayed back on the field. Geitir and his men caught up with the sons of Egil, and at once they dismounted and made a halt. Helgi and his men stood in the yard of the homestead at Hof and saw them lingering.

Then Helgi spoke up. "Understanding comes late to fools," he said. "We have been in this contest all day. Now in hindsight, I see that none of Geitir's champions were present. They must have taken the bodies away in the coal-baskets. It is always the case that Geitir is the wisest of us, although time and again he is overcome by sheer force."

There was no prosecution for the killing of Thormod, and Geitir got no justice from Helgi in any court case. Thorkel, Geitir's son, traveled abroad as soon as he was of age and was constantly going between lands. He was little involved in the lawsuits of Brodd-Helgi and Geitir his father. At Krossavik the illness of Halla Lytingsdottir grew severe and dangerous.

CHAPTER 8 VOCABULARY

allfár <-fá, -fátt> adj very few

allr <ǫll, allt> adj/indef pron all, entire, whole; **at ǫllu** in all respects, in every way; **með ǫllu** wholly, completely

annarr <ǫnnur, annat; acc m annan, f aðra, dat m ǫðrum, n ǫðru; pl nom m aðrir> adj/ indef pron other, another

auðsýnn adj clear, evident

auka <eykr; jók, jóku; aukinn> vb increase, augment; [w dat] add; exceed, surpass; **auka [e-u] við** add [sth]

áverki m bodily injury, bloody wound

bak prep [w dat] behind

blíða f friendliness

draga <dregr; dró, drógu; dreginn> vb drag, draw; **draga saman lið** collect troops

dreggjar f pl dregs, dust

dregit n ppart of **draga**

dvelja <dvalð~dvald-; ppart dvalðr~ dvaldr~dvalinn> vb stay, dwell; delay; refl **dveljask** linger, stay, be delayed

dvǫlðusk 3pl past of **dveljask**

eptir prep [w acc] after (time); [w dat] after, along; according to; adv after, afterwards; **vera eptir** stay back, remain behind

engi <engi, ekki> adj/indef pron no one, none, no

engr adj no, not any (var of **engi**)

Þeir þœfask þannig við um daginn, ok reiðir þrøngðina ýmsa vega eptir vellinum.[1]

Þá tekr maðr til orða ór flokki Helga: "Menn fara þarna, eigi allfáir, ok með klyfjahross."

Annarr svarar: "Eigi eru þat síðr kolamenn ok fara ór skógi, ok eru laupar á hrossunum, ok sá ek þá í dag, er þeir í skóginn fóru." Nú fellr þetta mál niðr.

Þá mælti Geitir: "Nú mun enn fara sem optar,[2] at vér munum bera lægra hlut ór, því at vér nám eigi at flytja í brott lík frænda várra."

"Hví lætr þú þannig?"[3] kvað Helgi. "Þat er enn líkligra, at inn lægri verði at lúta.[4] En þó er þat vænst, at hvárigir taki nú óvirðing af ǫðrum á þessum fundi, ok viljum vér nú slíta þessi þœfð, ef yðr sýnisk, en eigi viljum vér kvámu yðra nær húsi en nú eru þér komnir."

Eptir þat slíta þeir þrøngðinni, ok fóru þeir Geitir til hesta sinna, en þeir Helgi váru eptir á vellinum. Þeir Geitir kómu til móts við þá Egilssonu ok stíga þegar af baki ok gefa upp reiðina, en þeir Helgi stóðu heima á hlaðinu á Hofi ok sáu, at þeir dvǫlðusk.

Þá tók Helgi til orða: "Eptir koma ósvinnum ráð í hug,"[5] segir hann. "Vér hǫfum verit allan dag í þrǫng þessari. Ek sé nú eptir, at kappar Geitis váru hjá engir, ok munu þeir hafa borit í brott líkin í kollaupunum, ok er ávallt, at Geitir er vitrastr vár,[6] þótt hann verði jafnan ofríki borinn."

Ekki varð eptirmál um víg Þormóðar, ok at engu máli fekk Geitir jǫfnuð af Helga. Þorkell, sonr Geitis, fór útan ok jafnan landa í millum, þegar er hann hafði aldr til þess, ok varð hann lítt við riðinn[7] mál þeira Brodd-Helga ok Geitis, fǫður síns. Vanmáttr Hǫllu Lýtingsdóttur í Krossavík gerðisk mikill ok hættiligr.

---

engri *f dat sg of* **engr**
eptirmál *n* prosecution after a slaying
eru *3pl pres of* **vera**

flokkr <-s; -ar> *m* group, company, party, 'flock'
fram *adv* forward

---

[1] **reiðir þrøngðina ýmsa vega eptir vellinum:** 'the crowd drifts this way and that across the fields'.

[2] **nú mun enn fara sem oftar:** 'now again it will go as many times before'.

[3] **hví lætr þú þannig?:** 'why are you carrying on so?'

[4] **inn lægri verða at lúta:** 'the one who is lower has to bow down', a commonplace Icelandic expression.

[5] **eptir koma ósvinnum ráð í hug:** 'understanding comes to fools in hindsight (too late)'.

[6] **vitrastr vár:** 'the wisest of us'.

[7] **riðinn:** 'wound up, involved', past participle of *ríða* 'twist, wind'. Although spelled the same as *ríða* 'ride', this verb are unrelated. Alliterative patterns in poetry preserved from the Viking Age show that *ríða* 'twist, wind' earlier had an initial *v-* (from Germanic *w-*). The English cognates 'writhe' and 'wreath' still preserve the spelling with initial *w-*.

framar *comp adv* further, more (*see* **fram**); **enn framar** still further, once more

fyrir *prep* [*w acc* or *dat*] before, in front of; **vera þar fyrir** be present there

fyrirsǫgn <*gen* -sagnar; *pl* -sagnir> *f* instruction

gefa <gefr; gaf, gáfu; gefinn> *vb* give; **gefa upp** give up, leave off

geta <getr; gat, gátu; getinn> *vb* get; [*w gen*] guess, reckon, expect

hestr <-s; -ar> *m* stallion; horse

hugr <-ar; -ir> *m* mind; [e-m] **koma í hug** occur to [sb]

hvárigr *adj/indef pron* neither (of two) (= **hvárgi**)

hvert *interrog adv* to where, whither?

hví *interrog adv* why, for what?

hættiligr *adj* dangerous, serious

jafnan *adv* constantly, always

jafnaðr (*also* **jǫfnuðr**) <*gen* -ar> *m* justice, equality, equal share

jǫfnuðr *var of* **jafnaðr**

kappi *m* hero, champion

klyfjahross *n* pack-horse

kolamaðr <*pl* -menn> *m* charcoal-maker

kollaupr <-s; -ar> *m* box or basket for carrying coal or charcoal

kvaðning *f* greeting

laupr <-s; -ar> *m* box, basket

láta <lætr; lét, létu; látinn> *vb* let; express, say; *refl* **látask** declare (of oneself)

lágr <*comp* lægri, *superl* lægstr> *adj* low

leggja <lagð-; *ppart* lag(i)ðr~laginn> *vb* lay; **leggja af** leave, remove, take off (clothing)

leyniliga *adv* secretly

lézk *2/3sg past of* **látask**

lið *n* band of men, following, troops

líkami *m* body

líkligr *adj* likely, probable; fit, suitable

líkligri *comp of* **líkligr**

lítt *adv* little

lúta <lýtr; laut, lutu; lotinn> *vb* bow down; give way, yield

lægri *comp adj* lower (*see* **lágr**); **bera lægra hlut ór** get the worst of it

mál *n* (*leg*) suit, action, case; **at engu máli** in no legal case

milli (*also* **millum**) *prep* [*w gen*] between

millum *var of* **milli**; **fara í millum landa** travel from one land to another (i.e., trade)

mót *n* meeting; manner, way; **í mót** *prep* [*w dat*] towards, against; in return;

koma/fara til móts við [e-n] come/go to meet with [sb]

móti (*also* **á móti**, **í móti**) *prep* [*w dat*] towards, against; in return

nær *comp adv* nearer

ofríki *n* sheer force; **bera** [e-n] **ofríki** overcome [sb] by sheer force

optar *comp adv* more often, oftener; **sem optar** as many times before

ófriðr <*gen* -ar> *m* attack; violence; **bjóða ófrið** do battle

ósvinnr *adj* unwise

óvirðing *f* disgrace, dishonor

ráða <ræðr; réð, réðu; ráðinn> *vb* [*w dat*] advise, counsel; rule, govern, manage; undertake; **ráða frá** give up, abandon; **ráða í mót** go against (in a fight), confront, withstand; *refl* **ráðask** undertake; be resolved, settled; turn out; **ráðask á** attack, set upon; **ráðask á móti** [e-m] charge against [sb]

reið <-ar> *f* ride, the act of riding (a horse)

reiða <-dd-> *vb impers* [*acc subj*] drift, be carried about

rézk *2/3sg past of* **ráðask**

riðinn *ppart* involved, concerned (with) (*see* **ríða**); **verða við** [e-t] **riðinn** become involved in, concerned with [sth]

ríða <ríðr; reið, riðu; riðinn> *vb* twist, wind

sáu *3pl past of* **sjá**

sinn *n* time (*instance or repetition*); **at (því) sinni** at this time, at present

síðr *comp adv* less; **eigi ... síðr** *conj* nothing else ... but

sjá <sér; sá, sá(u); sénn> *vb* see

skikkja *f* cloak, mantle

snúðugt *n adj as adv* swiftly; **ganga snúðugt** march, walk at a swinging pace

standa <stendr; stóð, stóðu; staðinn> *vb* stand

stefna <-d-> *vb* aim at, go in a certain direction; **stefna leið** head toward, head for

stíga <stígr; steig, stigu; stiginn> *vb* step, walk; **stíga af baki** dismount (from a horse)

stóðu *3pl past of* **standa**

sæta <-tt-> *vb* [*w dat*] bring about, cause; **sæta áverkum við** [e-m] **fyrri** be the first to injure [sb]

tómliga *adv* slowly, leisurely

tómr *adj* empty

tún *n* enclosure; hayfield, homefield

túngarðr <-s; -ar> *m* fence, wall of a **tún**

vanmáttr *m* helplessness; illness

vara <-að-> *vb* warn; *refl* **varask** be aware of, be on one's guard against

vápn *n* weapon; **bera vápn á [e-n]** raise weapons agains [sb]

vár *gen of* **vér**

vegr <*gen* vegar~vegs; *pl* vegir~vegar, *acc* vegu~vega> *m* way, road; mode, manner; direction; side

velli *dat sg of* **vǫllr**

vera <er; var, váru; verit> *vb* be

verða <verðr; varð, urðu; orðinn> *vb* become; happen, come to pass; **verða at** [*w inf*] must, have to, be obliged to [do sth]

vér <*acc/dat* oss, *gen* vár> *pron 1pl* we

vitr <vitr, vitrt> *adj* wise

vitrastr *superl of* **vitr**

vænn *adj* likely, to be expected

vænstr *superl of* **vænn**

vǫllr <*dat* velli, *gen* vallar; *pl* vellir, *acc*

vǫllu, *gen* valla> *m* field, plain

ýmiss <*pl* ýmsir> *adj* various; **ýmsa vega** in various directions, this way and that

ýmsa *m acc pl of* **ýmiss**

þannig *adv* this way, thus

þarna *adv* there

þegar *adv* at once, immediately; **þegar er** *conj* as soon as

þótt *conj* [*w subjunct*] although, even though

þrǫng (*also* **þrøngð**) <-var> *f* crowd, throng

þrøngð *var of* **þrǫng**

þœfa <-að-> *vb* press, put pressure on; beat, stamp (cloth); *refl* **þœfask** quarrel, squabble; **þœfask við** struggle clumsily and inconclusively, delay, drag things out

þœfð *f* quarrel, long tedious struggle

þœfizk *2pl pres of* **þœfask**

œrinn <-in, -it; *acc m* œrnan> *adj* sufficient

ǫðrum *m dat sg & all dat pl of* **annarr**

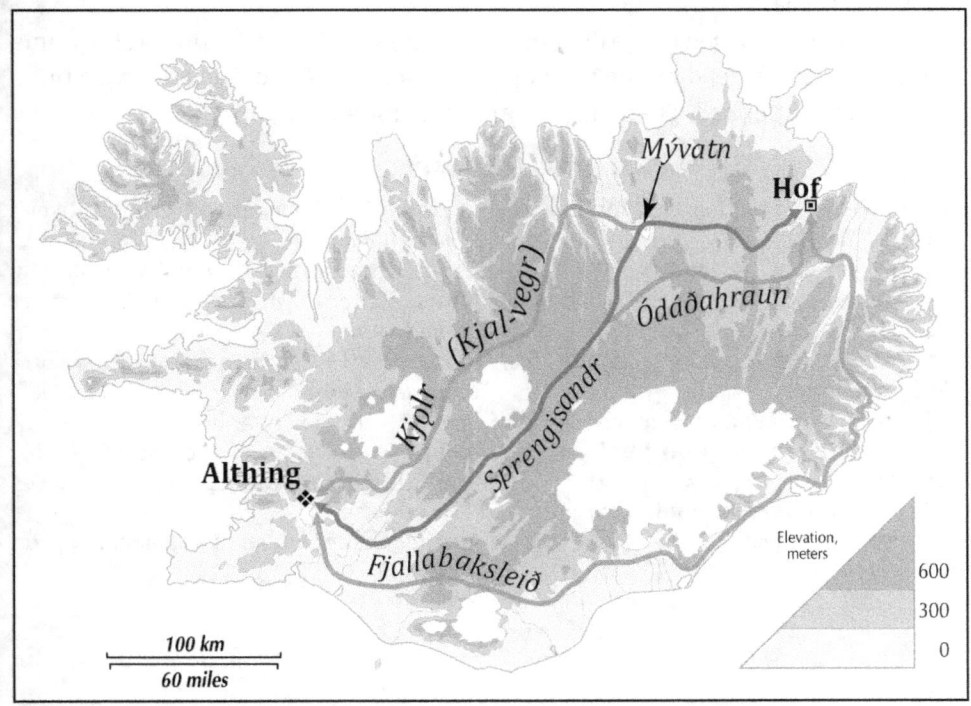

Map 7. Routes to the Althing. The shortest route between Weapon's Fjord and the Althing could be a journey of two-weeks or more on horseback. Riders might choose a longer route in order to meet and ride with kinsmen, friends, or allies, or to avoid crossing paths with a dangerous enemy.

9. BRODD-HELGI VISITS HALLA ON HER DEATH-BED

It is told that Geitir left home for a visit to Eyvindará ('Eyvind's River') in the Fljotsdal district and was away more than a week.[1] When he was gone, Halla sent a man to Helgi requesting that he should meet her.

He went immediately to Krossavik. Halla greeted him, and he received her greeting warmly. She asked him to look at her sore. He did so and said he had a grave foreboding.

He pressed out a lot of fluid from the boil, and she grew weak afterward. She asked him to remain there overnight, but he did not want to do so.

Both because she was weak and because she was distressed with him, she said, "There is no more need to ask you to stay here. You are almost done with your duties now. But I suspect that very few men would finish with their wives the way you will with me."

Brodd-Helgi returned home ill-content with his lot. Halla lived only a short time after that and was dead by the time Geitir arrived home. He was told everything just as it had happened. Then things were quiet for a while.

CHAPTER 9 VOCABULARY

anda <-að-> *vb* breathe; *refl* **andask** die, breathe one's last

andaðr *ppart* dead (*see* **anda**)

angrsamr <-sǫm, -samt> *adj* sorrowful, anguished

báðir <báðar, bæði, *gen* beggja> *adj/indef dual pron* both

biðja <biðr; bað, báðu; beðinn> *vb* ask, beg; command, tell; **biðja [e-n] [e-s]** ask [sb] for [sth]

bæði *adv* both; **bæði ... enda** *conj* both ... and also, and indeed

bæði *n of* **báðir**

Eyvindará *f* Eyvindará ('Eyvind's River') (*place name*)

fár <fá, fátt; *comp* fær(r)i, *superl* fæstr> *adj* few

Fljótsdalsherað *n* the Fljotsdal district (*place name*)

fæstir *superl adj* (*m nom pl*) fewest (*see* **fár**)

hana *acc of* **hon**

hérvist <-ir> *f* lodgings here

hleypa <-t-> *vb* [*w dat*] cause to escape, emit; **hleypa út vatni** press out fluid (*as from a sore*)

hon <*acc* hana, *dat* henni, *gen* hennar> *pron 3sg f* she

---

[1] Geitir's visit would have been to his sister-in-law, Groa of Eyvindará (see Genealogy 3). Groa, a wealthy and strong-minded widow, has a larger role in *Droplaugarsona saga* and *Fljótsdæla saga*. She is referred to directly in Ch. 18.

9. KAPÍTULI

Summary of Chapter 9. Geitir leaves home for a few days. In his absence, Halla sends for Brodd-Helgi. He comes and nurses her but refuses to stay by her side for the night. Distraught by his rejection, she sends him on his way with a final insult. She dies soon after.

Þat er sagt, at Geitir fór heiman í Fljótsdalsherað til Eyvindarár á kynnisleið ok var í brottu meir en viku. Ok er hann var heiman farinn, þá sendi Halla mann eptir Helga ok bað hann, at hann skyldi hitta hana.

Hann fór þegar í Krossavík. Halla kvaddi hann. Hann tók vel kveðju hennar. Hon bað hann, at hann skyldi sjá meinit. Hann gerði svá, ok kvazk honum þungt hugr um segja.[1]

Hann hleypir út vatni miklu ór sullinum, ok varð hon máttlítil eptir þetta. Hon bað hann þar vera um nóttina, en hann vildi þat eigi.

Þat var bæði, at hon var máttlítil, enda var hon angrsǫm við hann ok mælti: "Eigi þarf nú at biðja þik hérvistar.[2] Þú munt nú mjǫk lokit hafa verkum,[3] ok get ek, at fæstir munu lúka við sínar konur svá sem þú munt við mik."

Brodd-Helgi fór heim ok unði illa við sinn hlut. Halla lifði litla stund síðan, ok var hon ǫnduð,[4] er Geitir kom heim, ok var honum sagt allt, svá sem farit hafði. Ok er nú kyrrt um hríð.

---

hríð <-ir> *f* a time, while; **um hríð** for a while

hugr <-ar; -ir> *m* heart, mind; **svá segir honum hugr um** *impers* so his heart tells him, he forebodes

kveðja *f* welcome, greeting

kynnisleið <-ir> *f* visit

kyrr <kyrr, kyrrt> *adj* still, calm

lifa <-ð-, *n ppart* lifat> *vb* live

lúka <lýkr; lauk, luku; lokinn> *vb* [*w dat*] close; end, conclude; shut; **lúka við** end, finish with

máttlítill <-lítil, -lítit> *adj* weak, faint, feeble, exhausted

mein *n* sore, disease

stund *f* a while, a time; hour; **litla stund** a little while, for a short time

sullr <*pl* -ir> *m* boil

vatn <*gen* vatns~vatz~vaz; *pl* vǫtn> *n* water, liquid, fluid

vika <*pl gen* vikna> *f* week

þarf 1/3*sg pres of* **þurfa**

þungr *adj* heavy

þungt *n adj as adv* heavily, gravely

þurfa <þarf, þurfu; þurfti; þurft> *pret-pres vb* [*aux*] need

---

[1] **Hann ... kvazk honum þungt hugr um segja:** 'He ... said he felt a grave foreboding' (lit. 'his mind [heart] spoke heavily to him'). *Hugr* is 'mind', but with the quality of an emotion of the heart.

[2] **Eigi þarf nú at biðja þik hérvistar:** 'There is no need now to ask you to stay here' (i.e., because I know how you will answer).

[3] **Þú munt nú mjǫk lokit hafa verkum:** 'You're almost done with your chores now'.

[4] **var hon ǫnduð:** 'she was dead'.

10. BRODD-HELGI CHEATS GUDMUND THE POWERFUL

After this great animosity increased between Brodd-Helgi and Geitir.

One summer Helgi was short of supporters at the assembly, so he asked Gudmund for support.[1] Gudmund answered that he had no desire to grant Helgi support at every assembly, making himself unpopular with other chieftains while receiving no benefit from him in return. They settled on this agreement, that Gudmund promised him support, and Helgi was to give him half a hundred pieces of silver.[2]

When the court had ended – and the cases had gone well for Helgi – Gudmund and Helgi met by the booths[3] and Gudmund claimed the money from Helgi. But Helgi said he had nothing to pay him, and said also that he didn't see why he needed to pay money, considering their bond of friendship.

Gudmund answered, "This is poorly done by you. You always have need of others, but don't pay what you promise. I consider you friendship worth little. I will not claim the money again, nor ever again provide you support."

With that they parted, and their friendship was ended.

Geitir heard about this and went to see Gudmund to offer him money for his friendship. Gudmund said that he did not want Geitir's money and declared himself little inclined to give support to men who were always willing to come out the worse in every case against Helgi.

People went home from the assembly, and now it was quiet for a while.

CHAPTER 10 VOCABULARY

aðra *f acc sg & m acc pl of* **annarr**
aflafár <-fá, -fátt> *adj* short of strength;
[e-m] **verðr aflafátt** *impers* [sb] is short of
support (or supporters)

annarr <ǫnnur, annat; *acc m* annan, *f* aðra,
dat m ǫðrum, *n* ǫðru; *pl nom m* aðrir>
adj/indef pron other, another

---

[1] As local conflicts escalated, rival parties frequently sought allies from outside the immediate district in order to get the upper hand. Here Helgi seeks support from Gudmund the Powerful of Modruvellir, a prominent chieftain from the Eyjafjord region of northern Iceland.

[2] "Half a hundred" was about 60 ounces (*aurar*, singular *eyrir*) of silver. The "long hundred," a duodecimal hundred equal to 120, remained in common use in Iceland until well into the 19th century. Without native coinage in Iceland, homespun woolen cloth (*vaðmál*) became the standard unit of exchange, with a value relative to that of silver. During the 10th century, six ells (approximately three yards) of homespun, two ells across, were equal to one ounce of silver. As to livestock, one milk-cow or six sheep were worth just under 16 ounces of silver, or two marks (*merkr*, singular *mǫrk*). Helgi is thus in debt for 180 yards of cloth, or roughly four cows or 24 sheep. For background discussion, see Bruce E. Gelsinger, *Icelandic Enterprise: Commerce and Economy in the Middle Ages*.

[3] The *goðar* maintained booths at the assembly sites as temporary dwellings for themselves and their attending thingmen. The walls were constructed of turf and stone on a timber frame, and the roof was made of homespun cloth. Thingmen were legally required to supply the roofing cloth, receiving a place in the booth in return (*Grágás* Ia, 44).

10. KAPÍTULI

Summary of Chapter 10. One summer Brodd-Helgi is short of manpower at the Althing. He asks for support from the chieftain Gudmund, who grants it reluctantly in exchange for silver. When it comes time to pay, Brodd-Helgi refuses, and their alliance is broken. Geitir approaches Gudmund afterward and offers to pay in exchange for support. Gudmund refuses. He wants no ties to a chieftain who constantly loses to Brodd-Helgi.

Eptir þetta óx mikil óþykkja með þeim Brodd-Helga ok Geiti.

Eitthvert sumar varð Helga aflafátt á þingi, ok bað hann Guðmund liðs. En hann kvazk eigi nenna at veita honum lið á hverju þingi ok óvinsæla sik við aðra hǫfðingja, en taka af honum engi gœði í móti. Þeir skilðu svá með þetta mál, at Guðmundr hét honum liði, en Helgi skyldi gefa honum hálft hundrað silfrs.[1]

Er dómum var lokit[2]– ok hǫfðu Helga málin vel gengit –, þá mœttusk þeir Guðmundr við búðir, ok heimti Guðmundr féit at Helga. En Helgi kvazk ekki eiga at gjalda honum ok kvazk eigi sjá, at hann þyrfti fé at gefa í milli vinfengis þeira.[3]

Guðmundr svarar: "Þat er þér illa farit," segir hann, "þarft annarra ávallt, en geldr eigi þat, er þú ert heitbundinn. En vinfengi þitt þykki mér lítils vert. Mun ek ok eigi optar heimta þetta fé, enda vera þér aldri at liði síðan."

Ok skilðu við svá búit, ok er nú lokit vinfengi þeira.

Geitir spyrr þetta ok ferr til fundar við Guðmund ok býðr honum at taka fé til vinfengis. Guðmundr lézk eigi vilja hafa fé hans ok kvað sér lítit um at veita þeim mǫnnum lið, er ávallt vildu inn lægra hlut ór hverju máli bera fyrir Helga.

Fara menn nú heim af þingi, ok var nú kyrrt um hríð.

búð <-ir> *f* tent, booth

farit *n ppart* of a certain disposition (*from* **fara** 'go'); **[e-m] er illa farit** *impers* [sb] has an ill disposition, is acting unworthily

fundr <-ar; -ir> *m* meeting; **fara til fundar við [e-n]** go see, meet with [sb]

ganga <gengr; gekk, gengu; genginn> *vb* go, walk

geldr *2/3sg pres of* **gjalda**

gengit *n ppart of* **ganga**

gjalda <geldr; galt, guldu; goldinn> *vb* pay

gœði *n pl* profit, wealth

kvað sér = **kvazk**

heitbundit *n ppart* bound by a promise, oath-bound (*from* **heit** 'oath' *and* **binda** 'bind')

hundrað <hundruð> *n* hundred (*usu followed by noun in gen*); **tólfrætt hundrað** = 120, **tírætt hundrað** = 100

hǫfðingi <*gen* -ja; *pl* -jar> *m* chieftain; leader

lið *n* support, assistance

lítit *n indef pron* little (*see* **lítill**); **sjá lítit um** see little (advantage) in

mál *n* agreement

mœta <-tt-> *vb* [*w dat*] meet; *refl* **mœtask** meet one another

skilja <-d~ð-; *ppart* skiliðr~skildr~ skilinn> *vb* decide, settle

taka <tekr; tók, tóku; tekinn> *vb* take; **taka af** get, receive, accept

óvinsæla <-d-> *vb and refl* **óvinsælask** make (oneself) disliked, unpopular

óvinsæla sik = **óvinsælask**

þarft *2sg pres of* **þurfa**

þurfa <þarf, þurfu; þurfti; þurft> *pret-pres vb* [*w gen*] need, have need of

---

[1] **hálft hundrað silfrs**: 'half a hundred pieces of silver'.

[2] **er dómum var lokit**: 'when the court had ended'.

[3] **í milli vinfengis þeira**: 'considering their bond of friendship'.

11. GEITIR RETREATS

It is told that a ship came out to Weapon's Fjord, and on the ship was Thorarin Egilsson, who was then called the finest and most accomplished trader.

Brodd-Helgi rode to the ship and invited Thorarin to stay with him, along with such men as he wished. Thorarin said that he would accept. Helgi went home and said that Thorarin the shipmaster was expected to take up lodging there.

Geitir went to the ship to meet Thorarin and asked if he intended to go to Hof. Thorarin said that it had been discussed but not decided. Geitir said to him that it was surely more advisable to go to Krossavik, "because I reckon that few of my men[1] do well in accepting lodging with Helgi." From this it was decided that Thorarin would go to Krossavik.

Brodd-Helgi learned of this and immediately rode to the ship with saddled horses, intending to bring Thorarin home with him. Thorarin told him that it had now been decided otherwise.

"I want to show," said Helgi, "that I have not invited you to my home with false motives, because I will not hold it against you, if you go there."[2]

The following day Helgi rode to the ship and gave Thorarin some stud-horses for his friendship – five in total, and all of them dandelion-yellow. Geitir came for Thorarin and asked whether he had received the stud-horses from Brodd-Helgi. He said that that was the case.

"I advise you," said Geitir, "to send the stud-horses back."

Thorarin did so, and Helgi took back the stud-horses.

---

[1] Thorarin is the son of Egil of Egilsstadir, a thingman of Geitir (Ch. 3).

[2] That is, to Krossavik. This lack of offense contrasts markedly with Helgi's reaction to Hrafn's rejection of his offer of lodging in Ch. 4.

11. KAPÍTULI

Summary of Chapter 11. Thorarin, an important merchant with ties to Geitir, arrives one summer. Brodd-Helgi offers to host him and gives him a gift of five stud-horses. Geitir advises Thorarin to decline the offer, and Thorarin returns the horses. Thorarin leaves the following summer to continue trading, but when he returns, Geitir has moved his home to a remote and defensive location to avoid a confrontation with Brodd-Helgi. Geitir's supporters see little value in a chieftain who retreats when threatened, so Thorarin and the other farmers deliver an ultimatum to Geitir, threatening to withdraw their allegiance and join Brodd-Helgi's supporters.

Þat er sagt, at skip kom út í Vápnafirði, ok var á því skipi Þórarinn Egilsson, er þá var kallaðr vænstr maðr í forum ok gørviligastr.

Brodd-Helgi reið til skips, ok bauð hann Þórarni til vistar með sér ok þeim monnum með honum, sem hann vildi, en hann kvazk þat mundu þiggja. Helgi fór heim ok sagði, at ván væri Þórarins stýrimanns þangat til vistar.

Geitir fór til skips ok hitti Þórarin ok spyrr, ef hann ætlaði til Hofs.[1] Hann kvað þat rœtt, en ráðit eigi. Geitir kvað honum heldr ráðligra at fara í Krossavík, – "því at fám ætla ek mínum monnum vel gefisk at þiggja vist hjá Helga."[2] Þat rézk ór,[3] at Þórarinn fór í Krossavík.

Brodd-Helgi spyrr þetta, ok ríðr hann þegar til skips með soðlaða hesta ok ætlar at hafa Þórarin heim með sér. Þórarinn segir, at þá var annat ráðit.

"Þat vil ek sýna," kvað Helgi, "at ek hefi þér eigi með flærð heim boðit, því at ek vil vera vandalauss af,[4] þótt þú farir þangat."

Annan dag eptir[5] reið Helgi til skips ok gaf Þórarni stóðhross, fimm saman, til vinfengis, ok váru oll fífilbleik. Geitir ferr eptir Þórarni ok spyrr, hvárt[6] hann hefir þegit stóðhrossin at Brodd-Helga. Hann kvað þat satt vera.

"Þat ræð ek þér," segir Geitir, "at þú skilir aptr stóðhrossunum."

Hann gerði svá, ok tók Helgi aptr við stóðhrossunum.

---

[1] **ef hann ætlaði til Hofs:** 'if he intended [to go] to Hof'. The infinitive of motion (*at fara*) is left understood. Compare archaic English expressions such as "I must away," "I must to bed," etc.

[2] **því at fám ætla ek mínum monnum vel gefisk at þiggja vist hjá Helga:** 'because I reckon it turns out well for few of my men to accept lodging with Helgi'.

[3] **þat rézk ór:** 'it was decided from this'.

[4] **vera vandalauss af:** lit. 'be free from obligation or responsibility', meaning that Helgi will not hold it against Thorarin if he lodges with Geitir.

[5] **Annan dag eptir:** 'The following day' (lit. 'second day after').

[6] **hvárt:** 'whether'. As in English, this word is used in Icelandic as a conjunction to introduce an indirect yes/no question. *Geitir ... spyrr, **hvárt** hann hefir þegit stóðhrossin at Brodd-Helga:* 'Geitir asks **whether** he has accepted the studhorses from Brodd-Helgi'.

Thorarin stayed with Geitir over the winter and went abroad the summer after. By the time he came back, Geitir had moved his homestead and was living in the place called Fagradal. So Thorarin took up lodging at Egilsstadir.

Geitir's thingmen took counsel together, thinking that they could no longer bear Brodd-Helgi's injustice, and then they went to meet with Geitir. Thorarin spoke for the thingmen. "How long must it go on like this?" he said. "Until everything falls apart completely? Many people are leaving you, and all are allying themselves with Helgi. And we consider cowardice alone to be the reason you hold yourself back from confronting Helgi. You are the smarter of the two, and besides, you have men of no less courage on your side than he has on his.

"And now we offer you two choices. Either you go back home to your farm at Krossavik, never to move from there again, and you take action against Helgi if he ever does you any dishonor from now on, or else we will sell our farmsteads and move away. Some of us will move from the country and others from the district."

CHAPTER 11 VOCABULARY

annan m acc sg of **annarr**

annarr <ǫnnur, annat; acc m annan, f aðra, dat m ǫðrum, n ǫðru; pl nom m aðrir> adj/indef pron one of two, other, another; ord second; **annan dag eptir** the following day

bjóða <býðr; bauð, buðu; boðinn> vb [w acc] offer; [w dat] invite

boðit n ppart of **bjóða**

bústaðr <-ar; -ir> m farmstead, household

einn <ein, eitt> num one; adj (following the noun it modifies) alone, only, mere

Fagradalr <dat -dal, gen -dals> m Fagradal ('Fair Dale' or 'Beautiful Valley') (place name)

fara <ferr; fór, fóru; farinn> vb go, travel; move; **fara at** go, proceed; **fara fram** go on, take place

fám m dat sg & all dat pl of **fár**

fár <fá, fátt; pl dat fám> adj/indef pron few

fimm num five

fífilbleikr adj dandelion-yellow (only of horses)

flutt n ppart of **flytja**

flytja <flutt-> vb convey, move, carry; **flytja bústað sinn** move one's farm, change one's dwelling-place

flærð f deceit, false pretenses

fyrir prep [w acc] for, on behalf of

ganga <gengr; gekk, gengu; genginn> vb walk; go; [e-m] **gengr [e-t] til [e-s]** impers [sth] is [sb's] reason for [sth]; **ganga undan [e-m]** leave, withdraw support from [sb]

gefa <gefr; gaf, gáfu; gefinn> vb give, grant; refl **gefask** happen, turn out, come to pass; **gefask vel [e-m]** impers to prove good, turn out well for [sb]

gørviligastr superl of **gørviligr**

gørviligr adj accomplished, able, brave

hlífa <-ð-> vb [w dat] shelter, protect; spare, deal gently with; refl **hlífask** spare, refrain, hold back; **hlífask við [e-n]** spare [sb], hold oneself back from [sb]

hvárt interrog adv whether; conj whether

kostr <-ar; -ir, pl acc -i~u> m choice

laga <-að-> vb arrange; adjust, mend refl **lagask** adjust oneself; **lagask til [e-s]** enter into agreement with [sb], ally oneself with [sb]

lítill <lítil, lítit; comp minni, superl minnstr> adj little

lúka <lýkr; lauk, luku; lokinn> vb [w dat] close; end, conclude; **lýkr yfir** impers an end is reached

lýkr 2/3sg pres of **lúka**

minni comp adj less, lesser, smaller (see **lítill**)

mót n meeting; manner, way; **í mót** prep [w dat] towards, against; in return; **gera í mót [e-m]** move, act against [sb], oppose [sb]

ósómi m dishonor, disgrace; **gera [e-m] ósóma** treat [sb] dishonorably

ráð n advice, counsel; **bera ráð saman** take counsel among themselves; consult together

Þórarinn var með Geiti um vetrinn ok fór útan um sumarit eptir. Ok er hann kom út aptr, þá hafði Geitir flutt bústað sinn ok bjó þar, er heitir í Fagradal. Þórarinn fór á Egilsstaði til vistar.

Þeir bera ráð saman, þingmenn Geitis, ok þóttusk eigi þola mega lengr ójafnað Brodd-Helga, fóru nú til fundar við Geiti, ok mælti Þórarinn fyrir þingmenn: "Hversu lengi skal svá fram fara," segir hann, "hvárt[1] þar til er yfir lýkr með ǫllu? Nú gengr margt manna undan þér, ok lagask allir til Helga, ok virðum vér þér þrekleysi eitt til ganga,[2] er þú hlífisk við Helga. Þú ert ykkar snarari, en þó hefir þú eigi með þér minni garpa en hann hefir með sér.

"Ok eru nú tveir kostir af várri hendi,[3] at þú farir heim í Krossavík á bú þitt, ok flyt þaðan aldri síðan, en ger í mót Helga, ef hann gerir þér nǫkkurn ósóma heðan í frá, elligar munum vér selja bústaði vára ok ráðask í brottu, sumir af landi, en sumir ór heraði."

ráða <ræðr; réð, réðu; ráðinn> *vb* [*w dat*] decide, determine; *refl* **ráðask** undertake; be resolved, settled; turn out; **ráðask í brottu** move away

ráðligr *adj* advisable

ráðligri *comp adj* more advisable (*see* **ráðligr**)

ræð *1sg pres of* **ráða**

rœða <-dd-> *vb* speak; **rœða um [e-t]** discuss [sth]

rœtt *n ppart* discussed (*see* **rœða**)

skila <-að-> *vb* [*w dat*] give back, return; **skila aptr [e-u]** bring or take [sth] back

snarr <snǫr, snart> *adj* swift; gallant, bold, smart; keen

stóðhross *n* stud-horse

sumr <sum, sumt> *adj/indef pron* some

sǫðla <-að-> *vb* saddle

undan *prep* [*w dat*] from under; away from; **ganga undan [e-m]** leave, withdraw support from [sb]

vandalauss *adj* standing under no obligation to another; **vera vandalauss af** be free of obligation or responsibility, have no concern

virða <-ð-> *vb* value; consider, estimate; honor, respect

vænn *adj* beautiful, fine, handsome; hopeful, promising; **vænn í fǫrum** promising in trade

yfir *adv* over

ykkar *gen of* **þit**

þar *adv* there; **þar til** there to, to that point

þegit *n ppart of* **þiggja**

þiggja <þiggr; þá, þágu; þeginn> *vb* accept; receive; accept lodgings

þit <*acc/dat* ykkr, *gen* ykkarr> *pron 2dual* you (two)

þola <-d-, *n ppart* þol(a)t> *vb* suffer, endure, bear

þó *adv* yet, though, nevertheless; **en þó** nevertheless, and besides, moreover

þóttusk *3pl past of* **þykkjask**

þrekleysi *n* lack of courage, lack of resolve

þykkja <þykkir, þótt-> *vb impers* [*dat subj*] think, seem (to one); *refl* **þykkjask** think, consider oneself

---

[1] **hvárt:** In Icelandic, *hvárt* can also be used as an interrogative adverb which introduces a direct yes/no question. English has no equivalent, and in this usage *hvárt* is not translated: *hversu lengi skal svá fram fara, hvárt þar til er yfir lýkr með ǫllu?* 'how long must it go on like this – until everything falls apart altogether?'

[2] **virðum vér þér þrekleysi eitt til ganga:** 'we consider cowardice alone (*þrekleysi eitt*) to be your reason (*þér ... til ganga*)'.

[3] **ok eru nú tveir kostir af várri hendi:** 'and now we offer you two choices'.

CULTURE SECTION – DISPUTED PROPERTY

Disputes over property, often involving one family's gain and another's loss, are frequent in *Vápnfirðinga saga*. The motivation behind Thorarin's refusal of Brodd-Helgi's horses hinges on information found in the saga's introductory passages. The story behind this gift involves a simmering enmity between a farmer's family and a chieftain's family over property.

The farm at Sunnudal was owned by Thormod, one of Geitir's thingmen, whom Brodd-Helgi killed in the dispute over the woodland (Ch. 7). Although a good farm, Sunnudal is of far less value than Hof, the richest farmstead in the valley. Hof was originally owned by Thormod's father, Steinbjorn, who squandered his wealth. After that the land at Hof was sold to Thorstein the White, Brodd-Helgi's grandfather (Ch. 1). With little explanation but a careful use of geographical description, the saga captures the animosity underlying Thormod's alliance with the chieftains at Krossavik, rivals of the chieftains at Hof. From Sunnudal, Steinbjorn had a clear view across the valley to Hof, a picture of wealth and status. This sight must have continually galled Steinbjorn's descendants as they contemplated their family's loss.

This enmity may explain why Thormod from Sunnudal and his brother Egil of Egilsstadir were Geitir's thingmen. It may also explain why Brodd-Helgi treated Thormod harshly in the woodland dispute, and why Brodd-Helgi now makes such a handsome offer of matched horses to the newly arrived ship's captain, Thorarin the son of Egil of Egilsstadir.

The gift looks harmless on the surface, but Thorarin is the grandson of Steinbjorn, who lost Hof, and the nephew of Thormod from Sunnudal. Accepting the gift would publicly signal that Thorarin was willing to put aside his family's opposition to Brodd-Helgi over the loss of land and Thormod's death. His acceptance would make him indebted to Brodd-Helgi as part of the process of gift-giving, and it might set Thorarin against his own family. Any reconciliation between Brodd-Helgi and Thorarin would weaken Geitir's support from the families at Sunnudal and Egilsstadir. Helgi seeks to rob Geitir of his best thingmen, and Geitir wisely advises Thorarin to return the gift.

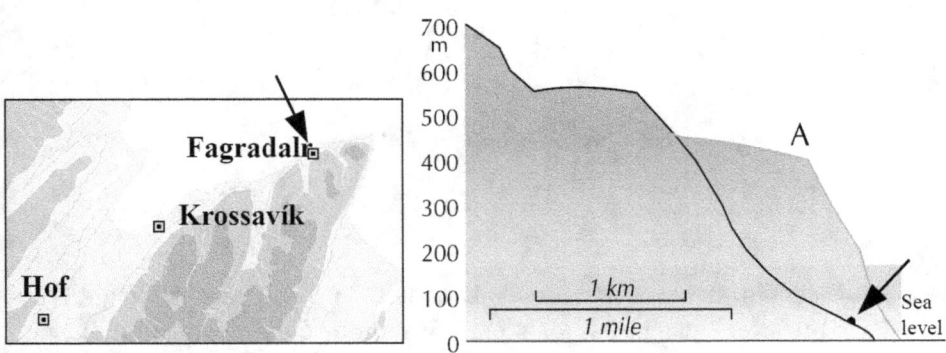

Map 8. The Location of Fagradal. Fagradal (Fair Dale), Geitir's retreat, is a natural fortress. The high outcrop, marked A on the geological profile, descends precipitously to the sea and separates Fagradal from the inland portion of Weapon's Fjord. The single path to Fagradal leading down the steep mountains could be watched from a great distance and easily blocked. Serious attack was possible only from the sea, where attackers could be sighted and lose the element of surprise.

12. GEITIR RIDES NORTH

Geitir journeyed from home and traveled north[1] to Ljosavatnsskard ('Light Water Lake Pass') to Ofeig Jarngerdarson's place.[2] Gudmund the Powerful met Geitir, and they sat in conversation all day.

After that they parted, and Geitir stayed overnight at Myvatn ('Midge' or 'Mosquito Lake') at Olvir the Wise's place.[3] Olvir questioned him closely about Brodd-Helgi. Geitir spoke well of him and said he was a great leader, unyielding and difficult, but nonetheless a good and courageous man in many respects.

"Isn't he an excessively overbearing man?" asked Olvir.

Giteir answered, "It has mainly befallen me, with regard to Helgi's injustice, that he begrudges me the same sky over my head as he has over his."

Olvir answered, "Does all this have to be endured from him?"

"It has been up to now," said Geitir.

They now ended this conversation. Geitir went home, and everything was quiet over the winter.

CHAPTER 12 VOCABULARY

gista <-t-> *vb* spend the night; **gista at [e-s]** spend the night at [sb's] (place)

heldr <*superl* helzt> *comp adv* more, rather

helzt *superl adv* most of all, especially (*see* **heldr**)

hér *adv* here (*location*); **hér til** until now, hereto

himinn <*dat* himni, *gen* himins; *pl* himnar> *m* sky; heaven

hætta <-tt-> *vb* [*w dat*] leave off, quit; [*w inf*] cease [doing sth]

jafn <jǫfn, jafnt> *adj* equal, even

Járngerðr <*acc/dat* Járngerði, *gen* Járngerðar> *f* Jarngerd (*personal name*)

lag <lǫg> *n* layer; **at mǫrgu lagi** in many respects

láta <lætr; lét, létu; látinn> *vb* let, allow, permit; express, say; **láta vel (illa) yfir [e-m]/[e-u]** to speak well (ill) of [sb]/[sth], express approval (disapproval) of [sb]/[sth]

Ljósavatnsskarð *n* Ljosavatnsskard ('Light Water Lake Pass') (*place name*)

---

[1] In medieval Icelandic texts (and modern ones also), directional references are largely contextual. Here Geitir is actually traveling northwest, but he is said to be traveling north because he is going into the northern quarter of Iceland.

[2] Ofeig was an instrumental ally of Geitir's and a thingman of chieftain Gudmund the Powerful. Ofeig is mentioned in *Reykdæla saga* (Ch. 19), *Vǫðu-Brands þáttr* (Ch. 4), and *Ljósvetninga saga*, where he helps arrange the marriage of Geitir's son Thorkel and Jorunn, Gudmund's niece.

[3] Apart from this reference, Olvir the Wise is known only in *Reykdæla saga* (Chs. 17 and 30). Here he is referred to as if he were a well-known figure in northeastern Iceland at the time that the saga is said to take place.

12. KAPÍTULI

Summary of Chapter 12. Geitir seeks powerful alliances. He visits important men in the northern quarter, Olvir the Wise from Myvatn, Gudmund the Powerful from Modruvellir (Mǫðruvellir), and Ofeig Jarngerdarson at Ljosavatnsskard. These distant leaders have, as yet, had no part in the feud, but they now lend a sympathetic ear to Geitir's account of his troubles with Brodd-Helgi. Although Geitir complains of Brodd-Helgi's injustice, he does not slander his old friend.

Geitir gerir heiman fǫr sína ok ferr norðr í Ljósavatnsskarð til Ófeigs Járngerðarsonar. Guðmundr inn ríki hitti Geiti, ok sátu þeir á tali allan dag.

Skiljask þeir síðan, ok gistir Geitir at Mývatni at Qlvis ins spaka, ok spurði hann at Brodd-Helga vandliga. Geitir lét vel yfir honum ok kvað hann vera stórmenni mikit, óvæginn ok ódælan ok þó góðan dreng at mǫrgu lagi.

"Er hann eigi ójafnaðarmaðr mikill?" segir Qlvir.

Geitir svarar: "Þat er helzt á mér orðit um ójafnaðinn Helga, at[1] hann unni mér eigi at hafa himininn jafnan yfir hǫfði mér sem hann hefir sjálfr."

Qlvir svarar: "Skal honum þá allt þola?"

"Svá hefir enn verit hér til," segir Geitir.

Nú hætta þeir þessu tali. Ferr Geitir heim, ok er nú allt kyrrt um vetrinn.

Mývatn *n* Myvatn ('Midge' or 'Mosquito Lake') (*place name*)

norðr *adv* north, northwards

Ófeigr <-s> *m* Ofeig (*personal name*)

ójafnaðarmaðr *m* unjust man, one who is quarrelsome and overbearing, difficult to deal with

óvæginn <-in, -it> *adj* unyielding, head-strong

sjálfr *adj* self, him-/her-/it-/oneself, themselves

skarð <skǫrð> *n* mountain pass

spakr <spǫk, spakt> *adj* wise

stórmenni *n* great man, leader

tal <tǫl> *n* conversation, talk; **á tali** in conversation, talking

unna <ann, unnu; unni; unn(a)t> *pret-pres vb* grant, allow, bestow; **unna [e-m] eigi** begrudge [sb]

vandliga *adv* carefully; completely, fully

verða <verðr; varð, urðu; orðinn> *vb* become, happen; **verða á [e-m]** *impers* befall [sb]

þola <-d-, *n ppart* þol(a)t> *vb* suffer, endure, bear; **þola [e-m] [e-t]** endure [sth] from [sb]

CULTURE SECTION – ÓJAFNAÐARMENN AND HÓFSMENN

In this chapter, Olvir asks Geitir about Brodd-Helgi, *"Er hann eigi ójafnaðar-maðr mikill?"* ('Isn't he a great *ójafnaðarmaðr* – an overbearing, unjust man?'). Brodd-Helgi often uses force to deny people their property and

---

[1] **Þat er helzt á mér orðit um ójafnaðinn Helga, at…:** 'It has mostly befallen me, with regard to Helgi's injustice, that…'.

rights. He cheats allies, takes advantage of his own thingmen's problems, kills without compensation, and prevents courts and arbitrators from settling disputes.

The sagas use the specific term *ójafnaðarmaðr*, meaning an 'unjust or overbearing man', for a ruthless and ambitious man of this sort. Such people were a source of severe tension in the sagas. They often refused to pay compensation, and hence did not allow others to even accounts with them. *Ójafnaðarmenn* took advantage of the fact that the social defenses against a thoroughly ruthless individual were cumbersome and potentially inadequate. Overbearing people such as Brodd-Helgi posed a major threat to the stability of Icelandic legal and social systems, because they acted without moderation and circumvented the dispute resolution process.

Brodd-Helgi ignores the Icelandic code of moderation, called *hóf*. By contrast, Geitir plays the role of *hófsmaðr*, a 'man of moderation'. *Hófsmenn* were not altogether peaceful, since small-scale feuding was permissible under Icelandic social parameters. For the common good, however, the *goðar* and important farmers shouldered a public responsibility to prevent feud from growing into warfare. Brodd-Helgi is willing to ignore this responsibility while Geitir attempts to ensure a modicum of peace and stability in the community.

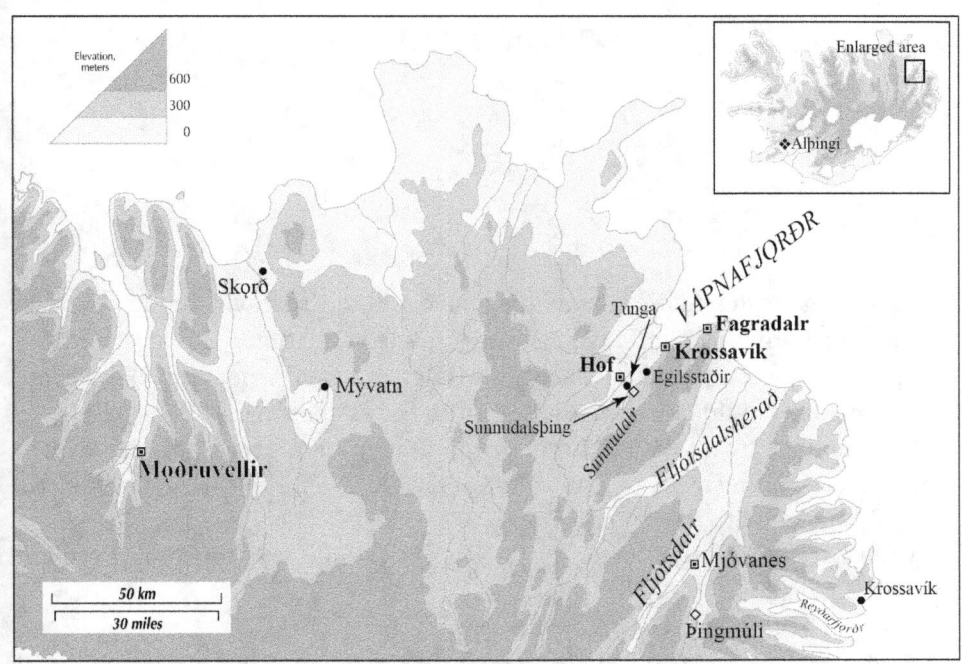

Map 9. Geitir's trip to Ljosavatnsskard. At this point in the saga Greitir sets out on a journey in search of support. He travels from his farm at Krossavík to the farm of Ofeig at Ljósavatnsskarð (the 'Pass at 'Light' or 'Clear Water Lake'). His goal is to strike an alliance with the chieftain (*goði*) Gudmund the Powerful, who lives at Mǫðruvellir. The distances are considerable, and the future allies meet at Ofeig's farm at Ljósavatn ('Clear Water') while Geitir later spends a night at Myvatn ('Midge' or 'Mosquito Lake') with Olvir the Wise. As in the other maps, the farms of chieftains (*goðar*) are marked by squares (▣), while the farmsteads of farmers (*bœndr*) are marked by dots (●).

13. A PROPHETIC DREAM

The following spring, Geiter moved his household to Krossavik and kept a large force of men with him. There was a severe famine at the time.[1]

When the assembly drew near, Brodd-Helgi and Geitir met, and Helgi asked how many men would be riding with Geitir to the assembly.

"Why should I travel with a larger group of men than necessary," he replied, "when I have no business to attend to there? I will ride to the opening of the assembly and go with few men."

"When I set out, we will meet," said Helgi, "and both ride together. I too will ride with few men."

"That will be fine," said Geitir.

Brodd-Helgi's son Bjarni rode from home at the opening of the assembly with his and Helgi's thingmen. Lyting, however, waited for Helgi because Helgi loved him much more. Geitir set a lookout for Brodd-Helgi's departure.

As soon as he was ready, Brodd-Helgi rode from home with his son Lyting. With them were Thorgils Skin, Lyting's foster-father, Eyjolf the Fat, Koll the Easterner, Thorgerd Silver, and her daughter by Helgi, who was named Hallbera. Geitir also rode from home and with him the sons of Egil – Thorarin, Hallbjorn, and Throst – Big Tjorvi and seven other men.

Some people say that Helgi had a foresighted foster-mother, and it was always his custom to look her up before leaving from home. He did so this time too. But when he came to her, she was sitting with her face in her hands, weeping.

Helgi asked why she was crying and why she was in such low spirits. She said that she was crying about her dreams.

---

[1] If this account refers to the first famine recorded in the Icelandic annals, the year must be 975. The annals, however, say that Helgi was killed in 974.

13. KAPÍTULI

Summary of Chapter 13. Geitir returns to his home in Krossavík. When the assembly draws near, Brodd-Helgi asks Geitir how many men will ride with him to the assembly. Geitir says only a few, and they agree to ride to the assembly together. Before Brodd-Helgi leaves, he visits his foster-mother, who relates a prophetic dream to him. The meaning of the dream is unquestionable: Geitir and his men will kill Brodd-Helgi.

Um várit eptir fœrir Geitir bústað sinn í Krossavík ok hafði mjǫk mannmargt. Hallæri var mikit.

En er dró at þingi, þá hittask þeir Brodd-Helgi ok Geitir, ok spurði Helgi, hversu fjǫlmennr hann vildi ríða til þingsins.

"Hví skal nú fjǫlmennari fara," segir hann, "þar ek á ekki[1] um at vera? Ek mun ríða til ǫndverðs þings ok ríða við fá menn."

"Þá er ek fer, munum vit hittask," kvað Helgi, "ok ríða báðir saman. Ek mun ok með fá menn ríða."

"Vel mun þat mega,"[2] segir Geitir.

Bjarni, sonr Brodd-Helga, ríðr heiman á ǫndvert þing með þingmenn þeira Helga, en Lýtingr beið Helga, því at hann unni honum miklu meira. Geitir hefir njósn af um fǫr Brodd-Helga.

Brodd-Helgi ríðr heiman ok með honum Lýtingr, sonr hans, þegar er hann var búinn, ok Þorgils skinni, fóstri Lýtings,[3] Eyjólfr feiti, Kollr Austmaðr, Þorgerðr silfra ok dóttir þeira Helga, er Hallbera hét. Geitir ríðr ok heiman ok með honum þeir Egilssynir: Þórarinn, Hallbjǫrn, Þrǫstr, – Tjǫrvi inn mikli ok sjau menn aðrir.

Þat segja sumir menn, at Helgi ætti fóstru[4] framvísa, ok var hann vanr at finna hana jafnan, áðr hann fór heiman, ok svá gerði hann enn. Ok er hann kom til hennar, sat hon ok sá í gaupnir sér ok grét.

Helgi spyrr, hví hon gréti eða hví henni væri svá skapþungt. Hon kvazk gráta drauma sína.

---

[1] **þar ek á ekki…:** This construction is rather unusual, as *þar* normally requires a relative pronoun *sem* or *er* when used as a conjunction (*þar sem, þar er* 'where'). Occasionally, however, the expected relative pronoun is dropped, indicating that, at least in colloquial speech, this rule was not inviolable.

[2] **Vel mun þat mega:** 'That will be fine'.

[3] **fóstri:** 'foster-father', 'foster-son', or 'foster-brother'. Thorgils is Lyting's foster-father.

[4] **fóstra:** 'foster-mother', 'foster-daughter', or 'foster-sister'. It is unclear which of these was intended here, and this woman is unknown. Perhaps she was an old nursemaid. Once again relationships that seem vague to us would have been plain to the medieval Icelandic audience, who were familiar with the stories of the families involved.

"I dreamed," she said, "that I saw a pale ox rise up here at Hof, great and splendid and carrying his horns high, and he went onto the sand out by the mouth of Sunnudal. But then I saw cattle coming up through the district,[1] big and not a few. In the lead went a red-flecked ox, neither great nor beautiful, but very strong. These cattle gored the pale ox to death.

"Then a red ox rose up here at Hof with bone-colored horns. He was the most splendid of all cattle. This one gored the red-flecked ox to death.

"Then a bull rose up in Krossavik which was the color of a sea-cow.[2] He went bellowing through all the district and all the heaths, always seeking for the red ox. And then I woke up."[3]

"You must mean," said Helgi, "that I represent the pale ox and Geitir the red-flecked ox, and he will be the one to kill me."

"That is surely what I mean," said she.

"You must mean that Lyting will be that red ox, and he will avenge me."

"No," she said, "Bjarni will avenge you."

"Then you know nothing of it," he said, and rushed out angrily.

CHAPTER 13 VOCABULARY

allfá *n nom/acc pl of* **allfár**

allfár <-fá, -fátt; *pl nom/acc n* -fá> *adj* very few

allsterkligr *adj* very strong-looking

bani *m* death; that which causes death, 'bane'; **til bana** to death; **verða [e-m] at bana** kill [sb]

bar *1/3sg past of* **bera**

beið *1/3sg past of* **bíða**

beinlitr *m* the color of bone

belja <-að-> *vb* bellow

bera <berr; bar, báru; borinn> *vb* carry, bear

bíða <bíðr; beið, biðu; beðinn> *vb* wait; [*w gen*] wait for

bleikr *adj* fawn-colored (*of animals*), pale

draga <dregr; dró, drógu; dreginn> *vb* drag, draw; **dregr at [e-u]** *impers* [sth] draws near

draumr <-s; -ar> *m* dream

dregr *2/3sg pres of* **draga**

---

[1] **up through the district:** *útan eptir heraðinu*. Here it is helpful to keep the Icelandic geography in mind. *Útan* denotes direction inward 'from outside'; *eptir* means 'along', for example, along the line of a river or a valley, which in Iceland often defined the area of a *herað* or 'district'. Hof lies inland up the valley to the southwest of Krossavik, which is located near the edge of the fjord.

[2] Sea bulls were folkloristic creatures. They are often described as gray, a color traditionally associated with the supernatural in Old Norse literature. According to Icelandic folk tales, they were said to come ashore to mate with domestic cows, and their progeny were highly prized. A variety of arctic sea cow, related to the manatee and dugong of tropical waters, did flourish in the far north, and particularly in the White Sea, until it was hunted to extinction in the early modern period.

[3] The bulls the woman sees in her dream are *fylgjur*, the spirits that were believed to accompany individuals and families. The term *fylgja* is often translated into English as 'fetch'. Literally, *flygja* means 'one who accompanies' (compare the verb *fylgja* 'follow, accompany'). *Fylgjur* appeared in a number of different forms, but most often as animals. Their appearance was ominous, often foreshadowng the death of those with whom they were associated. See E. O. G. Turville-Petre, *Myth and Religion of the North: The Religion of Ancient Scandinavia*, pp. 227–30.

"Mik dreymði þat,"[1] segir hon, "at ek sá hér upp rísa at Hofi uxa bleikan, mikinn ok skrautligan, ok bar hann hátt hornin, ok gekk hann á sandinn fram hjá Sunnudalsmynni. Enn sá ek fara naut útan eptir heraðinu, stór ok eigi allfá, ok gekk þar fyrir uxi rauðflekkóttr, ekki mikill né fagr, en allsterkligr var hann. Nautin stǫnguðu uxann til bana.

"Þá reis hér upp at Hofi rauðr uxi, ok var beinlitr á hornunum, ok var allra nauta skrautligastr. Sá stangaði rauðflekkótta uxann til bana.

"Þá reis upp í Krossavík þjórr nǫkkurr, ok var sænautalitr á. Hann fór beljandi um allt heraðit ok allar heiðarnar ok leitaði ávallt ins rauða uxans, enda vaknaða ek þá."

"Þat muntu ætla," segir Helgi, "at ek muna eiga inn bleika uxann,[2] en Geitir rauðflekkóttan[3] ok muni hann verða mér at bana."

"Þat ætla ek víst," kvað hon.

"Þat muntu ætla, at Lýtingr muni sá rauði uxinn[4] ok muni hann hefna mín."

"Nei," sagði hon, "Bjarni mun hefna þín."

"Þá veiztu ekki til,"[5] segir hann, ok hljóp hann þá út reiðr.

---

dreyma <-ð~d-> *vb* [*acc sub and obj*] dream; **[e-n] dreymr [e-t]** *impers* [sb] dreams [sth]

dró *1/3sg past of* **draga**

eiga <á, eigu; átti; áttr> *pret-pres vb* be the one represented by something

Eyjólfr <-s> *m* Eyjolf (*personal name*); **Eyjólfr feiti** *m* Eyjolf the Fat

fagr <fǫgr, fagrt> *adj* fair, fine, beautiful

fá *m acc pl & n nom/acc pl of* **fár**

fár <fá, fátt; *pl* nom/acc n & acc m fá> *adj/indef pron* few

feitr *adj* fat

fóstra *f* foster-mother/daughter/sister

fóstri *m* foster-father/son/brother

fram *adv* forward, outward; **fram hjá** [*w dat*] out by, out beside

framvíss *adj* prescient, prophetic, fore-sighted

gaupnir *f pl* both hands cupped together; **sjá í gaupnir sér** cover one's face with the palms

gráta <grætr; grét, grétu; grátinn> *vb* cry, weep; [*w acc*] weep for

grét *1/3sg past of* **gráta**

Hallbera *f* Hallbera (*personal name*)

hallæri *n* famine

hefna <-d-> *vb* [*w gen*] avenge, take revenge

hennar *gen of* **hon**

hon <*acc* hana, *dat* henni, *gen* hennar> *pron 3sg f* she

horn *n* horn

hversu *interrog adv* how?; **hversu fjǫl-**

---

[1] **Mik dreymði þat:** 'I dreamed that' or 'it was dreamed to me'. *Dreyma* 'to dream' is an impersonal verb, with both the logical subject (*mik*) and the object (*þat*) in the accusative.

[2] **inn bleika uxann ... sá rauði uxinn:** This type of definite construction, in which the suffixed article occurs in conjunction with an independent article or demonstrative pronoun, is noteworthy: **inn** *bleika ux**ann** 'the pale bull', or perhaps 'the bull, the pale one'; and **sá** *rauði ux**inn** 'that bull, the red one'. Sometimes called a "double definite," this construction is uncommon in the sagas and little used in Modern Icelandic, and is not found in Danish. However, the double definite construction is regular in Norwegian, Faroese, and Swedish when an adjective occurs with a definite noun.

[3] The verb phrase *munu eiga* is left understood in the second clause: *ek muna eiga inn bleika uxann, en Geitir [muni eiga] rauðflekkóttan* 'I will be (lit. have) the pale bull, and Geitir will be the red-speckled bull'.

[4] See footnote 3 on p. 102.

[5] **Þá veiztu ekki til**: 'Then you know nothing of it'.

mennr with how many men

Kollr <-s> *m* Koll (*personal name*)

litr <-ar; -ir, *pl acc* -u> *m* color

mannmargr <-mǫrg, -margt> *adj* with many men; **hafa mannmargt** have many people or forces

mega <má, megu; mátti; mátt> *pret-pres vb* can, may; be able; **mega vel** be well

mynni *n* mouth (of a river or fjord)

njósn <-ir> *f* spying, scouting, looking out; news; **hafa njósn af um fǫr [e-s]** spy on, have a watch kept on [sb]'s movements

rauðflekkóttr *adj* spotted, speckled with red, 'red-flecked'

reiðr <reið, reitt> *adj* angry

sandr <-s; -ar> *m* sand

sjau *num* seven

skapþungr *adj* depressed, heavy-hearted, in low spirits; **[e-m] er skapþungt** *impers* [sb] is heavy-hearted, in low spirits

skrautligr *adj* splendid

Sunnudalsmynni *m* Sunnudalsmynni ('the mouth of South (or Sun) Dale') (*place name*)

sænautalitr *m* the color of a sea-cow

unna <ann, unnu; unni; unn(a)t> *pret-pres vb* [*w dat*] love

vanr <vǫn, vant> *adj* accustomed, wont

veizt *2sg pres of* **vita**

veiztu = **veizt þú**, you (*sg*) know (*2sg pres of* **vita** *w encl pron*)

vera <er; var, váru; verit> *vb* be; last; stay; **eiga [e-t] um at vera** have [sth] to be troubled about

víst *n adj as adv* certainly, for certain

vita <veit, vitu; vissi; vitaðr> *pret-pres vb* know

þjórr <-s; -ar> *m* bull, young bull

ætti *3sg/pl past subjunct of* **eiga**

ǫndverðr *adj* in the earlier, former part of (*time*); **til ǫndverðs þings** for the opening of the assembly

At this point in the text, there is a lacuna (or gap) in all the paper manuscripts. From what comes before and after the missing text, we can surmise that Geitir and Brodd-Helgi meet in battle on the sandy flats at the mouth of Sunnudal. There Brodd-Helgi is killed along with his son Lyting and others. Big Tjorvi bears a major responsibility in the killings.

A single leaf of the original calfskin manuscript was discovered in the 17th century, but its significance was not determined until the middle of the 19th century. The leaf supplies part of the gap that exists in all the paper manuscripts. This vellum leaf is damaged, but much of the text can still be read. Chapter 14 begins with text preserved on the damaged leaf.[1]

---

[1] The version of the text presented here follows the reconstruction of Jón Helgason in "Syv sagablade: AM 162 C fol, bl. 1–7".

14. AN HONORABLE SETTLEMENT BROKEN BY VENGEANCE

The first two lines are so badly damaged that little sense can be made of them. Following these lines, most of the remaining text is clear enough to be reconstructed without a break in the story flow.

... who is in need of money and wants something ... but ... journey abroad (funeral?) ... the case was concluded that so much should be done quickly ... of Gudmund Eyjolfsson to the Althing. These stipulations were declared first and foremost that Big Tjorvi should remain at his farm that year but be gone before the first Moving-Day,[1] and that he should never afterwards be at liberty to reside within the district.

Then they traveled to the Althing and Gudmund arranged a settlement between them. He assessed a hundred pieces of silver for Brodd-Helgi's killing, with thirty more in addition.[2] Geitir asked Gudmund if Bjarni would be content with this.

"For his part, he will hold to the settlement," he said.

Afterwards they went home from the assembly, and all was now quiet.

Bjarni stayed that year with Thorgerd Silver, his stepmother ... and Bjarni and Thorgerd's children grew up as siblings. The kinsmen Bjarni and Geitir met often. Geitir paid the hundred pieces of silver as had been stipulated, but the thirty remained unpaid. Geitir did not offer it, and neither did Bjarni demand it.

---

[1] The Moving-Days (*fardagar*) were four days at the end of May in which the members of a household might change their dwelling place if forced to do so by economic or legal circumstances, or if they simply were so inclined (*Grágás* Ia, 128–39). Geitir's thingman Tjorvi was sentenced to district outlawry, but was allowed to remain at his homestead until the next spring. The implication is that Tjorvi is responsible for the death of Helgi (or Lyting).

[2] Payment of compensation in lieu of outlawry was the lightest penalty that Icelandic courts could impose. It was the fixed penalty for many crimes. A 'hundred of silver' (*hundrað silfrs*) is widely reckoned as the price of a single 'weregild' (*manngjǫld*), the compensation for a man's life. Here an additional 30 ounces of silver were awarded in recognition of Helgi's status. As it turned out, Geitir never paid this extra sum, but Bjarni did not seek to enforce the verdict.

14. KAPÍTULI

Summary of Chapter 14. The narrative moves to litigation at the Althing for Helgi's killing. The chieftain Gudmund the Powerful arranges terms of settlement and brokers a binding agreement that includes compensation to Brodd-Helgi's son Bjarni for his losses as well as the penalty of exile from the district for Big Tjorvi, Geitir's follower, who killed Brodd-Helgi. Following this settlement, Bjarni takes vengeance on Big Tjorvi and kills him.

Geitir, who has the right to act, chooses not to prosecute his cousin Bjarni. Instead, the two kinsmen act as though the matter of Brodd-Helgi's killing is completely settled. The two maintain a close relationship until Thorgerd Silver, Brodd-Helgi's second wife and aggrieved widow, demands vengeance. She taunts Bjarni with Brodd-Helgi's blood-stained clothes, shaming the dead man's son into taking revenge.

Bjarni kills Geitir without provocation at a public meeting and is widely condemned. Next, Geitir's son Thorkel returns to Iceland, and tensions mount between Thorkel and his kinsman Bjarni. The threat of further blood vengeance is imminent.

... er féþurfi er og vill nǫkkut ... en ... útanferð[1] ... var máli lokit, at bráðla skyldi gera svá mikit f... Guðmundar Eyjólfssonar til alþingis. Mæltar váru í fyrstu at fyrirmun greinir þær[2] at Tjǫrvi hinn mikli skyldi sitja á búi sínu þau misseri, en vera í brottu fyrir inn fyrsta fardag[3] ok þar aldri eiga heraðsvært síðan.

Nú fara þeir til alþingis ok semr Guðmundr sátt þeira. Gerir hann fyrir dráp Brodd-Helga hundrað silfrs ok þrjá tigu um fram. Geitir spurði Guðmund, ef Bjarni myndi við una.

"Sjálfr mun hann halda sáttina,"[4] segir hann.

Fara þeir síðan heim af þingi, ok er nú allt kyrrt.

Bjarni býr þau misseri með Þorgerði silfru, stjúpmóður sinni ... ok upp systkin, Bjarni ok bǫrn Þorgerðar. Þeir finnask opt frændr ok galt Geitir hundrað silfrs sem skilit var,[5] en þrír tigir stóðu eptir. Bauð Geitir þat ekki fram enda heimti Bjarni þat ekki.

---

[1] **útanferð:** lit. 'journey abroad', but here a figurative meaning 'funeral' may be appropriate. Because the surrounding text is disrupted, it is not clear who this refers to.

[2] **Mæltar váru í fyrstu at fyrirmun greinir þær:** 'These stipulations were declared first and foremost'.

[3] **vera í brottu fyrir inn fyrsta fardag:** 'be gone before the first Moving-Day'.

[4] **Sjálfr mun hann halda sáttina:** 'For his part, he will hold to the settlement'.

[5] **galt Geitir hundrað silfrs sem skilit var:** 'Geitir paid the hundred pieces of silver that had been stipulated'.

Now time drew on to the Moving-Days. Big Tjorvi had disposed of his land, and his whole household . . . It was on a Saturday morning.[1] Tjorvi's horse was tethered by the wall, and he was intending to go alone later and ride unencumbered.

At that moment at Hof, a shepherd came indoors, and Bjarni asked what news he had to tell.

He answered, "Tjorvi's possessions are on the move."

Bjarni stood up and took his shield and spear. He mounted on the shepherd's horse and came to Gudmundarstadir.

Tjorvi had gone to fetch his horse when he saw Bjarni approaching. At once he turned briskly toward the house. Such was the difference in their speeds that as Tjorvi was riding into the homefield, Bjarni had reached the homefield wall. Bjarni rushed after him and thrust his spear through him. Bjarni rode home after this and told Thorgerd about Tjorvi's killing.

She said, "That is better than nothing."

Geitir learned of Tjorvi's killing and had him buried, but did not require compensation from Bjarni for it.[2] They were both at feasts together, Bjarni was invited to Krossavik, and he followed Geitir's advice in all matters. Things continued this way for a long time . . . it was quiet for a while.

Bjarni[3] got married, taking as his wife a woman named Rannveig, the daughter of Thorgeir Eiriksson from Guddalir ('God Valleys'). Before that she was married to Ingimund Ulfsson, and their son was Skidi the Elegant. Rannveig was a good-looking and accomplished woman, and had an abundance of wealth.

The next thing to be told is that Bjarni was at a feast at Krossavik, and men were sitting by the fire. The kinsmen Bjarni and Geitir were lying in one of the sleeping-closets, both together in the same bed. There was a partition in the house with two openings in it, and Geitir looked out through one of the openings. Bjarni asked him what he could see.

Geitir said, "It is strange what appeared before me. It seemed to me as if a cloth were hung up, drenched with blood, and the redness from the cloth is so great that it seems to me . . . all here in the house."[4]

---

[1] The day of the week is important here. According to *Grágás* (I, 128), the first Moving-Day would have been a Thursday. As Jón Helgason notes ("Syv sagablade: AM 162 C fol, bl. 1– 7," p. 65, n. 10), if Tjorvi was sentenced to be gone before the first Moving-Day, then by remaining until Saturday morning (*þváttdagsmorgin* 'wash-day morning'), he was in violation of the provision. This made him *óheilagr* 'without protection of law', and he could be killed with impunity, see footnote 2 just below.

[2] Because Tjorvi was an outlaw (see footnote 1 just above), Bjarni was within his legal rights to kill him, and Geitir had no right to sue for violence directed at Tjorvi.

[3] A new chapter originally began with the name *Bjarni*. However, for the sake of consistency with the *Íslenzk fornrit* edition, we have not inserted a chapter break here.

[4] This is a typical saga premonition: Geitir foresees his own violent death at the hands of Bjarni. Compare Njál seeing the room and food covered in blood just before the burning in *Njáls saga* (Ch. 127).

Nú líðr at fardǫgum,[1] ok hefir Tjǫrvi inn mikli lógat landi sínu, ok allt lið . . . Þat var á þváttdagsmorgin. Hestr Tjǫrva var heptr hjá garði, ok ætlaði hann at fara einn saman síðar ok ríða lauss.

Í þetta mund kom smalamaðr inn at Hofi, ok spurði Bjarni, hvat hann segi tíðenda.

En hann svarar: "Nú leysisk varningr Tjǫrva."

Bjarni stendr upp ok tekr skjǫld sinn ok spjót ok stígr á bak smalahestinum ok kemr á Guðmundarstaði.

Tjǫrvi var farinn at sœkja hest sinn, ok sér hann nú fǫr Bjarna, ok snýr hann þegar heim hvatliga. Sá verðr misfari þeira, at þá ríðr Tjǫrvi í túnit at Bjarni kemr at túngarðinum Hann strýkr eptir honum ok rekr í gegnum hann spjótit, ok ríðr heim eptir þetta ok segir Þorgerði víg Tjǫrva.

Hon segir: "Betra er þat en ekki."

Geitir spyrr víg Tjǫrva ok lætr jarða hann ok gaf ekki Bjarna skuld fyrir þetta.[2] Þeir váru at veizlum báðir saman, ok var Bjarni at heimboðum í Krossavík, ok váru þar ráð hans ǫll, er Geitir var.[3] Nú fer svá fram lengi at . . . var kyrrt um hríð.

Bjarni[4] kvángaðisk ok fekk konu þeirar,[5] er Rannveig hét ok var dóttir Þorgeirs Eiríkssonar ór Guðdǫlum. Hana hafði átt Ingmundr Úlfsson, ok var þeira sonr Skíði inn prúði. Rannveig var væn kona ok vel at sér, ok hafði hon auð fjár.

Frá því er at segja þessu næst, at Bjarni var at boði í Krossavík, ok sátu menn við elda. En þeir frændr lágu í svefnbúri nǫkkuru í einni sæng báðir. Bjórþili var á húsinu, ok váru gluggar tveir á. Geitir leit út um glugginn. Bjarni spurði, hvat hann sæi.

Geitir segir: "Kynligt er þat, er fyrir mik bar. Mér sýndisk sem klæði væri fest fyrir blóði drifit,[6] ok er roði svá mikill af klæðinu, at mér þykkir . . . allt hingat í húsit."

---

[1] **Nú líðr at farðǫgum:** 'Now time draws on to the Moving-Days'.

[2] **Geitir ... gaf ekki Bjarna skuld fyrir þetta:** 'Geitir did not require compensation from Bjarni for this'.

[3] **váru þar ráð hans ǫll, er Geitir var:** lit. 'all his decisions/plans were where Geitir was', i.e., in all his undertakings Bjarni followed Geitir's advice or acted as Geitir's ally.

[4] In the manuscript, the initial letter of *Bjarni* is two lines in height, indicating that a new chapter originally began here. We have not inserted a chapter division in this edition, however, so as to maintain consistency with the *Íslenzk fornrit*.

[5] **fekk konu þeirar:** 'took that woman' (to be his wife). Usually *fá* 'get, take' takes an accusative object, but it can sometimes take genitive, particularly in reference to marriage. Compare *biðja* [e-s] 'ask for someone's hand in marriage'.

[6] **Mér sýndisk sem klæði væri fest fyrir blóði drifit:** 'It seemed to me as if a cloth were hung up, drenched with blood'.

"I see nothing of that," said Bjarni. "Blood must be sinking into your eyes on account of the fire."

"It may be that," said Geitir.

Then they went in after that, and was ... Bjarni went home afterwards and everything was quiet for some time.

It was a custom in the district for men to hold an assembly at the beginning of the last month of winter[1] at the farm called Thorbrandsstadir ('Thorbrand's Farmstead'). There work was to be divided among the farmers, and all matters were to be discussed that seemed necessary and should ... were between them. Geitir was a respectable man, and many men had pressing matters to discuss with him, and he sat ...

... but the driving snow was not heavy, and Bjarni asked what he should wear to cover himself.

Thorgerd ... cloak ... folded up into Bjarni's hand.[2] He took it and spread it out, and it was both ... and cut in pieces ...[3]

Bjarni struck her and said, "Take that, you most wretched of all women."

Bjarni was then red as blood[4] ... went out hastily.

She said, "You don't need to turn away because ... who was equally hard as you and was not a lesser warrior than you, and he would ..."[5]

Bjarni paid no heed to her words. He had in his hand a small wood-axe. When he came to the meeting, many men were also there.

Geitir was sitting at a little door next to the homefield wall itself ... asked ... Bjarni greeted the men of distinction also rather coldly.

"You look to me," said Geitir, "as if noisy rumors[6] will ... for you before you left home, that you have grown angry on account of what happened between us. And yet we would not want that."

Bjarni was very silent.

---

[1] The medieval Icelandic calendar was based on the lunar month. According to modern reckoning, *einmánuðr* (the last month of winter) corresponds to a period in March and April. The *einmánaðr* gatherings were the oldest meetings of the *hreppr*, a communal unit made up of at least twenty householders with sufficient property to pay the assembly attendance tax. (This corresponds to the parish of later times.) Each *hreppr* was responsible for the maintenance of the poor in the district and other communal projects. They functioned independently of the *goði-thingmaðr* structures (see *Grágás* Ib, 171–80, II, 249–61).

[2] Thorgerd has kept the cloak that Brodd-Helgi was wearing when he was killed, and she now hands it to Bjarni.

[3] Accounts of women inciting vengeance with blood-stained clothes occur in other sagas (for example, *Njáls saga*, Ch. 116, and *Laxdæla saga*, Chs. 59–60). Women often goaded their menfolk into action in the sagas, especially when conflicts settled at law were not to the satisfaction of honor.

[4] At times of high emotional drama, the sagas describe psychological crises in terms of observable external symptoms, such as flushing red, silence, and tragic laughter, rather than through any subjective description of internal feeling.

[5] Presumably Thorgerd is telling Bjarni that Brodd-Helgi would not have neglected to take vengeance if he (Bjarni) were the one who had been killed.

[6] **noisy rumors:** *hávarðar*. The meaning is unclear in this context. Perhaps it means 'rumors', 'quarrels', or 'troublesome people'.

"Ekki sé ek af því," segir Bjarni, "ok mun síga blóð í augu þér fyrir sakar elds."[1]

"Vera má þat," segir Geitir.

Nú gengu þeir inn eptir þat ok var . . .lat var. Bjarni fer heim síðan, ok er nú enn kyrrt allt nǫkkura hríð.

Þat var vanði í heraði, at menn hǫfðu samkvámu í ǫndverðan einmánað á bœ þeim, er á Þorbrandsstǫðum heitir. Skyldi þar skipta vinnum á bændr ok mæla þeim málum ǫllum, er þá þótti nauðsyn til, ok skyldi . . . millum váru. Geitir var maðr skilríkr, ok áttu margir menn við hann málþarfir,[2] ok sat hann . . .

. . . en eigi drífan á mikil,[3] ok spurði Bjarni, hvat hann skyldi yfir sér hafa.[4]

Þorgerðr . . . skikkju . . . saman vafða í hǫnd Bjarna. Hann tekr við ok rekr í sundr, ok var hon[5] bæði . . . ok í sundr hǫggvin.

Bjarni laust til hennar ok mælti: "Sel þú allra kvenna ǫrmust."[6]

Bjarni var þá rauðr sem blóð . . . gengr út skyndiliga.

Hon segir: "Eigi þarftu at snarask á brott fyrir því at . . . er þér var jafnharðr,[7] er ekki var minni garpr en þú ok myndi sá . . ."

Bjarni gaf engan gaum at orðum hennar. Hann hefir í hendi sér viðarøxi litla. En er hann kemr til fundarins, var þar fjǫlmenni.

Geitir sat á hurð lítilli við túngarðinn sjálfan . . . bað . . . Bjarni heilsar á fyrirmenn ok heldr fáliga.

"Svá lízk mér á þik," segir Geitir, "sem muni hávaðar . . . fyrir þér áðr þú fórt heiman, at[8] þér mun í skap hafa runnit við oss, ok vildum vér þat þó eigi."

Bjarni var fámálugr mjǫk.

---

[1] **mun síga blóð í augu þér fyrir sakar elds:** 'it must be blood sinking into your eyes on account of the fire', i.e., blood must be clouding your vision because of the heat.

[2] **áttu margir menn við hann málþarfir:** 'many men had pressing matters to discuss with him'.

[3] **eigi drífan á mikil:** 'the driving snow was not heavy'.

[4] **spurði Bjarni, hvat hann skyldi yfir sér hafa:** 'Bjarni asked what he should wear to cover himself'.

[5] **hon:** i.e., the cloak.

[6] **Sel þú allra kvenna ǫrmust:** 'Take that, you most wretched of all women'.

[7] **er þér var jafnharðr:** 'who was equally hard as you'.

[8] At this point, the textual witness of the paper manuscripts resumes after the lacuna.

Kolfinn had accompanied Bjarni from home. He spoke up by ill luck,[1] and looking up to the sky, he said, "The weather is variable now. This morning it seemed to me to be somewhat threatening and was very cold, but now it seems to me to be making as if it will thaw."

Bjarni said, "There will be a thaw for all time, if this coldness of mine begins to thaw."

Bjarni stood up and said, "My leg has fallen asleep."

"Then go easy on it," said Geitir.

Bjarni then struck Geitir on the head, and he was dead in a moment. But as soon as he had struck the blow, Bjarni regretted it. He sat down with Geitir's head on his lap, and Geitir died on Bjarni's knees.

Geitir was buried then. After this men went away, and no compensation was fixed. This killing was spoken badly of and was thought to have been done in an unmanly fashion.[2]

Bjarni went home to Hof, and when he arrived home, he drove Thorgerd Silver away and told her never again to come within his sight.

Thorkel Geitisson was not in Iceland when his father was killed, but Blaeng took care of the farm at Krossavik with the assistance of the Egilssons, who were then brothers-in-law of Thorkel Geitisson.[3] In the spring, the farmers called off the assembly,[4] not wishing to hold it, as it seemed hopeless to intercede between those men who had part in such grave matters.

It is said that Bjarni appointed a man named Birning to keep a lookout and give him warning if there was any threat of violence, so that it would not take him by surprise.

There was a man named Thorvard, a popular man who was reputed to be the best healer in the district. He lived at Sireksstadir.

---

[1] It is "bad luck" or perhaps an "evil omen" that Kolfinn, the brother of Thorgerd Silver, Helgi's second wife (see ch. 6), speaks about the weather. The weather in Kolfinn's remark is symbolically linked to Bjarni's foul and silent mood.

[2] This sort of public response from the surrounding community is an integral part of Icelandic feuding.

[3] The Egilssons are Thorkel's in-laws because he was married to their sister, Hallfrid (Ch. 3). At some later time not disclosed in the saga, Thorkel marries Jorunn Einarsdottir from Thverá. (See Ch. 19.) The wedding is described in Vǫðu-Brands þáttr (Ch. 4) a short tale in Ljósvetninga saga.

[4] The Sunnudal assembly seems never to have been convened again. After deciding to disband the Sunnudal assembly, the people of Weapon's Fjord begin to attend the várþing í Fljótsdalsherað 'spring assembly in the Fljotsdal district', which was most likely the Múla-assembly (see Ch. 18) or possibly the Kiðjafell assembly. The latter was held at Þingmúli, a short distance from where Helgi Asbjarnarson was then living.

Kolfinnr fór heiman með Bjarna. Hann tók til orða illu heilli[1] ok mælti ok sá í himininn upp: "Nú er margháttat um veðrin, í morgun þótti mér nǫkkut élligt vera ok var afarkalt, en nú þykkir mér þvílíkt gera sem þeyja muni."

Bjarni segir: "Þá mun ávallt þeyja, ef þetta verðr at þey."[2]

Bjarni stóð þá upp ok mælti: "Dofinn er mér fótr minn."[3]
"Ligg þú þá kyrr á,"[4] segir Geitir.
Bjarni hjó þá í hǫfuð Geiti, ok fekk hann þegar bana. Ok jafnskjótt sem hann hafði hǫggit, iðraðisk hann, ok settisk undir hǫfuð Geiti, ok andaðisk hann í knjám Bjarna.
Geitir var nú jarðaðr síðan. Eptir þetta fara menn á brott. Var þar ekki mælt til líka.[5] Þetta verk mæltisk illa fyrir, ok þótti ómannligt orðit verkit.[6]

Bjarni fór heim til Hofs. Ok er hann kom heim, rak hann braut Þorgerði silfru ok mælti, at hon skyldi aldri koma í augsýn honum.

Þorkell Geitisson var eigi á Íslandi, er faðir hans var veginn, en Blængr varðveitti bú í Krossavík með umsjá Egilssona, er þá váru mágar Þorkels Geitissonar. Um várit tóku bændr af þingit ok vildu eigi hafa ok þótti óvænt í millum at ganga þeira manna,[7] er í slíkum stórmælum áttu hlut.

Þat er sagt, at Bjarni setti til mann, er Birningr hét, at hafa njósn af, ef nǫkkurs ófriðar væri ván,[8] ok gera Bjarna varan við, svá at eigi mætti honum á óvart koma.

Þorvarðr hét maðr. Hann var vinsæll, ok var þá kallat, at hann væri beztr læknir þar í heraði. Hann bjó á Síreksstǫðum.

---

[1] **illu heilli:** 'unluckily' or 'by ill omen'.

[2] **Þá mun ávallt þeyja, ef þetta verðr at þey:** 'There will be a thaw for all time, if this coldness of mine begins to thaw'. There is a play on words between the thawing of the weather and Bjarni's silence. Þeyja 'to thaw' is a homonym of the fem. noun þeyja 'silent mood' while þey (from the masc. noun þeyr 'a thaw') is a homonym of the neut. noun þey, a variant of the fem. noun þeyja.

[3] **Dofinn er mér fótr minn:** 'My leg has fallen asleep'.

[4] **Ligg þú þá kyrr á [fætinum]:** 'Then go easy on [your leg]'. The object, fótr 'leg', is left understood in this sentence. Liggja kyrr á literally means 'lie quietly on' and in this sentence means 'sit and rest – don't stand up'.

[5] **Var þar ekki mælt til líka:** 'No compensation was fixed'.

[6] **Þetta verk mæltisk illa fyrir, ok þótti ómannligt orðit verkit:** 'This killing/work was spoken badly of, and the deed was thought to have been done in an unmanly fashion'.

[7] **þótti óvænt í millum at ganga þeira manna:** 'it seemed hopeless to intercede between those men'.

[8] **ef nǫkkurs ófriðar væri ván:** 'if there were threat of any violence'.

Now Thorkel Geitisson came back to Iceland and went at once to his farm at Krossavik. He acted as if he had nothing to be concerned about. Bjarni then sent men who were friends of them both to meet Thorkel and offer him a settlement, honor, and self-judgment.[1] But when they brought their errand to Thorkel, he acted as if he did not hear them and continued speaking without interrupting what he had been saying before. The messengers returned to tell Bjarni how matters stood. As a result, people assumed that Thorkel was preparing for vengeance.

Bjarni was accustomed to go to the mountains every autumn as his father had done, trusting that no one would do others harm at that time. Thorvard the Healer learned that Thorkel was preparing a trip to the mountains and had selected men to go with him as support. He informed Bjarni of this, so Bjarni stayed back and sent other men in his stead.

Then the men went to the mountains, but the encounter between Bjarni and Thorkel did not take place as Thorkel had intended. They remained quiet over the winter.

CHAPTER 14 VOCABULARY

afarkaldr <-kǫld, -kalt> *adj* very cold

armr <ǫrm, armt> *adj* vile, wretched, wicked

auga <*pl gen* augna> *n* eye

augsýn *f* sight

auðr *m* wealth; **hafa auð fjár** to be very wealthy, have an abundance of wealth

bani *m* death; that which causes death, 'bane'; **fá bana** die

báðir <báðar, bæði, *gen* beggja> *adj/indef dual pron* both

báru *3pl past of* **bera**

beggja *gen of* **báðir**

bera <berr; bar, báru; borinn> *vb* carry, bear; **bera fyrir [e-n]** *impers* appear to [sb] (*of a dream or vision*); **bera ørendi sín (upp) fyrir [e-n]** plead one's case before [sb], tell one's errand to [sb]

Birningr <-s> *m* Birning (*personal name*)

bjóða <býðr; bauð, buðu; boðinn> *vb* [*w acc*] offer; **bjóða [e-t] fram** offer, proffer, produce [sth]

bjórþili *n* partition, dividing wall (*perh of animal skin*)

blóð *n* blood

bóndi <*gen* bónda; *pl* bœndr> *m* farmer; head of a household

braut (*var of* **brott**) *adv* away

brautargengi *n* (*leg*) help, furtherance

bráðla *var of* **bráðliga**

bráðliga (*also* **bráðla**) *adv* soon, quickly

bregða <bregðr; brá, brugðu; brugðinn> *vb* [*w dat*] move quickly; turn, alter, change; break off, leave off, give up; **bregða tali** break off speaking

bændr (*var of* **bœndr**) *nom/acc pl of* **bóndi**

dofinn <-in, -it> *adj* dead, numb (*of a limb*)

dráp *n* slaying, killing

drifit *n ppart of* **drífa**; **blóði drifit** covered with blood

drífa *f* driving snow; sleet; snowfall

drífa <drífr; dreif, drifu; drifinn> *vb* drive (*of wind, snow, etc.*), shower

eiga <á, eigu; átti; áttr> *pret-pres vb* own, have, possess; **eiga mál við [e-n]** speak, converse with [sb]

---

[1] **self-judgment:** *sjálfdœmi.* Instead of submitting a case to arbitration or to the judgment of a court, one party could agree to give the other the sole judgment in the matter. *Sjálfdœmi* was the greatest satisfaction that could be given to a legal opponent. Although sometimes it represented a confirmation of mutual trust and interest in attaining peace, it could also be extorted from the weak or used as the last appeal to the justice and generosity of a much more powerful adversary. There was an expectation that the party awarded self-judgment would show moderation and forbearance in reaching a decision, but this ideal was not always respected.

Nú kemr Þorkell Geitisson út, ok ferr hann þegar til bús síns til Krossavíkr[1] ok lætr sem hann eigi ekki um at vera.[2] Þá sendir Bjarni menn á fund Þorkels, þá er beggja þeira vinir váru, at bjóða Þorkatli[3] sætt ok sœmð ok sjálfdœmi. En er þeir báru þessi ørendi upp fyrir Þorkel, lét hann sem hann heyrði eigi, ok eigi brá hann tali sínu, því er hann hafði áðr. Nú fara sendimenn aptr at segja Bjarna svá búit. Svá virðu menn, at Þorkell myndi til hefnda hyggja.

Bjarni var vanr hvert haust at fara á fjall, sem faðir hans hafði gǫrt, ok treysti þá engi ǫðrum rangt at gera. Þorvarðr læknir varð varr, at Þorkell bjósk til fjallgǫngu ok valdi menn með sér til brautargengis. Þorvarðr gerði Bjarna varan við. Bjarni settisk aptr ok fær aðra menn í stað sinn.

Nú gengu menn á fjallit. Fundr þeira Bjarna varð eigi sem Þorkell hafði ætlat, ok sátu þeir um kyrrt um vetrinn.

einmánaðr *m* the last month of winter (from mid-March to mid-April)
Eiríkr <-s> *m* Eirik (*personal name*)
eldr <-s; -ar> *m* fire
élligr *adj* threatening to storm
fara <ferr; fór, fóru; farinn> *vb* go, travel; move
fardagar *m pl* Moving-Days (i.e., four successive days in spring, at the end of May, in which householders in Iceland changed their abode)
fá <fær; fekk, fengu; fenginn> *vb* get; **fá bana** die
fáliga *adv* coldly
fámálugr *adj* silent, tight-lipped
fest *n ppart of* **festa**
festa <-t-> *vb* fasten, attach; **festa fyrir** hang up
fé <*gen* fjár; *pl gen* fjá> *n* wealth, money
féþurfi *adj indecl* in need of money
finna <finnr; fann, fundu; fundinn> *vb* find; *refl* **finnask** meet one another
fjall <fjǫll> *n* mountain
fjallganga <*acc/dat/gen* -gǫngu> *f* trip into the mountains (to gather sheep from the highland pastures)
fjár *gen sg of* **fé**
fjǫlmenni *n* many people, a crowd
fórt *2sg past of* **fara**
fyrirmaðr <*pl* -menn> *m* leader, man in charge; *pl* men of distinction
fyrirmunr <-ar; -ir> *m* most important point of distinction; **at fyrirmun** most importantly
fyrsta *wk f of* **fyrstr**; **í fyrstu** in the beginning, at first
fyrstr *superl adj* first
fær *2/3sg pres of* **fá**
galt *1/3sg past of* **gjalda**
ganga <gengr; gekk, gengu; genginn> *vb* walk; go; **ganga í millum** intercede
gaumr *m* heed, attention, *only in the phrase* **gefa gaum at [e-u]** give heed to [sth]
gera <-ð-; *ppart* gerðr~gerr> *vb* make, build; do, act; (*leg*) to set the amount of a fine
gjalda <geldr; galt, guldu; goldinn> *vb* pay
gluggr <-s; -ar> *m* opening, hole; window
grein <-ar~ir> *f* branch, division; point, particular

---

[1] **til Krossavíkr:** *víkr* is the gen. sing. of *vík* (fem.) 'inlet, bay'.

[2] **sem hann eigi ekki um at vera:** 'as if he has nothing to be concerned about'. Here *eigi* is the 3sg. pres. subjunct. of *eiga*.

[3] **Þorkatli:** this is the original dat. sg. of Þorkell, i.e. of the full form of the name, Þorketill, contrasting with gen. sg., Þorkels, coined from the fused form, Þorkell. In this saga, this is the only occurrence of this form, elsewhere the new dat. sg. Þorkeli is used. In other sagas, and also in the case of other names with the second element *Ketill* (e.g. *Arnkell*, *Grímkell* etc., all originally *Arnketill*, *Grímketill* etc.), the regular dat. sg. is -*katli*, while gen. sg. is still -*kels*.

Guðdalir *m pl* Guddalir ('God Valleys') (*place name*)

hafa <hef(i)r; -ð-> *vb* have; **hafa yfir sér** wear, put over oneself

harðr <hǫrð, hart> *adj* hard, difficult, severe

haust *n* autumn, fall, harvest season

hávaði *m* loud noise, tumult; loud self-assertion; (= **hávaðamaðr**) a noisy, self-assertive man

hefnd <-ir> *f* revenge; *esp pl* blood revenge

heill *n* (good) luck; omen; **illu heilli** unfortunately, by ill omen

heilsa <-að-> *vb* [*w dat*] greet; **heilsa á [e-n]** greet [sb]

heimboð *n* invitation to one's home

hepta <-t-> *vb* tether (a horse)

heraðsvært *n* freedom to live in a district; **eiga heraðsvært** (*leg*) be at liberty to reside within a district without threat of attack

hinn (*var of* **inn**) *art* the

hurð <-ir> *f* door

hvatliga *adv* quickly

hǫggva <hǫggr; hjó, hjoggu; hǫgg(v)inn> *vb* strike (a blow), chop, hack, hew; **hǫggva í hǫfuð [e-m]** strike [sb] on the head

iðra <-að-> *vb* repent; *refl* **iðrask** [*w gen*] repent of, regret

iðraðisk *2/3 sg past of* **iðrask**

Ingmundr <-s> *m* Ingmund (*personal name*)

jafn <jǫfn, jafnt> *adj* equal, even; *in cpds* equally, as

jafnharðr <-hǫrð, -hart> *adj* equally hard, as severe

jafnskjótt *adv* as soon, just as quickly

klæði <*pl gen* klæða> *n* cloth; garment, clothes

kné <*dat* kné, *gen* knés; *pl dat* knjám~ knjóm, *gen* knjá> *n* knee

knjám *dat pl of* **kné**

koma <kemr~kømr; kom, kómu~kvámu; kominn> *vb* come; **koma inn** enter, come in

kona <*pl gen* kvenna> *f* woman; wife

kvenna *gen pl of* **kona**

kynligr *adj* strange, extraordinary

laun *f* secrecy; **á laun** secretly, alone

laust *1/3sg past of* **ljósta**

lágu *3pl past of* **liggja**

leit *1/3sg past of* **líta**

leysa <-t-> *vb* loose, set free; *refl* **leysask** depart, remove oneself

lið *n* household

liggja <liggr; lá, lágu; leginn> *vb* lie (down); **liggja kyrr á [e-u]** sit and rest [sth], go easy on [sth]

líki *m* compensation

líta <lítr; leit, litu; litinn> *vb* look, see; *refl* **lítask** appear, seem; **[e-m] lízk á [e-n]/ [e-t]** *impers* [sb/sth] looks to [sb]

lízk *2/3sg pres of* **lítask**

ljósta <lýstr; laust, lustu; lostinn> *vb* strike; **ljósta til** (= **ljósta**) strike

lóga <-að-> *vb* [*w dat*] part with

læknir <-is; -ar> *m* doctor, physician, healer

margháttaðr <-háttuð, -háttat> *adj* of many kinds, varied

mágr <-s; -ar> *m* male in-law

málþorf <*gen* -þarfar; *pl* -þarfir> *f* matter requiring discussion

mega <má, megu; mátti; mátt> *pret-pres vb* can, may; be able

misfari *m* difference in speed

misseri *n* season, period of six months; *pl* cycle of seasons, year

morginn (*also* **morgunn**) <*gen* morgins, *pl* mor(g)nar> *m* morning; **í morgun** this morning

morgunn *var of* **morginn**

mund *n* (*in sg*) *or f* (*in pl*) moment; situation, circumstance; **í þetta mund** at that moment

mæla <-t-> *vb* say, speak; **mæla málum** plead a cause; **mæla til [e-s]** stipulate, fix [sth]; *refl* **mælask** be spoken of; **mælask illa fyrir** be ill spoken of, condemned

mæltisk *2/3 sg past of* **mælask**

mætti *3sg/pl past subjunct of* **mega**

næst *superl adv* next; **þessu næst** thereafter

og (*var of* **ok**) *conj* and

ómannligr *adj* unmanly; inhuman

óvarr <óvǫr, óvart> *adj* unaware, unwary

óvart *n adj as adv* unawares, by surprise; **koma [e-m] á óvart** take [sb] by surprise

óvænn *adj* hopeless, with little chance of success

prúðr *adj* fine, magnificent; gallant, brave

rak *1/3sg past of* **reka**

rangr <rǫng, rangt> *adj* wrong

rangt *n adj as adv* wrongly, unjustly

ráð *n pl* affairs, business

reka <rekr; rak, ráku; rekinn> *vb* drive, herd; drive onto shore, wreck; **reka braut** drive away; **reka [e-t] í gegnum [e-n]** drive [sth] through [sb]

rekja <rakð~rakt-; *ppart* rak(i)ðr~raktr> *vb* spread out, unfold; **rekja í sundr** (= **rekja**) spread out, unfold

renna <rennr; rann, runnu; runninn> *vb* run; **rennr [e-m] í skap** *impers* [sb] grows angry

roði *m* redness

runnit *n ppart of* **renna**

samkváma *f* meeting, assembly, 'coming together'

sátt (*also* **sætt**) <sættir> *f* settlement, agreement

selja <-d-> *vb* hand over (to another)

semja <samð-; *ppart* samiðr~samdr> *vb* arrange, compose, settle; **semja sátt** arrange a settlement

setja <-tt-> *vb* set, place, put; **setja [e-n] til** to appoint [sb]; **setjask** *refl* set oneself; **setjask aptr** hold back, stay back (*esp* from a journey)

sitja <sitr; sat, sátu; setinn> *vb* sit; reside; stay; **sitja um [e-t/e-n]** watch for [sth] (*as an opportunity*), lie in wait for, plot against [sb]

síga <sígr; seig, sigu; siginn> *vb* sink

sjá <sér; sá, sá(u); sénn> *vb* see

sjálfdœmi *n* (*leg*) self-judgment

skap <skǫp> *n* condition of mind, temper, mood; **rennr [e-m] í skap** *impers* [sb] grows angry

skikkja *f* cloak, mantle

skilríkr <*acc m* -jan> *adj* trustworthy, respectable

skuld <-ir> *f* debt, obligation to pay; **gefa [e-m] skuld** require compensation from [sb]

skyndiliga *adv* hastily, speedily

smalahestr *m* shepherd's horse

smalamaðr *m* shepherd

snara <-að-> *vb* turn quickly, twist; *refl* **snarask** turn oneself quickly, turn around

snúa <snýr; snøri~sneri; snúinn> *vb* turn, go

snýr *2/3sg pres of* **snúa**

spjót *n* spear

staðr <*dat* stað~staði, *gen* -ar; *pl* -ir> *m* stead, place; **í stað sinn** instead of one, in one's place

stíga <stígr; steig, stigu; stiginn> *vb* step, walk; **stíga á bak** mount (a horse)

stjúpmóðir <*acc/dat/gen* -móður; *pl* -mœðr, *dat* -mœðrum, *gen* -mœðra> *f* stepmother

stórmæli *n pl* great or grave affairs

strjúka <strýkr; strauk, struku; strokinn> *vb* run, rush, dash off

sundr (*also* **í sundr**) *adv* apart, asunder

svefnbúr *n* sleeping closet, stall

systkin *n pl* brother and sisters (*coll*)

sæi *3sg/pl past subjunct of* **sjá**

sæng <*gen* sængar~sængr; *pl* sængr> *f* bed

sætt (*also* **sátt**) <sættir> *f* settlement, reconciliation

sœmð *f* honor

taka <tekr; tók, tóku; tekinn> *vb* take; **taka [e-t] af** cancel, abolish, do away with [sth]; **treysta** <-t-> *vb* trust; **treysta [e-m]** trust, rely on [sb]

um *prep* [*w acc*] about; **um fram** in addition

umsjá *f* supervision, care over; assistance

Úlfr <-s> *m* Ulf ('Wolf') (*personal name*)

vafðr *ppart of* **vefja**

valði *3sg past of* **velja**

vandi (*also* **vanði**) *m* custom, habit

vanði *var of* **vandi**

varr <vǫr, vart> *adj* aware; **gera [e-n] varan við [e-t]** warn [sb], make [sb] aware of [sth]

vefja <vafð-; *ppart* vaf(i)ðr~vafinn> *vb* wrap, fold; **vefja [e-t] saman** wrap [sth] up, fold [sth] together

veizla *f* banquet, feast, party

vel *adv* well; **vel at sér** accomplished, gifted

velja <valð~vald-; *ppart* val(i)ðr~valdr~valinn> *vb* choose, select, pick out

viðarøx <*acc/dat* -i; *pl* -ar> *f* wood-axe

vinna *f* work, labor

þarftu = **þarft þú**, do you (*sg*) need (*2sg pres of* **þurfa** *w encl pron*)

þeyja <-; þá, -; -> *defect vb* thaw

þeyr <*dat* þey; *gen* þeys; *pl* þeyir> *m* thaw

Þorbrandsstaðir *m pl* Thorbrandsstadir ('Thorbrand's Farmstead') (*place name*)

Þorgeirr <-s> *m* Thorgeir (*personal name*)

þurfa <þarf, þurfu; þurfti; þurft> *pret-pres vb* need

þváttdagr *m* Saturday, *lit* washing-day

þvílíkt *adv* such, in such a manner

ǫrmust *nom f sg of* **armastr**, *superl of* **armr**

CULTURE SECTION – THE CYCLE OF SEASONS AND FEUD

Despite its far northern location and frequently hard winters, the climate in Weapon's Fjord is often mild and sunny in the summers. The saga tells of communal activity in the region as dictated by the progress of the seasons. Patterns of economic and social activity reflect the seasonal revolutions of each passing year.

Each year a stage of life began with the spring thaw, and life around the farms quickened noticeably. The sheep were kept around the farmsteads until the spring lambs were born, and then they were released into the highest mountain pastures as soon as the departing snow permitted. This practice hastened soil erosion. It allowed the sheep to graze on the new and vulnerable shoots of grass, destroying much of the highland vegetation as it was rejuvenating from winter.

Cattle were generally driven to the low highlands. They grazed mostly on grass and were much less destructive to the ecosystem than the sheep, pigs, and goats, which dug out roots and ate shoots and the bark of small trees. The cows, which were smaller than today's, were kept alive during the winter by feeding them the limited amount of hay that each farm could produce and store. Their milk dried up over the long dark months of confinement. By spring the cows were often so weak that they had to be carried from their byres in order to be given the first grass in the lowlands.

During the winter most horses fended for themselves out of doors. Their thick fur protected them, but by mid-winter, few were well enough fed to be ridden for any length of time. With the paths and rivers clear of snow and ice in the spring and with fresh grass available for the horses, kinsmen, allies, and friends met and exchanged news after the relative isolation of the winter. Concerns and strategies were discussed and preparations laid for the coming meetings and assemblies, especially for the major event of the year, the meeting of the Althing in June. By then the horses were well enough fed, and the weather was mild enough for traveling the long distance to southwestern Iceland.

Sheep and cattle grazed in common pastures in the mountains during the summer months, so that the hay in the grazing areas around the main farmhouses could be manured, harvested, and saved for winter. This type of cultivation, which can be characterized as settled pastoralism, was not very labor intensive. Usually there was one hay harvest per year, and the farmers were left with free time on their hands. During the early and middle summer, people traveled and met at social gatherings, and men engaged in the legal work and other business of the assemblies and courts. After spending the long winter nursing their animosities, remembering the wrongs done to them, and planning redress, characters like those in *Vápnfirðinga saga* took the opportunity of the summer months to engage in feud.

In the fall, the annual roundup of livestock in the highlands was a key event of the social calendar. Participants in the roundup were vulnerable to attack, but such was the economic importance of sheep and cattle to a family's subsistence that an unspoken period of peace – or at least a cessation of outright hostilities – was observed during this time of the year. Still, for those like Thorkel, the opportunity to settle old scores was too tempting to pass up. When Thorkel plans to break the customary peace by attacking Bjarni in the highlands, Thorvard the Healer warns Bjarni of the impending danger. Thorvard, a member of the community, has no role in the feud and yet intervenes to preserve the peace in this crucial season.

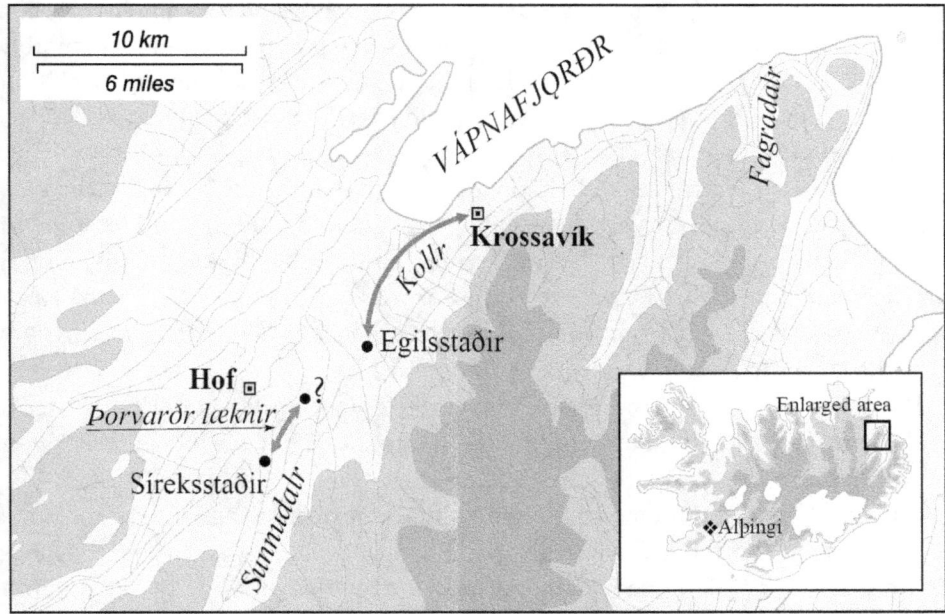

Map 10. A Problem of Geography. Sireksstadir is located in Sunnudal, but the saga writer assumes that Sireksstadir lies between Egilsstadir and Krossavik. The map shows the route of Thorvard of Sireksstadir, the best healer or leech (*læknir*) in the district, on his way home from the next farm. On this journey, Thorvard meets Koll, who is on his way from Egilstadir to Krossavik.

15. THORKEL SENDS A SPY NAMED KOLL

Next to be told is that Thorkel sent a man out one day from Krossavik to Egilsstadir to meet Thorarin. The man that was sent was named Koll. Koll's mission was to find out how many men were at Hof.

When he reached Egilsstadir, he met Thorarin outside and told him his mission. Thorarin said, "It will not seem to you that you are being welcomed hospitably. Go home as quickly as possible and let no one know of your journey. I will find out what Thorkel wants to know." And he said that he himself would tell Thorkel.

Then Koll turned back toward home and had to travel late.

But this same afternoon, it so happened that a man broke his leg at the farm next to Sireksstadir. Thorvard the Healer was called for, and he came to bind up the leg. He was invited to stay, but he wanted to ride home that night. He met Koll on the road, and they greeted each other and asked the news. Thorvard asked where Koll was coming from, and Koll in turn asked why Thorvard was traveling at night. Thorvard said it was nothing of importance.

"Now tell me your errand," said Thorvard. "I went up through the district to look for some sheep, but I did not find them," he said. They parted, and Koll went home that night.

Thorvard also went home that night, and the next morning he took his horse and rode up to Hof, where he was given a warm welcome. He was asked the news, and he said that a man had broken his leg. He drew Bjarni aside to talk and told him about meeting Koll, who likely had been returning from Egilsstadir. He said he was certain that Koll had not spoken the truth about his journey.

"I see now," said Bjarni, "that you do not want anything to happen in the district that I do not know about. You have my sincere thanks for that. Now return home and go to the farm named Faskrudsbakki ('Faskrud's Bank') in the middle of the district, where Thorkel's men are. If it happens to be asked how many men are here, tell them that some of our men arrived here this morning, and that not a few[1] horses were driven home, but that you do not know what they might be for."

.

---

[1] **Not a few** (*eigi alltfá*). The same phrase appears in Ch. 13, when Helgi's foster-mother dreams about a herd of "big and not a few" cattle roaming through the district.

15. KAPÍTULI

Summary of Chapter 15. Thorkel sends a man named Koll to Thorarin to find out how many men Bjarni has at Hof, hoping for a good opportunity at revenge. Thorarin promises to get an answer and sends Koll home, instructing him to keep a low profile. Thorvard the Healer meets Koll on the path at night and suspects that Koll is out spying for Thorkel. Thorvard loyally goes to Bjarni and shares his suspicions. Bjarni then uses Thorvard to spread a rumor around the district that he has many men at Hof ready to protect him. Thorarin believes the rumor and tells Thorkel to delay any attack.

Þat er nú næst frá at segja, at Þorkell sendir mann heiman um dag ór Krossavík ok til Egilsstaða at hitta Þórarin. Sá maðr hét Kollr, er sendr var. Þat var ørendi Kolls at vita, hversu fjǫlmennt væri at Hofi.

Ok er hann kom á Egilsstaði, hitti hann Þórarin úti ok sagði honum sín ørendi. Þórarinn mælti: "Eigi mun þér gestbeinliga þykkja boðit. Far þú heim sem tíðast ok lát eigi verða við vart,[1] en ek mun varr verða þess, er Þorkell vill forvitnask," – ok kvezk honum þat segja mundu.

Nú snýr Kollr heim á leið, ok varð honum síð farit.[2]

En á þessum sama aptni varð sá atburðr, at maðr braut fót sinn á næsta bœ frá Síreksstǫðum, ok var farit eptir Þorvarði lækni, ok kom hann at binda fótinn. Honum var boðit þar at vera, en hann vildi heim ríða um nóttina, ok hitti hann Koll á leið, ok kvǫddusk þeir ok spurðusk tíðenda, ok spyrr Þorvarðr, hvaðan Kollr væri at kominn, en Kollr spyrr móti, hví hann fari um nætr. Þorvarðr segir þat engu sæta.[3]

"Seg mér nú þitt ørendi, Kollr," segir Þorvarðr. "Ek fór upp í herað at leita sauða, ok fann ek eigi," segir hann. Skiljask, ok ferr Kollr heim um nóttina.

Þorvarðr fór ok heim um nóttina. Ok um morguninn eptir tók hann hest sinn ok reið upp til Hofs, ok var þar við honum vel tekit. Hann var spurðr at tíðendum, en hann sagði, at maðr braut fót sinn. Hann heimtir Bjarna á tal[4] ok segir, at hann hitti Koll ok hann mundi kominn frá Egilsstǫðum, ok sagðisk víst vita, at hann sagði honum ekki orð satt um sína ferð.

"Sé ek nú," kvað Bjarni, "attú vilt, at ekki gerisk þat út í heraði, at ek vita eigi, ok haf þú mikla þǫkk fyrir. Nú far þú heim ok kom á bœ þann, er heitir á Fáskrúðsbakka, í miðju heraðinu. Þar eru Þorkels menn fyrir. Ok ef at verðr spurt, hversu fjǫlmennt hér er, þá seg, at hér kómu í morgun nǫkkurir várir menn ok váru hross heim rekin ok eigi allfá,[5] en þú vissir eigi, hvat þau skyldu."

---

[1] **lát eigi verða við vart:** 'let no one become aware of [it]', i.e., the journey.

[2] **varð honum síð farit:** 'he had to travel late'.

[3] **Þorvarðr segir þat engu sæta:** 'Thorvard says it is nothing of importance'.

[4] **Hann heimtir Bjarna á tal:** 'He draws Bjarni [aside] to talk', i.e., in private.

[5] **ok eigi allfá**: 'and not just a few'. This phrasing may consciously echo the *eigi allfá oxen* of the dream in Ch. 13. Such mirroring of phrases is common in this and other sagas. See Rolf Heller, "Studien zu Aufbau und Stil der Vápnfirðinga saga," *Arkiv för nordisk filologi* 78, 1963, pp. 170–89.

Thorvard left and came to Bakki,[1] and he was asked how many men there were at Hof. He said what he was told to say, and went home afterwards.

But as soon as he had left, they sent mento Egilsstadir to report that a great body of men was at Hof. Thorarin then sent word to Thorkel that it would not be easy to attack Hof as things stood, and so the winter passed.

CHAPTER 15 VOCABULARY

aptann <*dat* aptni, *gen* aptans; *pl* aptnar> *m* evening

atburðr <-ar; -ir> *m* occurrence, event; **verðr sá atburðr** it so happened

attú = **at þú** that you (*sg*)

auðsóttr <-sótt, -sótt> *adj* easily won, easy to win

bakki *m* bank (of a river or chasm), slope

Bakki *m* Bakki ('Bank' or 'Slope') (*place name, esp a nickname for a place name ending with -bakki*)

binda <bindr; batt, bundu; bundinn> *vb* bind, tie, fasten; bind up (a wound, etc.)

braut *1/3sg past of* **brjóta**

brjóta <brýtr; braut, brutu; brotinn> *vb* break

búa <býr; bjó, bjoggu~bjuggu; búinn> *vb* prepare, make ready

búnu *n dat sg ppart of* **búa**; **at svá búnu** as matters stand, in the present state of things

fara <ferr; fór, fóru; farinn> *vb* go; **fara eptir [e-m]** send for [sb]

Fáskrúðsbakki *m* Faskrudsbakki ('Faskrud's Bank') (*place name*)

gera <-ð-; *ppart* gerðr~gerr> *vb* make, build; do, act; *refl* **gerask** occur, happen

gestbeinliga *adv* hospitably

heimta <-t-> *vb* draw, pull; claim; **heimta [e-n] á tal** engage [sb] in conversation, address [sb]; draw [sb] aside to speak with them

hvaðan *adv* from where, whence

koma <kemr~kømr; kom, kómu~kvámu; kominn> *vb* come; **koma at** arrive

leið <-ir> *f* road, path; way; **á leið** on the way; **fara leiðar sinnar** go (on) one's way; **heim á leið** on one's way home, homeward

miðju *n dat of* **miðr**

miðr <mið, mitt; *acc m* miðjan > *adj* middle

móti *adv* in return

segja <sagð-> *vb* say, tell; *refl* **segjask** say of oneself, declare of oneself

seta *f* body of men

síð *adv* late

sæta <-tt-> *vb* amount to, be of importance; **engu sæta** be of no importance, amount to nothing

tíðast *superl adv* most quickly; **sem tíðast** at once, with all speed

um *prep* [*w acc*] during, for, in, by (*time*); **um dag** one day; **um nætr** by night

vita <veit, vitu; vissi; vitaðr> *pret-pres vb* know; **vita [e-t] víst** know [sth] for sure

---

[1] That is, Faskrudsbakki. This feature, the so-called compund truncation, when the first element or elements of a compound noun, especially in place names, are cut away (here, *Faskrud-*) and only the final one (here, *-bakki*) is used instead of the whole, is common in both Old Norse and Modern Icelandic, as well as in other compound-rich languages.

Þorvarðr ferr ok kemr á Bakka, ok var hann spurðr, hversu fjǫlmennt væri at Hofi. En hann sagði slíkt, sem honum var sagt, ok ferr hann heim síðan.

En þegar er hann var í brottu, sendu þeir menn til Egilsstaða ok sǫgðu, at seta mikil var at Hofi. Síðan sendi Þórarinn Þorkeli orð, at eigi mundi at svá búnu auðsótt til Hofs, ok líðr nú enn vetrinn.

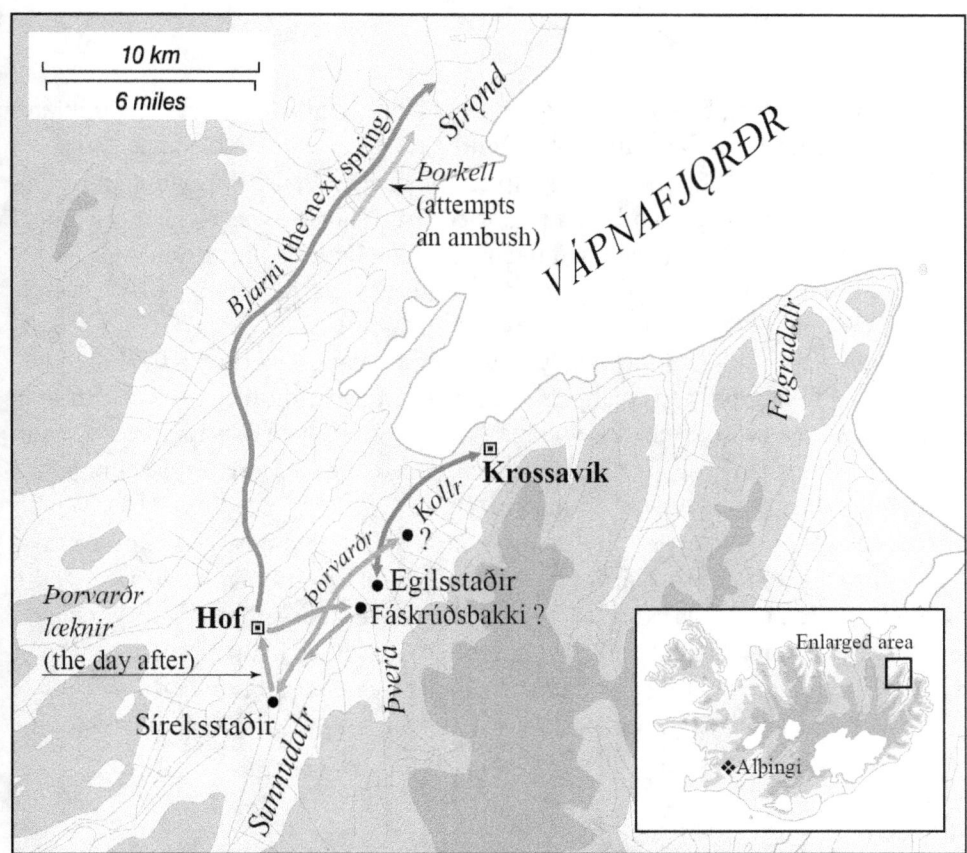

Map 11. Movements of Thorvard and Koll, and Thorkel's Attempt at Ambushing Bjarni Out on the Strands (Strönd). Coming into the fall season, Bjarni journeys to Strond on the northern coast of Weapon's fjord in order to round up his sheep, and Thorkel, Bjarni's enemy, attempts to ambush him there. The map also shows the movements of Thorvard and Koll recounted in the previous chapter.

16. Bjarni Brodd-Helgason
Deceives Thorkel Geitisson and Escapes

The following spring Bjarni had to go out to Strond[1] and was forced to go inland across the heath, because water was flooding the inlets.

There were summer milking huts[2] up on the heaths. Bjarni was riding past one of the huts with two men and did not notice until Thorkel was right there ahead of him with eight men. Thorkel had been watching Bjarni's movements.

In front of the milking hut there was a large three-legged chopping block. "Let us take the chopping-block," said Bjarni, "cover it with my cloak, and set it on my saddle. Then ride on both sides supporting it on the horse's back. You ride to the hill that is nearest the milking hut, and I will go inside the hut. If they ride after you and continue past the hut, then I will go into the woods and save myself. But if they turn this way and come to the hut, then I will defend myself according to the measure of my courage."

The men now did as they were instructed.

Thorkel was not a sharp-sighted man, but nonetheless he was wise and perceptive. As the distance between the parties grew less, Thorkel asked if they could see for sure that there were three men riding away from the hut, "because it would be a good plan for Bjarni to go into the hut and then into the woods if we happen to pass by." But they said they could see for sure that there were three men going away.

"I saw," said Thorkel, "that there were three horses, but I have doubts whether there were men on the backs of them all."

---

[1] Strond (the name means 'Shore') is the long stretch of coastline running northeast above the main fjord, now called Vopnafjarðarströnd ('Shore of Weapon's Fjord').

[2] The term *sel* was used for the summer grazing land as well as for huts that formed summer dairy stations in the highlands. *Sel* is often translated into English as 'shieling', a little-known Scottish word perhaps of Scandinavian origin. A *sel* was typically a simple hut of stones and turf, and such low, dirt-floored buildings can still be seen in Iceland's highlands. It provided shelter for the shepherds, cowherds, and dairymaids doing the milking and making of skyr and cheese. Other activities such as wood collection and charcoal burning also took place there.

16. KAPÍTULI

Summary of Chapter 16. Bjarni rides to his *sel* (summer dairy station in the highlands) with two other men and is taken by surprise when Thorkel arrives with eight men. Bjarni wraps his cloak around a chopping-block and sets it on the back of his horse. He instructs his men to ride on each side, keeping the block upright on the horse's back, so that it looks as if the horse is carrying a man. Bjarni meanwhile escapes through the forest. Thorkel has his suspicions about the three "riders," but his vision is poor. He and his men pursue the horses, and Bjarni gets away on foot.

Um várit eptir átti Bjarni ferð út á Strǫnd, ok varð hann at fara it efra um heiðina, því at vatn gengr fram um víkrnar.[1]

Sel váru á heiðunum, ok ríðr Bjarni hjá selinu við þriðja mann[2] ok finnr eigi, fyrr en þar var Þorkell fyrir honum við níunda mann, ok hafði hann haft njósn af um ferðir hans Bjarna.

Fyrir selinu stóð fjalhǫgg mikit ok þrífœtt. "Nú skulum vér taka fjalhǫggit," kvað Bjarni, "ok fœra þat í kápu mína[3] ok setja í sǫðul minn ok ríða á tvær hendr ok styðja á baki[4] ok ríða á þat leiti, er næst er selinu, en ek mun ganga inn í selit. Ok ef þeir ríða eptir yðr ok um fram selit, þá mun ek ganga í skóginn ok forða mér. En ef þeir víkja hingat at selinu, þá mun ek verjask eptir því, sem minn er drengskapr til."[5]

Nú gera þeir eptir því, sem þeim var fyrir sagt.

Þorkell var maðr eigi skyggn, en þó var hann vitr ok glǫggþekkinn, ok er saman dró með þeim,[6] þá spurði Þorkell, ef þeir sæi víst, at þrír riði mennirnir frá selinu fram, – "því at þat væri ráð at ganga inn í selit ok svá í skóginn, ef oss berr um fram."[7] En þeir kváðusk víst sjá, at þrír fóru mennirnir fram.

"Sá ek," kvað Þorkell, "at þrír váru hestarnir, en grunr er mér á,[8] hvárt menn váru á baki ǫllum."

---

[1] **vatn gengr fram um víkrnar:** 'water is flooding the inlets'. Generally *fram* applies to motion outward or toward the open, and *um* is often coupled with an adverb of motion to form a compound preposition (compare English *out to, out of*). The meaning here is that the water produced by the spring thaw is flooding the inlets and making the lowland routes near the shore impassable. The alternative high route (*it efra*) that Bjarni took must have wound around the hills to the north of the main valley.

[2] **við þriðja mann ... við níunda mann:** lit. 'with a third man ... with a ninth man', meaning 'as a party of three' and 'as a party of nine', i.e., the subject plus two or eight others. Such expressions may seem less peculiar to an English speaker when one considers that *annarr* 'other' also means 'second'; hence *við annan mann* 'with another man' also means 'with a second man', which is to say, as a party of two.

[3] **fœra þat í kápu mína:** 'cover it with my cloak', lit. 'bring it into my cloak'.

[4] **ríða á tvær hendr ok styðja á baki:** 'ride on both sides and support [it] on the horse's back'.

[5] **eptir því, sem minn er drengskapr til:** 'according to the measure of my courage'.

[6] **er saman dró með þeim:** 'as the distance between them grew less', lit. 'as it drew together with them'.

[7] **ef oss berr um fram:** 'if we happen to pass by'.

[8] **grunr er mér á:** 'I have doubts'.

"Not only were there men on the backs of them all," they replied, "but it was the biggest man who rode in the middle."

"We will trust," said Thorkel, "how it appears to you, but I do think it is ill-advised not to search the hut."

Thorkel and his companions now rode after the three horses, and when they had almost reached them, Bjarni's traveling companions let the chopping-block drop and then rode away. But Bjarni had already gotten away into the woods and so was saved from Thorkel and his men.

Thorkel now turned back and arrived home ill-pleased with his lot. Bjarni's traveling companions went to find him as soon as they thought he was out of danger, and they continued on their way. So again Bjarni and Thorkell were kept apart from each other at this time.

CHAPTER 16 VOCABULARY

allr <ǫll, allt> *adj/indef pron* all

bera <berr; bar, báru; borinn> *vb* carry, bear; *impers* [*acc subj*] be born or carried (*denoting involuntary motion*); befall, happen

draga <dregr; dró, drógu; dreginn> *vb* drag, draw; **dregr saman með [e-m]** *impers* [sb] draws together, comes close

drengskapr <*gen* -ar> *m* courage, honesty

efri *comp adj* upper, higher; **fara it efra** travel the higher or inland route

eiga <á, eigu; átti; áttr> *pret-pres vb* own, have, possess; **eiga ferð** have some errand

eptir *prep* [*w acc*] after (*time*); [*w dat*] after, along; according to

falla <fellr; fell, fellu; fallinn> *vb* fall; **láta [e-t] falla ofan** let [sth] fall down, drop [sth]

finna <finnr; fann, fundu; fundinn> *vb* find; notice, perceive;

fjalhǫgg *n* chopping-block

forða <-að-> *vb* [*w dat*] save; **forða sér** save oneself, escape danger

fram *adv* forward, outward; **fram um** *or* **um fram** [*w vb of motion*] on past, up beyond, out over

fǫrunautr <-s; -ar> *m* traveling companion, fellow-traveler

glǫggþekkinn <-in, -it> *adj* perceptive

grunr <-ar; -ir> *m* suspicion, uncertainty, doubt; **[e-m] er grunr á [e-u]** [sb] has doubts, is suspicious about [sth]

hafa <hef(i)r, -ð-> *vb* have; hold, keep; take; **hafa sik** take oneself

heldr *comp adv* more, rather; **at heldr ... at** not merely ... but rather, all the more

hjálpa <helpr; halp~hjalp, hulpu; hólpinn> *vb* [*w dat*] help, save

hlíta <-tt-> *vb* [*w dat*] rely on, trust

hólpinn *ppart of* **hjálpa**, safe, saved

hǫnd <*acc* hǫnd, *dat* hendi, *gen* handar; *pl* hendr, *dat* hǫndum, *gen* handa> *f* hand; (right or left) hand, side; **á tvær hendr** on both sides

kanna <-að-> *vb* search, explore

kápa *f* 'cape' or cloak with a hood

kváðusk *3pl past of* **kveðask**

kveða <kveðr; kvað, kváðu; kveðinn> *vb* speak, say; *refl* **kveðask** say of oneself

leiti *n* hill, elevation

mið *n* middle; **í miðit** in the middle

misráðit *n ppart* ill-advised (*from* **mis-** 'badly' *and* **ráða** 'advise')

níundi *ord num* ninth

óhættr <óhætt, óhætt> *adj* safe, out of danger; **er [e-m] óhætt** *impers* [sb] is out of danger

sel <*pl gen* selja> *n* shieling, hut or shed in a mountain pasture used in the summer for milking livestock

skyggn <skyggn, skyggnt> *adj* sharp-sighted

strǫnd <*dat* strǫnd(u), *gen* strandar; *pl* strendr~strandir> *f* shore, coast, 'strand'

Strǫnd *f* Strond ('Shore' *or* 'Strand') (*place name*)

sǫðull <sǫðuls; sǫðlar> *m* saddle

um *prep* [*w vb of motion*] over, past, beyond, across; **fram um** *or* **um fram** [*w vb of motion*] on past, up beyond, out over

verja <varð-, *ppart* var(i)ðr~varinn> *vb* defend; *refl* **verjask** defend onself

vitja <-að-> *vb* [*w gen*] call on, visit

vík <*gen* víkr; *pl* víkr, *gen* víkna> *f* inlet, bay

víkja <víkr; veik, viku; vikinn> *vb* turn, move, shift direction

víkr *gen sg & nom/acc pl of* **vík**

"At heldr váru menn á baki þeim ǫllum," kváðu þeir, "at sá var maðrinn mestr á baki, er í miðit reið."

"Þessu munum vér hlíta," segir Þorkell, "sem yðr sýnisk, en þat hygg ek, at þat muni misráðit, er eigi er kannat selit."

Ríða þeir Þorkell nú eptir þeim, ok er þeir eru mjǫk eptir komnir,[1] þá láta þeir fǫrunautar Bjarna falla ofan fjalhǫggit ok ríða undan síðan. En Bjarni hefir sik þegar í skóginn ok er nú hólpinn fyrir þeim Þorkeli.

Þorkell hverfr nú aptr ok kemr heim ok unir illa við sinn hlut. Fǫrunautar Bjarna vitja hans, þegar er þeim þykkir honum óhætt vera. Ok fara þeir leiðar sinnar, ok berr nú enn í sundr með þeim Þorkeli ok Bjarna at sinni.[2]

þrífœttr <-fœtt, -fœtt> *adj* three-legged   **ǫllum** *m dat sg & all dat pl of* **allr**

CULTURE SECTION – SUMMER DAIRY STATIONS

Much of the routine labor during the summer, including milking and dairy production, as well as the wool-working and weaving during the other times of the year, was performed by women. Men saw to the herding of animals, the annual maintenance of turf buildings, the gathering of foods, and the collection and transportation of driftage washed ashore on the coasts. Men fished during the winter when the above-mentioned chores were done.

During the summer all or part of a household, including a large number of the women, would move to temporary dwellings on the highland pastures known as shielings (*sel* or *sumarhús*). There they tended to their livestock. Dairy products, especially cheese, butter, and skyr (a form of coagulated milk that preserves well and is high in protein) were produced. Later in the autumn, these foodstuffs were transported from the highland *sel* to the lowland farmsteads for storage and usage during the winter.

The sheep intermingled over the summer months as the animals roamed the highland pastures and mountain valleys. The practice of letting the sheep run free required a high degree of cooperation, self-control, and honesty among neighboring farmers. The different farmers marked their sheep to distinguish them, and because there were no natural predators, every farmer's knowledge of his own and his neighbors' livestock meant that theft could not go undetected for long.

After the late summer or fall hay harvest, the local farmers as a collective group gathered their sheep from the highlands and drove them to the lowland valleys. In the lowlands, the sheep were sorted and herded back to their owners' farmsteads for the winter. Back in the hands of their rightful owners, the sheep that were not going to be kept over the winter were slaughtered. This activity brought a time of plenty. People consumed conspicuously at autumn feasts that heralded the onset of the long, dark winter.

---

[1] **er þeir eru mjǫk eptir komnir:** 'when they have almost reached them'.

[2] **berr nú enn í sundr með þeim Þorkeli ok Bjarna at sinni:** 'now again Thorkell and Bjarni keep apart at this time'.

17. THE SONS OF DROPLAUG OFFER TO BURN BJARNI

A little while later, Thorkel sent men to the Fljotsdal district for his kinsmen Helgi and Grim, the sons of Droplaug,[1] requesting that they should come to Krossavik. They left at once with the messengers, and when they arrived at Krossavik, they were given a warm welcome. Helgi asked what needed to be done, since Thorkel had sent word to them.

"Recently I made a journey and am ill-pleased with the way it turned out," said Thorkel. "I revealed openly that I wanted Bjarni dead, but I got nowhere. Now I want to go to Hof quckly and attack him, and we will overcome him with fire if we are unable to do so with weapons."[2]

Helgi expressed approval of this plan. But first they slept for the night.

Thorkel's health was always poor and he often fell sick without warning.

Helgi awoke early in the morning and dressed. He went to Thorkel's bed-closet and said, "It's time to get up, if you are still of the same mind as yesterday, because a sleeping man seldom gains the victory."[3]

Thorkel answered, "I am going to get little work done this day on account of my poor health."

Helgi volunteered to make the excursion and do what had been planned the evening before. Thorkel answered, "I do not think it right for anyone but me to be the leader of this excursion."

Helgi began to get angry and said, "You need not send word to me again, since you now act like a coward when I have come to give you aid, and you are not even willing to let others go."

With this they parted in anger. The brothers then went home, and things were now quiet for a while. Bjarni and Thorkel did not encounter each other on this occasion.

CHAPTER 17 VOCABULARY

athǫfn <athafnir> *f* business, work

bauzk *2/3sg past of* **bjóðask**

berr *adj* open, clear, manifest; **gera sik beran** show openly, reveal oneself

---

[1] The brothers Helgi and Grim, known as the *Droplaugarsynir* (the sons of Droplaug), were introduced in Ch. 3.

[2] Burning one's enemy in his own house was the last resort in feud and the most dramatic and impressive act of violence known in the sagas.

[3] Compare the following lines from *Hávamál* (*Sayings of the High One*) 58, which ends: "Seldom does a lying wolf / get the thigh bone / nor a sleeping man the victory" (*Sjaldan liggjandi úlfr / lær um getrat / né sofandi maðr sigr*). See Gustav Neckel and Hans Kuhn, *Edda. Die Lieder des Codex Regius nebst verwandten Denkmälern*, 2d. ed., p. 26.

17. KAPÍTULI

Summary of Chapter 17. Thorkel sends for his kinsmen Helgi and Grim Droplaugar-son to help him attack Bjarni. They are willing and come at once. However, Thorkel, who often suffers from sudden illnesses, is taken ill on the morning of the attack. Thorkel himself cannot go, and he refuses to let anyone take his place. Helgi accuses him of cowardice and returns home with Grim.

Litlu síðar sendir Þorkell menn í Fljótsdalsherað eptir frændum sínum, Helga ok Grími Droplaugarsonum, at þeir skyldi koma í Krossavík. Ok þeir fara þegar með sendimǫnnum Þorkels, ok er þeir kómu í Krossavík, var við þeim tekit vel, ok spyrr Helgi, hvat at skyldi hafask,[1] er hann hefði honum orð sent.

"Fyrir skǫmmu fór ek þá ferð, er ek uni illa við svá búit," segir Þorkell. "Gerða ek mik beran í því, at ek vilda Bjarna feigan, ok kom ek engu fram.[2] Nú vilda ek brátt fara til Hofs ok veita Bjarna heimsókn ok sœkja hann með eldi, ef vér getum eigi með vápnum"[3]

Helgi lét vel yfir þessari ætlan. Sofa þeir nú af nóttina fyrst.

Þorkell var lítt heill jafnan ok tók opt bráða sótt.[4]

Helgi vaknar þegar í elding ok klæðisk ok gengr til lokrekkju Þorkels ok mælti: "Mál er upp at standa,[5] ef nú er slíkt í hug sem í gær, fyrir því at sjaldan vegr sofandi maðr sigr."

Þorkell svarar: "Litla athǫfn mun ek drýgja daglangt fyrir sakar vanheilsu minnar."

Helgi bauzk til ferðar þessarar ok gera at slíkt, sem áðr var ætlat. Þorkell svarar: "Ekki þykki mér þat annarra manna en mín at vera foringinn þessarar ferðar."

Helgi mælti ok tók þá at styttask: "Eigi þarftu mér orð optar at senda, er þú skræfisk nú, er ek em hér kominn til liðs við þik, enda viltu eigi, at aðrir fari."

Skiljask þeir nú síðan með styttingi. Fara þeir brœðr nú heim, ok er nú kyrrt um hríð, ok fundusk þeir Bjarni ok Þorkell ekki í þessu sinni.

bjóða <býðr; bauð, buðu; boðinn> *vb* [*w acc*] offer; [*w dat*] invite; order, command; *refl* **bjóðask** offer oneself, volunteer one's service

bráðr <bráð, brátt> *adj* sudden, quick

brátt *n adj as adv* soon, shortly

daglangt *adv* through the day

drýgja <-ð-> *vb* accomplish, commit, perpetrate

elding *f* last part of the night before dawn,

---

[1] **hvat at skyldi hafask:** 'what needed to be done'.

[2] **kom ek engu fram:** 'I brought nothing about', i.e., 'I got nowhere'.

[3] **ef vér getum eigi með vápnum:** 'if we are unable [to overcome him] with weapons'.

[4] **tók ... sótt:** 'fell sick'. Compare the common English expression 'be taken ill' (or the colloquial regional variant 'take ill, take sick').

[5] **Mál er upp at standa:** 'It's time to get up'.

starting about 3 a.m., *lit* 'fire-lighting'

feigr *adj* death-bound, fated to die; **vilja [e-n] feigan** wish for [sb's] death, want [sb] dead

ferð <-ir> *f* journey, trip; **fara ferð** make a journey, take a trip

finna <finnr; fann, fundu; fundinn> *vb* find; *refl* **finnask** meet one another

foringi <*gen* -ja; *pl* -jar> *m* leader

fundusk *3pl past of* **finnask**

Grímr <-s> *m* Grim (*personal name*)

gær *adv*, *only in* **í gær** yesterday

hafa <hef(i)r, -ð-> *vb* have; hold, keep; take; **hafask at** do

heill *adj* healthy, 'hale'

heimsókn <-ir> *f* attack on one's home; visit; **veita [e-m] heimsókn** to attack [sb] in his home; visit

klæða <-dd-> *vb* clothe; *refl* **klæðask** get dressed (in the morning)

láta <lætr; lét, létu; látinn> *vb* let, allow, permit; express, say; **láta vel yfir [e-u]** express approval of [sth]

lokrekkja *f* locking bed-closet

mál *n* time

senda <-d-> *vb* send; **senda eptir [e-m]** send for [sb]

sigr <*gen* sigrs> *m* victory

sjaldan *adv* seldom

skræfask <-ð-> *refl vb* act like a coward

skammr <skǫmm, skam(m)t> *adj* short, brief; **fyrir skǫmmu** recently

skǫmmu *n dat sg of* **skammr**

sofa <sefr; svaf, sváfu; sofinn> *vb* sleep; **sofa af um nóttina** sleep through the night

sofandi *pres part of* **sofa**

sótt <-ir> *f* sickness, illness; **taka sótt** fall sick, be taken ill

stytta <-tt-> *vb* shorten; *refl* **styttask** get angry

styttingr *m* unfriendliness, abruptness; **skiljask með styttingi** part coldly, abruptly

sœkja <sótt-> *vb* seek; attack

vega <vegr; vá, vágu; veginn> *vb* kill, slay; fight; **vega sigr** gain the victory

ætlan <-ir> *f* plan, design

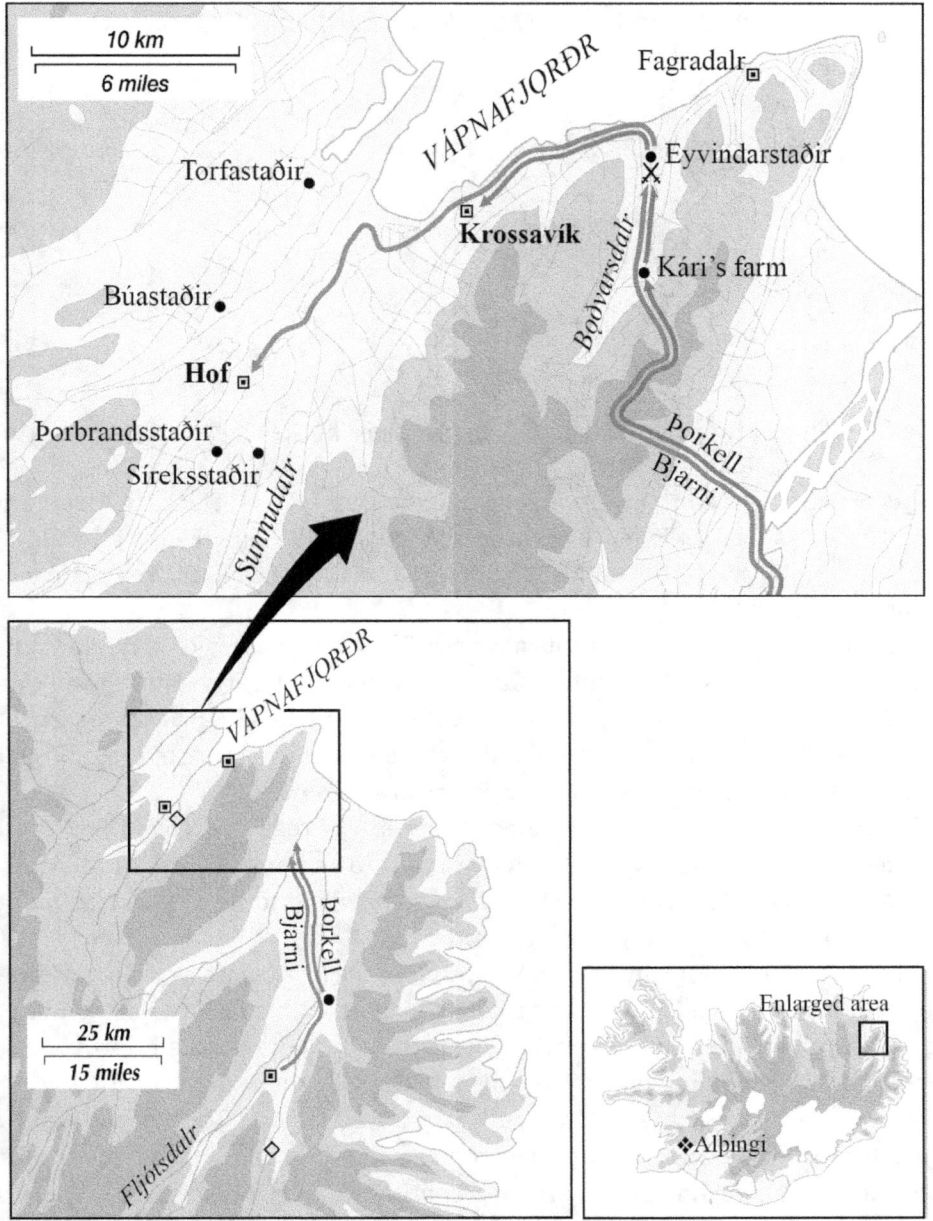

Map 12. The Battle of Bodvarsdal. The map shows the routes taken by the feuding chieftains, Bjarni and Thorkel, as they return to Weapon's Fjord from the local springtime assembly at Mjovanes. The riders first pass Kari's farm and then meet and battle at Eyvindarstadir ('Eyvind's Farmstead'). The exact location of Kari's farm is uncertain today, but remains of summer milking sites (*sel*) in Bodvarsdal indicate where the route over the hills from the south came down to the valley floor.

18. BLOOD IS SHED AND WOUNDS NEED HEALING

The following spring, both chieftains, Bjarni and Thorkel, traveled to the spring assembly in the Fljotstal district.

Accompanying Thorkel were Blaeng and the sons of Egil, Thorarin, Hallbjorn, and Throst, as well as Eyjolf who lived at Vidivellir ('Willow Fields'). Including Thorkel, they were fifteen in all. They went to Eyvindará, and Groa[1] provided what they needed.

Accompanying Bjarni on the journey were Thorvard the Healer of Sireksstadir, Bruni of Thorbrandsstadir, Eilif Torfason of Torfastadir ('Torfi's Farmstead'), the two brothers Berg and Brand of Buastadir ('Bui's Farmstead'), Bjarni's foster-son Skidi, and Hauk Loptsson. They were eighteen in all. Helgi Asbjarnarson and Thordis Brodd-Helgadottir[2] gave them a warm welcome.[3]

When the assembly was concluded, Thorkel was ready to leave first, which pleased Bjarni well. And when Bjarni was ready to go home, Thordis Todda gave him a fine necklace, saying she would take no payment for it. She fastened it on his neck and made sure it was firmly fixed.

Thorkel and his company now traveled across the heath. Afterwards they came down into Bodvarsdal, where they took up lodging with a farmer named Kari, a thingman of Thorkel. But when they went to bed, Thorkel asked Kari to keep watch and warn him immediately if any men came down from the heath.

Bjarni traveled slowly across the heath and was glad that Thorkel had made a track through the heath, because the path was in poor condition. Bjarni came at night to a woman named Freygerd, and continued afterwards across the heath, coming down early in the morning into Bodvardsal near Kari's farm.

---

[1] Groa was Thorkel's aunt, his mother's sister (see footnote 1, page 86, and Genealogy 3.)

[2] This is Thordis Todda, Bjarni's sister (Ch. 3).

[3] One manuscript adds *er þeir kómu til Mjóvaness* 'when they came to Mjovanes'. Most likely this phrase is a scribal addition, as it only appears in the one manuscript. The saga's author would likely have expected the reader to know where Helgi and Thordis lived. Helgi and Thordis moved several times in the course of *Droplaugarsona saga*, much of which is contemporaneous with the events in *Vápnfirðinga saga*. They first lived at Oddstadir, then, pressured by the sons of Droplaug, they moved to Mjovanes. Eventually they settled farther north at Eidar, where Helgi was killed by Grim Droplaugarson.

18. KAPÍTULI

Summary of Chapter 18. Thorkel is first to leave for home after the spring assembly. He rests for the night at Kari's farm and tells Kari to keep watch through the night. Bjarni and his men ride past the farm during the night, but Kari says nothing, not wishing to take part in the feud. Thorkel and his men rise early the next morning and recognize the tracks outside. They pursue Bjarni and easily catch up to him. Battle breaks out near the farm of a man named Eyvind, with casualties on both sides. Eyvind rushes out of his house and breaks up the fight before either Bjarni or Thorkel is killed. Afterwards both parties see to their wounds and their dead. Once Bjarni and his men have begun to heal through Thorvard's care, Bjarni sends him to heal Thorkel's wounds. Thorkel recovers with Thorvard's help and thanks him with gifts and kind words.

Um várit eptir fara þeir báðir hǫfðingjar, Bjarni ok Þorkell, til várþings í Fljótsdalsherað.

Með Þorkeli var Blængr ok þeir Egilssynir, Þórarinn, Hallbjǫrn ok Þrǫstr, Eyjólfr, er bjó á Víðivǫllum, ok váru þeir Þorkell fimmtán saman ok fóru til Eyvindarár til Gróu, ok annaðisk hon þat, er þeir þurftu.

Með Bjarna váru í fǫr Þorvarðr læknir af Síreksstǫðum, Brúni af Þorbrandsstǫðum, Eilífr Torfason af Torfastǫðum, brœðr tveir af Búastǫðum, Bergr ok Brandr, Skíði, fóstri Bjarna, Haukr Loptsson, ok váru þeir átján saman. Þau Helgi Ásbjarnarson ok Þórdís Brodd-Helgadóttir tóku við þeim vel.

Ok er þinginu var lokit, þá varð Þorkell fyrr á braut búinn,[1] ok þótti Bjarna þat vel. En er hann var búinn til heimferðar, þá gaf Þórdís todda honum men gott ok kvazk eigi laun vilja fyrir hafa, bjó svá um, at var fest á háls honum, ok festi rammliga.

Þorkell ferr nú með því fǫruneyti um heiðina. Þeir Þorkell kómu síðan ofan í Bǫðvarsdal. Tóku þeir þar gisting hjá bónda þeim, er Kári hét, ok var hann þingmaðr Þorkels. En er þeir gengu at sofa, þá bauð Þorkell Kára um, at hann skyldi vǫrð halda, ef menn nǫkkurir kœmi af heiðinni, ok gera hann þegar varan við.

Bjarni fór tómliga um heiðina, ok þótti vel, at Þorkell gerði feril um heiðina, fyrir því at fœrð var ill. Hann kom til konu þeirar um nóttina, er Freygerðr hét, ok fór síðan um heiðina ok kom snimma um morguninn ofan í Bǫðvarsdal hjá bœ Kára.

---

[1] **varð Þorkell fyrr á braut búinn:** 'Thorkel was sooner ready to be away', i.e., he left ahead of Bjarni.

Seeing Thorkel's tracks leading to the farm, Bjarni said that three of them should go side by side, followed by a second three and after that a third three, and so on, "so it will then appear to be the tracks of three men." And so they did.

Kari was outside when they went by the wall but he did not give warning, because the trouble between those kinsmen seemed serious, and he did not wish to get himself involved in it.

Thorkel awakened in his bed and woke up his company saying they had slept enough. They armed themselves and then went outside.

Thorkel told them to go back to the trail and see if any tracks led off the trail, They saw the tracks of three men leading away. Thorkel himself went to the trail. "These men were heavy," he said. "I believe that Bjarni and his companions must have gone here. Now let us follow hard after them."

When they had made it some distance away from the farm, they saw that the tracks divided. They traveled as fast as they could until they came almost to the mouth of the valley, where a little farm named Eyvindarstadir ('Eyvind's Farmstead') stood. There lived a man named Eyvind.

Bjarni and his companions had nearly reached the homefield wall of this farm when they took a rest. Bjarni said, "I will not run from Thorkel any longer. Here we must wait for whatever may come about."

As soon as Thorkel caught up, he said, "Now let us attack valiantly. My kinsman Bjarni and I will see to each other, as will Blaeng and Birning, Thorvard and Throst."

Now the battle began.[1] Bjarni and his men defended themselves most valiantly, and for a while it went on in such a way that no men were wounded. Then Thorkel said, "We are attacking now like such cowards that nothing tale-worthy will come of it."

Bjarni answered, "You have courage enough."

A certain woman came outside at Eyvindarstadir and saw the men fighting. She quickly turned and ran back inside. "Eyvind," she said, "I think that those kinsmen Thorkel and Bjarni are fighting here close to the wall. I saw a man lying under the wall, and he seemed very much afraid."

Eyvind answered, "Let us go as quickly as possible and take clothes with us to throw over the weapons."[2]

Eyvind picked up a pole and, carrying it on his shoulder, he leapt out beyond the wall where the man was lying. This man was Thorvard, who now sprang up greatly alarmed.

---

[1] The battle was supposedly fought at a spot which is still called Vígaflötur, just outside the *tún* at Eyvindarstadir.

[2] Women throw cloth over men's weapons to prevent violence in *Eyrbyggja saga* (Ch. 18) and *Víga-Glúms saga* (Ch. 22).

Ok er spor þeira Þorkels lágu til bœjarins, þá mælti Bjarni, at þeir þrír skyldi ganga jafnframt ok þar eptir aðrir þrír ok síðan inir þriðju þrír, – "ok munu þá sýnask þriggja manna spor," – ok svá gerðu þeir.

Kári var úti, er þeir gengu hjá garði, ok gerði ekki vart við, ok þótti mikill vandi með þeim frændum, ok vildi hann þat ekki til sín taka láta.

Þorkell vaknaði í sæng sinni ok vakði upp fǫrunauta sína ok kvað fullsofit. Nú vápnask þeir ok ganga síðan út.

Þorkell bað þá ganga aptr á ferilinn ok sjá, ef nǫkkur spor lægi af ferlinum, ok sjá þeir liggja þriggja manna spor af í brott. Hann ferr sjálfr til ferilsins ok mælti: "Þungir hafa þessir menn verit," segir Þorkell, "ok ætla ek, at þeir Bjarni muni hér farit hafa, ok hǫldum nú eptir hart."

Ok er þeir kómu nǫkkut svá í brott frá bœnum, sjá þeir, at sporin dreifðusk. Fara þeir nú sem þeir megu mest,[1] unz þeir koma mjǫk svá í ǫndverðan dalinn.[2] Bœr stendr þar lítill, er heitir á Eyvindarstǫðum. Þar bjó sá maðr, er Eyvindr hét.

En er þeir Bjarni áttu skammt til túngarðsins, þá tóku þeir hvíld. Bjarni mælti: "Eigi mun ek renna lengr fyrir Þorkeli, ok skulum vér hér þess bíða, er at hǫndum kemr."[3]

Þegar er Þorkell kemr eptir, mælti hann: "Gǫngum nú at drengiliga. Vit Bjarni, frændrnir, munum á sjásk, en Blængr ok Birningr, Þorvarðr ok Þrǫstr."

Nú teksk bardagi, ok vǫrðusk þeir Bjarni it drengiligasta, ok gekk svá um stund, at menn urðu ekki sárir. Þá mælti Þorkell: "Klækiliga sœkjum vér nú at, er ekki verðr sǫguligt í."[4]

Bjarni svarar: "Œrinn hefir þú hug,"[5] segir hann.

Kona ein gekk út á Eyvindarstǫðum ok sér sameign manna, ok hverfr hon inn aptr skyndiliga ok mælti: "Eyvindr," segir hon, "ek hygg, at þeir frændr muni berjask hér skammt frá garði, Þorkell ok Bjarni, ok ek sá einn mann liggja undir garðinum, ok sýndisk mér sá allhræddr."

Eyvindr svarar: "Fǫrum vér sem skjótast ok hǫfum klæði með oss ok kǫstum á vápnin."

Eyvindr tók upp stokk ok reiðir um ǫxl sér ok hljóp þar út af garðinum, er maðrinn lá undir, ok var þetta Þorvarðr. Hann spratt upp ok varð felmtsfullr.

---

[1] **sem þeir megu mest:** 'as fast as they could'.

[2] **þeir koma mjǫk svá í ǫndverðan dalinn:** 'in this way they come almost to the mouth of the valley'.

[3] **er at hǫndum kemr:** 'whatever may happen/come about'.

[4] **er ekki verðr sǫguligt í:** 'that there will be nothing worthy of a tale in it'.

[5] **œrinn hefir þú hug:** 'You have courage enough'.

But as soon as he came to,[1] men began to fall in the battle. Thorvard had thrown himself down under the fence from exhaustion. Birning fell first, killed by Blaeng.

Then Blaeng struck at Bjarni. The blow fell on Bjarni's neck, and there was a loud crack as the necklace broke apart.[2] Bjarni was wounded slightly, and the whole necklace fell down in the snow. Bjarni reached out for the necklace and put it in his shirt.

Thorkel said, "You are still greedy, kinsman."

Bjarni replied, "The way you are managing things today, there will be need of the money."[3]

Then Thorkel sat down, but Blaeng attacked Bjarni resolutely and in earnest. The end of their fight was that Blaeng fell. Then Thorkel stood up and attacked sharply, but he received a wound on his arm so that he was unable to fight.

Both sons of Gliru-Halli fell there.[4] Eilif also fell before Hallbjorn, but still lived, if it could be called that.[5]

Then Eyvind arrived and charged forward between the men so hard with the beam that they fell back on both sides. There were women with him who threw clothes over the weapons, and the fighting was stopped.

By then four men of Bjarni's company had fallen, and many who survived were wounded. Four of Thorkel's men also fell.

Eyvind asked if Thorkel would permit Bjarni and his men to be carried home. He said he saw that Thorkel and his men would want to take care of themselves. Thorkel did not forbit it.

Afterwards the bodies of the men who had fallen were attended to.

---

[1] **as soon as he came to:** *þegar er hann kom til.* It is not clear to whom this refers. It might be Eyvind, in which case the fighting became more intense 'as soon as he arrived'. Yet Eyvind's arrival is announced clearly a few lines later, making this statement seem superfluous (at least to the eyes of the modern reader). In addition, the fact of Eyvind's arrival does not logically connect with the explanation that immediately follows about Thorvard's lack of participation in the battle. On the other hand, if *hann* (he) refers to Thorvard, then *hann kom til* means that 'he came to' his senses after having fallen down from sheer exhaustion, as stated in the next line. This could also be an example of a scribal error confusing the progression of events.

[2] The same necklace motif occurs in *Heiðarvíga saga* (Chs. 23 and 30). Bardi's nurse binds a necklace of stones about his neck. Later the necklace saves him from a sword blow, and "when the sword struck the stone of the necklace … there was an amazingly loud crack [*brast við furðu hátt*]." See *Hallfreðar saga* (Ch. 7) and *Eyrbyggja saga* (Chs. 44 and 45). See also Walter, *Studien zur Vápnfirðinga saga*, pp. 58–60.

[3] Bjarni is referring to Thorkel's apparent bloodthirstiness, commenting that the money will probably have to be used to pay for subsequent lawsuits and damages for killing.

[4] These men were Berg and Brand, mentioned at the beginning of the chapter. *Land-námabók* reports that Berg and Brand, the sons of Gliru-Halli, died in battle at Bodvarsdal, and *Þórðarbók* adds "by the side of Bjarni Brodd-Helgason, when he fought with Thorkel Geitisson." *Þórðarbók* also states that Egil's sons supported Thorkel in the battle.

[5] In other words, he was barely alive. This may be a play on words with the name *Eilífr*, which means 'ever-living'.

En þegar er hann kom til,[1] tóksk mannfallit í bardaganum, – ok hafði hann[2] kastat sér niðr af mœði undir garðinn. Fell þar fyrstr Birningr fyrir Blængi.

Þá hjó Blængr til Bjarna, ok kom á hálsinn, ok brast við hátt, fyrir því at menit brast í sundr. Bjarni skeindisk, ok allt menit fell niðr í snæinn. Bjarni seildisk eptir meninu ok lét þat í serk sinn.

Þorkell mælti: "Fégjarn ertu enn, frændi."
Bjarni mælti: "Svá muntu um búa í dag, at þurfa mun fjárins."[3]

Þorkell settisk þá niðr, en Blængr sótti at Bjarna allfast í ákafa. Lýkr svá þeira atgangi, at Blængr fellr. Þa stóð Þorkell upp ok sœkir snarpliga, ok fekk hann sár á hendi, svá at hann varð óvígr.

Synir Glíru-Halla fellu þar báðir. Eilífr fell ok fyrir Hallbirni, ok lifði hann þá at kalla.[4]

Þá kom at Eyvindr ok gekk svá hart fram með setstokkinn milli manna, at þeir hrukku hvárutveggju vegna. Konur váru með honum ok kǫstuðu klæðum á vápnin, ok stǫðvaðisk bardaginn.

Þá váru fallnir ór liði Bjarna fjórir menn, en þeir margir sárir, er eptir lifðu. Fjórir fellu af Þorkeli.

Eyvindr spurði, ef Þorkell lofaði at fœra Bjarna til húsa[5] ok hans menn, en kvazk sjá, at Þorkell vildi bjargask á sínar hendr ok hans menn. Þorkell bannaði þat eigi.

Þá var síðan búit um lík þeira manna, er þar fellu.

---

[1] **er hann kom til:** either 'when he [Thorvard] came to' (his senses) or 'when he [Eyvind] arrived'.

[2] That is, Thorvard.

[3] **Svá muntu um búa í dag, at þurfa mun fjárins:** 'You will take care of things in such a way today that there will be need for the money'.

[4] **lifði hann þá at kalla:** 'he was still alive, so to speak', or 'if it could be called that'.

[5] **til húsa** (pl.): 'to home', meaning that Bjarni and his men would be taken to their home.

After that, both sides left. Thorkel and his men went home to Krossavik, and Eyvind escorted Bjarni and his men up Weapon's Fjord until they arrived home at Hof.

Thorvard the Healer came to Hof and bound the men's wounds. Eilif Torfason lay wounded for a long time, yet he eventually recovered.

Bjarni went to meet Halli and told him of the death of his sons. He invited Halli to live with him, and said that he would take the place of his sons for him.[1]

Halli answered, "I consider the death of my sons a great loss, and yet I think it better to lose them than that they should bear the charge of cowardice like some of your companions.[2] I will remain content with my farm and not move to Hof, but you have my great thanks for the invitation to your home."

One day Bjarni said to Thorvard the Healer, "Now our wounds here at Hof have reached the point that we can look after ourselves with your supervision. But I know that Thorkel has a wound and no one is treating him, and he is growing weak. Now I would like you to go and tend to him."

Thorvard said that he would do as Bjarni wished.

Then he left and came to Krossavik at about midday. A board game[3] was in progress, and Thorkel was sitting up and looking at the game. He looked very pale. No one greeted Thorvard.

Thorvard went to Thorkel and said, "I want to see your wound. I am told bad things about it." Thorkel told him to do as he wished.

Thorvard was there seven nights, and the farmer Thorkel improved day by day. Then Thorvard left Krossavik, and Thorkel rewarded him well for his healing. He gave him a horse and a silver ring, and afterwards spoke friendly words to him.

After this Thorvard went to Hof and told Bjarni how matters stood. Bjarni thought things had turned out well, since Thorkel had recovered.

CHAPTER 18 VOCABULARY

allfast *adv* very firmly, steadfastly
allhræddr <-hrædd, -hrætt> *adj* very much afraid
annask <-að-> *refl vb* take care of; provide for

atgangr *m* fighting
ákafi *m* vehemence, fierceness, eagerness; **í ákafa** in earnest
átján *num* eighteen

---

[1] Compare the *Saga of Thorstein the White* (*Þorsteins saga hvíta*), Ch. 7: "But I will consider us reconciled on the condition that you move here to Hof as my helper with everything you own." See also the *Tale of Thorstein Staff-struck* (*Þorsteins þáttr stangarhǫggs*), Ch.6, where Bjarni, pretending he has killed Thorstein in combat, offers old Thorarin, Thorstein's father, a place at Hof: "I wish to invite you to Hof. You shall sit in the second seat of honor as long as you live, and I will be in place of a son to you." Thorarin replies, "It has turned out for me the same as for those who have control over nothing. Only a foolish man takes delight in promises. And the promises of you chieftains, when you wish to comfort a man after events like this, are such that the relief lasts for a month. But after that our value is like any other pauper's, and our sorrows are slowly forgotten."

[2] Referring to Thorvard.

[3] **a board game:** *tafl*. Though frequently translated as 'chess', *tafl* is really a generic word for to a variety of games that used a board, pieces, and/or dice. It often denoted the game of *hnefatafl* 'king's table', the rules of which are unknown. Checkerboards, peg boards, and playing pieces have been found in numerous Norse graves and settlements.

Eptir þat sneru á brottu hvárutveggju. Fóru þeir Þorkell heim til Krossavíkr ok hans menn, en Eyvindr flutti þá Bjarna inn eptir Vápnafirði, ok kómu þeir heim til Hofs.

Þorvarðr læknir kom til Hofs ok batt sár manna. Eilífr Torfason lá í sárum lengi ok varð þó grœddr.

Bjarni fór þegar á fund Halla ok sagði honum fall sona sinna ok bauð honum til sín ok kvazk skyldu vera honum í sona stað.[1]

Halli svarar: "Mikill skaði þykki mér at sonum mínum, en þó þykki mér betra at missa þeira en þat þeir[2] bæri bleyðiorð sem sumir fǫrunautar þínir. En ek mun enn hlíta búm mínum ok fara ekki til Hofs, en haf þú mikla þǫkk fyrir heimboðit."

Þat var einn dag, at Bjarni mælti við Þorvarð lækni: "Nú er svá komit sárum várum hér at Hofi, at vér munum verða sjálfbjargi með umsjá þinni, en ek veit, at Þorkell hefir sár, ok grœðir hann engi, ok gerisk hann máttlítill. Nú vil ek, at þú farir at lækna hann."

Þorvarðr segisk svá mundu gera sem hann vill.

Hann ferr nú ok kemr í Krossavík nær miðjum degi, ok er tafl uppi,[3] ok sat Þorkell uppi ok horfði á taflit. Hann var mjǫk fǫlleitr. Engi maðr heilsaði Þorvarði.

Hann gekk at Þorkeli ok mælti: "Sjá vil ek sár þitt. Mér er órífligt sagt frá því." Hann bað hann gera sem hann vildi.

Var hann þar sjau nætr, ok batnaði bónda dag frá degi. Nú ferr Þorvarðr í brott ór Krossavík, ok launaði Þorkell honum vel lækning sína, gaf honum hest ok silfrhring ok mælti síðan við hann vingjarnligum orðum.

Ferr hann nú síðan ok kemr til Hofs ok segir Bjarna til svá búins. Ok þótti honum vel hafa um ráðizk, er Þorkell varð heill.

---

banna <-að-> *vb* ban, forbid, prohibit
bardagi *m* battle
batna <-að-> *vb* improve; *impers* [*dat subj*] improve, get or feel better
batt *3sg past of* **binda**
bera <berr; bar, báru; borinn> *vb* carry, bear; bear, have, hold (a title)
Bergr <-s> *m* Berg (*personal name*)
binda <bindr; batt, bundu; bundinn> *vb* bind, tie; bind up (a wound, etc.)
bjarga <bergr; barg, burgu; borginn> *vb* [*w dat*] help, save; *refl* **bjargask** help, save oneself; **bjargask á sínar hendr** support oneself with one's own hands, take care of oneself

bjóða <býðr; bauð, buðu; boðinn> *vb* [*w acc*] offer; [*w dat*] invite; order, command; **bjóða [e-m] um** delegate to [sb], commit to [sb's] charge
bleyðiorð *n* charge of cowardice
Brandr <-s> *m* Brand (*personal name*)
brast *1/3sg past of* **bresta**
bresta <brestr; brast, brustu; brostinn> *vb* break; make a breaking sound
Brúni *m* Bruni (*personal name*)
bú <*pl dat* búm> *n* home, house, household; farm; estate
búa <býr; bjó, bjoggu~bjuggu; búinn> *vb* prepare, make ready; **búa svá um, at** arrange it so that; **búa um [e-n]** attend to,

---

[1] **kvazk skyldu vera honum í sona stað**: 'he said that he would take the place of his sons for him'. *Skyldu*, preterite infinitive of *skulu*; see footnote 4, page 41.

[2] *Þat* here is an object pronoun standing in apposition to the clause [*at*] *þeir bæri bleyðiorð* which follows. Exceptionally, the *at* of the clause seems to have merged with *þat*.

[3] **er tafl uppi**: 'a board game is in progress'.

take care of [sth]

Búastaðir *m pl* Buastadir ('Bui's Farm-stead') (*place name*)

búm *dat pl of* **bú**

bæri *3sg/pl past subjunct of* **bera**

bœjar *gen sg of* **bœr**

bœr <*gen* bœjar, *pl* bœir> *m* farm, farm-house, farmstead

Boðvarsdalr <*dat* -dal, *gen* -dals> *m* Bod-varsdal ('Bodvar's Valley') (*place name*)

dagr <*dat* degi, *gen* dags; *pl* dagar> *m* day; **dag frá degi** from day to day

dalr <*dat* dal, *gen* dals; *pl* dalar~dalir> *m* valley, dale

dreifa <-ð-> *vb* [*w dat*] scatter, disperse; *refl* **dreifask** spread out

drengiliga *adv* bravely, nobly

drengiligr *adj* brave, valiant; **it drengi-ligasta** in the most valiant fashion

Eilífr <-s> *m* Eilif ('Ever-Living') (*personal name*)

Eyvindarstaðir *m pl* Eyvindarstadir ('Eyvind's Farmstead') (*place name*)

fall <foll> *n* fall, death in battle

falla <fellr; fell, fellu; fallinn> *vb* fall

fellu *3pl past of* **falla**

felmtsfullr *adj* alarmed, frightened

ferill <*dat* ferli> *m* track, trace

fimmtán *num* fifteen

fjórir <fjórar, fjogur; *acc m* fjóra, *dat* fjórum, *gen* fjogurra> *num* four

flytja <flutt-> *vb* guide, escort

Freygerðr <*acc/dat* Freygerði, *gen* Frey-gerðar> *f* Freygerd (*personal name*)

fullsofit *n ppart* having slept enough (*from* full- 'fully' *and* sofa 'sleep')

fœrð *f* condition of a road or path

folleitr *adj* pale-looking

foruneyti *n* company of travelers, retinue

Glíru-Halli *m* Gliru-Halli (*personal name*)

Gróa *f* Groa (*personal name*)

grœða <-dd-> *vb* heal

halda <heldr; hélt, héldu; haldinn> *vb* [*w dat*] hold; **halda eptir [e-m]** pursue [sb]

Halli *m* Halli (*personal name*)

harðr <horð, hart> *adj* hard

hart *n adj as adv* hard; fast

Haukr <-s> *m* Hauk ('Hawk') (*personal name*)

háls <háls; hálsar> *m* neck

hár <há, hátt; *acc m* hávan; *pl dat* hávum> *adj* high, tall, long; loud

hátt *n adj as adv* loudly

heimferð <-ir> *f* homeward journey

hlíta <-tt-> *vb* [*w dat*] be content with

horfa <-ð-> *vb* (turn so as to) look upon, behold

hrukku *3pl past of* **hrokkva**

hrokkva <hrokkr; hrokk, hrukku; hrokkinn> *vb* fall back, be repelled

hugr <-ar; -ir> *m* courage, spirit

hvíld *f* rest, repose

hoggva <hoggr; hjó, hjoggu; hogg(v)inn> *vb* strike (a blow), chop, hack, hew; **hoggva til [e-s]** strike a blow at [sb]

hond <*acc* hond, *dat* hendi, *gen* handar; *pl* hendr, *dat* hondum, *gen* handa> *f* hand; arm and hand, arm; **koma at hondum** happen, come about

jafnframt *adv* side by side

kalla <-að-> *vb* call; **at kalla** so to speak, in a manner of speaking

kasta <-að-> *vb* [*w dat*] throw

Kári *m* Kari (*personal name*)

klækiliga *adv* in a cowardly fashion

koma <kemr~komr; kom, kómu~kvámu; kominn> *vb* come; **koma at hondum** happen, come about; **koma eptir** follow

kœmi *3sg/pl past subjunct of* **koma**

laun *n pl* reward, recompense

launa <-að-> *vb* [*w dat*] reward; **launa [e-m] [e-u]** reward [sb] with [sth]; **launa [e-m] [e-t]** reward [sb] for [sth]

liggja <liggr; lá, lágu; leginn> *vb* lie (down); go, lead (*of a trail*); **liggja í sárum** lie ill from one's wounds

lofa <-að-> *vb* allow, permit

Loptr <-s> *m* Lopt (*personal name*)

lægi *3sg/pl past subjunct of* **liggja**

lækna <-að-> *vb* cure, heal

lækning *f* cure; medicine, art of healing

mannfall *n* casualties (in battle)

máttlítill <-lítil, -lítit> *adj* weak, faint, feeble, exhausted

men <*pl dat* menjum, *gen* menja> *n* neck-lace

mest *superl adv* most (*see* **mjok**)

missa <-t-> *vb* [*w gen*] be without; lose, suffer loss of

mjok <*comp* meir(r), *superl* mest> *adv* much

mæla <-t-> *vb* speak; **mæla [e-u] við [e-n]** say [sth] to [sb]

mœði *f* weariness, exhaustion

órífligr *adj* bad, unfavorable

óvígr *adj* unable to fight

rammliga *adv* strongly

ráða <ræðr; réð, réðu; ráðinn> *vb* [*w dat*] advise, counsel; rule, govern, manage; undertake; *refl* **ráðask** undertake; be resolved, settled; turn out; **ráðask vel** turn out or end well

ráðizk *n ppart of* **ráðask**

reiða <-dd-> *vb* carry

saman *adv* together; [*w numbers*] all together, all told

sameign *f* conflict, fight

sár *n* wound; **liggja í sárum** lie ill from one's wounds

sárr *adj* wounded

seilask <-d-> *refl vb* stretch out one's hands; **seilask eptir [e-u]** to reach out for [sth]

serkr <-s~jar; -ir, *pl gen* -ja> *m* shirt

setja <-tt-> *vb* set, seat, place; *refl* **setjask** set onself; seat oneself, sit; **setjask niðr** sit down, set oneself down

setstokkr <-s; -ar> *m* partition-beam, post

silfrhringr <-s; -ar> *m* silver ring

sjálfbjargi *adj indecl* self-sufficient

sjá <sér; sá, sá(u); sénn> *vb* see, look; *refl* **sjásk** see one another; **sjásk á** see to, deal with one another

skaði *m* loss

skammr <skǫmm, skam(m)t> *adj* short

skammt *n adj as adv* a short distance, not far; **eiga skammt til** have a short distance to go until, be not far from

skeina <-d-> *vb* scratch, wound slightly; *refl* **skeinask** get a slight wound

skjótast *superl adv* most swiftly (*see* **skjótt**)

skjótr *adj* swift, quick

skjótt *n adj as adv* swiftly, quickly; soon

skulu <skal, skulu; skyldi; *pret inf* skyldu> *pret-pres vb* shall (*obligation, purpose, necessity, fate*)

skyldu *pret inf of* **skulu**

snarpliga *adv* sharply, with a dash

sneru *3pl past of* **snúa**

snúa <snýr; snøri~sneri; snúinn> *vb* turn, go

snær (*also* **snjór**) <*gen* snævar~snæfar> *m* snow

sótti *3sg past of* **sœkja**

spratt *1/3sg past of* **spretta**

spretta <sprettr; spratt, spruttu; sprottinn> *vb* start, spring; **spretta upp** spring up

stokkr <-s; -ar> *m* pole, log of wood

stund <*dat* -u> *f* a while, a time; **um stund** for a while

stǫðva <-að-> *vb* stop; *refl* **stǫðvask** stop oneself, calm down; be stopped

sœkja <sótt-> *vb* pursue; attack; **sœkja at** attack

sǫguligr <-lig, -ligt> *adj* important, worth telling

tafl <tǫfl> *n* a board game

taka <tekr; tók, tóku; tekinn> *vb* take; **taka til** concern; **láta [e-t] til sín taka** let [sth] concern oneself, involve oneself in [sth], meddle with [sth]; *refl* **takask** begin

teksk *2/3sg pres of* **takask**

Torfastaðir *m pl* Torfastadir ('Torfi's Farmstead') (*place name*)

Torfi *m* Torfi (*personal name*)

vandi *m* difficulty, difficult task, problem

vápna <-að-> *vb* furnish with arms; *refl* **vápnask** arm oneself

vegna *prep* [*w gen*] on account of, on behalf of; **hvárutveggja vegna** on both sides

verja <varð-, *ppart* var(i)ðr~varinn> *vb* defend; *refl* **verjask** defend onself

vingjarnligr *adj* friendly, kind

Víðivellir *m pl* Vidivellir ('Willow Fields') (*place name*)

vǫrðr <*dat* verði, *gen* varðar; *pl* verðir, *acc* vǫrðu> *m* watch, guard; **halda vǫrð** keep watch

vǫrðusk *3pl past of* **verjask**

þriggja *gen of* **þrír**

þrír <þrjár, þrjú; *acc m* þrjá, *dat* þrim(r), *gen* þriggja> *num* three

ǫndverðr *adj* fronting, in front of (*place*)

ǫxl <*gen* axlar; *pl* axlir> *f* shoulder

19. JORUNN, THORKEL'S WIFE, DEMANDS PEACE AND THE COUSINS SETTLE THEIR FEUD

That summer there was little haying done because Thorkel was hardly fit to manage the farm at Krossavik,[1] and matters looked so unpromising that the livestock was going to have to be slaughtered or killed off. Jorunn was his wife by that time.[2]

One of Thorkel's farmhands had to take a trip up into the district. He lodged overnight at Hof and was welcomed warmly. Bjarni asked him about the health of the people and the condition of the livestock.

The farmhand replied, "Things are coming along with people's health." But about the livestock, he said it was becoming utterly hopeless.

In the morning, when the farmhand was leaving, Bjarni saw him out of the yard and said, "Offer Thorkel the choice of either moving his household here, or I will send meat and fodder[3] there, so that he does not need to be concerned about loss of livestock. Now, be sure to convey the message."[4]

Then the farmhand left and arrived home just as men had sat down at the table and Jorunn was bringing the food out. He went to Thorkel and told him everything Bjarni had said. Jorunn halted on the floor, listening to what he said. Thorkel answered nothing.

Jorunn said, "Why do you remain silent about something that was so generously offered?"

Thorkel replied, "I will not give a hasty answer to this matter, because this generous offer would take most men by surprise."

Jorunn said, "I would like the two of us to go to Hof tomorrow and meet Bjarni. I think such an offer is very honorable from a man such as he is."

"You shall have your way," said Thorkel, "because I have often found that you are both wise and kind."

---

[1] This passage gives insight into the economic and social status of the Icelandic *goði*. Unlike a chieftain in a fully stratified society who could rely on his rank to co-opt the labor and produce of commoners, a *goði*'s status was much more fragile and depended heavily on his personal capabilities and his involvement in the day-to-day running of his own farmstead. His political concerns, especially in the organization of *þingmenn* into a coherent interest group, were part-time activities, taking place only after subsistence requirements had been met.

[2] Jorunn, Thorkel's wife, is mentioned here for the first time in the saga, without introduction. She was the daughter of Einar of Thverá. Their marriage is mentioned in *Vǫðu-Brands þáttr* (Ch. 4).

[3] Hay was vital to support livestock through the long Icelandic winters.

[4] Literally, 'now be a good messenger' (*vertu nú góðr ørendsreki*).

19. Kapítuli

Summary of Chapter 19. Bjarni hears that Thorkel is doing poorly with his farm and offers him provisions. Thorkel is initially reluctant to accept the offer, but at his wife's insistence, he meets Bjarni to discuss it. The two men come to terms, and a lasting settlement is established, ending the feud.

Sumar þetta var lítit forverk, því at Þorkell var lítt fœrr til umsýslu í Krossavík – Jórunn var þá húsfreyja hans –, ok horfðisk til óvænliga,[1] at skera myndi verða kvikfé niðr eða drepa.[2]

Húskarl Þorkels átti fǫr upp í herað. Tók hann gisting at Hofi. Var þar vel við honum tekit. Bjarni spurði hann um heilsun manna ok um búfjárhagi.

Húskarlinn mælti: "Vel þokar áleiðis um heilsun manna,"[3] – en um búfjárhagi kallaði hann gerask it óvænligasta.[4]

En um morguninn, er húskarlinn fór í brott, leiddi Bjarni hann ór garði ok mælti: "Bið þú Þorkel annathvárt flytja hingat hjú sín elligar mun ek þangat flytja slátr ok fjárfœði, svá at eigi þurfi at um huga fjárlát, ok vertu nú góðr ørendsreki."

Húskarlinn ferr nú ok kemr svá heim, at menn váru undir borð komnir, ok bar Jórunn mat fram. Hann gekk fyrir Þorkel ok segir honum ǫll orð Bjarna. Jórunn nam staðar á gólfinu ok hlýddi á, hvat hann mælti. Þorkell svarar engu.

Jórunn mælti: "Hví muntu þegja við því, er svá er drengiliga boðit?"

Þorkell svarar: "Eigi mun ek bráð svǫr veita þessu máli, því at kostaboð þessi munu flestum mǫnnum á óvart koma."

Jórunn mælti: "Þat vilda ek, at vit fœrim til Hofs á morgun ok hittim Bjarna, ok þykki mér þvílík boð allsœmilig af þvílíkum manni, sem hann er."

"Þú skalt ráða," segir Þorkell, "því at ek hefi opt reynt, at þú ert bæði vitr ok góðgjǫrn."

---

[1] **horfðisk til óvænliga:** 'matters looked so unpromising'.

[2] **at skera myndi verða kvikfé niðr eða drepa:** 'that the livestock should be slaughtered or killed'. The words *eða drepa* are perhaps redundant, since *skera niðr* and *drepa niðr* have the same meaning. This may have been an idiom, or it could be a scribal infelicity.

[3] **Vel þokar áleiðis um heilsun manna:** 'Things are coming along/improving with people's health'.

[4] **kallaði hann gerask it óvænligasta:** 'he said it was becoming utterly hopeless'.

The following morning, Thorkel and Jorunn set out with ten others. When their arrival was seen from Hof, Bjarni was told. He was pleased as soon as he heard it and went to meet them. He welcomed Thorkel.

And when these kinsmen talked with each other, they went over all their lawsuits thoroughly and earnestly. Afterwards Bjarni offered Thorkel a settlement and self-judgment,[1] and said he would let him have his will in all things from then on, as long as they both lived. Thorkel accepted this offer and they then agreed on a full settlement. Thorkel assessed a hundred pieces of silver for Geitir's killing,[2] and each of them granted the other pardon. They kept their truce faithfully afterward.

Bjarni was a man of courage. The people of Hof have not been men of great wisdom, and yet things have mostly gone well for them.

Thorkel was a great chieftain, the most valiant of men, and an important legal advocate. His money ran out in his old age, and when he gave up his farm, Bjarni invited him to live at Hof. There he grew old and stayed to the end of his life.

Thorkel was a man blessed with notable descendants. His daughter Ragnheid was married to Lopt Thorarinsson, and they had nine children. Their daughter was Halla, the mother of Steini, the mother of Halla, the mother of Bishop Thorlak the Holy.[3] Bishop Thorlak's sister was Ragnheid, the mother of Bishop Pal, Orm Jonsson, and the priest Jon Arnthorsson.[4]

CHAPTER 19 VOCABULARY

allsœmiligr adj very honorable

annathvárt adv either

Arnþórr <-s> m Arnthor (*personal name*)

áleiðis adv onward, forward; on the right path; **þoka áleiðis** improve

boð n bid, offer

borð n table; **koma undir borð** sit down at a table

bregða <bregðr; brá, brugðu; brugðinn> vb [w dat] break off, leave off, give up; **bregða búi** give up one's farm

búfjárhagr m condition of the livestock

byskup <-s; -ar> m bishop

drengiliga adv generously, nobly

drepa <drepr; drap, drápu; drepinn> vb kill, smite; strike, beat, knock; **drepa niðr** (= **skera niðr**) strike down; slaughter

eiga <á, eigu; átti; áttr> pret-pres vb own, have, possess; **eiga tal með sér** have a talk with each other, hold a discussion

einarðliga adv earnestly, firmly; **vel ok einarðliga** well and earnestly

eldask <-d-> refl vb grow old

elli f indecl old age

fara <ferr; fór, fóru; farinn> vb go, travel

fjárfœði n fodder

fjárlát n loss of money or livestock

flestr <flest, flest> superl adj most (*see* **margr**)

forverk n haying, hireling's work

fœrim 1pl past subjunct of **fara**

fœrr adj able, capable; **fœrr til [e-s]** capable of [sth]

ganga <gengr; gekk, gengu; genginn> vb walk; go; **ganga af** leave, depart from

gera <-ð-; ppart gerðr~gerr> vb make, build; do, act; (*leg*) set the amount of a fine; **gera vilja [e-s]** let [sb] have his/her will

---

[1] **self-judgment:** See footnote 1, page 114. Bjarni's offer is essentially the same as he initially offered when Thorkel first returned to Iceland following Geitir's killing.

[2] Thorkel chooses the same sum that Geitir paid Bjarni after the death of Helgi (Ch. 14).

[3] Although not officially declared a saint by the Church in Rome until 1984, Thorlak the Holy, Bishop of Skalholt (d. 1193), was regarded as a saint in Iceland around 1200.

[4] Pal and Orm were Ragnheid Thorhallsdottir's sons by her first husband, Jon Loftsson from Oddi. Her third son Jon was fathered by Arnthor the Norwegian.

Um morguninn eptir fara þau Þorkell heiman tólf saman, ok er fǫr þeira var sén frá Hofi, þá var sagt Bjarna. Því varð hann feginn, er hann spurði þat nú þegar, ok gekk í móti þeim ok kvaddi Þorkel vel.

Ok er þeir áttu tal með sér frændr, þá rippuðu þeir upp ǫll málaferli þeira vel ok einarðliga. Bauð Bjarni síðan Þorkeli sætt ok sjálfdœmi ok hans vilja at gera um alla hluti þaðan í frá, meðan þeir lifði báðir. Þorkell þekkðisk þessi boð, ok sættusk þeir nú heilum sáttum,[1] ok gerði hann hundrað silfrs fyrir víg Geitis, ok seldi hvárr ǫðrum grið, ok heldu vel síðan.[2]

Bjarni var rǫskr maðr. Ekki hafa Hofverjar verit spekingar miklir, en þó hefir þeim flest vel tekizk.

Þorkell var hǫfðingi mikill ok inn mesti hreystimaðr ok málafylgismaðr mikill. Fé gekk af hǫndum honum[3] í elli hans, ok er hann brá búi sínu, bauð Bjarni honum til Hofs, ok eldisk hann þar til lykða.

Þorkell var kynsæll maðr. Ragnheiði, dóttur hans, átti Loptr Þórarinsson, ok áttu þau níu bǫrn. Halla var dóttir þeira, móðir Steina, fǫður Hǫllu, móður Þorláks byskups ins helga. Ragnheiðr var systir Þorláks byskups, móðir Páls byskups ok Orms Jónssonar ok Jóns prests Arnþórssonar.

góðgjarn <-gjǫrn, -gjarnt> *adj* benevolent, kind
gólf *n* floor
grið *n pl* peace, pardon, truce; **halda grið** keep a truce; **selja grið** grant pardon
heilagr <heilǫg, heilagt; *acc m* helgan> *adj* holy
heill *adj* whole, complete
heilsan (*also* **heilsun**) *f* greeting; health
heilsun *var of* **heilsan**
helgi *wk m nom sg of* **heilagr**
hjú *n* household
hlýða <-dd-> *vb* [*w dat*] listen; **hlýða á [e-t]** listen to [sth]
horfa <-ð-> *vb* turn (in a certain direction); (turn so as to) look upon, behold; look (a certain way), have a certain appearance; *refl* **horfask** look, appear; **horfask til** look like, look as if
hreystimaðr *m* valiant man, man of valor
huga <-að-> *vb* mind; **huga um [e-t]** be concerned about [sth]

húsfreyja *f* housewife, lady
Jón <-s> *m* Jon (*personal name*)
kalla <-að-> *vb* say
kostaboð *n* favorable or generous offer
kvikfé *n* livestock, cattle
kynsæll *adj* blessed with notable descendants
lykð *var of* **lykt**
lykt (*also* **lykð**) <-ir> *f* (*usu in pl*) end, conclusion; **til lykta** until the end
margr <mǫrg, mar(g)t; *comp* fleiri, *superl* flestr> *adj* [*w sg*] many a (*in collective sense*); [*w pl*] many
matr <-ar; -ir> *m* food
málaferli *n pl* lawsuits, litigation
málafylgismaðr *m* lawyer, active participant in lawsuits
morginn (also **morgunn**) <*gen* morgins, *pl* mor(g)nar> *m* morning; **á morgun** tomorrow
móðir <*acc/dat/gen* móður; *pl* mœðr, *dat* mœðrum, *gen* mœðra> *f* mother

---

[1] **sættusk þeir nú heilum sáttum:** 'now they agreed on a full settlement'.

[2] **seldi hvárr ǫðrum grið, ok heldu:** 'each granted the other pardon and kept their truce'. *Grið* can mean both 'pardon' and 'peace' or 'truce', yielding the expressions *selja grið* 'grant pardon', and *halda grið* 'keep a truce'. Here both expressions are combined.

[3] **Fé gekk af hǫndum honum:** 'Wealth slipped through his fingers', i.e., his money ran out.

nam *1/3sg past of* **nema**

nema <nemr; nam, námu; numinn> *vb* take; **nema staðar** stop, halt

Ormr <-s> *m* Orm ('Snake') (*personal name*)

óvænliga *adv* unpromisingly, hopelessly

óvænligr *adj* unpromising, hopeless; **it óvænligasta** most unpromising

Páll <-s> *m* Pal (*personal name*)

prestr <-s; -ar> *m* priest

Ragnheiðr <*acc/dat* Ragnheiði, *gen* Ragnheiðar> *f* Ragnheid (*personal name*)

ráða <ræðr; réð, réðu; ráðinn> *vb* [*w dat*] decide, determine

reyna <-d-> *vb* experience, find out (from experience)

rippa <-að-> *vb* go over, sum up; **rippa [e-t] upp** go over [sth], sum [sth] up

rǫskr <*acc m* -van> *adj* vigorous, brave

sén *ppart of* **sjá**

sjá <sér; sá, sá(u); sénn> *vb* see

skera <skerr; skar, skáru; skorinn> *vb* cut; slaughter; **skera niðr** (= **drepa niðr**) cut down; slaughter

Steini *m* Steini (*personal name*)

sætta <-tt-> *vb* reconcile; make peace among; *refl* **sættask** come to terms, agree, be reconciled

taka <tekr; tók, tóku; tekinn> *vb* take; *refl* **takask** begin, happen; succeed; **[e-m] teksk vel** *impers* it goes well for [sb], [sb] succeeds

vili <*gen* vilja> *m* will, wish, desire; **gera vilja [e-s]** let [sb] have his/her will

vilja *acc/dat/gen sg of* **vili**

þaðan *adv* from there, thence; **þaðan í frá** from that time forward, from then on

þegja <þagð-, *n ppart* þagat> *vb* be silent

þekkja <-ð~t-> *vb* perceive, notice; comprehend; know, recognize; *refl* **þekkjask** agree with, accept, consent to

þoka <-að-> *vb* [*w dat*] go, move; **þoka áleiðis** improve

Þorlákr <-s> *m* Thorlak (*personal name*); **Þorlákr inn helgi** *m* Thorlak the Holy, Saint Thorlak

ørendsreki *m* messenger

CULTURE SECTION – WOMEN AND FEUD

In times of dispute and feud, Icelandic women were influential in forming the private consensus that underlay group decisions. Within the family, the importance of such influence, as in the cases of Thorgerd Silver or Jorunn, was considerable.

Earlier in the saga, in Ch. 14, Thorgerd Silver alters the course of her family's destiny. As a woman, she has been excluded from the legal process of settlement for her husband's death. Bjarni, the new head of the household, settles the conflict following Brodd-Helgi's killing. Afterwards Bjarni continues to maintain a strong friendship with his father's killer, his uncle Geitir, despite part of his father's compensation remaining unpaid. Bjarni's handling of the case affronts Thorgerd Silver, prompting her to act.

In Thorgerd's eyes, Bjarni's settlement has satisfied neither the demands of justice nor her need for retribution. She passionately defends her and her family's honor by seeking blood vengeance. Taking matters into her own hands, Thorgerd publicly shames Bjarni, humiliating Brodd-Helgi's son with the father's blood-stained cloak. Her action calls into question Bjarni's honor and causes him to act. Barred from a public role, Thorgerd Silver demonstrates that women still had the power to change the course of events.

The sagas contain numerous examples of women who incite their men to violence, but there are also examples of women who act as peacemakers. The feud of *Vápnfirðinga saga* is resolved in this chapter after Jorunn, Thorkel's wife, forcefully expresses her wishes. At the time of Jorunn's intervention, Thorkel's honor is at low ebb. He has been publicly humiliated by the utter failure of his springtime ambush. The attack brought about the deaths of several of Thorkel's own supporters, and the slow healing of his wounds keeps him from the summer farm work. Winter is coming and Thorkel is facing disaster. He has not put in a store of hay for his livestock, and he will be forced to kill off his precious cattle and sheep. With this loss, his wealth and status will drop.

Having learned of Thorkel's problems, Bjarni makes an unexpected offer of assistance, but the motive behind it can be interpreted in various ways. Either it is humiliating to the point of calculated mockery, or it is nobly generous. Thorkel hesitates. Perhaps his sense of honor, driven by shame, will not let him accept. His wife Jorunn sees the matter differently and steps in. Neither inciting nor passive, Jorunn is portrayed as an engaged participant in the decision-making process that leads to peace. Bjarni's messenger talks to Thorkel, the man of the house, but the woman of the house acts on her right to intervene and in so doing decides the outcome.

VOCABULARY
FROM *VÁPNFIRÐINGA SAGA*

ORDER OF THE ALPHABET

The alphabetical order of the vocabulary is: **a, á, b, d/ð, e, é, f, g, h, i, í, j, k, l, m, n, o, ó, p, r, s, t, u, ú, v, y, ý, x, z, þ, æ, œ, ǫ/ø.** Long vowels with accent are listed after the corresponding short vowels without accent (**a**, then **á**). At the end of the alphabet, **æ** and **œ** are listed separately while **ǫ** and **ø** are listed together.

WORD FREQUENCY

The symbol ❖ marks the 260 most common words in the sagas. These comprise the 50+ most common nouns, adjectives, and verbs, as well as the most common adverbs, prepositions, pronouns, conjunctions, and numerals.

NOTES ON THE VOCABULARY

STRONG NOUNS. The principal declension classes are indicated by the following conventions:

Masculine. The genitive singular and nominative plural endings are given. For example, **heimr** <-s; -ar> *m* world. **vinr** <-ar; -ir> *m* friend.

Feminine. The nominative plural ending is given. For example, **ferð** <-ir> *f* journey, trip; **reið** <-ar> *f* ride, the act of riding.

Neuter. The nominative/accusative plural is shown when there is vowel alternation. For example, **barn** <bǫrn> *n* child.

ADJECTIVES. The strong feminine and neuter nominative singular forms are provided. For example, **fagr** <fǫgr, fagrt> *adj* fair, beautiful; **feginn** <-in, -it> *adj* glad, happy, pleased; **góðr** <góð, gott> *adj* good; **sterkr** <sterk, sterkt> *adj* strong. In addition, the strong masculine accusative singular is given where necessary to indicate a stem-final -*j*- or -*v*- or syncope (loss of vowel). For example, **ríkr** <rík, ríkt; *acc m* -jan> *adj* powerful; **rǫskr** <rǫsk, rǫskt; *acc m* -van> *adj* vigorous, brave; **gǫfugr** <-ug, -ugt; *acc m* gǫfgan> *adj* noble, distinguished.

STRONG VERBS. The principal parts are given: 3sg pres; 3sg past, 3pl past; past participle. For example, **fara** <ferr; fór, fóru; farinn> *vb* go, travel.

WEAK VERBS. The notation -*að*- indicates a weak verb with the vocalic link -*a*-. For example, **kalla** <-að-> *vb* call (past *kallaði* 'called'). For weak verbs without vocalic link, the dental suffix alone is given (-*t*-, -*d*-, or -*ð*-). For example, **mæla** <-t-> *vb* speak (past *mælti* 'spoke'). When a past tense dental is added to a verb whose stem already ends in a dental, the two dentals often assimilate. In such instances, the vocabulary indicates the outcome. For example, **leiða** <-dd-> *vb* lead; **setja** <-tt-> *vb* set; **senda** <-nd-> *vb* send (past *leiddi* 'led', *setti* 'set', *sendi* 'sent'). Where the past-tense stem differs from that of the present, the vocabulary

provides the full stem. For example, **spyrja** <spurð-> *vb* ask (past ***spurði*** 'asked').
PRETERITE-PRESENT VERBS: The principal parts are given: 3sg pres, 3pl pres; 3sg past; past participle. For example, **eiga** <á, eigu; átti; áttr> *pret-pres vb* own, have, possess; **vita** <veit, vitu; vissi; vitaðr> *pret-pres vb* know.

PHRASES AND IDIOMS: Verbs and prepositions take their objects in various cases, depending on sometimes unpredictable usage. This vocabulary adopts the Icelandic convention of using the pronoun *einnhverr/eitthvat* 'somebody/some-thing' to indicate the object cases used in particular phrases. The notation is also useful for distinguishing whether the object is a person or thing.

[e-n] (einhvern) = [sb] (somebody), accusative
[e-t] (eitthvat) = [sth] (something), accusative
[e-m] (einhverjum) = (for) [sb], dative
[e-u] (einhverju) = (for) [sth], dative
[e-s] (einhvers) = (of) [sb] or [sth], genitive

Examples:
fala [e-t] af [e-m] offer to buy [sth] from [sb]
firra [e-n] [e-u] deprive [sb] of [sth]
mæla [e-t] við [e-n] say [sth] to [sb]
segja [e-m] frá [e-m] tell, inform [sb] about [sb]
segja [e-m] til [e-s] tell, inform [sb] where [sth/sb] is to be found

ABBREVIATIONS

1dual, 2dual	1st person dual, etc.		something' (*gen*)
1pl, 2pl, 3pl	1st person plural, etc.	*e-t*	*eitthvat* 'something' (*acc*)
1sg, 2sg, 3sg	1st person singular, etc.	*e-u*	*einhverju* 'for something'
acc	accusative		(*dat*)
adj	adjective	*encl*	enclitic
adv	adverb	*Eng*	English
art	article (*def*)	*esp*	especially
aux	auxiliary (*vb*)	*etc*	et cetera
coll	collectively	*f*	feminine
comp	comparative (*adj* or *adv*)	*f.ex.*	for example
conj	conjunction	*fig*	figurative
cpd	compound	*freq*	frequently
dat	dative	*gen*	genitive
def	definite (*art*)	*impers*	impersonal (*vb*)
defect	defective	*indecl*	indeclinable
dem	demonstrative (*pron*)	*indef*	indefinite (*pron*)
e-m	*einhverjum* 'for somebody' (*dat*)	*indic*	indicative
		inf	infinitive
e-n	*einhvern* 'somebody' (*acc*)	*interrog*	interrogative (*adv* or *pron*)
e-s	*einhvers* 'of somebody or	*intrans*	intransitive (*vb*)

leg	legal usage
lit	literally
m	masculine
MI	Modern Icelandic
n	neuter
neg	negative
neg suff	negative suffix
nom	nominative
num	number
obj	object
OE	Old English
OI	Old Icelandic
ON	Old Norse
ord	ordinal (*num*)
part	particle
perh	perhaps
pers	personal
pl	plural
poss	possessive (*pron*)
ppart	past participle
pref	prefix
prep	preposition
pres	present
pres part	present participle
pret-pres	preterite-present (*vb*)
pron	pronoun
refl	reflexive (*vb* or *pron*)
rel	relative (*pron* or *particle*)
sb	somebody
sg	singular
sth	something
str	strong (*adj* or *vb*)
subj	subject
subjunct	subjunctive
suff	suffix
superl	superlative (*adj* or *adv*)
trans	transitive (*verb*)
transl	translation
usu	usually
var	variant
vb	verb
w	with
wk	weak (*adj* or *vb*)
=	equals
~	alternative form
❖	256 most common words in sagas

A

aðra *f acc sg & m acc pl of* **annarr**

aðrir *m nom pl of* **annarr**

❖ **af** *prep* [*w dat*] of, by; off (of), out of, from; *adv* off, away

afar *adv* very

afarkaldr <-kǫld, -kalt> *adj* very cold

afbragð <-brǫgð> *n* outstanding example, paragon; **afbragð þeira manna allra** the most outstanding of all those men

afbrigði *n* deviation, transgression, offense

afl *n* physical strength, might, power; **rammr at afli** extremely strong

aflafár <-fá, -fátt> *adj* short of strength; [**e-m**] **verðr aflafátt** *impers* [sb] is short of support (or supporters)

afréttr *m* common pasture (in the mountains or wilderness)

albúa <albýr; albjó, albjoggu; albúinn> *vb* fit out, furnish or equip fully

albúinn *ppart* fully equipped (*see* **albúa**)

aldr <-rs, -rar> *m* age; **ungr at aldri** young, 'young in age'

❖ **aldri** *adv* never

aldri *dat sg of* **aldr**

allfast *adv* very firmly, steadfastly

allfár <-fá, -fátt> *adj* very few

allhjaldrjúgr <-drjúg, -drjúgt> *adj* very talkative; [**e-m**] **verðr allhjaldrjúgt** *impers* [sb] talks at very great length

allhræddr <-hrædd, -hrætt> *adj* very much afraid

❖ **allr** <ǫll, allt> *adj* all, entire, whole; *indef pron* all, everyone; **allt** *n* everything; **at ǫllu** in all respects, in every way; **með allt sitt** with all one's possessions; **með ǫllu** wholly, completely

allsíð *adv* very late

allsterkligr <-lig, -ligt> *adj* very strong-looking

allsœmiligr <-lig, -ligt> *adj* very honorable

allt *n adj as adv* all, entirely, altogether, completely; **allt saman** wholly, entirely,

altogether
alþingi *n* national assembly
alþýða *f* all the people, the majority of the people, the public, the common people
anda <-að-> *vb* breathe; *refl* **andask** die, breathe one's last
andaðr *ppart* dead (*see* **anda**)
andviðri *n* headwind
angr <*gen* -rs> *m* sorrow, grief
angrsamr <-sǫm, -samt> *adj* sorowful, anguished
❖ **annarr** <ǫnnur, annat; *acc m* annan, *f* aðra, *dat m* ǫðrum, *n* ǫðru; *pl* aðrir, etc.> *adj/indef pron* other, another; one of two; *ord* second; **annarr ... annarr** one ... the other; **annan dag eptir** the following day; **í annat sinn** the second time
annask <-að-> *refl vb* take care of; provide for
annathvárt *adv* either
aptann <*dat* aptni, *gen* aptans; *pl* aptnar> *m* evening
❖ **aptr** *adv* back
arfsal *n* (*leg*) transfer of one's right of inheritance; **seljask arfsali** (*leg*) cede one's right of inheritance
armr <ǫrm, armt> *adj* vile, wretched, wicked
Arnfinnr <-s> *m* Arnfinn (*personal name*)
Arnþórr <-s> *m* Arnthor (*personal name*)
at *prep* [*w dat*] at, in; as to, with respect to; on account of, by reason of; close up to, around, by
❖ **at** *conj* that
at *inf marker* to
atburðr <-ar; -ir> *m* occurrence, event; **af þessum atburði** because of this incident; **verðr sá atburðr** it so happened
atgangr *m* fighting
atgørvi *f & n* ability, talent, accomplishment; **at atgørvi** in ability (*esp* physical)
athǫfn <athafnir> *f* business, work
atsókn <-ir> *f* onslaught, attack
attú = **at þú** that you (*sg*)
❖ **auðigr** (*older* **auðugr**) <-ig, -igt; *acc m* auðgan> *adj* rich, wealthy; **auðigr at fé** very wealthy, 'rich in wealth'
auðr *m* wealth; **hafa auð fjár** to be very wealthy, have an abundance of wealth
auðsóttr <-sótt, -sótt> *adj* easily won, easy to win
auðsýnn <-sýn, -sýnt> *adj* clear, evident
auðugr *var of* **auðigr**
auga <*pl gen* augna> *n* eye
augsýn *f* sight
auka <eykr; jók, jóku; aukinn> *vb* increase, augment; [*w dat*] add; exceed, surpass; **auka [e-u] við** add [sth]
Austmaðr <*acc* -mann, *dat* -manni, etc.> *m* Easterner, person from the east (*esp* a Norwegian)

Á

❖ **á** *prep* [*w acc*] onto, on, towards (*motion*); with respect to; [*w dat*] on; upon; at; in (*location*)
á <*gen* ár; *pl* ár, *dat* ám, *gen* á> *f* river
á *1/3sg pres of* **eiga**
❖ **áðr** *adv* before; **áðr en** *conj* before
ágætavel *adv* excellently
❖ **ágætr** <ágæt, ágætt> *adj* excellent
ákafi *m* vehemence, fierceness, eagerness; **í ákafa** vehemently, eagerly, fiercely
ákveða <ákveðr; ákvað, ákváðu; ákveðinn> *vb* fix, decide, appoint
áleiðis *adv* onward, forward; on the right path; **þoka áleiðis** improve
ár *gen sg & nom/acc pl of* **á**
Ásbjǫrn <*gen* Ásbjarnar> *m* Asbjorn (*personal name*)
ástmaðr <*pl* -menn> *m* dear friend
Ásvaldr <-s> *m* Asvald (*personal name*)
átján *num* eighteen
átt *ppart of* **eiga**
átta *num* eight
áttan *m acc sg ppart of* **eiga**
átti *3sg past of* **eiga**
áttu *3pl past of* **eiga**
ávallt *adv* always
áverki *m* bodily injury, bloody wound

B

bað *1/3sg past of* **biðja**

❖ **bak** <bǫk> *n* back; horseback; **koma á bak** mount on horseback; **stíga af baki** dismount (from a horse); **stíga á bak** mount (a horse)

bak *prep* [*w dat*] back, behind

bakki *m* bank (of a river or chasm), slope

Bakki *m* Bakki ('Bank' or 'Slope') (*place name, esp a nickname for a place name ending with* -bakki)

banahǫgg *n* death-blow

banamaðr <*acc* -mann, *dat* -manni, etc.> *m* killer, slayer

bani *m* death; that which causes death, 'bane'; **fá bana** die; **til bana** to death; **verða [e-m] at bana** kill [sb]

banna <-að-> *vb* ban, forbid, prohibit

bar *1/3sg past of* **bera**

bardagi *m* battle

barði *3sg past of* **berja**

barn <bǫrn> *n* child

barnœska *f* childhood

batna <-að-> *vb* improve; *impers* [*dat subj*] improve, get or feel better

batt *3sg past of* **binda**

bauð *1/3sg past of* **bjóða**

bauzk *2/3sg past of* **bjóðask**

❖ **báðir** <báðar, bæði, *gen* beggja> *adj/ indef dual pron* both

báru *3pl past of* **bera**

bátr <-s; -ar> *m* boat

beggja *gen of* **báðir**

beið *1/3sg past of* **bíða**

beini *m* hospitality

beinlitr *m* the color of bone

beiting <-ar> *f* grazing, pasturage

belja <-að-> *vb* bellow

❖ **bera** <berr; bar, báru; borinn> *vb* carry, bear; have, hold (a title); *impers* [*acc subj*] be born or carried (*denoting passive or involuntary motion*); befall, happen; **bera fyrir [e-n]** *impers* appear to [sb] (*of a dream or vision*); **bera lægra hlut ór** get the worst of it; **bera ofan á [e-t]** place [sth] on top; **bera [e-n] ofríki** overcome [sb] by sheer force; **bera ráð saman** take counsel among themselves; consult to-

gether; **bera vápn á [e-n]** raise weapons against [sb]; **bera ørendi sín (upp) fyrir [e-n]** plead one's case before [sb], tell one's errand to [sb]

Bergr <-s> *m* Berg (*personal name*)

berja <barð-; *ppart* bar(i)ðr > *vb* strike; *refl* **berjask** fight

berr <ber, bert> *adj* bare, open, clear, manifest; **gera sik beran** to show openly, reveal oneself

betr *comp adv* better (*see* **vel**)

betri *comp adj* better (*see* **góðr**)

beztr *superl adj* best (*see* **góðr**)

❖ **biðja** <biðr; bað, báðu; beðinn> *vb* ask, beg; command, tell ([sb] to do [sth]); **biðja [e-n] [e-s]** ask [sb] for [sth]; *refl* **biðjask** request for oneself; **biðjask ór búi** request separation from the household

binda <bindr; batt, bundu; bundinn> *vb* bind, tie, fasten; bind up (a wound, etc.); pledge; **binda í [e-u]** bind to [sth], bind on [sth]; **binda vinfengi** pledge friendship

Birningr <-s> *m* Birning (*personal name*)

bíða <bíðr; beið, biðu; beðinn> *vb* wait; [*w gen*] wait for

bjarga <bergr; barg, burgu; borginn> *vb* [*w dat*] help, save; *refl* **bjargask** help, save oneself; **bjargask á sínar hendr** support oneself with one's own hands, take care of oneself

Bjarni *m* Bjarni (*personal name*); **Herlu-Bjarni** *m* Herlu-Bjarni ('Hood-Bjarni')

bjó *1/3sg past of* **búa**

❖ **bjóða** <býðr; bauð, buðu; boðinn> *vb* [*w acc*] offer; [*w dat*] invite; order, command; **bjóða [e-m] [e-t]** offer [sb] [sth]; **bjóða [e-m] at vera** invite [sb] to stay; **bjóða [e-t] fram** offer, proffer, produce [sth]; **bjóða mál** (*leg*) appeal a case; **bjóða [e-m] til sín** invite [sb] to one's house; **bjóða [e-m] til vistar** to invite [sb] to stay at one's house; **bjóða [e-m] um** delegate to [sb], commit to [sb's] charge; *refl* **bjóðask** offer oneself, volunteer one's service

bjórþili *n* partition, dividing wall (*perh of*

animal skin)

bjósk *1/3sg past of* **búask**

bjǫrg <*gen* bjargar; *pl* bjargir> *f* means of subsistence, store of food

bleikr <bleik, bleikt> *adj* fawn-colored (*of animals*), pale

bleyðiorð *n* charge of cowardice

blíða *f* friendliness

blóð *n* blood

Blængr <-s> *m* Blaeng (*personal name*)

boð *n* bid, offer; bidding, command, order; invitation (*as to a feast*); feast

boða <-að-> *vb* [*w dat*] order

boðit *ppart of* **bjóða**

boløx <*acc/dat* -i, *gen* -ar; *pl* -ar> *f* pole-axe, wood-axe

borð *n* table; **koma undir borð** sit down at a table

borinn *ppart of* **bera**

❖ bóndi <*pl* bœndr, *dat* bóndum~bœndum, *gen* bónda~bœnda> *m* farmer; husband; head of a household

Brandr <-s> *m* Brand (*personal name*)

brast *1/3sg past of* **bresta**

braut (*var of* **brott**) *adv* away

braut *1/3sg past of* **brjóta**

brautargengi *n* (*leg*) help, furtherance

brá *1/3sg past of* **bregða**

bráðgǫrr <-gǫr, -gǫrt> *adj* matured early in life, precocious

bráðla *var of* **bráðliga**

bráðliga (*also* **bráðla**) *adv* soon, quickly

bráðr <bráð, brátt> *adj* sudden, quick; hasty, rash

brátt *n adj as adv* soon, shortly

bregða <bregðr; brá, brugðu; brugðinn> *vb* [*w dat*] move quickly; draw, brandish (a weapon); break (faith or an oath); turn, alter, change; break off, leave off, give up; **bregða búi** give up one's household; **bregða tali** break off speaking; **bregða við [e-u]** ward off with, parry with [sth]; *refl* **bregðask** fail, come to nothing; **bregðask [e-m]** deceive, disappoint [sb]

bresta <brestr; brast, brustu; brostinn> *vb* break; make a breaking sound

brjóst *n* chest, breast

brjóta <brýtr; braut, brutu; brotinn> *vb* break; **brjóta saman** fold (clothes)

Brodd-Helgi *m* Brodd-Helgi ('Spike-Helgi') (*personal name*)

broddr <-s; -ar> *m* spike

brotna *f acc sg ppart of* **brjóta**

❖ brott (*also* **braut, á brott, í brott, í brottu**) *adv* away, off; **brott búinn** ready to start, prepared to depart

brottbúningr *m* preparation for departure

brottu *var of* **brott**

❖ bróðir <*acc/dat/gen* bróður; *pl* brœðr, *dat* brœðrum, *gen* brœðra> *m* brother

brugðizk *ppart of* **bregðask**

Brúni *m* Bruni (*personal name*)

brœðr *nom/acc pl of* **bróðir**

brœðra *gen pl of* **bróðir**

brœkr *f pl* breeches

bundit *ppart of* **binda**

❖ bú <*pl dat* búm> *n* home, house, household; farm; estate

❖ búa <býr; bjó, bjoggu~bjuggu; búinn> *vb* live (in a place), dwell; prepare, make ready; **búa svá um, at ...** arrange it so that ...; **búa [e-t] til [e-s]** to prepare [sth] for [sth]; **búa um [e-n]** attend to, take care of [sth]; **búa undir [e-u]** be the (hidden) reason behind [sth], be at the bottom of [sth]; *refl* **búask** make oneself ready, equip oneself

Búastaðir *m pl* Buastadir ('Bui's Farmstead') (*place name*)

búð <-ir> *f* tent, booth

búfjárhagr *m* condition of the livestock

búit *ppart* ready, set; finished, done (*see* **búa**); **er svá búit** it was thus set, matters so stood; **við svá búit** with matters thus, with that

búm *dat pl of* **bú**

búnu *n dat sg ppart of* **búa**; **at svá búnu** as matters stand, in the present state of things

bústaðr <-ar; -ir> *m* farmstead, household

byggja <-ð-> *vb* inhabit

byrr <-jar; -ir> *m* fair wind; **[e-m] gefr vel byr** *impers* [sb] gets a fair wind

byskup <-s; -ar> *m* bishop

býðr *2/3sg pres of* **bjóða**

❖ bæði *adv* both; **bæði ... enda** *conj* both ... and also, and indeed; **bæði ... ok** *conj* both ... and

bæði *n of* **báðir**

bændr *MI var of* **bœndr**

bæri *3sg/pl past subjunct of* **bera**

bœjar *gen sg of* **bœr**

bœndr *nom/acc pl of* **bóndi**

❖ bœr <*gen* bœjar, *pl* bœir> *m* farm, farmhouse, farmstead

Bǫðvarsdalr <*dat* -dal, *gen* -dals> *m* Bod-varsdal ('Bodvar's Valley') (*place name*)

bǫrn *nom/acc pl of* **barn**

D

daglangt *adv* through the day

❖ **dagr** <*dat* degi, *gen* dags; *pl* dagar> *m* day; **dag frá degi** from day to day; **einn-hvern dag** one day; **í dag** today; **um daginn eptir** (on) the day after, the next day

dalr <*dat* dal, *gen* dals; *pl* dalar~dalir> *m* valley, dale

dasa <-að-> *vb* exhaust

❖ **dauðr** <dauð, dautt> *adj* dead

deila <-d-> *vb* divide; quarrel; **deila um [e-t]** quarrel over [sth], take up a lawsuit over [sth]

digr <digr, digrt> *adj* big, stout

dofinn <-in, -it> *adj* dead, numb (*of a limb*)

dómr <-s; -ar> *m* (*leg*) court, court of judgment

❖ **dóttir** <*acc/dat/gen* dóttur; *pl* dœtr, *dat* dœtrum, *gen* dœtra> *f* daughter

draga <dregr; dró, drógu; dreginn> *vb* drag, draw; **dregr at [e-u]** *impers* [sth] draws near; **dregr saman með þeim** *impers* they draw together, come close; **draga saman lið** collect troops

draumr <-s; -ar> *m* dream

dráp *n* slaying, killing

dreggjar *f pl* dregs, dust

dregit *ppart of* **draga**

dregr *2/3sg pres of* **draga**

dreifa <-ð-> *vb* [*w dat*] scatter, disperse; *refl* **dreifask** spread out

drengiliga *adv* bravely; nobly

drengiligr <-lig, -ligt> *adj* brave, valiant; **it**

drengiligasta in the most valiant fashion

drengr <-s; -ir, *pl gen* drengja> *m* courageous person; **góðr drengr** honest and courageous person

drengskapr <*gen* -ar> *m* courage, honesty

❖ **drepa** <drepr; drap, drápu; drepinn> *vb* kill, smite; strike, beat, knock; **drepa niðr** (= **skera niðr**) strike down; slaughter

dreyma <-ð~d-> *vb* [*acc sub and obj*] dream; **[e-n] dreymr [e-t]** *impers* [sb] dreams [sth]

drifit *ppart of* **drífa**; **blóði drifit** covered with blood

drífa *f* snowstorm

drífa <drífr; dreif, drifu; drifinn> *vb* drive (*of wind, snow, etc.*), shower

Droplaugarsynir *m pl* the sons of Droplaug

dró *1/3sg past of* **draga**

drógu *3pl past of* **draga**

drýgja <-ð-> *vb* accomplish, commit, perpetrate

duga <-ð-, *n ppart* dugat> *vb* do, show prowess; **duga verr** come off badly, do worse (in a contest)

dul *f* self-conceit, arrogance

durum *dat pl of* **dyrr**

dvelja <dvalð~dvald-; *ppart* dvalðr~ dvaldr~dvalinn> *vb* stay, dwell; delay; *refl* **dveljask** linger, stay, be delayed

dvǫlðusk *3pl past of* **dveljask**

dyrr <*pl dat* durum, *gen* dura> *f pl* door, doorway

E

❖ **eða** *conj* or

❖ **ef** *conj* if

efri *comp adj* upper, higher; **fara it efra** travel the higher or inland route

Egill <*dat* Agli, *gen* Egils> *m* Egil (*personal name*)

Egilsstaðir *m pl* Egilsstadir ('Egil's Farm-stead') (*place name*)

❖ **eiga** <á, eigu; átti; áttr> *pret-pres vb* own, have, possess; be married or related to; be the one represented by something; [*aux*] must, owe, be obligated, have to; **eiga ferð** have some errand; **eiga mál við [e-n]** speak, converse with [sb]; **eiga tal**

með sér have a talk with each other

❖ **eigi** *adv* not

eigu *3pl pres of* **eiga**

Eilífr <-s> *m* Eilif ('Ever-Living') (*personal name*)

einarðliga *adv* earnestly, firmly; **vel ok einarðliga** well and earnestly

einkis *gen of* **engi**

einmánaðr *m* the last month of winter (from mid-March to mid-April)

❖ **einn** <ein, eitt> *num* one; *adj/indef pron* a, an, a certain one; *adj* (*following the noun it modifies*) alone, only, mere

❖ **einnhverr** *adj/indef pron* some, someone, a certain one; (*usu as two words*, **einn hverr**) each, each one; **einnhvern dag** one day

Eiríkr <-s> *m* Eirik (*personal name*)

❖ **ek** <*acc* mik, *dat* mér, *gen* mín> *pron 1sg*

ekki *n nom/acc sg of* **engi**

❖ **ekki** *n adj as adv* not

ekkja *f* widow

eldask <-d-> *refl vb* grow old

eldskáli *m* 'fire hall', main hall of a long house, where benches used for sitting and sleeping were warmed by a long fire that ran the length of the hall and was used for cooking

eldhús *n* 'fire house' (= **eldaskáli**)

elding *f* last part of the night before dawn, starting about 3 a.m., *lit* 'fire-lighting'

eldr <-s; -ar> *m* fire

elli *f indecl* old age

elligar *adv* otherwise, else

ellri *comp adj* older, elder (*see* **gamall**)

em *1sg pres of* **vera**

❖ **en** *conj* but; and (on the other hand);

[*w comp*] than

❖ **enda** *conj* and (etc.); and if; even; even if; and also, and so; and yet

endi <-is; -ar> *m* end

❖ **engi** <engi, ekki> *adj/indef pron* no one, none, no

engr *adj* no, not any (*var of* **engi**)

❖ **enn** *adv* yet, still; yet again

enni *n* forehead

❖ **eptir** *prep* [*w acc*] after (*time*); [*w dat*] after, along; according to; *adv* after, afterwards; **standa eptir** *or* **vera eptir** stay back, remain behind; **eptir þetta** after that, afterward

eptirmál *n* prosecution after a slaying

❖ **er** *rel particle* who, which, that; *conj* when; where; as

er *1/3sg pres of* **vera**

erfingi <*pl* erfingjar> *m* heir

ert *2sg pres of* **vera**

ertu = **ert þú** are you (*sg*) (*see* **vera**)

eru *3pl pres of* **vera**

eyða <-dd-> *vb* waste; spend; do away with, destroy; make empty; (*leg*) render void, annul; **eyða mál** nullify a lawsuit; *refl* **eyðask** be squandered, come to naught

Eyvindará *f* Eyvindará ('Eyvind's River') (*place name*)

Eyvindarstaðir *m pl* Eyvindarstadir ('Eyvind's Farmstead') (*place name*)

Eyvindr <-ar> *m* Eyvind (*personal name*)

eyzlumaðr *m* **a** wasteful person; wasteful farmer, one who consumes more than he produces [*eyzlumaðr mikill*]

É

élligr <-lig, -ligt> *adj* threatening to storm

F

❖ **faðir** <*acc* fǫður, *dat* fǫður~feðr, *gen* fǫður; *pl* feðr, *dat* feðrum, *gen* feðra> *m* father

❖ **fagr** <fǫgr, fagrt; *comp* fagrari~fegri,

superl fagrastr~fegrstr> *adj* fair, fine, beautiful

Fagradalr <*dat* -dal, *gen* -dals> *m* Fagradal ('Fair Dale' or 'Beautiful Valley') (*place* *name*)

fala <-að-> *vb* demand for purchase; **fala [e-t] af [e-m]** offer to buy [sth] from [sb]

fall <fǫll> *n* fall, death in battle

❖ **falla** <fellr; fell, fellu; fallinn> *vb* fall; fail, be foiled; **falla niðr** fall, drop, be forgotten; (*leg*) be dropped; **láta [e-t] falla ofan** let [sth] fall down, drop [sth]

fang <fǫng> *n* grasp, grip, hold; wrestling; **fá fang á [e-m]** to get hold of [sb]

fangstaðr <*gen* -ar> *m* something to grasp or lay hold of; **fá fangstað á [e-m]** to catch hold of [sb]

fann *1/3sg past of* **finna**

fannsk *1/3sg past of* **finnask**

❖ **fara** <ferr; fór, fóru; farinn> *vb* go, travel; move; **fara at** go, proceed; **fara eptir [e-m]** send for [sb]; **fara fram** go on, take place; **fara frá** leave, back off, back away; **fara í engan mun** amount to no importance; **fara í millum landa** travel from one land to another (i.e., trade); **[e-m] er illa farit** *impers* [sb] has an ill disposition, is acting unworthily

fardagar *m pl* Moving-Days (i.e., four successive days in spring, at the end of May, in which householders in Iceland changed their abode)

farit *ppart* gone; of a certain disposition (*see* **fara**); **[e-m] er illa farit** *impers* [sb] has an ill disposition, is acting unworthily

fastna <-að-> *vb* pledge, betroth

fastr <fǫst, fast> *adj* firm, fast

❖ **fá** <fær; fekk, fengu; fenginn> *vb* get, take, procure; grasp; [*usu w gen*] marry; **fá á [e-u]/[e-m]** get hold of, grasp [sth]/[sb]; **fá bana** die; *refl* **fásk** get (for) oneself; **fá(sk) fang á [e-m]** get hold of [sb]

fálátr <-lát, -látt> *adj* silent, reserved

fáliga *adv* coldly

fám *m dat sg & all dat pl of* **fár**

fámálugr <-ug, -ugt> *adj* silent, tight-lipped

❖ **fár** <fá, fátt; *acc m* fán, *f* fá, *dat m* fám, *n* fá; *pl nom/acc f* fár, *n* fá, *acc m* fá, etc.; *comp* fær(r)i, *superl* fæstr> *adj/indef pron* few; *adj* cold, reserved

Fáskrúðsbakki *m* Faskrudsbakki ('Faskrud's Bank') (*place name*)

❖ **feginn** <-in, -it> *adj* glad, happy, pleased

feigr <feig, feigt> *adj* death-bound, fated to die; **vilja [e-n] feigan** wish for [sb's] death, want [sb] dead

feitr <feit, feitt> *adj* fat

fekk *1/3sg past of* **fá**

fell *1/3sg past of* **falla**

fellr *2/3 pres of* **falla**

fellu *3pl past of* **falla**

felmtsfullr <-full, -fullt> *adj* alarmed, frightened

fengi *3sg/pl past subjunct of* **fá**

fengit *ppart of* **fá**

❖ **ferð** <-ir> *f* journey, trip; **eiga ferð** have some errand; **fara ferð** make a journey, take a trip

ferill <*dat* ferli, *gen* ferils; *pl* ferlar> *m* track, trace

ferr *2/3sg pres of* **fara**

fest *ppart of* **festa**

festa <-t-> *vb* fasten

❖ **fé** <*gen* fjár; *pl gen* fjá> *n* cattle, sheep; wealth, money

fégjarn <-gjǫrn, -gjarnt> *adj* greedy, avaricious

félagi *m* partner, comrade, companion, friend, 'fellow'

félauss <-laus, -laust> *adj* penniless

félítill <-lítil, -lítit; *acc m* -litlan> *adj* short of money, poor

fémætr <-mæt, -mætt> *adj* valuable

fénaðr <*gen* -ar> *m* sheep, cattle, livestock

féþurfi *adj indecl* in need of money

❖ **fimm** *num* five

fimmtán *num* fifteen

❖ **finna** <finnr; fann, fundu; fundinn> *vb* find; notice, perceive; *refl* **finnask** meet one another; *impers* [*dat subj*] be found, be perceived, noticed (by one)

firra <-ð-> *vb* deprive; **firra [e-n] [e-u]** deprive [sb] of [sth]

fífilbleikr <-bleik, -bleikt> *adj* dandelion-yellow (*only of horses*)

fjalhǫgg *n* chopping-block

fjall <fjǫll> *n* mountain

fjallganga <*acc/dat/gen* -gǫngu> *f* trip into the mountains (to gather sheep from the highland pastures)

fjár *gen sg of* **fé**

fjárfœði *n* fodder

fjárhlutr <-ar; -ir> *m* property, valuables

fjárlát *n* loss of money or livestock

fjárstaðr <-ar; -ir> *m* investment

❖ **fjórir** <fjórar, fjǫgur; *acc m* fjóra, *dat* fjórum, *gen* fjǫgurra> *num* four

fjǫlkunnugr <-ug, -ugt> *adj* well-known, renowned; (*usu*) skilled in magic

fjǫlmenna <-t-> *vb* assemble a following

fjǫlmennari *comp adj* with more men (*see* **fjǫlmennr**)

fjǫlmenni *n* many people, a crowd

❖ **fjǫlmennr** <-menn, -mennt> *adj* numerous, with many people, well-attended

fjǫrðr <*dat* firði, *gen* fjarðar; *pl* firðir, *acc* fjǫrðu> *m* fjord

flakka <-að-> *vb* roam, wander about (*as a shepherd with sheep*)

fleiri *comp adj* more (*see* **margr**)

flestr <flest, flest> *superl adj* most (*see* **margr**)

Fljótsdalr <*dat* -dal, *gen* -dals> *m* Fljotsdal ('River Dale') (*place name*)

Fljótsdalsherað *n* the Fljotsdal district (*place name*)

flokkr <-s; -ar> *m* group, company, party, 'flock'

flutt *ppart of* **flytja**

fluttu *3pl past of* **flytja**

flytja <flutt-> *vb* convey, move, carry; bring, deliver; guide, escort; **flytja bústað sinn** move one's farm, change one's dwelling-place

flærð *f* deceit, false pretenses

forað <foruð~forǫð> *n* dangerous place; precipice; pit

forða <-að-> *vb* [*w dat*] save; **forða sér** save oneself, escape danger

foringi <*gen* -ja; *pl* -jar> *m* leader

forverk *n* haying, hireling's work

forvista *f* leadership, management, authority

forvitna <-að-> *vb* pry into, inquire about; *refl* **forvitnask** inquire, find out; be curious about

fór *1/3sg past of* **fara**

fórt *2sg past of* **fara**

fóru *3pl past of* **fara**

fóstr <*gen* fóstrs> *n* fostering of a child; **vera at fóstri** be a foster-child, be in a fostering relationship

fóstra *f* foster-mother/daughter/sister

fóstri *m* foster-father/son/brother

❖ **fótr** <*dat* fœti, *gen* fótar; *pl* fœtr, *acc* fœtr> *m* foot, foot and leg

❖ **fram** *adv* forward, outward; **koma máli fram** (*leg*) prosecute (a case); **fram hjá** [*w dat*] out by, out beside; **fram um** *or* **um**

fram [*w vb of motion*] on past, up beyond, out over; **um fram** in addition

framar *comp adv* further, more (*see* **fram**); **enn framar** still further, once more

framvíss <-vís, -víst> *adj* prescient, prophetic, foresighted

❖ **frá** *prep* [*w dat*] from; about; *adv* away; **þaðan frá** from that point onward

frásǫgn <*gen* -sagnar; *pl* -sagnir> *f* story, narrative, account

fremst *superl adv* foremost, most, greatest (*see* **fram**)

frest *n pl* delay; **selja á frest** sell on credit

Freygerðr <*acc/dat* Freygerði, *gen* Freygerðar> *f* Freygerd (*personal name*)

frétta <-tt-> *vb* hear, find out about

❖ **frændi** <*pl* frændr> *m* kinsman

full- *pref* fully, quite, enough

❖ **fullr** <full, fullt> *adj* full

fullsofit *ppart* having slept enough (*see* **full-**, **sofa**)

❖ **fundr** <-ar; -ir> *m* meeting; **fara á fund [e-s]** go see, meet [sb]; **fara til fundar við [e-n]** go see, meet with [sb]

fundu *3pl past of* **finna**

fundusk *3pl past of* **finnask**

❖ **fyrir** *prep* [*w acc or dat*] before, in front of; along, against; before, preceding, ago; above, superior to; for, on behalf of; for, because of; by, by means of; [*w acc only*] in spite of, against; [*w dat only*] at the head of (leading); **fyrir innan** [*w acc*] inside; **fyrir neðan** [*w acc*] below; **fyrir ofan** [*w acc*] above; **fyrir útan** [*w acc*] outside; out beyond; **fyrir** *adv* ahead, in front, before; first, before; at hand, present; **vera þar fyrir** be there present; **fyrir því at** *conj* because

fyrirmaðr <*acc* -mann, *dat* -manni, etc.> *m* leader, man in charge; *pl* men of distinction

fyrirmunr <-ar; -ir> *m* most important point of distinction; **at fyrirmun** most importantly

fyrirsǫgn <*gen* -sagnar; *pl* -sagnir> *f* instruction

❖ **fyrr** *comp adv* before, previously, sooner; **fyrr en** *conj* before, sooner than, until

❖ **fyrri** *comp adj* former, previous; *comp adv* (= **fyrr**) before, previously, sooner

fyrst *superl adv* first (*see* **fyrr**)

fyrsta *wk f of* **fyrstr; í fyrstu** in the beginning, at first

❖ **fyrstr** <fyrst, fyrst> *superl adj* first (*see* **fyrri**)

fýsa <-t-> *vb* urge

fækka <-að-> *vb* make few, reduce in number; *refl* **fækkask** grow cold, unfriendly

fær *2/3sg pres of* **fá**

fæsk *1/3sg of* **fásk**

fæstir *nom m pl superl of adj* **fár**

fœða <-dd-> *vb* feed; rear, bring up; **fœða upp** bring up; *refl* **fœðask** grow up, be brought up; be born; feed oneself, be fed; **fœðask upp** grow up, be brought up

fœra <-ð-> *vb* bring, present, convey, send, give; **fœra [e-m] [e-t]** bring [sb] [sth]

fœrð *f* condition of a road or path

fœri *3sg/pl past subjunct of* **fara**

fœrim *1pl past subjunct of* **fara**

fœrr <fœr, fœrt> *adj* able, capable; **fœrr til [e-s]** capable of [sth]

fǫðursystir <*acc/dat/gen* -systur; *pl* -systr> *f* aunt, father's sister

fǫlleitr <-leit, -leitt> *adj* pale-looking

fǫr <*gen* farar; *pl* farar~farir> *f* journey, trip

fǫrunautr <-s; -ar> *m* traveling companion, fellow-traveler

fǫruneyti *n* company of travelers, retinue

G

gaf *1/3sg past of* **gefa**

galt *1/3sg past of* **gjalda**

❖ **gamall** <gǫmul, gamalt; *acc m* gamlan; *comp* ellri~eldri, *superl* ellztr~elztr~ ellstr~eldstr> *adj* old

gaman <*dat* gamni> *n* fun, amusement

ganga <*acc/dat/gen* gǫngu; *pl nom/acc* gǫngur, *dat* gǫngum, *gen* gangna> *f* walking, going; **hallr í gǫngu** stooped, walking with a stoop

❖ **ganga** <gengr; gekk, gengu; genginn> *vb* walk; go; **ganga af** leave, depart from; **ganga [e-m] betr** go better for [sb]; **ganga inn** to go indoors; **ganga í millum** intercede; **[e-m] gengr [e-t] til [e-s]** *impers* [sth] is [sb's] reason for [sth]; **ganga undan [e-m]** leave, withdraw support from [sb]; **ganga upp** go up, ascend

garðr <-s; -ar> *m* enclosed space, yard; fence, wall; **í garði [e-s]** in [sb's] keeping, hands

garpr <-s; -ar> *m* a bold, daring, courageous, or warlike man or woman

gaumr *m* heed, attention, *only in the phrase* **gefa gaum at [e-u]** give heed to [sth]

gaupnir *f pl* both hands cupped together; **sjá í gaupnir sér** cover one's face with the palms

gáfu *3pl past of* **gefa**

❖ **gefa** <gefr; gaf, gáfu; gefinn> *vb* give, grant; **gefa [e-m] [e-t]** give [sb] [sth]; **gefa upp** give up, leave off; *refl* **gefask** happen, turn out, come to pass; **gefask vel [e-m]** prove good, turn out well for [sb]

gegnum (*also* **í gegnum**) *adv* through

Geitir <-is> *m* Geitir (*personal name*)

gekk *1/3sg past of* **ganga**

geldfé *n* castrated sheep, goats, or cattle

geldingr <-s; -ar> *m* wether, gelded sheep

geldr *2/3sg pres of* **gjalda**

gengit *ppart of* **ganga**

gengr *2/3sg pres of* **ganga**

gengu *3pl past of* **ganga**

❖ **gera** <-ð-; *ppart* gerðr~gerr> *vb* make, build; do, act; (*leg*) set the amount of a fine; **gera af** accomplish, do; **gera ... at** do ...; **gera hríð** attack, 'do battle'; **gera [e-n] sekan** (*leg*) condemn [sb] to outlawry, make [sb] an outlaw; **gera um** (*leg*) judge, arbitrate in a case; **gera vilja [e-s]** let [sb] have his/her will; *refl* **gerask** become, grow; occur, happen

gerr <ger, gert> *adj & ppart* skilled, accomplished; ready, willing; done (*see* **gera**)

gersemi *f* costly thing, jewel, treasure; **auðugr at gersemum** rich in treasures; **fjǫlkunnugr at gersemum** well-known for one's riches

gert *ppart of* **gera**

gestbeinliga *adv* hospitably

gestr <-s; -ir> *m* guest

❖ **geta** <getr; gat, gátu; getinn> *vb* get; [*w gen*] guess, reckon, expect; speak of, mention; **þess er getit** it is told; [*w ppart of another vb*] be able to

geyma <-d-> *vb* keep, store

ginna <-t-> *vb* dupe, fool; **ginna [e-n] at sér** fall out with [sb]

gipta <-t-> *vb* give away in marriage

gista <-t-> *vb* spend the night; **gista at [e-s]** spend the night at [sb's] (place)

gisting *f* lodging for the night; **at gisting** stay overnight

gjalda <geldr; galt, guldu; goldinn> *vb* pay

gjarna *adv* willingly, rather

Glíru-Halli *m* Gliru-Halli (*personal name*)

gluggr <-s; -ar> *m* opening, hole; window

gløggþekkinn <-in, -it> *adj* perceptive

goldit *ppart of* **gjalda**

góðgjarn <-gjǫrn, -gjarnt> *adj* benevolent, kind

❖ **góðr** <góð, gott; *comp* betri, *superl* beztr> *adj* good

gólf *n* floor

graðungr <-s; -ar> *m* bull

gráta <grætr; grét, grétu; grátinn> *vb* cry, weep; [*w acc*] weep for

greiða <-dd-> *vb* pay; **greiða af hǫndum** pay out, discharge, turn over

greiðr <greið, greitt> *adj* clear, unencumbered, free from obstacles

grein <-ar~ir> *f* branch, division; point, particular

greina <-d-> *vb* divide; *impers* [*acc subj*] fall out, disagree

grét *1/3sg past of* **gráta**

grið *n pl* peace, pardon; **halda grið** keep a truce; **selja grið** grant pardon, truce

gripr <-ar; -ir> *m* costly thing; property, possession

Grímr <-s> *m* Grim (*personal name*)

Gróa *f* Groa (*personal name*)

grunr <-ar; -ir> *m* suspicion, uncertainty, doubt; **[e-m] er grunr á [e-u]** [sb] has doubts, is suspicious about [sth]

grœða <-dd-> *vb* heal

grǫf <*gen* grafar; *pl* grafir~grafar> *f* grave

Guðdalir *m pl* Guddalir ('God Valleys') (*place name*)

Guðmundarstaðir *m pl* Gudmundarstadir ('Gudmund's Farmstead') (*place name*)

Guðmundr <-ar> *m* Gudmund (*personal name*); **Guðmundr inn ríki** *m* Gudmund the Powerful

gull *n* gold

gullhringr <-s; -ar> *m* gold ring

gyldi *3sg/pl past subjunct of* **gjalda**

gæfumunr <-ar; -ir> *m* difference in fortune, turn or shift of luck

gær *adv, only in* **í gær** yesterday

gæti *3sg/pl past subjunct of* **geta**

gœði *n pl* profit, wealth

gǫfgastur *superl of* **gǫfugr**

❖ **gǫfugr** <-ug, -ugt; *acc m* gǫfgan> *adj* noble

gǫrr *var of* **gerr**

gǫrt *var of* **gert**, *ppart of* **gera**

gǫrvibúr *n* storehouse

gǫrviligastr *superl of* **gǫrviligr**

gǫrviligr <-lig, -ligt> *adj* accomplished, able, brave

H

❖ **hafa** <hef(i)r, -ð-> *vb* have; hold, keep; take; **hafa [e-t] fyrir satt** believe [sth] to be true, be convinced of [sth]; **hafa [e-t] í hendi** hold [sth] in one's hand; **hafa [e-t] með sér** take, bring [sth] with one; **hafa sik** take oneself; **hafa yfir sér** wear, put over oneself; **hafask at** do

hafi *3sg/pl pres subjunct of* **hafa**

Hagi *m* Hagi ('Meadow') (*place name*)

hagr <-s; -ir> *m* state, condition

❖ **halda** <heldr; hélt, héldu; haldinn> *vb* [*w dat*] hold; keep, retain; maintain; **halda eptir [e-m]** pursue [sb]

Halla <*acc/dat/gen* Hǫllu> *f* Halla (*personal name*)

Hallbera *f* Hallbera (*personal name*)

Hallbjǫrn <-bjarnar> *m* Hallbjorn (*personal name*)

Hallfríðr *f* Hallfrid (*personal name*)

Halli *m* Halli (*personal name*)

Hallkatla *f* Hallkatla (*personal name*)

hallr <hǫll, hallt> *adj* leaning, sloping; **hallr í gǫngu** stooped, walking with a stoop

hallæri *n* famine

hana *acc of* **hon**

handsala <-að-> *vb* (*leg*) transfer one's rights to something (by shaking hands)

❖ **hann** <*acc* hann, *dat* honum, *gen* hans> *pron 3sg m* he

hans *poss pron 3sg m indecl* his

hans *gen of* **hann**

harðna <-að-> *vb* harden; become severe (*of weather*); grow worse

❖ **harðr** <hǫrð, hart> *adj* hard, difficult, severe

hart *n adj as adv* hard; fast

haukr <-s; -ar> *m* hawk

Haukr <-s> *m* Hauk ('Hawk') (*personal name*)

haust *n* autumn, fall, harvest season

haustboð *n* autumn feast, harvest feast

Hákon <-ar> *m* Hakon (*personal name*); **Hákon jarl Grjótgarðsson** *m* Earl Hakon, son of Grjotgard ('Stone-Fence')

❖ **hálfr** <hálf, hálft> *adj* half

háls <háls; hálsar> *m* neck

hár <há, hátt; *acc m* hávan; *pl dat* hávum; *comp* hæri, *superl* hæstr> *adj* high, tall, long; loud

hásetar *m pl* crew (of a ship) (*see* **háseti**)

háseti *m* oarsman

hátt *n adj as adv* loudly

hávaðamaðr <*acc* -mann, *dat* -manni, etc.> *m* a noisy, self-assertive man

hávaði *m* loud noise, tumult; loud self-assertion; (= **hávaðamaðr**) a noisy, self-assertive man

hávi *wk m of* **hár**

hávu *n dat of* **hár**

heðan *adv* from here, hence; **heðan af** from now on, henceforth; **heðan í frá** hereafter, henceforth

Heðinn <*dat* Heðni, *gen* Heðins> *m* Hedin (*personal name*)

hefða *1sg past subjunct of* **hafa**

hefði *3sg/pl past subjunct of* **hafa**

hefir *2/3sg pres of* **hafa**

hefja <hefr; hóf, hófu; hafinn> *vb* begin

hefna <-d-> *vb* [*w gen*] avenge, take revenge

hefnd <-ir> *f* revenge; *esp pl* blood revenge

heiðr <*acc/dat* heiði, *gen* heiðar, *pl* heiðar> *f* heath, moor

heilagr <heilǫg, heilagt; *acc m* helgan> *adj* holy

heill *n* (good) luck; omen; **illu heilli** unfortunately, by ill omen

❖ **heill** <heil, heilt> *adj* healthy, sound, 'hale'; unscathed; healed; blessed, happy; whole, complete

heilsa <-að-> *vb* [*w dat*] greet; **heilsa á [e-n]** greet [sb]

heilsan (*also* **heilsun**) *f* greeting; health

heilsun *var of* **heilsan**

❖ **heim** *adv* home, homeward (*motion*)

heima *adv* home, at home (*location*)

heiman *adv* from home

heimboð *n* invitation to one's home

heimferð <-ir> *f* homeward journey

heimili *n* home, house, homestead

heimsókn <-ir> *f* attack on one's home; visit; **veita [e-m] heimsókn** to attack [sb] in his home; visit

heimta <-t-> *vb* draw, pull; recover; claim, collect; **heimta [e-t] at [e-m]** to claim [sth] from [sb]; **heimta [e-n] á tal** engage [sb] in conversation, address [sb]; draw [sb] aside to speak with them

heit *n* solemn vow, oath

❖ **heita** <heitr; hét, hétu; heitinn> *vb* call, give a name to; call, call on; (*intrans, 2/3sg pres* heitir) be named, be called; [*w dat*] promise; **heita á [e-n]** call upon, pray to, invoke [sb]

heitbundit *ppart* (*see* **binda, heit**) bound by a promise, oath-bound

❖ **heldr** <*superl* helzt> *comp adv* more, rather; **at heldr … at** not merely … but rather, all the more; (*after a neg*) but, on the contrary; **heldr … en** rather … than

helgi *wk m nom sg of* **heilagr**

Helgi *m* Helgi (*personal name*); **Brodd-Helgi** *m* Brodd-Helgi ('Spike-Helgi')

hella <*pl gen* hellna> *f* flat stone, slate

hellusteinn *m* flat slab of rock, flagstone

helzt *superl adv* most of all, especially (*see* **heldr**)

hendi *dat of* **hǫnd**

hendr *nom/acc pl of* **hǫnd**

hennar *gen of* **hon**

hennar *poss pron 3sg f indecl* her

henni *dat of* **hon**

hepta <-t-> *vb* tether (a horse)

herað <heruð~herǫð> *n* district; county; (*in Iceland*) a valley region

heraðsvært *n* freedom to live in a district; **eiga heraðsvært** (*leg*) be at liberty to reside within a district without threat of attack

❖ **hestr** <-s; -ar> *m* stallion; horse

heyra <-ð-> *vb* hear

❖ **hér** *adv* here (*location*); **hér til** until now, hereto

hérvist <-ir> *f* lodgings here

hét *1/3sg past of* **heita**

hétu *3pl past of* **heita**

himinn <*dat* himni, *gen* himins, *pl* himnar> *m* sky; heaven

hingat *adv* to here, hither

❖ **hinn** <hin, hitt> *dem pron* the other one; **á hinn fótinn** on the other foot

hinn <hin, hit> (*var of* **inn**) *art* the

hirða <-ð-> *vb* mind, care for; **hirða eigi (um) [e-t]** not care about [sth]

hitta <-tt-> *vb* meet with, hit upon; hit; *refl* **hittask** meet one another

hjaldrjúgr <-drjúg, -drjúgt> *adj* talkative; aggressively demanding; **[e-m] verðr hjaldrjúgt um [e-t]** *impers* [sb] talks much or at length about [sth]

❖ **hjá** *prep* [*w dat*] by, near; at one's place

hjálpa <helpr; halp~hjalp, hulpu; hólpinn> *vb* [*w dat*] help, save

hjó *1/3sg past of* **hǫggva**

hjuggu *var of* **hjoggu**, *3pl past of* **hǫggva**

hjú *n* household

hlað <hlǫð> *n* courtyard, the paved area in front of a farmhouse

❖ **hlaupa** <hleypr; hljóp, hljópu; hlaupinn> *vb* leap, spring; run; **hlaupa at [e-m]** leap at, assault [sb]

hleypa <-t-> *vb* [*w dat*] cause to escape, emit; **hleypa út vatni** press out fluid (*as from a sore*)

hleypr *2/3 pres of* **hlaupa**

hlífa <-ð-> *vb* [*w dat*] shelter, protect; spare, deal gently with; *refl* **hlífask** spare, refrain, hold back; **hlífask við [e-n]** spare [sb], hold oneself back from [sb]

hlíta <-tt-> *vb* [*w dat*] rely on, trust; be content with

hljóp *1/3sg past of* **hlaupa**

hljóta <hlýtr; hlaut, hlutu; hlotinn> *vb* get, be allotted; undergo, suffer; **hljóta [e-t] af [e-m]** get, suffer [sth] on account of [sb]

hlotit *ppart of* **hljóta**

hlunnr <-s; -ar> *m* piece of wood put under the keel of a ship when ashore; **ráða skipi til hlunns** drag a ship ashore (during winter)

❖ **hlutr** <*dat* hlut, *gen* -ar; *pl* -ir> *m* lot; thing; **bera lægra hlut ór** get the worst of it; **eiga hlut í [e-u]** take part in, interfere in [sth]

hlýða <-dd-> *vb* [*w dat*] listen; **hlýða á [e-t]** listen to [sth]

hof *n* temple (*freq a name for a farm*)

Hof *n* Hof ('Temple') (*place name*)

hofgyðja *f* priestess

Hofsland *n* the Hof estate

Hofsverjar *m pl* the people of Hof

hoftollr <-s; -ar> *m* temple tax, temple 'toll'

❖ **hon** <*acc* hana, *dat* henni, *gen* hennar> *pron 3sg f* she

honum *dat of* **hann**

horfa <-ð-> *vb* turn (in a certain direction); (turn so as to) look upon, behold; look (a certain way), have a certain appearance; *refl* **horfask** look, appear; **horfask til** look like, look as if

horfinn *ppart* lost, missing, nowhere to be found (*see* **hverfa**)

horn *n* horn

hólpinn *ppart* safe, saved (*see* **hjálpa**)

hraðfara *adj indecl* swift, speedy, 'quick-faring'; **verða vel hraðfara** be very swift in travelling, have a speedy journey

Hrafn <-s> *m* Hrafn ('Raven') (*personal name*)

Hreiðarr <-s> *m* Hreidar (*personal name*)

hreyfing *f* movement, motion

hreystimaðr <*acc* -mann, *dat* -manni, etc.> *m* valiant man, man of valor

hringr <-s; -ar> *m* ring

hríð <-ir> *f* a time, while; storm; attack, battle; **gera hríð** attack, 'do battle'; **um hríð** for a while

hrís *n* shrubbery, brushwood

hross *n* horse

Hróðgeirr <-s> *m* Hrodgeir (*personal name*); **Hróðgeirr inn hvíti** *m* Hrodgeir the White

hrukku *3pl past of* **hrøkkva**

hræ <*pl gen* hræva> *n* dead body, corpse, carrion

hrøkkva <hrøkkr; hrøkk, hrukku; hrokkinn> *vb* fall back, be repelled

huga <-að-> *vb* mind; **huga um [e-t]** be concerned about [sth]

hugðu *3pl past of* **hyggja**

hugkvæmr <-kvæm, -kvæmt> *adj* clever, cunning

hugr <-ar; -ir> *m* heart, mind; courage,

spirit; **[e-m] koma í hug** occur to [sb]; **svá segir honum hugr um** *impers* so his heart tells him, he forebodes

hulðu *3pl past of* **hylja**

hundrað <hundruð> *n* hundred (*usu followed by noun in gen*) (**tólfrætt hundrað** = 120, **tírætt hundrað** = 100)

hurð <-ir> *f* door

❖ **hús** *n* house, building; *pl* the group of buildings on a farm

húsfreyja *f* housewife, lady

❖ **húskarl** *m* farmhand

hvaðan *adv* from where, whence

❖ **hvar** *interrog adv* where?; **hvar er komit um [e-t]** what has become of [sth]

hvat *interrog pron* what?; *rel pron* what, that which

hvatliga *adv* quickly

❖ **hvárgi** <*n* hvárki~hvártki> *adj/indef pron* neither (of two); *conj* **hvárki ... né** neither ... nor

hvárigr *adj/indef pron* neither (of two) (= **hvárgi**)

hvárki *n of* **hvárgi**

❖ **hvárr** *interrog pron* who, which (of two)?; *indef pron* each (of two)

❖ **hvárrtveggi** *indef pron* each of the two

❖ **hvárt** *interrog adv* whether; *conj* whether

hverfa <hverfr; hvarf, hurfu; horfinn> *vb intrans* turn (in a circular motion), rotate; be lost, be missing; disappear; **hverfa aptr** return, turn around, turn back

hvergi *adv* by no means, not at all

❖ **hverr** <hver, hvat> *interrog pron* who, which?; <hver, hvert> *adj/indef pron* each, every, all; **hvern dag** every day

❖ **hversu** *interrog adv* how, just how?; **hversu fjǫlmennr** with how many men

hvert *interrog adv* to where, whither?

hvé *interrog adv* how?; **hvé nær** *conj* when

hví *interrog adv* why, for what?

hvíld *f* rest, repose

hvítr <hvít, hvítt> *adj* white

hyggja <hugð-; *ppart* hug(a)ðr> *vb* think, believe; **hyggja (sér) til [e-s]** anticipate, prepare (oneself) for [sth]

hylja <hulð~huld-; *ppart* huliðr~huldr> *vb* bury, cover over, conceal, hide

hætta <-tt-> *vb* [*w dat*] leave off, quit; [*w inf*] cease [doing sth]

hættiligr <-lig, -ligt> *adj* dangerous, serious

hǫfðingi <*gen* -ja, *pl* -jar> *m* chieftain; leader

❖ **hǫfuð** <*dat* hǫfði, *pl dat* hǫfðum, *gen* hǫfða> *n* head

hǫfuðhof *n* chief temple

hǫggspjót *n* broad-bladed spear

❖ **hǫggva** <hǫggr; hjó, hjoggu; hǫgg(v)inn> *vb* strike (a blow), chop, hack, hew; **hǫggva af** chop off; **hǫggva í hǫfuð [e-m]** strike [sb] on the head; **hǫggva til [e-s]** strike a blow at [sb]; **hǫggva upp** cut down (trees)

❖ **hǫnd** <*acc* hǫnd, *dat* hendi, *gen* handar, *pl* hendr, *dat* hǫndum, *gen* handa> *f* hand; arm and hand, arm; (right or left) hand, side; **á tvær hendr** on both sides; **hafa [e-t] í hendi** hold [sth] in one's hand; **á hendr [e-m]** against [sb]; **telja á hendr [e-m]** lay the blame on [sb]; **koma at hǫndum** happen, come about

hǫrfa <-að-> *vb* give way, retreat, withdraw

I

iðra <-að-> *vb* repent; *refl* **iðrask** [*w gen*] repent of, regret

iðraðisk *2/3 sg past of* **iðrask**

❖ **illa** <*comp* verr, *superl* verst> *adv* badly, ill

❖ **illr** <ill, illt; *comp* værri, *superl* verstr> *adj* bad, evil

illviðri *n* bad weather

Ingibjǫrg <*acc/dat* -bjǫrgu, *gen* -bjargar> *f*

Ingiborg (*personal name*); **Ingibjǫrg Hróðgeirsdóttir ins hvíta** *f* Ingibjorg, daughter of Hrodgeir the White

Ingmundr <-s> *m* Ingmund (*personal name*)

❖ **inn** <*comp* innarr, *superl* innst> *adv* in, into (*motion*)

inn <in, it> *art* the

inni *adv* in (*location*), inside, indoors

innri *comp adj* inner, inmost, farther in

Í

❖ **í** *prep* [*w acc*] into (*motion*); during (*time*); [*w dat*] in, within; at (*location*)

Ísland *n* Iceland

J

jafn <jǫfn, jafnt> *adj* equal, even; *in cpds* equally, as

jafnaðr (*also* **jǫfnuðr**) <*gen* -ar> *m* justice, equality, equal share

jafnan *adv* constantly, always

jafnframt *adv* side by side

jafngamall <-gǫmul, -gamalt; *acc m* -gamlan> *adj* as old, of the same age

jafnharðr <-hǫrð, -hart> *adj* equally hard, as severe

jafnskjótt *adv* as soon, just as quickly

jafnungr <-ung, -ungt> *adj* as young

jagmál *n* (petty) quarrel

jarða <-að-> *vb* bury

❖ **jarl** <-s; -ar> *m* earl

já *adv* yes

járn *n* iron; *pl* irons, fetters, chains

Járngerðr <*acc/dat* Járngerði, *gen* Járn-gerðar> *f* Jarngerd (*personal name*)

Jón <-s> *m* Jon (*personal name*)

jǫfnuðr *var of* **jafnaðr**

jǫrð <*dat* jǫrðu, *gen* jarðar; *pl* jarðir> *f* earth; ground

K

kaldr <kǫld, kalt> *adj* cold

❖ **kalla** <-að-> *vb* call; say; **at kalla** so to speak, in a manner of speaking

kallaðr *ppart of* **kalla**

kanna <-að-> *vb* search, explore

kappi *m* hero, champion

karl <-s; -ar> *m* man; old man; **Þorsteinn karl** old Thorstein, old man Thorstein

kasta <-að-> *vb* [*w dat*] throw

kaup *n* bargain, trade

kaupa <keypt-> *vb* buy

kaupmaðr <*acc* -mann, *dat* -manni, etc.> *m* trader, merchant

kaus *1/3sg past of* **kjósa**

kápa *f* 'cape' or cloak with a hood

Kári *m* Kari (*personal name*)

kemr *2/3sg pres of* **koma**

kenna <-d-> *vb* know, recognize; feel; attribute; teach

Ketill <-ils> *m* Ketil (*personal name*); **Digr-Ketill** *m* Stout-Ketil

keypti *3sg past of* **kaupa**

kistill <*dat* kistli, *gen* kistils, *pl* kistlar> *m* little chest, small box

kjósa <kýss; kaus~kǫri, kusu~kuru; kosinn~kjǫrinn> *vb* choose

Klifshagi *m* Klifshagi ('Cliff Meadow') (*place name*)

klyfjahross *n* pack-horse

klæða <-dd-> *vb* clothe; *refl* **klæðask** get dressed (in the morning)

klæði <*pl gen* klæða> *n* cloth; garment, clothes

klækiliga *adv* in a cowardly fashion

knáligr <-lig, -ligt> *adj* hardy, vigorous

kné <*dat* kné, *gen* knés; *pl dat* knjám~ knjóm, *gen* knjá> *n* knee

knjám *dat pl of* **kné**

kolamaðr <*acc* -mann, *dat* -manni, etc.> *m* charcoal-maker

Kolfinnr <-s> *m* Kolfinn (*personal name*)

kollaupr <-s; -ar> *m* box or basket for carrying coal or charcoal

Kollr <-s> *m* Koll (*personal name*)

kom *1/3sg past of* **koma**

❖ **koma** <kemr~kømr; kom, kómu~ kvámu; kominn> *vb* come; **koma aptr** come back, return; **koma at** arrive; **koma at hondum** happen, come about; **koma á** hit; **koma á bak** mount on horseback; **koma á tal við [e-n]** come to speak with [sb]; **koma ásamt** be agreed; **koma eptir** follow; **koma [e-u] fram** bring [sth] about, bring [sth] to a successful conclusion; **koma inn** enter, come in; **koma máli fram** (*leg*) prosecute (a case); **koma út til Íslands** come out to Iceland (*usu* from Norway); **koma við þessa sogu** appear in this saga; **vel/illa komit** well/ poorly placed, in good/bad hands; *refl* **komask** get through, arrive at an end, reach; **komask undan** escape, get away

kominn, komit *ppart of* **koma**; **vel (illa) komit** well (poorly) placed, in good (bad) hands

komnir *m nom pl ppart of* **koma**

❖ **kona** <*pl gen* kvenna> *f* woman; wife

❖ **konungr** <-s; -ar> *m* king

kostaboð *n* favorable or generous offer

❖ **kostr** <-ar; -ir, *pl acc* -i~u> *m* choice; opportunity; match; state, condition; cost, expense

kómu *3pl past of* **koma**

kómusk *3pl past of* **komask**

kristinn <*f* kristin; *wk m* kristni, *f* kristna> *adj* Christian

Krossavík *f* Krossavik ('Cross Bay' or 'Cross Inlet', presumably an inlet where a cross was erected) (*place name*); **Krossavík in ýtri** Outer Krossavik

kunna <kann, kunnu; kunni; kunnat> *pret-pres vb* can, know how to; feel (an emotion); **kunna [e-m] þokk fyrir [e-t]** be thankful to [sb] for [sth]

❖ **kunnigr** <-ig, -igt> *adj* known; wise; versed in magic

kvaddi *3sg past of* **kveðja**

kvað *1/3sg past of* **kveða**

kvað sér = **kvazk**

kvaðning *f* greeting; order, command

kvazk *2/3sg past of* **kveðask**

kváðusk *3pl past of* **kveðask**

kváma *f* coming, approach, arrival

kvánga <-að-> *vb* cause (a man) to marry; *refl* **kvángask** marry (*of a man*), take a wife

kvángaðr *ppart* married (*of a man*) (*see* **kvánga**)

❖ **kveða** <kveðr; kvað, kváðu; kveðinn> *vb* speak, say; *refl* **kveðask** say of oneself

kveðja *f* welcome, greeting

kveðja <kvadd-> *vb* greet; call on, summon; **kveðja [e-n] vel** greet [sb] well, welcome [sb]; *refl* **kveðjask** greet one another

❖ **kveld** *n* evening; **um kveldit** in the evening

kvenna *gen pl of* **kona**

kvezk *2/3sg pres of* **kveðask**

kvikfé *n* livestock, cattle

kvoddu *3pl past of* **kveðja**

kvoddusk *3pl past of* **kveðjask**

kyn <*pl dat* kynjum, *gen* kynja> *n* kin; kindred; **at kyni** by extraction or birth

kynligr <-lig, -ligt> *adj* strange, extraordinary

kynnisleið <-ir> *f* visit

kynsæll <-sæl, -sælt> *adj* blessed with notable descendants

❖ **kyrr** <kyrr, kyrrt; *comp* kyrrari, *superl* kyrrastr> *adj* still, calm

kœmi *3sg/pl past subjunct of* **koma**

kortr <*gen* kartar~korts> *m* short, stocky, sturdy man (*nickname*)

L

lag <log> *n* layer; thrust, stab; **at morgu lagi** in many respects

laga *gen of* **log**

laga <-að-> *vb* arrange; adjust, mend *refl* **lagask** adjust oneself; **lagask til [e-s]** enter into agreement with [sb], ally oneself with [sb]

lagðisk *2/3sg past of* **leggjask**

❖ **land** <lond> *n* land; country; estate

landseti *m* tenant

langa <-að-> *vb* long (for) (*usu impers* [*acc subj*]); **langa til [e-s]** long for [sth]

langfeðgar *m pl* forefathers, ancestors (through the father's line)

langháls <-ls> *m* long-neck (*nickname*)

❖ **langr** <lǫng, langt; *comp* lengri, *superl* lengstr> *adj* long (*of distance and time*)

lauk *1/3sg past of* **lúka**

laun *f* secrecy; **á laun** secretly, alone

laun *n pl* reward, recompense

launa <-að-> *vb* [*w dat*] reward; **launa [e-m] [e-u]** reward [sb] with [sth]; **launa [e-m] [e-t]** reward [sb] for [sth]

laupr <-s; -ar> *m* box, basket

❖ **lauss** <laus, laust> *adj* loose; free, unimpeded

laust *1/3sg past of* **ljósta**

lá *1/3sg pret of* **liggja**

lágr <lág, lágt; *comp* lægri, *superl* lægstr> *adj* low

lágu *3pl past of* **liggja**

❖ **láta** <lætr; lét, létu; látinn> *vb* let, allow, permit; put, place, set; behave; express, say; [*w inf*] have something done; **láta at landi** put back to land; **láta fram** let go, yield, hand over; **láta laust** 'let loose', yield, give up, hand over; **láta sem** 'let on as if', pretend, behave or make as if; **láta [e-t] til sín taka** let [sth] concern oneself, involve oneself in [sth], meddle with [sth]; **láta vel (illa) yfir [e-m]/[e-u]** to speak well (ill) of [sb]/[sth], express approval (disapproval) of [sb]/[sth]; **láta við [e-u]** agree, yield, give in to [sth]; *refl* **látask** declare (of oneself)

❖ **leggja** <lagð-; *ppart* lag(i)ðr~laginn> *vb* lay, place, put; stab, thrust; **leggja af** leave, remove, take off (clothing); **leggja í gegnum [e-n]** impale [sb], run [sb] through; **leggja ráð til** offer advice; **leggja til [e-s] með [e-u]** attack [sb] with [sth]; *refl* **leggjask** lay, set oneself; **leggjask á** arise; **leggjask á [e-t]** prey upon (*of robbers, beasts of prey, etc.*), fall upon, attack [sth]; **leggjask til** contribute; **leggjask út** set out (into the wilderness to live as an outlaw)

❖ **leið** <-ir> *f* road, path; way; **á leið** on the way; **fara leiðar sinnar** go (on) one's way; **heim á leið** on one's way home, homeward

leið *1/3sg past of* **líða**

leiða <-dd-> *vb* lead; *refl* **leiðask** be led, be persuaded

leiðrétta <-tt-> *vb* correct, put right, redress; **geta leiðrétt** be able to put right, succeed in correcting

leiga *f* rent, pay; interest; **með leigum** with interest

leikr <*dat* leik, *gen* -s; *pl* -ar> *m* game, play, sport; **með illan leik** narrowly, by a narrow escape; in poor condition

leit *1/3sg past of* **líta**

❖ **leita** <-að-> *vb* [*w gen*] seek, search for

leitat *ppart* sought for, intended (*see* **leita**)

leiti *n* hill, elevation

lendr *adj* 'landed', describing one who has received a grant of land from a king

❖ **lengi** <*comp* lengr (*time*), lengra (*distance*)> *adv* long, for a long time

lengr *comp adv* longer (*time*), for a longer time (*see* **lengi**)

leyniliga *adv* secretly

leysa <-t-> *vb* loose, set free; *refl* **leysask** depart, remove oneself

lét *1/3sg past of* **láta**

létu *3pl past of* **láta**

lézk *2/3sg past of* **látask**

❖ **lið** *n* band of men, following, troops; support, assistance; family, household

liðveizla *f* support

lifa <-ð-, *n ppart* lifat> *vb* live

❖ **liggja** <liggr; lá, lágu; leginn> *vb* lie (down); go, lead (*of a trail*); **liggja í sárum** lie ill from one's wounds; **liggja kyrr á [e-u]** sit and rest [sth], go easy on [sth]

litr <-ar; -ir, *pl acc* -u> *m* color

líða <líðr; leið, liðu; liðinn> *vb* pass (*usu of time*); **líða á** pass, draw to a close

líf *n* life

líflát *n* loss of life, death (*esp violent*)

lífláta <líflætr; líflét, líflétu; líflátinn> *vb* put to death, kill

lík *n* body, corpse

líka <-að-> *vb impers* [*dat subj*] like, be pleasing (to one)

líkami *m* body

líki *m* compensation

❖ **líkligr** <-lig, -ligt> *adj* likely, probable; fit, suitable

líkligri *comp of* **líkligr**

❖ **líkr** <lík, líkt> *adj* like, resembling; probable; promising

líta <lítr; leit, litu; litinn> *vb* look, see; *refl* **lítask** appear, seem; **[e-m] lízk á [e-n]/ [e-t]** *impers* [sb/sth] looks to [sb]

lítilhæfr <-hæf, -hæft> *adj* humble, moderate

❖ **lítill** <lítil, lítit; *acc m* litlan, *f* litla, *dat n* litlu; *pl* litlir, etc.; *comp* minni, *superl* minnst> *adj* little; short, brief (*time*); **litlu síðar** shortly afterward, a little while later

lítit *n indef pron* little (*see* **lítill**); **sjá lítit um** see little (advantage) in

lítt *adv* little

lízk *2/3sg pres of* **lítask**

Ljósavatnsskarð *n* Ljosavatnsskard ('Light Water Lake Pass') (*place name*)

ljósta <lýstr; laust, lustu; lostinn> *vb* strike; **ljósta til** (= **ljósta**) strike

loðinhǫfði *m* shaggy head (*nickname*)

lofa <-að-> *vb* praise; allow, permit; promise

lokit *ppart of* **lúka**

lokrekkja *f* locking bed-closet

lokrekkjugólf *n* locking bed-closet

Loptr <-s> *m* Lopt (*personal name*)

lóga <-að-> *vb* [*w dat*] part with

luku *3pl past of* **lúka**

lúka <lýkr; lauk, luku; lokinn> *vb* [*w dat*] close; end, conclude; shut; **lúka [e-t/e-u] upp** open [sth]; **lúka við** end, finish with; **lýkr yfir** *impers* an end is reached

lúta <lýtr; laut, lutu; lotinn> *vb* bow down; give way, yield

lykð *var of* **lykt**

lykt (*also* **lykð**) <-ir> *f* (*usu in pl*) end, conclusion; **til lykta** until the end

lýkr *2/3sg pres of* **lúka**

Lýtingr <-s> *m* Lyting (*personal name*)

lægi *3sg/pl past subjunct of* **liggja**

lægri *comp adj* lower (*see* **lágr**); **bera lægra hlut ór** get the worst of it

lækna <-að-> *vb* cure, heal

lækning *f* cure; medicine, art of healing

læknir <-is; -ar> *m* doctor, physician, healer

lær *n* upper leg, thigh

læsa <-t-> *vb* [*w dat*] lock, shut

lætr *2/3sg pres of* **láta**

lǫg <*gen* laga> *n pl* laws, law

lǫgskyld <-ir> *f* legal dues

lǫgvillr <-vill, -villt> *adj* mistaken in point of law, confused about the law

M

❖ **maðr** <*acc* mann, *dat* manni, *gen* manns; *pl nom/acc* menn, *dat* mǫnnum, *gen* manna> *m* man; person, human being

mann *acc sg of* **maðr**

manna *gen pl of* **maðr**

mannbroddr <-s; -ar> *m* spike

mannfall *n* casualties (in battle)

mannfundr <-ar; -ir> *m* meeting, gathering

manni *dat sg of* **maðr**

mannmargr <-mǫrg, -margt> *adj* with many men; **hafa mannmargt** to have many people or forces

mannval *n* choice people, select body of men

margbreytinn <-in, -it> *adj* fickle, capricious, unpredictable

margháttaðr <-háttuð, -háttat> *adj* of many kinds, varied

❖ **margr** <mǫrg, mar(g)t; *comp* fleiri, *superl* flestr> *adj* [*w sg*] many a (*in collective sense*); [*w pl*] many

markaðr (*also* **marknaðr**) <*gen* -ar> *m* market; monetary claim; **eiga marknað í annars garði** have a claim against another

marknaðr *var of* **markaðr**

matr <-ar; -ir> *m* food

má *1/3sg pres of* **mega**

mágr <-s; -ar> *m* male in-law

❖ **mál** *n* speech, narrative, talk; language; saying; deliberation, discussion; case, matter, affair; agreement; (*leg*) suit, action, case; **at engu máli** in no legal case; **eiga mál við [e-n]** speak, converse with [sb]

mál *n* time

málaferli *n pl* lawsuits, litigation

málafylgismaðr <*acc* -mann, *dat* -manni, etc.> *m* lawyer, active participant in lawsuits

málaleitan (*also* **málaleitun**) *f* negotiation

málaleitun *var of* **málaleitan**

málalok *n pl* end, conclusion of a case or matter

málugr <-ug, -ugt> *adj* talkative

málþǫrf <*gen* -þarfar; *pl* -þarfir> *f* matter requiring discussion

máttlítill <-lítil, -lítit; *acc m* -litlan> *adj* weak, faint, feeble, exhausted

❖ **með** *prep* [*w acc*] with (*in the sense of bringing, carrying, or forcing*); [*w dat*] with (*in the sense of accompanying or togetherness*)

meðan *adv* meanwhile; *conj* while, as long as; **á meðan** in the mean time, meanwhile

❖ **mega** <má, megu; mátti; mátt> *pret-pres vb* can, may; be able; **má vera** maybe; **mega vel** be well

megin *adv* on the side; **þeim megin** on that side

mein *n* sore, disease

meir *comp adv* more (*see* **mjǫk**)

meiri *comp adj* more (*see* **mikill**)

men <*pl dat* menjum, *gen* menja> *n* necklace; *pl* treasures, jewels

menn *nom/acc pl of* **maðr**

merr <*acc/dat* meri, *gen* merar, *pl* merar> mare

mest *superl adv* most (*see* **mjǫk**)

mestr <mest, mest> *superl adj* greatest, biggest (*see* **mikill**)

mér *dat of* **ek**

mið *n* middle; **í miðit** in the middle

miðju *n dat of* **miðr**

❖ **miðr** <mið, mitt; *acc m* -jan> *adj* middle

mik *acc of* **ek**

❖ **mikill** <mikil, mikit; *acc m* mikinn, *dat m* miklum, *n* miklu; *pl* miklir, etc.; *comp* meiri, *superl* mestr> *adj* big, tall, great; much

miklu *adv* much [*w comp*] (*see* **mikill**)

❖ **milli** (*also* **millum, á milli, í milli**) *prep* [*w gen*] between

millum *var of* **milli**; **fara í millum landa** travel from one land to another (i.e., trade)

❖ **minn** <mín, mitt> *poss pron 1sg* my

minni *comp adj* less, lesser, smaller (*see* **lítill**)

minnka <-að-> *vb* lessen, diminish; *refl* **minnkask** grow less, decrease

mis- *pref* unequal, alternately; amiss, wrong. wrongly; bad, badly; mis-

misfari *m* difference in speed

misráðit *ppart* ill-advised (*see* **mis-, ráða**)

missa <-t-> *vb* [*w gen*] miss, fail to hit; be without; miss, feel the want of; lose, suffer loss of

misseri *n* season, period of six months; *pl* cycle of seasons, year

❖ **mjǫk** <*comp* meir(r), *superl* mest> *adv* much, very; almost, very nearly

❖ **morginn** (*also* **morgunn**) <*gen* morgins, *pl* mor(g)nar> *m* morning; **á morgin** (**á morgun**) tomorrow; **í morgin** (**í morgun**) this morning

morgunn *var of* **morginn**

❖ **móðir** <*acc/dat/gen* móður, *pl* mœðr, *dat* mœðrum, *gen* mœðra> *f* mother

mót *n* meeting; manner, way; **í mót** *prep* [*w dat*] towards, against; in return; **gera í mót [e-m]** move, act against [sb], oppose [sb]; **koma/fara til móts við [e-n]** come/go to meet with [sb]

❖ **móti** (*also* **á móti, í móti**) *prep* [*w dat*] towards, against; in return

mun *1/3sg pres of* **munu**

mund *n* (*in sg*) or *f* (*in pl*) moment; situation, circumstance; **í þær mundir** in those times; in those circumstances; **í þetta mund** at that moment

mundi (*var of* **myndi**) *3sg/pl past subjunct of* **munu**

mundu *pret inf of* **munu**

munnr <-s; -ar> *m* mouth

munr <-ar; -ir> *m* difference, importance; **fara í engan mun** amount to no importance

muntu = **munt þú**, will you (*sg*) (*see* **munu**)

❖ **munu** <mun, munu; mundi; *pret inf* mundu> *pret-pres vb* will, shall (*futurity*); to be sure to, must (*probability*); (*past tense*) would, must

myndi (*also* **mundi**) *3sg/pl past subjunct of* **munu**

mynni *n* mouth (of a river or fjord)

Mývatn *n* Myvatn ('Midge' or 'Mosquito Lake') (*place name*)

❖ **mæla** <-t-> *vb* say, speak; **mæla eptir [e-t]/[e-n]** (*leg*) take up the prosecution for [sth]/[sb] (who was murdered or wronged); **mæla fyrir [e-u]** declare [sth]; **mæla illa fyrir [e-u]** speak ill of, condemn [sth]; **mæla málum** plead a cause; **mæla til [e-s]** stipulate, fix [sth]; **mæla við [e-n]** speak to or with [sb], say to [sb]; **mæla [e-u] við [e-n]** say [sth] to [sb]; *refl*

mælask be spoken of; **mælask illa fyrir** be ill spoken of, condemned

mæltisk *2/3 sg past of* **mælask**, *refl of* **mæla**

mætti *3sg/pl past subjunct of* **mega**

mœði *f* weariness, exhaustion

mœta <-tt-> *vb* [*w dat*] meet; *refl* **mœtask** meet one another

mǫnnum *dat pl of* **maðr**

N

nam *1/3sg past of* **nema**

nauðsyn <-jar> *f* necessity

naut *n* ox; *pl* cattle, oxen

nautr <-s; -ar> *m* partaker (with another person)

ná <2/3sg pres náir, *past* -ð-> *vb* [*w dat*] reach, catch, overtake; get, obtain; [*w inf*] be able to [do sth]

nefna <-d-> *vb* name, call

nei *adv* no

neita <-að-> *vb* [*w dat*] deny, refuse, reject

nema <nemr; nam, námu; numinn> *vb* take; **nema staðar** stop, halt

❖ **nema** *conj* except, unless, but (that)

nenna <-t-> *vb* [*w dat or inf*] have a desire to, be disposed to

neyta <-tt-> *vb* [*w gen*] use, make use of

❖ **né** *conj* nor

❖ **niðr** *adv* down (*motion or direction*); **falla niðr** fall, drop, be forgotten; (*leg*) be dropped

níu *num* nine

níundi *ord num* ninth

njósn <-ir> *f* spying, scouting, look out; news; **hafa njósn af um fǫr [e-s]** spy on, have a watch kept on [sb's] movements

norðr *adv* north, northwards

norrœnn <norrœn, norrœnt> *adj* Norse, Norwegian

Nóregr <-s> *m* Norway

❖ **nótt** <*gen* nætr; *pl* nætr> *f* night

❖ **nú** *adv*

❖ **nær** *adv* nearly; **hvé nær** *conj* when; *comp adv* nearer

næst *superl adv* next; **þessu næst** thereafter

❖ **næstr** <næst, næst> *superl adj* next; nearest

nætr *gen sg & nom/acc pl of* **nótt**

❖ **nǫkkurr** <nǫkkur, nǫkkut; *acc m* nǫkkurn> *adj/indef pron* any, anybody; some, a certain

nǫkkut *n adj as adv* some

O

of *adv* too

❖ **ofan** *adv* down, downwards; down from above

ofgangr *m* excess, abuse

ofríki *n* sheer force; **bera [e-n] ofríki** overcome [sb] by sheer force

ofrlið *n* superior force; **bera [e-n] ofrliði** overpower [sb]

og (*var of* **ok**) *conj* and

❖ **ok** *conj* and; *adv* also

okkar *gen of* **vit**

❖ **okkarr** <okkur, okka(r)t; *dat m* okkrum, *n* okkru; *pl m* okkrir, *f* okkrar, *dat* okkrum, *gen* okkarra> *poss pron 1dual* our (two)

okkr *acc/dat of* **vit**

opt *adv* often

optar *comp adv* more often, oftener (*see* **opt**); **eigi optar** no more, not again; **sem optar** as many times before

❖ **orð** *n* word; repute, fame, report; message; **orð var á því** it was said

orðit *ppart of* **verða**

ormr <-s; -ar> *m* snake, serpent

Ormr <-s> *m* Orm ('Snake') (*personal name*)

oss *acc/dat of* **vér**

Ó

ó- *neg pref* un-

ódæll <ódæl, ódælt> *adj* difficult, quarrelsome, stubborn

óeirðarmaðr <*acc* -mann, *dat* -manni, etc.> *m* unruly man

Ófeigr <-s> *m* Ofeig (*personal name*)

ófriðr <*gen* -ar> *m* attack; violence; **bjóða ófrið** do battle

ógreiðligr <-lig, -ligt> *adj* unpayable, uncollectible; difficult; unclear

óheilagr <-heilog, -heilagt; *acc m* -helgan> *adj* without protection of law

óhættr <óhætt, óhætt> *adj* safe, out of danger; **er [e-m] óhætt** *impers* [sb] is out of danger

ójafnaðarmaðr <*acc* -mann, *dat* -manni, etc.> *m* unjust man, one who is quarrelsome and overbearing, difficult to deal with

ójafnaðr (*also* **ójǫfnuðr**) <*gen* -ar> *m* injustice, unfairness

ójǫfnuðr *var of* **ójafnaðr**

ókátr *adj* morose, gloomy

Óláfr <-s> *m* Olaf (*personal name*); **Ólafr langháls** *m* Olaf Long-Neck

ómannligr <-lig, -ligt> *adj* unmanly; inhuman

❖ **ór** *prep* [*w dat*] out of, from, from inside of; made of

órífligr <-lig, -ligt> *adj* bad, unfavorable

ósamfœrr <-fœr, -fœrt> *adj* incompatible, unable to be mixed together

ósómi *m* dishonor, disgrace; **gera [e-m] ósóma** treat [sb] dishonorably

ósvinnr *adj* unwise

ótrúligr <-lig, -ligt> *adj* undependable, unsafe, not to be relied upon

óvarr <óvǫr, óvart> *adj* unaware, unwary

óvart *n adj as adv* unawares, by surprise; **koma [e-m] á óvart** take [sb] by surprise

óvinsæla <-d-> *vb* make (oneself) disliked, unpopular; *refl* **óvinsælask** make onself disliked, unpopular

óvinsæla sik = **óvinsælask**

óvirðing *f* disgrace, dishonor

óvitrliga *adv* foolishly, unwisely

óvitrligr <-lig, -ligt> *adj* foolish, unwise

óvígr <óvíg, óvígt> *adj* unable to fight

óvæginn <-in, -it> *adj* unyielding, headstrong

óvægr <óvæg, óvægt> *adj* harsh, unmerciful

óvænliga *adv* unpromisingly, hopelessly

óvænligr <-lig, -ligt> *adj* unpromising, hopeless; **it óvænligasta** most unpromising

óvænn <óvæn, óvænt> *adj* hopeless, with little chance of success

óx *1/3sg past of* **vaxa**

óþykkja *f* discord, dislike, ill-will

P

Páll <-s> *m* Pal (*personal name*)

penningr <-s; -ar> *m* coin, penny; piece of property, article

prestr <-s; -ar> *m* priest

prúðr <prúð, prútt> *adj* fine, magnificent; gallant, brave

R

Ragnheiðr <*acc/dat* Ragnheiði, *gen* Ragnheiðar> *f* Ragnheid (*personal name*)

rak *1/3sg past of* **reka**

rammliga *adv* strongly

rammr <rǫmm, rammt> *adj* strong; mighty, powerful; **rammr at afli** extremely strong

rangr <rǫng, rangt> *adj* wrong

rangt *n adj as adv* wrongly, unjustly

Rannveig *f* Rannveig (*personal name*)

rauðflekkóttr <-ótt, -ótt> *adj* spotted, speckled with red, 'red-flecked'

rauðr <rauð, rautt> *adj* red

❖ **ráð** *n* advice, counsel; plan; *pl* affairs, business; **at ráði** wise, advisable; **bera ráð saman** take counsel among themselves; consult together; **vera [e-m] ráð** be advisable for [sb]

❖ **ráða** <ræðr; réð, réðu; ráðinn> *vb* [*w dat*] advise, counsel; rule, govern, manage; undertake; decide, determine; **ráða frá** give up, abandon; **ráða í mót** go against (in a fight), confront, withstand; **ráða skipi til hlunns** drag a ship ashore (during winter); *refl* **ráðask** undertake; be resolved, settled; turn out; **ráðask á** attack, set upon; **ráðask á móti [e-m]** charge against [sb]; **ráðask í brottu** move away; **ráðask vel** turn out or end well

ráðizk *ppart of* **ráðask**

ráðligr <-lig, -ligt> *adj* advisable

ráðligri *comp adj* more advisable (*see* ráðligr)

Refr <-s> *m* Ref ('Fox') (*personal name*); **Refr inn rauði** *m* Ref the Red

Refsstaðir *m pl* Refsstadir ('Ref's Farmstead') (*place name*)

reið <-ar> *f* ride, the act of riding (a horse)

reið *1/3sg past of* **ríða**

reiða <-dd-> *vb* carry; *impers* [*acc subj*] drift, be carried about

❖ **reiðr** <reið, reitt> *adj* angry

reis *1/3sg past of* **rísa**

reka <rekr; rak, ráku; rekinn> *vb* drive, herd; drive onto shore, wreck; **reka braut** drive away; **reka [e-t] í gegnum [e-n]** drive [sth] through [sb]; **rekr [e-n/e-t] upp** *impers* [sb/sth] is driven ashore

rekja <rakð~rakt-; *ppart* rak(i)ðr~raktr> *vb* track, trace; spread out, unfold; **rekja í sundr** (= **rekja**) spread out, unfold

rekkja *f* bed; **fara í rekkju** go to bed

renna <rennr; rann, runnu; runninn> *vb* run; **[e-m] rennr í skap** *impers* [sb] grows angry

reru *3pl past of* **róa**

Reyðarfjǫrðr <*dat* -firði, *gen* -fjarðar> *m* Reydarfjord (*place name*)

reyna <-d-> *vb* try, prove; experience, find out (from experience); *refl* **reynask** prove to be

reynzk *ppart of* **reynask**

réð *1/3sg past of* **ráða**

rétta <-tt-> *vb* make right; (*leg*) right (a wrong); **rétta hluta [e-s]** obtain redress for [sb]

❖ **réttr** <rétt, rétt> *adj* straight; correct, right, just

rézk *2/3sg past of* **ráðask**

riðinn *ppart* involved, concerned (with) (*see* ríða); **verða við [e-t] riðinn** become involved in, concerned with [sth]

rippa <-að-> *vb* go over, sum up; **rippa [e-t] upp** go over [sth], sum [sth] up

❖ **ríða** <ríðr; reið, riðu; riðinn> *vb* ride

ríða <ríðr; reið, riðu; riðinn> *vb* twist, wind

❖ **ríkr** <rík, ríkt; *acc m* -jan; *comp* -(a)ri, *superl* -(a)str> *adj* powerful

rísa <ríss; reis, risu; risinn> *vb* arise, rise, stand up; **rísa upp** rise up, get up

roði *m* redness

róa <rær; reri, reru; róinn> *vb* row

rómr *m* voice; cheering, acclamation; **illr rómr** criticism, voiced disapproval

runnit *ppart of* **renna**

rúm *n* bed; space, seat

ræð *1sg pres of* **ráða**

rœða <-dd-> *vb* speak; **rœða um [e-t]** discuss [sth]

rœtt *ppart of* **rœða**

rǫkðu *3pl past of* **rekja**

rǫskr <rǫsk, rǫskt; *acc m* -van> *adj* vigorous, brave

S

safna <-að-> *vb* [*w dat*] gather, collect

saga <*acc/dat/gen* sǫgu; *pl nom/acc* sǫgur, *dat* sǫgum, *gen* sagna> *f* story, saga

sagði *1/3sg past of* **segja**

sagðisk *2/3sg past of* **segjask**

sagt *ppart of* **segja**

sakar *gen sg of* **sǫk**

❖ **saman** *adv* together; [*w numbers*] all

together, all told; **allt saman** wholly, entirely, altogether

sameign *f* conflict, fight

samfarar *gen sg & nom/acc pl of* **samfǫr**

samfǫr <-farar> *f* (*usu in pl*) relationship, marriage

samkváma *f* meeting, assembly, 'coming together'

❖ **samr** <sǫm, samt> *adj/indef pron* same

sandr <-s; -ar> *m* sand

❖ **sannr** <sǫnn, satt> *adj* true; **hafa [e-t] fyrir satt** believe [sth] to be true, be convinced of [sth]; **it sanna** the truth

sat *1/3sg past of* **sitja**

satt *n sg of* **sannr**

sauðahús *n* sheep-pen, sheep-fold

sauðamaðr <*acc* -mann, *dat* -manni, etc.> *m* shepherd

sauðr <-ar; -ir> *m* sheep

sax <sǫx> *n* short sword

❖ **sá** <sú, þat> *dem pron* that (one); *pl* those

sá *1/3sg past of* **sjá**

sár *n* wound; **liggja í sárum** lie ill from one's wounds

❖ **sárr** <sár, sárt> *adj* wounded

sátt (*also* **sætt**) <sættir> *f* settlement, agreement

❖ **sáttr** <sátt, sátt> *adj* reconciled, at peace

sátu *3pl past of* **sitja**

sáu *3pl past of* **sjá**

❖ **segja** <sagð-> *vb* say, tell; **segja frá [e-u]** reveal, tell about [sth]; **segja it sanna** tell the truth; **segja [e-m] til [e-s]** tell, inform [sb] of [sth]; **segja til sín** give one's name; *refl* **segjask** say of oneself, declare of oneself

seilask <-d-> *refl vb* stretch out one's hands; **seilask eptir [e-u]** to reach out for [sth]

❖ **sekr** <sek, sekt; *acc m* sekan~sekjan> *adj* guilty; convicted, condemned to outlawry; **gera [e-n] sekan** condemn [sb] to outlawry, make [sb] an outlaw

sel <*pl gen* selja> *n* shieling, hut or shed in a mountain pasture used in the summer for milking livestock

selja <-d-> *vb* hand over (to another); sell; **selja á frest** sell on credit; **selja smátt** sell piece by piece, bit by bit; *refl* **seljask** give oneself up, submit oneself; **seljask arfsali** (*leg*) cede one's right of inheritance (i.e., perform an **arfsal**)

❖ **sem** *rel particle* who, which, that; *conj* as; [*w superl*] as ... as possible; where; **þar sem** where

semja <samð-; *ppart* samiðr~samdr> *vb* arrange, compose, settle; **semja sátt** arrange a settlement

❖ **senda** <-nd-> *vb* send; **senda eptir [e-m]** send for [sb]

sendimaðr <*acc* -mann, *dat* -manni, etc.> *m* messenger

serkr <-s~jar; -ir, *pl gen* -ja> *m* shirt

seta *f* body of men

❖ **setja** <-tt-> *vb* set, seat, place; **setja [e-n] til** appoint [sb]; *refl* **setjask** set onself; seat oneself, sit; **setjask aptr** hold back, stay back (*esp* from a journey); **setjask niðr** sit down, set oneself down

setstokkr <-s; -ar> *m* partition-beam, post

❖ **sex** *num* six

sé *1sg pres of* **sjá**

sé *1/3sg pres subjunct of* **vera**

sém *1pl pres subjunct of* **vera**

sén *ppart of* **sjá**

sér *dat of* **sik**

sér *2/3sg pres of* **sjá**

sét *ppart of* **sjá**

siðvenja *f* custom, practice; **at siðvenju** according to custom

sigr <*gen* sigrs> *m* victory

❖ **sik** <*dat* sér, *gen* sín> *refl acc pron* him-/her-/it-/oneself, themselves

silfr *n* silver

silfra *f* Silver (*nickname*)

silfrhringr <-s; -ar> *m* silver ring

❖ **sinn** <sín, sitt> *refl poss pron* his, her, its, their (own)

❖ **sinn** *n* time (*instance or repetition*); **at (því) sinni** at this time, at present; **í fyrsta sinni** the first time; **annat sinn** the second time

❖ **sitja** <sitr; sat, sátu; setinn> *vb* sit; reside; stay; **sitja um [e-t/e-n]** watch for [sth] (*as an opportunity*), lie in wait for, plot against [sb]

síð *adv* late

❖ **síðan** *adv* then, later, afterwards

síðar *comp adv* later, afterwards (*see* **síð**); **litlu síðar** shortly afterward, a little while later

síðr *comp adv* less; **eigi ... síðr** *conj* nothing else ... but

síga <sígr; seig, sigu; siginn> *vb* sink

sín *gen of* **sik**

sínkr <sink, sínkt> *adj* avaricious, covetous

Síreksstaðir *m pl* Sireksstadir ('Sirek's Farmstead') (*place name*)

sjaldan <*comp* sjaldnar, *superl* sjaldnast> *adv* seldom

❖ **sjau** *num* seven

❖ **sjá** (= **þessi**) *dem pron m/f* this

❖ **sjá** <sér; sá, sá(u); sénn> *vb* see, look; understand; **sjá á [e-m]** look upon [sb]; **sjá yfir** look over, survey, look after; *refl* **sjásk** see one another; **sjásk á** see to, deal with one another

sjálfbjargi *adj indecl* self-sufficient

sjálfdœmi *n* (*leg*) self-judgment

❖ **sjálfr** <sjálf, sjálft> *adj/indef pron* self, him-/her-/it-/oneself, themselves

sjónlauss <-laus, -laust> *adj* blind, sightless

skaði *m* harm, damage; loss

skaðlauss <-laus, -laust> *adj* without loss, unscathed

skal *1/3sg pres of* **skulu**

❖ **skammr** <skǫmm, skam(m)t; *comp* skemri, *superl* skemstr> *adj* short, brief; **fyrir skǫmmu** recently

skammt *n adj as adv* a short distance, not far (*place*); a short while, not long (*time*); **eiga skammt til** have a short distance to go until, be not far from

skap <skǫp> *n* condition of mind, temper, mood; **[e-m] rennr í skap** *impers* [sb] grows angry

skapt <skǫpt> *n* handle, shaft; **á hávu skapti** on a long shaft

skapþungr <-þung, -þungt> *adj* depressed, heavy-hearted, in low spirits; **[e-m] er skapþungt** *impers* [sb] is heavy-hearted, in low spirits

skarð <skǫrð> *n* notch; gap; mountain pass

skeina <-d-> *vb* scratch, wound slightly; *refl* **skeinask** get a slight wound

skera <skerr; skar, skáru; skorinn> *vb* cut; slaughter; **skera niðr** (= **drepa niðr**) cut down; slaughter

skikkja *f* cloak, mantle

skila <-að-> *vb* [*w dat*] give back, return; **skila aptr [e-u]** bring or take [sth] back

skildi *dat sg of* **skjǫldr**

skilði *3sg past of* **skilja**

❖ **skilja** <-d~ð-; *ppart* skiliðr~skildr~skilinn> *vb* part, separate, divide; discern, understand; decide, settle; **þá skilr á um [e-t]** *impers* they fall out over, differ, disagree about [sth]; *refl* **skiljask** part company

skilríkr <-rík, -ríkt; *acc m* -jan> *adj* trustworthy, respectable

skinni *m* skin, skinner (*nickname*)

❖ **skip** *n* ship

skipta <-t-> *vb* [*w dat*] divide, share; shift, change; happen; **skipta sér engu af [e-u]** take no part in [sth]

skipverjar *m pl* ship's crew

Skíði *m* Skidi (*personal name*); **Skíði inn prúði** *m* Skidi the Elegant

skjótast *superl adv* most swiftly (*see* **skjótt**)

skjótr <skjót, skjótt> *adj* swift, quick

skjótt *n adj as adv* swiftly, quickly; soon

❖ **skjǫldr** <*dat* skildi, *gen* skjaldar; *pl* skildir, *acc* skjǫldu> *m* shield

skógarhǫgg *n* tree felling, wood cutting

skógr <-ar, -ar> *m* forest, woods

skrautligr <-lig, -ligt> *adj* splendid

skrautmaðr <*acc* -mann, *dat* -manni, etc.> *m* showy person, show-off, one who loves fine clothes and adornments

skrautmenni *n* showy person (= **skrautmaðr**)

skræfask <-ð-> *refl vb* act like a coward

skuld <-ir> *f* debt, obligation to pay; **gefa [e-m] skuld** require compensation from [sb]

skuldunautr <-s; -ar> *m* debtor

❖ **skulu** <skal, skulu; skyldi; *pret inf* skyldu> *pret-pres vb* shall (*obligation, purpose, necessity, fate*); (*past tense*) should

skyggn <skyggn, skyggnt> *adj* sharpsighted

skyldi *3sg past indic & 3sg/pl past subjunct of* **skulu**

❖ **skyldr** <skyld, skylt; *comp* -(a)ri, *superl* skyldastr~skylztr> *adj* related by kinship

skyldu *3pl past indic & pret inf of* **skulu**

skyndiliga *adv* hastily, speedily

skyndir *m* haste

skǫmmu *n dat sg of* **skammr**; **fyrir skǫmmu** recently

slátr *n* butchered meat

slitit *ppart of* **slíta**

❖ **slíkr** <slík, slíkt> *adj* such

slíkt *n adj as adv* in such a way

slíta <slítr; sleit, slitu; slitinn> *vb* [*w dat*] break; break up, dissolve (a meeting or confrontation)

smalahestr *m* shepherd's horse

smalamaðr <*acc* -mann, *dat* -manni, etc.> *m* shepherd

smálátr <-lát, -látt> *adj* content with little

smálæti *n* stinginess

smár <smá, smátt; *acc m* smán, *f* smá, *dat m* smám, *n* smá; *pl f* smár; *comp* smæri, *superl* smæstr> *adj* small

smáskip *n* small ship

smátt *adv* in small quantities; **selja smátt** sell piece by piece, bit by bit

Smjǫrvatnsheiðr *f* Smjorvatnsheid ('Butter-Water Heath') (*place name*)

smæligr *adj* humiliating, dishonorable

snara <-að-> *vb* turn quickly, twist; *refl* **snarask** turn oneself quickly, turn around

snarpliga *adv* sharply, with a dash

snarr <snǫr, snart> *adj* swift; gallant, bold, smart; keen

sneiða <-dd-> *vb* slice; glance off

sneri *1/3sg past of* **snúa**

sneru *3pl past of* **snúa**

snimma *adv* early; **snimma dags** early in the day

snimmt *adv* early (= **snimma**)

snjór (*also* **snær**) <*gen* snjóvar~snjófar> *m* snow

snúa <snýr; snøri~sneri; snúinn> *vb* turn, go

snúðugr <-ug, -ugt> *adj* swift

snúðugt *n adj as adv* swiftly; **ganga snúðugt** march, walk at a swinging pace

snýr *2/3sg pres of* **snúa**

snær (also **snjór**) <*gen* snævar~snæfar> *m* snow

sofa <sefr; svaf, sváfu; sofinn> *vb* sleep; **sofa af um nóttina** sleep through the night

sofandi *pres part of* **sofa**

sofna <-að-> *vb* fall asleep; **vera sofnaðr** be asleep

sonarsonr *m* grandson

❖ **sonr** <*dat* syni, *gen* sonar, *pl* synir, *acc* sonu> *m* son

sótt <-ir> *f* sickness, illness; **taka sótt** fall sick, be taken ill

sótti *3sg past of* **sœkja**

spakr <spǫk, spakt> *adj* wise

spekingr <-s; -ar> *m* wise person, sage

❖ **spjót** *n* spear

spor *n* track, footprint, trail

spratt *1/3sg past of* **spretta**

spretta <sprettr; spratt, spruttu; sprottinn> *vb* start, spring; **spretta upp** spring up

spurði *3sg past of* **spyrja**

spurðr *ppart of* **spyrja**

spurðu *3pl past of* **spyrja**

spurðusk *3pl past of* **spyrjask**

❖ **spyrja** <spurð-> *vb* ask; hear, hear of, learn, be informed of, find out; **spyrja at [e-m/e-u]** ask after, inquire about [sb/sth]; *refl* **spyrjask** be heard of, be reported

❖ **staðr** <*dat* stað(i), *gen* -ar; *pl* -ir> *m* stead, parcel of land; place, spot; abode, dwelling; *pl* (*in place names*) farmstead; **í stað sinn** instead of one, in one's place; **nema staðar** stop, halt

stafr <-s; -ar~ir> *m* staff, stick

❖ **standa** <stendr; stóð, stóðu; staðinn> *vb* stand; **standa eptir** stay back, remain

stanga <-að-> *vb* ram, butt with the head, gore (*of cattle*); *refl* **stangask** butt each other

stefna <-d-> *vb* aim at, go in a certain direction; call, call together, summon; (*leg*) summon, serve notice to; **stefna leið** head toward, head for

stefna *f* (*leg*) summons, citation

stefnufǫr <*gen* -farar; *pl* -farar~farir> *f* journey to serve a legal summons

Steinbjǫrn *m* Steinbjorn ('Stone-Bear') (*personal name*); **Steinbjǫrn kǫrtr** *m* Steinbjorn Sturdy

Steini *m* Steini (*personal name*)

Steinn <-s> *m* Stein ('Stone') (*personal name*)

Steinvǫr <*acc/dat* Steinvǫru, *gen* Steinvarar> *f* Steinvor (*personal name*)

stendr *2/3sg pres of* **standa**

❖ **sterkr** <sterk, sterkt> *adj* strong

stigu *3pl past of* **stíga**

stikublígr *m* 'stick-gazer', miser (*nickname*)

stilla <-t-> *vb* arrange, settle; still, calm; **stilla til** arrange

stilltr <stillt, stillt> *adj* calm, composed, self-contained

stíga <stígr; steig, stigu; stiginn> *vb* step, walk; **stíga af baki** dismount (from a horse); **stíga á bak** mount (a horse); **stíga á (skip, bát)** board (a ship, a boat)

stjúpmóðir <*acc/dat/gen* -móður; *pl* -mœðr, *dat* -mœðrum, *gen* -mœðra> *f* stepmother

stjúpsonr <*dat* -syni, *gen* -sonar, *pl* -synir, *acc* -sonu> *m* stepson

stoða <-að-> *vb* support

stofa *f* 'stove room', a room in a long house, secondary to the **eldaskáli** and warmed by a stove of flat stones, which served as a living room where women worked the looms, families sat in the evenings, and feasts were held

stokkr <-s; -ar> *m* pole, log of wood

stóð *1/3sg past of* **standa**

stóðhross *n* stud-horse

stóðu *3pl past of* **standa**

stórilla *adv* very badly

stórlátr <-lát, -látt> *adj* proud, haughty; munificent; not content with little

stórmannligr <-lig, -ligt> *adj* magnificent, grand, imposing

stórmenni *n* great man, leader

stórmæli *n pl* great or grave affairs

❖ **stórr** <stór, stórt; *comp* stœrri, *superl* stœrstr> *adj* big

strjúka <strýkr; strauk, struku; strokinn> *vb* stroke, rub, wipe; caress; smooth, brush; run, rush, dash off

strǫnd <*dat* strǫnd(u), *gen* strandar; *pl* strendr~strandir> *f* shore, coast, 'strand'

Strǫnd *f* Strond ('Shore' or 'Strand') (*place name*)

stund <*dat* -u; *pl* -ir> *f* a while, a time; hour; **litla stund** a little while, for a short time; **um stund** for a while

styðja <studd-> *vb* support

stytta <-tt-> *vb* shorten; *refl* **styttask** get angry

styttingr *m* unfriendliness, abruptness; **skiljask með styttingi** part coldly, abruptly

stýra <-ð-> *vb* [*w dat*] steer, command; rule, govern; manage

stýrimaðr <*acc* -mann, *dat* -manni, etc.> *m* captain of a ship, skipper

stǫðull <*dat* stǫðli, *gen* stǫðuls, *pl* stǫðlar> *m* milking pen (for cows)

stǫðva <-að-> *vb* stop; *refl* **stǫðvask** stop oneself, calm down; be stopped

stǫnguðusk *3pl past mid of* **stanga**

suðr (*gen* suðrs) *n* the south; *adv* southwards

Suðrmaðr <*acc* -mann, *dat* -manni, etc.> *m* Southerner, person from the south (*esp* a German or a Saxon)

sullr <*pl* -ir> *m* boil

❖ **sumar** <*dat* sumri; *pl* sumur, *dat* sumrum, *gen* sumra> *n* summer; **um sumarit** in, during the summer; **um sumarit eptir** the following summer

❖ **sumr** <sum, sumt> *adj/indef pron* some; **sumra manna** of some people

sundr (*also* **í sundr**) *adv* apart, asunder

sunna *f* sun

Sunnudalr <*dat* -dal, *gen* -dals> *m* Sunnudal ('South Dale', 'South Valley', *or perh* 'Sun Dale') (*place name*)

Sunnudalsmynni *m* Sunnudalsmynni ('the mouth of South (or Sun) Dale') (*place name*)

sú *f nom sg of dem pron* **sá**

svar <svǫr> *n* answer, reply

❖ **svara** <-að-> *vb* [*w dat*] answer, reply

svartr <svǫrt, svart> *adj* black

Svartr <-s> *m* Svart ('Black') (*personal name*)

❖ **svá** *adv* so, thus; such; then; so (*denoting degree*); **svá at** such that, with the result that

svefn <*gen* svefns> *m* sleep

svefnbúr *n* sleeping closet, stall

❖ **sveinn** <-s; -ar> *m* boy, lad

❖ **sverð** *n* sword

svigi *m* switch

sviptir *m* loss

svíða <svíðr; sveið, sviðu; sviðinn> *vb* burn, singe; *impers* [*dat subj*] be hurt

svívirðing *f* disgrace, humiliation

svǫr *nom/acc pl of* **svar**

synir *nom pl of* **sonr**

synja <-að-> *vb* [*w gen*] deny, refuse

systir <*acc/dat/gen* systur, *pl* systr> *f* sister

systkin *n pl* brother and sisters (*coll*)

sýna <-d-> *vb* show; *refl* **sýnask** seem, appear; seem fitting

sýnn <sýn, sýnt> *adj* clear, evident, certain

sýnt *n adj as adv* evidently, clearly

sæi *3sg/pl past subjunct of* **sjá**

sæll <sæl, sælt; *comp* sælli, *superl*

sæl(a)str> *adj* well-off; happy, fortunate; blessed

sænautalitr *m* the color of a sea-cow

sæng <*gen* sængar~sængr; *pl* sængr> *f* bed

sæta <-tt-> *vb* [*w dat*] bring about, cause; amount to, be of importance; **engu sæta** be of no importance, amount to nothing; **sæta áverkum við [e-m] fyrri** be the first to injure [sb]

sætt (*also* **sátt**) <sættir> *f* settlement, reconciliation

sætta <-tt-> *vb* reconcile; make peace among; *refl* **sættask** come to terms, agree, be reconciled

❖ **sœkja** <sótt-> *vb* seek; pursue; (*leg*) prosecute; attack; **sœkja at** attack

sœmð *f* honor

sœmiligr <-lig, -ligt> *adj* honorable, becoming

sǫðla <-að-> *vb* saddle

sǫðull <sǫðuls; sǫðlar> *m* saddle

sǫguligr <-lig, -ligt> *adj* important, worth telling

❖ **sǫk** <*gen* sakar; *pl* sakar~sakir> *f* cause, reason, sake; (*leg*) charge, the offence charged; (*leg*) case, lawsuit, prosecution; **fyrir [e-s] sakar** on account of, because of [sth]; **gefa [e-m] sǫk** prosecute, make a charge against [sb]

sǫmu *str n dat sg & wk f acc/dat/gen sg & wk all nom/acc/gen pl of* **samr**

T

tafl <tǫfl> *n* a board game

❖ **taka** <tekr; tók, tóku; tekinn> *vb* take, catch, seize; take hold of, grasp; reach, touch; [*w inf*] begin [to do sth]; **taka af** get, receive, accept; **taka [e-t] af** cancel, abolish, do away with [sth]; *impers* **[e-t] taka af** [sth] comes loose, comes off; **taka at** [*w inf*] begin to [do sth]; **taka mál** (*leg*) take up a case; **taka til** begin; concern; **taka til orða** speak up; **láta [e-t] til sín taka** let [sth] concern oneself, involve oneself in [sth], meddle with [sth]; **taka upp** interpret, think, take a position (on a question); **taka upp [e-t]** take, pick up [sth]; **taka vel við [e-m]** give [sb] a warm welcome; **taka við [e-m]** take in, receive, or welcome [sb] into one's house; **taka við [e-u]** receive, take possession of, acquire, inherit [sth]; *refl* **takask** begin; happen; succeed; **[e-m] teksk vel** *impers* it goes well for [sb], [sb] succeeds

tal <tǫl> *n* conversation, talk; **á tali** in conversation, talking, **bregða tali** break off speaking; **eiga tal með sér** have a talk with each other; **heimta [e-n] á tal** engage [sb] in conversation, address [sb]; draw someone aside; **koma á tal við [e-n]** come to speak with [sb]

❖ **tala** <-að-> *vb* talk, speak; **tala við [e-n]** speak to [sb]; *refl* **talask** speak to one another

talazk *ppart of* **talask**

talði *3sg past of* **telja**

tekinn *ppart of* **taka**

tekizk *ppart of* **takask**

teksk *2/3sg pres of* **takask**

telja <talð~tald-; *ppart* taliðr~taldr~ talinn> *vb* count; reckon, consider; **telja á hendr [e-m]** lay the blame on [sb]

tigr <*gen* tigar; *pl* tigir, *acc* tigu> *m* ten; a decade; **sex tigir** *num* sixty; **þrír tigir** *num* thirty

❖ **til** *prep* [*w gen*] to

tíðast *superl adv* most quickly; **sem tíðast** at once, with all speed

tíðendi *var of* **tíðindi**

❖ **tíðindi** (*also* **tíðendi**) *n pl* news, tidings

tíðr <tíð, títt> *adj* frequent; usual

tíðrœtt *ppart* discussed much (*see* **rœða**, **tíðr**); **þeim var tíðrœtt** *impers* they spoke much together

tími *m* time; **í þann tíma** at that time; **þykkja [e-m] tími til** *impers* [sb] thinks the time is right

títt *n adj as adv* frequently; quickly (*see* **tíðr**)

❖ **tíu** *num* ten

Tjǫrvi *m* Tjorvi (*personal name*); **Tjǫrvi inn mikli** *m* Big Tjorvi

todda *f* Todda (*abbreviation for the name* **Þórdís** *and a nickname; see also* **toddi**)

toddi *m* bit, piece, morsel

tollr <-s; -ar> *m* toll, duty, tax

topt <-ir> *f* 'toft', site of a house; foundation or bare walls, *esp* the ruins of a house

Toptavǫllr *m* Toptavoll ('Field of Wall-Ruins') (*place name*)

Torfastaðir *m pl* Torfastadir ('Torfi's Farmstead') (*place name*)

Torfi *m* Torfi (*personal name*)

tók *1/3sg past of* **taka**

tóksk *1/3sg past of* **takask**

❖ **tólf** *num* twelve

tómliga *adv* slowly, leisurely

tómr <tóm, tómt> *adj* empty

treysta <-t-> *vb* make trusty, firm; test; trust; dare; **treysta [e-m]** trust, rely on [sb]

tré <*dat* tré, *pl* tré, *dat* trjám, *gen* trjá> *n* tree

tunga *f* tongue; language; tongue of land at the meeting of two rivers

Tunga *f* Tunga ('Tongue') (*place name*)

tún *n* enclosure; hayfield, homefield

túngarðr <-s; -ar> *m* fence, wall of a **tún**

tvá *m acc of* **tveir**

❖ **tveir** <tvær, tvau; *acc m* tvá, *dat* tveim(r), *gen* tveggja> *num* two

tvær *f nom/acc of* **tveir**

týna <-d-> *vb* lose; *refl* **týnask** perish

týnzk *ppart of* **týnask**

tœki *3sg/pl past subjunct of* **taka**

U

❖ **um** *prep* [*w acc*] about; around; across; for, because of; beyond; during, for, in, by (*time*); [*w dat in poetic and older texts*] over; by, in (*time*); [*w vb of motion*] over, past, beyond, across; **fram um** *or* **um fram** [*w vb of motion*] on past, up beyond, out over; **um dag** one day; **um fram** in addition; **um nætr** by night

umsjá *f* supervision, care over; assistance

umsýsla *f* management; **vera at umsýsla** manage, oversee

una <-ð-, *n ppart* unat> *vb* dwell, stay, abide; [*w dat*] enjoy, be happy in, be content with; **una við [e-t]** to be content with [sth]

❖ **undan** *prep* [*w dat*] from under; away from; *adv* away; **ganga undan [e-m]** leave, withdraw support from [sb]

❖ **undir** *prep* [*w acc*] under, underneath; [sb]

[*w dat*] under, depending upon; **undir sér** with him

unðu *3pl past of* **una**

❖ **ungr** <ung, ungt; *comp* yngri, *superl* yngstr> *adj* young; **ungr at aldri** young, at a young age, 'young in age'

unna <ann, unnu; unni; unn(a)t> *pret-pres vb* grant, allow, bestow; [*w dat*] love; **unna [e-m] eigi** begrudge [sb]

unnit *ppart of* **vinna**

unz *conj* until

❖ **upp** *adv* up, upward (*motion*)

uppi *adv* up (*location*); **vera uppi** live, last

urðu *3pl past of* **verða**

uxaslátr *n* meat of oxen, beef

uxi (*also* **oxi**) <*pl* (*often irregularly n*) yxn~øxn, *dat* yxnum~øxnum, *gen* yxna~øxna> *m* ox

Ú

úlfr <-s; -ar> *m* wolf

Úlfr <-s> *m* Ulf ('Wolf') (*personal name*)

❖ **út** *adv* out, outward (*motion*)

❖ **útan** *adv* from without, from outside; **fara útan** go abroad, away from Iceland (*usu* to Norway)

útanferð <-ir> *f* journey abroad

útanverðr <-verð, -vert> *adj* the outward, outside, outer part of

útferð <-ir> *f* journey to a remote place; funeral, burial

úti *adv* out (*location*), outside, outdoors

útibúr *n* outside storehouse

V

vafðr *ppart of* **vefja**

vakna <-að-> *vb* awaken (*intrans*), get up

val <vǫl> *n* choice

valði *3sg past of* **velja**

van- *prefix* lacking, under-, un-

vandalauss <-laus, -laust> *adj* standing under no obligation to another; **vera vandalauss af** be free of obligation or responsibility, have no concern

vandi *m* difficulty, difficult task, problem

vandi (*also* **vanði**) *m* custom, habit

vanði *var of* **vandi**

vandliga *adv* carefully; completely, fully

vandræði *n* trouble, difficulty

vanhaldinn *ppart* wronged, getting less than one's due (*see* **halda, van-**)

vanheilsa *f* poor health, illness

vanmáttr *m* helplessness; illness

vanmenni *n* worthless person

❖ **vanr** <vǫn, vant> *adj* accustomed, wont; **vera vanr [e-u]** be accustomed to [sth]

var *1/3sg past of* **vera**

vara <*pl* vǫrur, *gen* varna> *f* wares

vara <-að-> *vb* warn; *refl* **varask** be aware of, be on one's guard against

varð *1/3sg past of* **verða**

varða <-að-> *vb* warrant, guarantee, answer for; (*leg*) be liable, punishable, incur a penalty

varðveita <-tt-> *vb* keep, take care of

varit *ppart* of a certain disposition (*see* **verja**; *see also* **farit**); **[e-m] er illa varit** *impers* [sb] has an ill disposition, is acting unworthily

varla *adv* hardly, scarcely

varningr <*gen* -s> *m* wares, goods, cargo

❖ **varr** <vǫr, vart> *adj* aware; **gera [e-n] varan við [e-t]** warn [sb], make [sb] aware of [sth]; **verða varr við [e-t]** become aware of, learn of [sth]

vatn <*gen* vatns~vatz~vaz, *pl* vǫtn> *n* water, liquid, fluid; fresh water; lake

vaxa <vex; óx, óxu; vaxinn> *vb* grow; **vaxa upp** grow up

vá *1/3sg past of* **vega**

vágu *3pl past of* **vega**

ván <-ir> *f* hope; expectation; **er ván [e-s]**

impers [sb]/[sth] is expected

❖ **vápn** *n* weapon; **bera vápn á [e-n]** raise weapons against [sb]

vápna <-að-> *vb* furnish with arms; *refl* **vápnask** arm oneself

Vápnafjǫrðr <*dat* -firði, *gen* -fjarðar> *m* Vapnafjord ('Weapon's Fjord') (*place name*)

❖ **vár** *n* spring (season); **um várit** in the spring

vár *gen of* **vér**

várkunn *f* that which is excusable; excuse

❖ **várr** *poss pron 1pl* our

váru *3pl past of* **vera**

várþing *n* spring assembly

váttr <-s; -ar> *m* witness

veðr *n* weather

veðrfastr <-fǫst, -fast> *adj* weatherbound

vefja <vafð-; *ppart* vaf(i)ðr~vafinn> *vb* wrap, fold; **vefja [e-t] saman** wrap [sth] up, fold [sth] together

vega <vegr; vá, vágu; veginn> *vb* kill, slay; fight; **vega sigr** gain the victory

vegandi *m* killer

vegna *prep* [*w gen*] on account of, on behalf of; **hvárutveggja vegna** on both sides

❖ **vegr** <*gen* vegar~vegs, *pl* vegir~vegar, *acc* vegu~vega> *m* way, road; mode; manner; direction; side

veit *1/3sg pres of* **vita**

❖ **veita** <-tt-> *vb* grant, give, offer; assist; **veita [e-m] [e-t]** grant [sb] [sth]; **veita [e-m] atsókn** attack [sb]

veizla *f* banquet, feast, party

veizt *2sg pres of* **vita**

veiztu = **veizt þú**, you (*sg*) know (*see* **vita**)

vekja <vakð~vakt-, vakiðr~vaktr~vakinn> *vb* wake, awake (*trans*); **vekja [e-n] upp** wake [sb] up

❖ **vel** <*comp* betr, *superl* bezt> *adv* well; very; **vel at sér** accomplished, gifted

velja <valð~vald-; *ppart* val(i)ðr~valdr~ valinn> *vb* choose, select, pick out

velli *dat sg of* **vǫllr**

❖ **vera** <er; var, váru; verit> *vb* be; last; stay; **vera eptir** stay back, remain behind; **vera til** exist, stand; **eiga [e-t] um at vera** have [sth] to be troubled about; **vera um nóttina** stay for the night; **vera þar fyrir** be present there

❖ **verða** <verðr; varð, urðu; orðinn> *vb* become, happen; **verða at** [*w inf*] must, have to, be obliged to [do sth]; **verða á [e-m]** befall [sb]

❖ **verðr** <verð, vert> *adj* [*w gen*] worth, of value; worthy, deserving; **vera [e-s] verðr** be worthy, deserving of [sth]

verja <varð-, *ppart* var(i)ðr~varinn> *vb* defend; wrap, enclose; **[e-m] er illa varit** *impers* [sb] has an ill disposition, is acting unworthily (*see also* **fara**); *refl* **verjask** defend onself

-verjar *m pl suff* people of (a place)

verk *n* work, a deed, business

verr *comp adv* worse (*see* **illa**)

verst *superl adv* worst (*see* **illa**); **sem verst** as bad as it can be, as bad as possible

❖ **vetr** <*gen* vetrar, *pl* vetr> *m* winter; **um vetrinn** in, during the winter

vetrnætr *f pl* Winter Nights (the three days which begin the winter season)

vér <*acc/dat* oss, *gen* vár> *pron 1pl* we

❖ **við** *prep* [*w acc*] at, by, close to; with; according to, after; [*w dat*] against; toward; with

viðarøx <*acc/dat* -i; *pl* -ar> *f* wood-axe

viðr <*gen* viðar, *pl* viðir, *acc* viðu> *m* tree; forest, wood; timber

vika <*pl gen* vikna> *f* week

vildu *pret inf of* **vilja**

vili <*gen* vilja> *m* will, wish, desire; **gera vilja [e-s]** let [sb] have his/her will

vilja *acc/dat/gen sg of* **vili**

❖ **vilja** <vill; vildi; viljat; *pret inf* vildu> *vb* wish, want

viltu = **vill þú**, do you (*sg*) want (*see* **vilja**)

vinátta *f* friendship (*esp* a sincere, personal friendship)

vinfengi *n* friendship (*esp* a contractual alliance)

vingjarnligr <-lig, -ligt> *adj* friendly, kind

vingóðr <-góð, -gott> *adj* good towards one's friends, friendly

vinna *f* work, labor

vinna <vinnr; vann, unnu; unninn> *vb* gain, win; work; perform, accomplish; *refl* **vinnask** last

❖ **vinr** <-ar; -ir> *m* friend

❖ **vinsæll** <-sæl, -sælt; *comp* vinsælli, *superl* vinsæl(a)str> *adj* much liked, popular

virða <-ð-> *vb* value; consider, estimate; honor, respect

vissi *3sg past indic & 3sg/pl past subjunct of* **vita**

vist <-ir> *f* stay; lodging; **til vistar** to lodge, stay (at one's house)

vista <-að-> *vb* (*trans*) lodge (someone), find lodging for; furnish with food and provisions; *refl* **vistask** lodge (*intrans*), stay, take up lodging

vit <*acc/dat* okkr, *gen* okkar> *pron 1dual* we (two)

vit *n pl* place where a thing is kept, case; (*fig*) possession

❖ **vita** <veit, vitu; vissi; vitaðr> *pret-pres vb* know; **vita til [e-s]** know of [sth]; **vita [e-t] víst** know [sth] for sure

vitja <-að-> *vb* [*w gen*] call on, visit; claim the fulfillment of an agreement or promise

❖ **vitr** <vitr, vitrt> *adj* wise

vitrastr *superl of* **vitr**

víðfrægr *adj* widely renowned, famous

víðir <-is; -ar> *m* willow

Víðivellir *m pl* Vidivellir ('Willow Fields') (*place name*)

❖ **víg** *n* battle; (*leg*) homicide, manslaughter, killing

vígr <víg, vígt> *adj* able to fight; **vel vígr** skilled at fighting

vík <*gen* víkr; *pl* víkr, *gen* víkna> *f* inlet, bay

víkja <víkr; veik, viku; vikinn> *vb* turn, move, shift direction

víkr *gen sg & nom/acc pl of* **vík**

vísa <-að-> *vb* show, point out, indicate; **vísa [e-m] á [e-t]** direct or lead [sb] into [sth]

❖ **víss** <vís, víst> *adj* certain, sure; **at vísu** surely

víst *n adj as adv* certainly, for sure; **vita [e-t] víst** know [sth] for sure

❖ **vænn** <væn, vænt> *adj* beautiful, fine, handsome; hopeful, promising; likely, to be expected; **vænn í fǫrum** promising in trade

vænstr *superl of* **vænn**

væri *3sg/pl past subjunct of* **vera**

vǫllr <*dat* velli, *gen* vallar, *pl* vellir, *acc* vǫllu, *gen* valla> *m* field, plain

vǫrðr <*dat* verði, *gen* varðar; *pl* verðir, *acc*

vǫrðu> *m* watch, guard; **halda vǫrð** keep watch

vǫrðusk *3pl past of* **verjask**

Y

yðar *gen of* **þér**

yðarr (*also* **yðvarr**) <yður, yðart; *dat m* yðrum, *n* yðru; *pl m* yðrir, *f* yðrar, *n* yður, *acc m* yðra, *all dat* yðrum> *pron 2pl poss* your, yours (*pl*)

❖ yðr *acc/dat of pl pron* **þér**

❖ yfir *prep* [*w acc/dat*] over, above, across; *adv* over

ykkar *gen of* **þit**

ykkarr <ykkur, ykkart; *acc m* ykkarn, *dat m* ykkrum, *n* ykkru; *pl m* ykkrir, *f* ykkrar, *n* ykkur, *acc m* ykkra, *all dat* ykkrum> *poss pron 2dual* your, yours

ykkr *acc/dat of* **þit**

yngri *comp of* **ungr**

yxn *pl* (*often irregularly* n) *of* **uxi**

Ý

ýmiss <*pl* ýmsir> *adj* various; **ýmsa vega** in various directions, this way and that

ýmsa *m acc pl of* **ýmiss**

ýtri <*superl* ýztr> *comp adj* outer

Þ

þaðan *adv* from there, thence; **þaðan frá** from that point onward; **þaðan í frá** from that time forward, from then on

❖ þangat *adv* to there, thither (*motion*)

þann *m acc sg of dem pron* **sá**

þannig *adv* this way, thus

❖ þar *adv* there; **þar til** thereto, to that point; **þar sem** *conj* where

þarf *1/3sg pres of* **þurfa**

þarft *2sg pres of* **þurfa**

þarftu = **þarft þú** (*see* **þurfa**)

þarna *adv* there

þat <*acc* þat, *dat* því, *gen* þess> *pron 3sg n* it

þat *n nom/acc of dem pron* **sá**

þau <*acc* þau, *dat* þeim, *gen* þeira~þeirra> *pron 3pl n* they

þau *n nom/acc pl of dem pron* **sá**

þá *acc of* **þeir**

þá *f acc sg of dem pron* **sá**

❖ þá *adv* then; **þá er** *conj* when

þáttr <*dat* þætti, *gen* þáttar, *pl* þættir, *acc* þáttu> *m* tale, short saga

❖ þegar *adv* at once, immediately; already; **þegar á unga aldri** already by a young age; **þegar er** *conj* as soon as

þegit *ppart of* **þiggja**

þegja <þagð-, *n ppart* þagat> *vb* be silent

þegnskapr <-ar> *m* generosity, open-handedness

þeim *m dat sg & all dat pl of dem pron* **sá**

þeir <*acc* þá, *dat* þeim, *gen* þeira~þeirra> *pron 3pl m* they

þeir *m nom pl of dem pron* **sá**

þeira *gen pl of dem pron* **sá**; *gen of* **þeir**

þeira *poss pron 3pl indecl* their, theirs

þekkja <-ð~t-> *vb* perceive, notice; comprehend; know, recognize; *refl* **þekkjask** agree with, accept, consent to

þenna *m acc sg of* **þessi**

þess *gen of* **þat**, (of) it

þess *poss pron 3sg n indecl* its

❖ þessi <þessi, þetta; *dat m* þessum, *n* þessu, *gen m/n* þessa; *pl n* þessi> *dem pron* this, *pl* these

þeyja <-, þá, -, -> *defect vb* thaw

þeyr <*dat* þey; *gen* þeys, *pl* þeyir> *m* thaw

þér *dat of* **þú**

þér <*acc/dat* yðr, *gen* yðarr~yðvarr> *pron 2pl* you (*pl*)you

Þiðrandi *m* Thidrandi (*personal name*)

þiggja <þiggr; þá, þágu; þeginn> *vb* accept; receive; accept lodgings

þik *acc of* **þú**

❖ **þing** *n* assembly, meeting

þingmaðr <*acc* -mann, *dat* -manni, etc.> *m* 'thingman', the follower of an Icelandic chieftain

❖ **þinn** <þín, þitt> *poss pron 2sg* your (*sg*)

þit <*acc/dat* ykkr, *gen* ykkarr> *pron 2dual* you (two)

þjórr <-s; -ar> *m* bull, young bull

þoka <-að-> *vb* [*w dat*] go, move; **þoka áleiðis** improve

þola <-d-, *n* ppart þol(a)t> *vb* suffer, endure, bear; **þola [e-m] [e-t]** endure [sth] from [sb]

Þorbrandsstaðir *m pl* Thorbrandsstadir ('Thorbrand's Farmstead') (*place name*)

Þorgeirr <-s> *m* Thorgeir (*personal name*)

Þorgerðarstaðir *m pl* Thorgerdarstadir ('Thorgerd's Farmstead') (*place name*)

Þorgerðr <*acc/dat* Þorgerði, *gen* Þorgerðar> *f* Thorgerd (*personal name*); **Þorgerðr silfra** *f* Thorgerd Silver

Þorgils <*gen* Þorgils> *m* Thorgils (*personal name*); **Þorgils skinni** *m* Thorgils Skin; **Þorgils Þorsteinsson** *m* Thorgils, son of Thorstein

Þorkell <-s> *m* Thorkel (*personal name*)

Þorlákr <-s> *m* Thorlak (*personal name*); **Þorlákr inn helgi** *m* Thorlak the Holy, Saint Thorlak

Þormóðr <-ar> *m* Thormod (*personal name*); **Þormóðr stikublígr** *m* Thormod Stick-Gazer

Þorsteinn <-s> *m* Thorstein (*personal name*); **Þorsteinn hvíti** *m* Thorstein the White

Þorvaldr <-s> *m* Thorvald (*personal name*); **Þorvaldr inn hávi** *m* Thorvald the Tall

❖ **þó** *adv* yet, though, nevertheless; **en þó** nevertheless, and besides, moreover

Þórarinn <-s> *m* Thorarin (*personal name*)

Þórdís *f* Thordis (*personal name*)

Þórðr <-ar> *m* Thord (*personal name*)

Þórir <*gen* Þóris> *m* Thorir (*personal name*)

Þórleifr <-s> *m* Thorleif (*personal name*); **Þorleifr inn kristni** *m* Thorleif the Christian

❖ **þótt** *conj* [*w subjunct*] although, even though

þótti *1/3sg past of* **þykkja**

þóttisk *2/3sg past of* **þykkjask**

þóttusk *3pl past of* **þykkjask**

þrekleysi *n* lack of courage, lack of resolve

þrekvirki *n* courageous a deed, feat of strength

þriði <-ja, -ju> *ord num* third; **við þriðja mann** 'with a third person', being three altogether

þriggja *gen of* **þrír**

þrífœttr <-fœtt, -fœtt> *adj* three-legged

❖ **þrír** <þrjár, þrjú; *acc m* þrjá, *dat* þrim(r), *gen* þriggja> *num* three

þrǫng (*also* **þrøngð**) <-var> *f* crowd, throng

þrøngð *var of* **þrǫng**

Þrǫstr <-s> *m* Throst (*personal name*)

❖ **þungr** <þung, þungt> *adj* heavy

þungt *n adj as adv* heavily, gravely

þunnr <þunn, þunnt; *comp* þynnri~ þunnari, *superl* þynnstr~þunnastr> *adj* thin

þurfa <þarf, þurfu; þurfti; þurft> *pret-pres vb* [*aux*] need; [*w gen*] need, have need of

❖ **þú** <*acc* þik, *dat* þér, *gen* þín> *pron 2sg* you (*sg*)

þváttdagr *m* Saturday, *lit* washing-day

þverra <þverr; þvarr, þurru; þorrinn> *vb* decrease

því *dat of* **þat**; **því at** *conj* because

því *n dat sg of dem pron* **sá**

þvílíkr <-lík, -líkt> *adj* such; **þvílíkr ok** the same as

þvílíkt *n adj as adv* such, in such a manner

❖ **þykkja** <þykkir, þótt-> *vb impers* seem to be; [*dat subj*] think, seem (to one); **[e-m] þykkir sviptir** *impers* [sb] feels bereft; **[e-m] þykkir undir** it seems important to [sb]; *refl* **þykkjask** seem to oneself, think, consider oneself

þyrfti *3sg/pl past subjunct of* **þurfa**

þær <*acc* þær, *dat* þeim, *gen* þeira~þeirra> *pron 3pl f* they

þær *f nom/acc pl of dem pron* **sá**

þœfa <-að-> *vb* press, put pressure on; beat, stamp (cloth); *refl* **þœfask** quarrel, squabble; **þœfask við** struggle clumsily and inconclusively, delay, drag things out

þœfð *f* quarrel, long tedious struggle

þœfizk *2pl pres of* **þœfask**

þœtti *3sg/pl past subjunct of* **þykkja**

þǫkk *<gen* þakkar; *pl* þakkir> *f* thanks

Æ

❖ **ætla** <-að-> *vb* intend, purpose, mean; think, consider

ætlan <-ir> *f* plan, design

ætt <-ir> *f* family

ættangr *<gen* -rs> *m* family calamity, family misfortune

ætti *3sg/pl past subjunct of* **eiga**

ævi *f indecl* age, time; **alla ævi** for all time, forever

Œ

❖ **œrinn** <-in, -it; *acc m* œrnan> *adj* sufficient

Ǫ/Ø

ǫðru *n dat sg of* **annarr**

ǫðrum *m dat sg & all dat pl of* **annarr**

ǫll *f nom sg & n nom/acc pl of* **allr**

ǫllum *m dat sg & all dat pl of* **allr**

Ǫlvir *<gen* Ǫlvis> *m* Olvir (*personal name*); **Ǫlvir inn spaki** *m* Olvir the Wise

ǫndvegi *n* high-seat

ǫndverðr <-verð, -vert> *adj* fronting, in front of (*place*); in the earlier, former part of (*time*); **til ǫndverðs þings** for the opening of the thing

ǫnnur *f nom sg of* **annarr**

ørendi *n* errand, mission, purpose

ørendislauss <-laus, -laust> *adj* without effect, purposeless, *lit* errand-less

ørendislaust *n adj as adv* without purpose, in vain, for nothing; **fara ørendislaust** go in vain, without a purpose or reason

ørendsreki *m* messenger

ǫrmust *nom f sg of* **armastr**, *superl of* **armr**

øx *<acc/dat* -i; *pl* -ar> *f* axe

Øxarfjǫrðr *<dat* -firði, *gen* -fjarðar> *m* Oxarfjord ('Axe Fjord') (*place name*)

ǫxl *<gen* axlar, *pl* axlir> *f* shoulder

Øxna-Þórir *m* Thorir 'of the Oxen' (*personal name*)

GLOSSARY OF NAMES AND PLACES
IN *VÁPNFIRÐINGA SAGA*

This glossary is a tool for locating people and places appearing in *Vápnfirðinga saga*. The entries are alphabetized and the numbers refer to the chapters in the saga. Epithets (that is, terms used to characterize a person) are used throughout the glossary in order to distinguish the different characters. In the sagas, epithets are sometimes used as nicknames.

TRANSLATION OF NICKNAMES (EPITHETS)

Brodd-Helgi Þorgilsson, Brodd-Helgi ('Spike-Helgi') Thorgilsson
Digr-Ketill, Stout-Ketil
Eyjólfr feiti, Eyjolf the Fat
Guðmundr inn ríki Eyjólfsson, Gudmund the Powerful Eyjolfsson
Herlu-Bjarni Arnfinnsson, Herlu-Bjarni ('Hood-Bjarni') Arnfinnsson
Hróðgeirr inn hvíti Hrappsson, Hrodgeir the White Hrappsson
Óláfr langháls, Olaf Long-Neck
Páll Jónsson byskup, Bishop Pal Jonsson
Refr inn rauði Steinbjarnarson, Ref the Red Steinbjarnarson
Skíði inn prúði, Skidi the Elegant
Steinbjǫrn kǫrtr Refsson ins rauða, Steinbjorn Sturdy, son of Ref the Red
Tjǫrvi inn mikli, Big Tjorvi
Þorgerðr silfra, Thorgerd Silver
Þorgils skinni, Thorgils Skin
Þorlákr byskup inn helgi, Bishop Thorlak the Holy
Þorleifr inn kristni, Thorleif the Christian
Þormóðr stikublígr Steinbjarnarson, Thormod Stick-Gazer Steinbjarnarson
Þorsteinn hvíti Ǫlvisson, Thorstein the White Olvisson
Þorvaldr inn hávi, Thorvald the Tall
Þorvarðr læknir, Thorvard the Healer
Ǫlvir inn spaki, Olvir the Wise

INDEX OF NAMES AND PLACES
(Saga chapters where characters appear are noted by numerals)

Ásbjǫrn Óláfsson langháls (Asbjorn son of Olaf Long-Neck): **3**, father of Lyting Asbjarnarson, father of Geitir.

Ásvaldr Øxna-Þórisson (Asvald son of Thorir 'of the oxen'): **1**, father of Olvir the White, father of Thorstein the White, grandfather of Brodd-Helgi.

Bergr Glíru-Hallason (Berg Gliru-Hallason), farmer at Buastadir and son of Gliru-Halli: **18**, travels with Bjarni to Mula-thing; is killed in battle at Bodvarsdal.

Birningr (Birning): **14**, hired by Bjarni to keep lookout over Krossavík and Thorkel; **18**, killed by Blaeng in battle at Bodvarsdal.

Bjarni Brodd-Helgason, younger son of Brodd-Helgi: **3**, fostered at Krossavík by his uncle Geitir; **13**, rides home from assembly with his men and his father's men; Brodd-

Helgi's foster-mother predicts Bjarni will avenge Brodd-Helgi's death; (lacuna) **14**, (still lacuna), receives 100 pieces of silver for Brodd-Helgi's slaying from Geitir as per Gudmund the Powerful's judgment at the Althing, but not the extra 30 they had agreed upon, which he does not demand; stays with Thorgerd Silver for a year; slays Big Tjorvi as he is trying to move covertly out of the valley; tells Thorgerd Silver, who approves; is not charged for Big Tjorvi's death; feasts with Geitir; marries Rannveig, daughter of Thorgeir Eiriksson; at feast with Geitir at Krossavík, Geitir has vision of blood, which Bjarni does not see; at assembly at Thorbrandsstadir (lacunae; Kolfinn and a woman mentioned) Bjarni kills Geitir, which is condemned; repents immediately, with no talk of compensation; returns to Hof; drives away Thorgerd Silver, telling her never to return; hires Birning to spy on Krossavík; sends men to Thorkel Geitisson at Krossavík when he returns, to offer settlement; sends men in his place to the mountains as planned upon hearing that Thorkel plans to go as well with a company of men; **15**, informed by Thorvard the Healer that Thorkel is counting his men, tells him to go to Faskrudsbakki where Thorkel's men were to say that many men were at Hof, in order to avoid attack; **16**, at Strond, encounters Thorkel but hides successfully from him; **18**, goes to Mula-thing with seventeen others including Thorvard the Healer, Bruni of Thorbrandsstadir, Eilif Torfason from Torfastadir, Berg and Brand, Bjarni's foster-son Skidi, and Hauk Loptsson; stay with Helgi Asbjarnarson and Bjarni's sister Thordis Todda; is given a necklace by Thordis Todda; follows Thorkel across the heath; stays the night with Freygerd; walks past farm where Thorkel is staying, has his men step in each other's steps to give the appearance of only three men's paths; is followed by Thorkel to Eyvindarstadir, where he decides to face Thorkel; they battle; Blaeng strikes at Bjarni, knocking off the necklace, which he picks up; Thorkel tells him he is still greedy for money; kills Blaeng; four of his men die; taken by Eyvind to Hof, where Thorvard the Healer takes care of him and his men; tells Gliru-Halli of the death of his sons; sends Thorvard the Healer to Krossavík to take care of Thorkel's wounds; **19**, farmhand of Thorkel's moves to Hof; learns that the people of Krossvík (Krossvíkingar) are healthy but their livestock are ill; invites Thorkel to Hof via farmhand; offers Thorkel a settlement, self-judgment and 100 pieces of silver for the killing of Geitir, which he accepts; they make peace; live together at Hof in their old age.

Blængr Lýtingsson (Blaeng Lytingsson), son of Lyting Asbjarnarson: **3**, son of Lyting Asbjarnarson, brother of Geitir, Halla and Rannveig; **14**, runs farm at Krossavík with the sons of Egil (Egilssynir); **18**, attends Mula-thing with Thorkel and stays with Groa at Eyvindará; travels across heath to Bodvarsdal, where they stay with Kari; kills Birning; strikes off Bjarni's necklace; killed by Bjarni.

Brandr Glíru-Hallason (Brand Gliru-Hallason), farmer at Buastadir and son of Gliru-Halli: **18**, travels with Bjarni to Mula-thing; is killed in battle at Bodvarsdal.

Brodd-Helgi's foster-mother: **13**, Brodd-Helgi's foster-mother dreams that Geitir will kill Brodd-Helgi; Brodd-Helgi thinks dream means that Lyting will avenge him, but mother says Bjarni will avenge him (lacuna).

Brodd-Helgi Thorgilsson, son of Thorgils Thorsteinsson: **1**, reared by his grandfather Thorstein the White; fastens iron spike to the head of his kinsmen's bull to help it get the better of another bull, and from then on is called Brodd- or Spike-Helgi; **2**, takes up the lawsuit against Svart after he kills his neighbor Skidi, and succeeds in having Svart outlawed; seeks out and kills Svart after he traces some of their missing sheep to Svart's cave; receives Svart's curse that kin-hurt will persist in Brodd-Helgi's family; is much praised for his precocity in dealing with Svart; **3**, marries Halla and has two sons and one daughter, Lyting, Bjarni, and Thordis Todda; fosters his younger son Bjarni with Geitir at Krossavík, and elder son Lyting at Oxarfjord with Thorgils Skin; becomes great friends with Geitir; **4**, is refused the sale of valuables from Hrafn, the Norwegian skipper, and is offended; takes the most valued seat at the feast for the Winter Nights (vetrnætum) with the sons of Egil and speaks only with Geitir; attends the games at Hagi and condemns Hrafn's murder; intends to share the slain Hrafn's goods with Geitir; is convinced by Geitir not to attack Thorleif the Christian when he takes the goods; **5**, is dispirited during the summer and a coldness develops between him and Geitir on account of the Norwegian's goods; learns Thorleif the Christian has given Hrafn's goods over to the Norwegian's heirs; visits Stout-Ketil in Fljotsdal and exchanges friendship with him in return for Stout-Ketil's promise to prosecute Thorleif the Christian for failing to pay temple tax; ends friendship with Stout-Ketil when he drops the case against Thorleif the Christian; blames Geitir for the affair; **6**, Halla divorces him; betrothes himself to Thorgerd Silver; hostility arises between him and Geitir when he refuses to return Halla's dowry; still refuses to give Halla her money back; is summoned by Geitir at Sunnudal-thing but wins due to his having a larger company; wins suit again at Althing, primarily on account of support from Gudmund the Powerful; there is hostility between him and Geitir; **7**, at first denies his thingman Thord, farmer at Tunga, support in dispute with farmer Thormod Stick-Gazer about grazing rights and tree-cutting; when Thord moves to Hof, Brodd-Helgi cuts off the heads of all Thormod Stick-Gazer's oxen; cuts down Thormod Stick-Gazer's trees on the communal property, when Thormod Stick-Gazer comes on a summoning trip to Hof, Brodd-Helgi is unexpectedly at home and ambushes the men, some of whom die; places them in his field; **8**, while talking to Geitir, does not see Geitir's men reclaiming the bodies of their slain companions; notices and admits Geitir to be wiser than himself; no legal action taken against him for death of Thormod Stick-Gazer; **9**, visits Halla at Krossavík; refuses her offer to stay the night, and on that night she dies; **10**, needing support at the Assembly, promises Gudmund the Powerful half a hundred pieces of silver for his friendship after Gudmund the Powerful will not do it free of charge; Gudmund the Powerful retracts friendship upon Brodd-Helgi's failure to pay; **11**, meets Thorarin Egilsson the skipper in Vapnafjord and asks him to stay at Hof; when Geitir asks him to stay at Krossavík, Brodd-Helgi offers Thorarin five stud-horses, which are returned to him on Geitir's counsel; **13**, rides to assembly with Geitir; rides home with Bjarni Brodd-Helgason, Lyting Brodd-Helgason, Thorgils Skin, Eyjolf the Fat, Koll the Norwegian, Thorgerd Silver and her daughter Hallbera Brodd-Helgadottir; foster-mother dreams he will find death at hands of Geitir; Brodd-Helgi thinks dream means Lyting avenges him, but mother says Bjarni will avenge him (lacuna); **14**, (lacuna; apparently Big Tjorvi kills Brodd-Helgi); at Althing, Gudmund the Powerful makes peace between Geitir and Bjarni and judges that Geitir pay 130 pieces of silver for Brodd-Helgi's death.

Brúni (Bruni), farmer at Thorbrandsstadir: **18**, thingman of Bjarni's, travels with him to Mula-thing.

Búastaðir (Buastadir 'Bui's Farmstead'), farm in Vapnafjord: **18**, Berg and Brand Gliru-Hallason travel from Buastadir to the Mula assembly with Bjarni.

Bǫðvarsdalr (Bodvarsdal), deep mountain valley in the mountains on the south shore of Vapnafjord: **18**, Bjarni and Thorkel travel over the heath to Bodvarsdal, where they battle.

Digr-Ketill (Stout-Ketil): **5**, Brodd-Helgi visits him in Fljotsdal, begins a friendship (*vinfengi*) with him in exchange for the promise that he will prosecute Thorleif the Christian for failing to pay his temple tax; summons Thorleif the Christian, but after accepting hospitality drops the case against him; Brodd-Helgi ends their friendship.

Egill (Egil) **Steinbjarnarson**, farmer at Egilsstadir in Sunnudal: **3**, son of Steinbjorn Sturdy and brother of Ref the Red and Thormod Stick-Gazer; has three sons, Thorarin, Hallbjorn and Throst, and one daughter, Hallfríðr, who marries Thorkel Geitisson.

Egilsstaðir (Egilsstadir 'Egil's Farmstead'), farm in Sunnudal: owned by Egil Steinbjarnarson and his sons Thorarin, Hallbjorn and Throst.

Eilífr (Eilif) **Torfason**, farmer at Torfastadir: **18**, thingman of Bjarni's, travels with him to Mula-thing; stays with Helgi Asbjarnarson and Thordis Todda; follows Thorkel and men over the heath to Bodvarsdal; in battle, disabled by Hallbjorn; cured at Hof by Thorvard the Healer.

Eyjólfr feiti (Eyjolf the Fat), foster-father of Lyting: **13**, returns from Assembly with Brodd-Helgi.

Eyjólfr (Eyjolf) **from Víðivellir** (Vidivellir): **18**, thingman of Thorkel's, travels with him to Mula-thing.

Eyvindará (Eyvindará 'Eyvind's River'), home of Groa; **9**, Geitir visits Groa **18**, Thorkel and his men stay here with Groa

Eyvindarstaðir (Eyvindarstadir 'Eyvind's Farmstead'), site of Eyvind's farm

Eyvindr (Eyvind), farmer in Bodvarsdal at Eyvindarstadir: **18**, notified by a woman at his farm that Bjarni and Thorkel are in battle; joins battle; allowed by Thorkel to bring wounded home to Hof; takes Bjarni and his men to Hof.

Fagradalr (Fagradal 'Fair Dale'), homestead at the southern point of Vapnafjord: **11**, Geitir moves his household to Fagradal because of its inaccessibility; his thingmen travel there to demand that he return to Krossavík.

Fáskrúðsbakki (Faskrudsbakki 'Faskrud's Bank'), farm in Sunnudal (exact location unknown): **15**, Bjarni tells Thorvard the Healer to pass by this farm, which was likely on the western bank of the Thver River.

Fljótsdalr (Fljotsdal 'River Dale'): river valley in the east fjords southeast of Sunnudal.

Freygerðr (Freygerd): **18**, woman with whom Bjarni and his men spend the night while they are following Thorkel to Bodvarsdal.

Geitir Lýtingsson (Lytingsson), son of Lyting Asbjarnarson: **3**, brother of Blaeng, Rannveig, and Halla, Brodd-Helgi's wife; fosters Brodd-Helgi's son Bjarni at Krossavík; marries Hallkatla, Thidrandi's daughter, aunt of the sons of Droplaug (Droplaugarsynir); has great friendship with Brodd-Helgi; **4**, meets Hrafn at his ship after he has refused Brodd-Helgi's attempt to purchase valuables from him, and tells Hrafn he has offended an important man in the district; lodges Hrafn for the winter; attends feast for the Winter Nights at the house of Egil's sons and speaks only with Brodd-Helgi; attends games at Hagi; intending to share slain Hrafn's goods with Brodd-Helgi, locks them in his warehouse; attends Sunnudal-thing with Brodd-Helgi; goods removed from his warehouse by Thorleif the Christian; with Brodd-Helgi, confronts Thorleif the Christian in the harbor; convinces Brodd-Helgi not to attack Thorleif the Christian; **5**, antagonism develops between him and Brodd-Helgi on account of Hrafn's goods; learns that Thorleif the Christian has given the goods to Hrafn's Norwegian heirs; is blamed by Brodd-Helgi when the action against Thorleif the Christian collapses; friendship between him and Brodd-Helgi diminishes; **6**, travels to Hof to return Halla to Krossavík; summons and loses to Brodd-Helgi twice, at Sunnudal-thing and at Althing, to return Halla's dowry; **7**, pays for Thormod Stick-Gazer's oxen, which Brodd-Helgi beheaded, but will not support Thormod Stick-Gazer in his dispute about grazing rights and tree-cutting; when Brodd-Helgi cuts down Thormod Stick-Gazer's trees on the communal property, Geitir provides Thormod Stick-Gazer with support; advises Thormod Stick-Gazer to find Stein and Hreidar, sons of Ref the Red, and Big Tjorvi from Gudmundarstadir and go to Hof to summon Thord while Brodd-Helgi is away; Brodd-Helgi learns of this plan, ambushes Thormod Stick-Gazer and men when they arrive; loses some men, kinsmen very dissatisfied; advises them to bide their time; **8**, summons thingmen to go to Hof; sends men through fields to collect bodies of their men with charcoal pails, so that Brodd-Helgi does not notice; Geitir admitted by Brodd-Helgi to be the wiser of them; takes no legal action for death of Thormod Stick-Gazer; **9**, visits Groa in Eyvindará, returns home to find Halla dead and that Brodd-Helgi had visited in his absence; **10**, denied friendship by Gudmund the Powerful, who does not want allies who are Brodd-Helgi's enemies; **11**, convinces Thorarin Egilsson to lodge with him instead of Brodd-Helgi; counsels Thorarin to return five stud-horses to Brodd-Helgi that he had offered for Thorarin's friendship; moves to Fagradal; called back to Krossavík by his thingmen; **12**, visits Ofeig at Ljosavatn Pass; meets with Gudmund the Powerful; stays with Olvir the Wise at Myvatn; says he has endured Brodd-Helgi thus far; **13**, in springtime, moves back to Krossavík; rides to assembly with Brodd-Helgi; goes home with Thorarin, Hallbjorn, Throst, the sons of Egil, Big Tjorvi and seven others; Brodd-Helgi's foster-mother dreams Geitir will kill Brodd-Helgi; **14**, (lacuna; apparently Geitir's thingman Big Tjorvi killed Brodd-Helgi); at Althing, Gudmund the Powerful makes peace between Geitir and Bjarni and judges that Geitir must pay 130 pieces of silver for Brodd-Helgi's slaying; pays 100 pieces of silver to Bjarni, but not the extra 30, which Bjarni does not demand; buries Big Tjorvi; does not charge Bjarni for Big Tjorvi's slaying; feasts with Bjarni; has vision of blood at feast with Bjarni at Krossavík; killed by Bjarni at assembly at Thorbrandsstadir, which is condemned; there is no talk of compensation.

Glíru-Halli Sigurðarson (Gliru-Halli Sigurdarson), farmer at Buastadir and thingman of Bjarni's: **18**, visited by Bjarni, who informs him of the death of his sons Berg and Brand in battle.

Grímr (Grim) **Droplaugarson**: **17**, summoned by Thorkel to Krossavík for purpose of killing Bjarni; leaves with brother Grim when the latter is denied permission to lead the attack when Thorkel feels unwell and does not want to proceed.

Gróa (Groa), kinswoman of Geitir at Eyvindará: **9**, visited by Geitir; **18**, Thorkel and fourteen men stay with her during the Mula-thing.

Guðdalir í Skagafjǫrð (Guddalir in Skagafjord): **14**, Rannveig, daughter of Thorgeir Eiriksson from Guddalir, marries Bjarni.

Guðmundarstaðir (Gudmundarstadir 'Gudmund's Farmstead'), farm in Sunnudal owned by Big Tjorvi.

Guðmundr inn ríki (Gudmund the Powerful) son of Eyjolf, chieftain in Modruvellir (Mǫðruvellir): **6**, with his support, Brodd-Helgi able to win case against Geitir at the Althing over Halla's money; **10**, does not accept Brodd-Helgi's friendship until he offers half a hundred pieces of silver; retracts friendship at Althing when he does not receive the money; refuses Geitir's offer of friendship as well; **12**, meets with Geitir; **14**, makes peace between Geitir and Brodd-Helgi's family at Althing and adjudges that Geitir must pay 130 pieces of silver for Brodd-Helgi's slaying.

Hagi, farm in Vapnafjord: **4**, Hrafn slain there.

Halla Steinadóttir (Steinadottir): **19**, daughter of Steini, the son of Halla Loptsdottir, the daughter of Lopt Thorarinsson and Ragnheid Thorkelsdottir.

Halla Loptsdóttir (Loptsdottir): **19**, daughter of Lopt Thorarinsson and Ragnheid Thorkelsdottir; mother of Steini, the father of Halla, the mother of Bishop Thorlak the Holy.

Halla Lýtingsdóttir (Lytingsdottir): **3**, sister of Geitir, Blaeng and Rannveig; marries Brodd-Helgi; **4**, sees Thorleif the Christian and his men taking Hrafn's goods from Geitir's storehouse but does not attempt to stop them; **6**, requests divorce from Brodd-Helgi; finds Brodd-Helgi has betrothed himself to Thorgerd Silver; leaves Hof with her brothers and valuables (lacuna; apparently Brodd-Helgi will not return Halla's valuables); Geitir tries twice to get Halla's money, at the Sunnudal-thing and the Althing, but Brodd-Helgi wins both suits; **8**, health declines at Krossavík; **9**, invites Brodd-Helgi to Krossavík while Geitir is away; offers him to stay the night, which he refuses; dies in the morning.

Hallbjǫrn (Hallbjorn) **Egilsson**, farmer at Egilsstadir and son of Egil Steinbjarnarson; **13**, returns from assembly with Geitir; **18**, attends Mula-thing with Thorkel; stays with Groa at Eyvindará; crosses heath to Bodvarsdal; company stays with Kari; Thorkel and his men awake, get their weapons and go to the trail; follow them to Eyvindarstadir, where they battle; disables Eilif.

Hallkatla Þiðrandadóttir (Thidrandadottir), daughter of Thidrandi: **3**, married to Geitir Lytingsson; aunt of Droplaugarsynir.

Haukr (Hauk) **Loptsson**: **18**, thingman of Bjarni's, travels with him to Mula-thing.

Hákon jarl Grjótgarðsson (Earl Hakon Grjotgardsson): **1**, was earl in Norway when Olvir the White Asvaldsson, the father of Thorstein the White, was landholder in Norway.

Heðinn Þorfinnsson (Hedin Thorfinnsson): **1**, together with Thorkel kills Thorgils, the father of Brodd-Helgi.

Helgi Ásbjarnarson (Asbjarnarson), chieftain in Fljotsdal: **3**, married to Thordis Todda, daughter of Brodd-Helgi and Halla Lytingsdottir; **18**, lodges brother-in-law Bjarni and his men, Thorvard the Healer, Bruni of Thorbrandsstadir, Eilif Torfason from Torfastadir, Berg and Brand, Bjarni's foster-son Skidi, and Hauk Loptsson and ten others while they attend the Mula-thing.

Helgi Droplaugarson: **17**, invited by Thorkel with brother Grim to Krossavík to kill Bjarni; volunteers to supervise mission in Thorkel's place when he is sick the next day, but is denied; becomes angry with him because of his cowardice, and the brothers leave.

Herlu-Bjarni (Hood-Bjarni) **Arnfinnsson**: **3**, father of Thordis, the wife of Lyting Asbjarnarson and mother of Geitir, Blaeng, Halla, and Rannveig.

Hof, farm in Sunnudal owned by Brodd-Helgi's family: Steinbjorn Sturdy, Thorstein the White, Thorgils, Brodd-Helgi and Bjarni live there.

Hrafn, Norwegian merchant: **4**, comes to Iceland with Thorleif the Christian; refuses to stay with or sell valuables to Brodd-Helgi; stays with Geitir and stores his wares in a storehouse at Krossavík; is slain at the farm Hagi by an unknown person, and Geitir and Bjarni intend to share his goods between themselves, but Thorleif the Christian claims them secretly instead.

Hreiðarr Refsson ins rauða (Hreidar son of Ref the Red): **3**, son of Ref the Red and brother of Steinbjorn (Stein); **7**, goes with Thormod Stick-Gazer to Hof to summon Thord; ambushed by Brodd-Helgi.

Hróðgeirr inn hvíti (Hrodgeir the White) **Hrappsson**: **1**, father of Ingibjorg, who married Thorstein the White.

Ingibjǫrg Hróðgeirsdóttir ins hvíta (Ingibjorg daughter of Hrodgeir the White): **1**, marries Thorstein the White.

Ingimundr Úlfsson (Ingimund Ulfsson): **14**, former husband of Rannveig, who marries Bjarni, and father of Skidi the Elegant.

Jón Arnþórsson (Jon Arnthorsson), priest: **19**, son of Ragnheid, who is sister of Bishop Thorlak the Holy, who is great-grandson of Ragnheid Thorkelsdottir; half-brother of Orm Jonsson and Bishop Pal Jonsson.

Jórunn Einarsdóttir (Jorunn Einarsdottir): **19**, second wife of Thorkel Geitisson; convinces Thorkel to discuss settlement of Geitir's death with Bjarni when he offers it.

Kári (Kari), farmer in Bodvarsdal and thingman of Thorkel's: **18**, lodges Thorkel and his companions on their way back from the Mula-thing; agrees to inform Thorkel if men are following them; sees Bjarni and his companions, but does not alert Thorkel.

Klifshagi í Qxarfjǫrð (Oxarfjord): **3**, Olaf of Klifshagi marries Rannveig Lýtingsdottir.

Kolfinnr Þorvaldsson ins háva (Kolfinn son of Thorvald the Tall), brother of Thorgerd

Silver: 14, mentioned between lacunae, possibly involved with Geitir's death.

Kollr (Koll): **15**, sent from Krossavík by Thorkel to meet with Thorarin at Egilsstadir to see how many men were at Hof; told by Thorarin at Egilsstadir that he will tell Thorkel himself; on the way back to Krossavík, meets Thorvard the Healer, who is riding back to Sireksstadir from the next farm over; does not tell Thorvard the Healer why he is riding at night.

Krossavík í Reyðarfjǫrð (Krossavík in Reydarfjord): **4, 5**, home of Thorleif the Christian.

Krossavík in ýtri (Outer Krossavík), farm in Vapnafjord owned by Geitir's family: Lyting, Geitir Lytingsson, Thorkel Geitisson.

Ljósavatnsskarð (Ljosavatnsskard, 'Light Water Lake Pass'): **12**, home of Ofeig.

Loptr Þórarinsson (Lopt Thorarinsson): **19**, marries Ragnheid Thorkelsdottir, daughter of Thorkel Geitisson.

Lýtingr Ásbjarnarson (Lyting Asbjarnarson): **3**, lives at Outer-Krossavík; husband of Thordis and father of Geitir, Blaeng, Halla, and Rannveig.

Lýtingr (Lyting) **Brodd-Helgason**, elder son of Brodd-Helgi: **13**, returns from assembly with Brodd-Helgi; in Brodd-Helgi's foster-mother's dream, Brodd-Helgi thinks Lyting will avenge his death, though his foster-mother says it will be Bjarni (lacuna).

Múlaþing (Mula Assembly), assembly site; **18**, see, várþing í Fljótsdalshérað, visited by Bjarni and Thorkel and their followers.

Mývatn (Myvatn 'Midge' or 'Mosquito Lake'): **12**, home of Olvir the Wise, who is visited by Geitir.

Ormr Jónsson (Orm Jonsson): **19**, half-brother of Jon Arnthorsson and brother of Bishop Pal Jonsson; son of Ragnheid, who is daughter of Halla, who is great-granddaughter of Ragnheid Thorkelsdottir.

Ófeigr Járngerðarson (Ofeig Jarngerdarson), at Ljosavatnsskard: **12**, visited by Geitir.

Óláfr langháls (Olaf Long-Neck): **3**, father of Asbjorn, father of Lyting, father of Geitir.

Páll byskup Jónsson (Bishop Pal Jonsson): **19**, son of Ragnheid, the sister of Bishop Thorlak the Holy, son of Halla, daughter of Steini, son of Halla, daughter of Ragnheid Thorkelsdottir and Lopt Thorarinsson.

Ragnheiðr (Ragnheid): **19**, sister of Bishop Thorlak the Holy and mother of Bishop Pal Jonsson, Orm Jonsson and Jon Arnthorsson; great-great-granddaughter of Ragnheid Thorkelsdottir.

Ragnheiðr Þorkelsdóttir (Ragnheid Thorkelsdottir), daughter of Thorkel Geitisson: **19**, marries Lopt Thorarinsson, has nine children, including daughter Halla, the mother of Steini, the father of Halla, the mother of Bishop Thorlak the Holy; Bishop Thorlak's sister, Ragnheid, is mother of Bishop Pal Jonsson, Orm Jonsson, and priest Jon Arnthorsson.

Rannveig, daughter of Thorgeir Eiriksson of Guddalir: **14**, marries Bjarni; already has been married to Ingimund Ulfsson, with whom she has a child, Skidi the Elegant.

Refr inn rauði (Ref the Red): **1**, father of Steinbjorn Sturdy, the first settler at Hof.

Refr inn rauði (Ref the Red) **Steinbjarnarson**, farmer at Refsstadir in Sunnudal, son of Steinbjorn Sturdy and grandson of Ref the Red: **3**, has two sons, Steinbjorn (Stein) and Hreidar; he and his sons are all thingmen of Geitir Lytingsson.

Refsstaðir (Refsstadir), farm in Vapnafjord: **3**, home of Ref the Red Steinbjarnarson and his sons Steinbjorn (Stein) and Hreidar.

Síreksstaðir (Sireksstadir 'Sirek's Farmstead'), farm in Sunnudal: **14**, Thorvard the Healer lives there.

Skíði (Skidi), poor farmer: **2**, is killed by his neighbor Svart.

Skíði (Skidi): **18**, Bjarni's foster-son and thingman, travels with him to Mula-thing.

Skíði inn prúði (Skidi the Elegant): **14**, son of Ingimund Ulfsson and Rannveig, who marries Bjarni (this Skidi may be the same as Skidi in **18**).

Smjǫrvatnsheiðr (Smjorvatnsheid 'Butter-Water Heath'), heath east of Sunnudal.

Steinbjǫrn kǫrtr Refsson ins rauða (Steinbjorn Sturdy, son of Ref the Red): **1**, first settler at Hof; squanders his wealth; sells the farm to Thorstein the White.

Steinbjǫrn (also called Stein) **Refsson ins rauða Steinbjarnarsonar** (Steinbjorn [Stein], son of Ref the Red Steinbjarnarson): **3**, son of Ref the Red and brother of Hreidar; **7**, goes with Thormod Stick-Gazer to Hof to summon Thord; ambushed by Brodd-Helgi.

Steini: **19**, son of Halla, the daughter of Ragnheid Thorkelsdottir and Lopt Thorarinsson, and mother of Halla, the mother of Bishop Thorlak the Holy and Ragnheid.

Steinvǫr (Steinvor): temple priestess in Vapnafjord and relative of Brodd-Helgi: **5**, goes to Brodd-Helgi to tell him that Thorleif the Christian has not paid his temple tax.

Strǫnd (Strond): an area on northern shore of Vapnafjord.

Sunnudalr (Sunnudal 'South Dale' or 'Sun Dale'): inland river valley that opens into Vapnafjord from the south.

Sunnudalr (Sunnudal 'South Dale' or 'Sun Dale'): farm in Sunnudal river valley: **7**, home of farmer Thormod Stick-Gazer.

Svartr (Svart 'Black'): **2**, kills his neighbor Skidi, whereupon Brodd-Helgi takes up the lawsuit and has Svart outlawed; steals sheep in retaliation, for which he is hunted down and killed by Brodd-Helgi; as he dies utters a curse that kin-hurt will plague Brodd-Helgi's family.

Tjǫrvi inn mikli (Big Tjorvi), farmer at Gudmundarstadir: **4**, friend of Geitir and Brodd-Helgi; was nowhere to be seen when Hrafn slain at Hagi; **7**, goes to Hof with Thormod Stick-Gazer to summon Thord, but is ambushed by Brodd-Helgi; **13**, returns from Assembly with Geitir; **14**, (lacuna; apparently Big Tjorvi kills Brodd-Helgi); allowed to stay at Gudmundarstadir one year, but must leave before Moving-Days (*fardagar*) and never return to Vapnafjord; slain by Bjarni as he is trying to move covertly out of the valley; buried by Geitir, who does not charge Bjarni for the death of Big Tjorvi.

Toptavǫllr (Toptavoll), farm in Sunnudal: **1**, Thorstein the White first lives at Toptavoll.

Torfastaðir (Torfastadir 'Torfi's Farmstead'), farm in Vapnafjord: **18**, home of Eilif Torfason, a thingman of Bjarni's.

Tunga, farm at the entrance to Sunnudal: **7**, home of Thord.

Vápnafjǫrðr (Vapnafjord 'Weapon's Fjord') the setting of Vápnfirðinga saga.

Várþing í Fljótsdalsherað: **18**, most likely the Mula-thing and possibly the Kidjafells-thing

Víðivellir (Vidivellir), location unknown: **18**, home of Eyjolf, a thingman of Thorkel's.

Þiðrandi (Thidrandi), father of Hallkatla

Þorbrandsstaðir (Thorbrandstadir 'Thorbrand's Farmstead'): farm on the bank of Hofs River in Vapnafjord: **18**, home of Bruni, a thingman of Bjarni's who travels with him to Mula-thing.

Þorgeirr Eiríksson (Thorgeir Eiriksson) of Guddalir in Skagafjord: **14**, father of Rannveig, who marries Bjarni Brodd-Helgason.

Þorgerðr silfra (Thorgerd Silver), widow in Fljotsdal at Thorgerdarstadir: **6**, Brodd-Helgi visits her after Halla requests a divorce from him; they become engaged, Brodd-Helgi returns to Hof and Thorgerd Silver follows him; **13**, returns from Assembly with Brodd-Helgi and their daughter Hallbera Helgadottir; **14**, Bjarni lives with her for a year following Brodd-Helgi's death; approves of Bjarni's slaying Big Tjorvi as he tries to move covertly out of the valley; driven away from Hof by Bjarni and told never to return after he kills Geitir and repents (due to a lacuna, it is unclear exactly what happens, but Thorgerd Silver evidently goads Bjarni into avenging his father's death; Thorgerd Silver's brother Kolfinn is mentioned as well).

Þorgerðarstaðir (Thorgerdarstadir 'Thorgerd's Farmstead'), farm in Fljotsdal: **6**, widow Thorgerd Silver's home.

Þorgils Þorsteinsson ins hvíta (Thorgils, son of Thorstein the White), father of Brodd-Helgi: **1**, killed by Thorkel and Hedin.

Þorgils skinni (Thorgils Skin), thingman of Brodd-Helgi's: **13**, returns from Assembly with Brodd-Helgi.

Þorkell Þorfinnsson (Thorkel Thorfinnsson): **1**, together with Hedin kills Thorgils, the father of Brodd-Helgi.

Þorkell (Thorkel) **Geitisson**, son of Geitir Lytingsson: **8**, travels abroad, not involved in dispute between Geitir and Brodd-Helgi; **14**, abroad when Geitir killed; returns to Krossavík; does not respond to Bjarni's offers of settlement; is assumed by men at Hof to be formulating revenge; goes to the mountains, which is discovered by Bjarni, who sends men in his own place to avoid meeting Thorkel; **15**, sends Koll from Krossavík to meet with Thorarin at Egilsstadir to see how many men were at Hof; receives message from Thorarin that there are many men, due to Thorvard the Healer telling Thorkel's men at Faskrudsbakki that; **16**, finds Bjarni is planning to travel to Strond and tries to intercept him on the path, but does not encounter him because Bjarni hides in a milking hut on the side of the road; **17**, invites the sons of Droplaug, Helgi and Grim, to Krossavík because he wishes to kill Bjarni with fire; becomes sick the following day and does not wish to go or let Helgi lead, causing Helgi to become angry with him and the sons of Droplaug to leave; **18**, attends the Mula-thing with Blaeng and the sons of Egil, Thorarin, Hallbjorn, and Throst, and Eyjolf from Vidivellir, fifteen all together; stays with Groa at Eyvindará; leaves the assembly first; with his companions, travels across the heath until Bodvarsdal, where they stay with Thorkel's thingman Kari; asks Kari to watch for people following them; is not alerted by Kari when Bjarni passes; awakes and ascertains that more than three men walked on the path; follows Bjarni and his men to Eyvindarstadir, where they battle; tells Bjarni he is still greedy for money when he picks up the necklace that Thordis Todda gave him which has fallen in battle; four of his men fall in battle; he is disabled by a wound on his arm; allows Eyvind to bring the wounded home to Hof; is visited and cured by Thorvard the Healer on Bjarni's command; gives Thorvard the Healer gifts and words of friendship; **19**, marries Jorunn; unable to manage Krossavík properly; receives Bjarni's offer to live at Hof with indecision; visits Bjarni with twelve men and accepts Bjarni's settlement and self-judgment along with 100 pieces of silver from Geitir, and there is peace between them; runs out of money late in life and moves to Hof; has daughter Ragnheid.

Þorlákr byskup inn helgi (Bishop Thorlak the Holy), a descendant of Ragnheid Thorkelsdottir: **19**, Ragnheid Thorkelsdottir and Loft Thorarinsson have nine children, including daughter Halla, the mother of Steini, the father of Halla, the mother of Bishop Thorlak the Holy; Thorlak's sister, Ragnheid, is the mother of Bishop Pal Jonsson, Orm Jonsson, and priest Jon Arnthorsson.

Þorleifr inn kristni (Thorleif the Christian), skipper of a Norwegian merchant ship; **4**, returns to his farm at Krossavík in Reydarfjord; goes to Krossavík during the Sunnudal-thing the spring after Hrafn is murdered, and removes Hrafn's goods from Geitir's storehouse; is confronted by Brodd-Helgi and Geitir in the harbor, but they decide not to attack then; returns goods to Hrafn's Norwegian heirs; **5**, Brodd-Helgi informed by the priestess Steinvor that Thorleif the Christian does not pay temple tax, so Brodd-Helgi has Stout-Ketil prosecute Thorleif the Christian; gives hospitality to Stout-Ketil and his men, as a result of which Stout-Ketil drops the case against him.

Þormóðr stikublígr (Thormod Stick-Gazer) **Steinbjarnarson**, farmer at Sunnudal: **3**, brother of Ref the Red and Egil, has two sons, Thorstein and Eyvind; **7**, has dispute with Thord, farmer at Tunga, about grazing rights and tree-cutting; Brodd-Helgi beheads Thormod Stick-Gazer's oxen; asks Geitir for support, which Geitir denies but pays for his oxen; Brodd-Helgi learns of Thormod Stick-Gazer's actions and fells his trees on the communal property; asks Geitir again for support and receives it; according to Geitir's counsel, goes to Hof with Stein and Hreidar Refssynir ins rauða and Big Tjorvi from Gudmundarstadir to summon Thord, provided Brodd-Helgi is not at home; when Brodd-Helgi learns of their intended visit and ambushes them, Thormod Stick-Gazer is killed in resulting battle; **8**, no legal actions are taken for his death.

Þorsteinn inn hvíti Qlvisson (Thorstein the White Olvisson), grandfather of Brodd-Helgi: **1**, one of the first settlers of Iceland, lives at Toptavoll; takes over the farm at Hof and rears Brodd-Helgi when his son Thorgils is killed; **2**, is blind and cannot watch over the farm, so entrusts it generally to Brodd-Helgi; when a shepherd gives him bad news about his flock, tells him not to tell Brodd-Helgi; tells farmhands to follow Brodd-Helgi's trail after he kills Svart.

Þorvaldr inn hávi (Thorvald the Tall): **6**, father of Thorgerd Silver.

Þorvarðr læknir (Thorvard the Healer), farmer at Sireksstadir and thingman of Bjarni's: **14**, lives at Sireksstadir; **15**, on his way back to Sireksstadir from a nearby farm, encounters Koll, who is on his way back to Krossavík from Egilsstadir; suspects Koll was spying on Bjarni and his men; tells Bjarni who thanks him and tells him to pass by Faskrudsbakki where Thorkel's men are, and to misinform them that there are many men at Hof to prevent a confrontation; **18**, attends Mula-thing with Bjarni and his men; stays with Helgi Asbjarnarson and Thordis Todda; follows Thorkel over the heath to Bodvarsdal; stays the night with a woman named Freygerd; approaches Kari's farm, where Thorkel and his men are staying, in the morning; Bjarni and his men proceed in each other's steps to make it appear that there are paths of only three men; is followed by Thorkel and his men to Eyvindarstadir where they battle; cares for wounded at Hof; sent by Bjarni to Krossavík; cures Thorkel and is rewarded with gifts and words of friendship.

Þórarinn (Thorarin) **Egilsson**: farmer at Egilsstadir and thingman of Geitir and Thorkel: **3**, son of Egil Steinbjarnarson and brother of Throst, Hallbjorn and Hallfrid (Hallfríðr); **4**, sons of Egil have feast, which Brodd-Helgi and Geitir attend; **11**, sails to Vapnafjord and agrees to stay with Brodd-Helgi; convinced by Geitir to come to Krossavík instead; offered five stud-horses by Brodd-Helgi for his friendship; returns them according to Geitir's counsel; stays at Krossavík and sails abroad the next summer; returns to find Geitir has moved to Fagradal; lives at Egilsstadir; **13**, returns from Assembly with Geitir and his brothers Hallbjorn and Throst; **15**, Koll sent by Thorkel from Krossavík to meet with Thorarin at Egilsstadir to see how many men were at Hof; meets Koll, says he will tell Thorkel himself; Thorvard the Healer goes to Faskrudsbakki to tell Thorkel's men that there are many men at Hof, which is then reported to Thorarin; **18**, thingman of Thorkel's, travels with him to Mula-thing.

Þórdís (Thordis) **todda**: **3**, daughter of Brodd-Helgi and Halla Lytingsdottir, wife of Helgi Asbjarnarson; **18**, lodges brother Bjarni and his companions while they attend Mula-thing; gives Bjarni a necklace; does not want anything in return for it.

Þórdís Herlu-Bjarnadóttir, daughter of Herlu-Bjarni Arnfinnsson: **3**, wife of Lyting Asbjarnarson and mother of Geitir, Blaeng, Rannveig and Halla.

Þórðr (Thord), farmer in Sunnudal and thingman of Brodd-Helgi's: **7**, seeks Brodd-Helgi's support in a property dispute between him and farmer Thormod Stick-Gazer about grazing rights and tree-cutting; is denied support; accepts Brodd-Helgi's offer to move to Hof with all his possessions; Geitir plans to summon him after Brodd-Helgi cuts down Thormod Stick-Gazer's trees on communal property, but Brodd-Helgi learns of this and ambushes Geitir's men.

Þrǫstr (Throst) **Egilsson**, son of Egil Steinbjarnarson: **13**, returns from assembly with Geitir; **18**, thingman of Thorkel's, travels with him to Mula-thing.

Ǫlvir inn hvíti Ásvaldsson (Olvir the White Asvaldson), father of Thorstein the White, the grandfather of Brodd-Helgi: **1**, was landholder in Norway in the time of Earl Hakon Grjotgardsson.

Ǫlvir inn spaki (Olvir the Wise), sage at Myvatn: **12**, visited by Geitir; asks if Brodd-Helgi must be endured, and Geitir says he has endured him thus far.

Ǫxarfjǫrðr (Oxarfjord), fjord in north Iceland: **3**, Brodd-Helgi and Halla's son Lyting fostered there with Thorgils Skin.

Øxna-Þórir (Thorir 'of the Oxen'): **1**, father of Asvald, the father of Olvir the White, the father of Thorstein the White, the grandfather of Brodd-Helgi.

THE SAGA OF PEOPLE OF WEAPON'S FJORD :
SELECT BUBLIOGRAPHY

Editions:

Ásmundarson, Valdimar, ed., *Vápnfirðinga saga*. Reykjavík: Kostnaðarmaður: Sigurður Kristjánsson, 1898.

Halldórsson, Bragi et al., eds., *Íslendinga sögur*. Reykjavík: Svart á hvítu, 1987, pp. 1987–2007.

Jakobsen, Jakob, ed., *Vápnfirðinga saga*. In *Austfirðinga sǫgur*, Samfund til udgivelse af gammel nordisk litteratur 29. Copenhagen: S. L. Møller, 1902–1903, pp. 21–72.

Jóhannesson, Jón, ed., *Vápnfirðinga saga*. In *Austfirðinga sögur*, Íslenzk fornrit XI. Reykjavík: Hið íslenzka fornritafélag, 1950, pp. 23–65.

Þórðarson, Gunnlaugur, ed., *Vápnfirðinga saga*, Nordiske Oldskrifter 5. Copenhagen: Berling, 1848, pp. 1–31.

Translations:

Boucher, Alan, transl., *The Tale of Thorstein Rod-Stroke*. In *Tales from the Eastfirths*. Reykjavík: Iceland Review, 1981, pp. 31–59.

Jones, Gwyn, transl., *Erik the Red and Other Icelandic Sagas*. London: Oxford University Press, 1961, repr. 1966, pp. 39–77.

Magnusson, Magnus and Hermann Pálsson, transl., *Njal's Saga*. London: Penguin Books, 1960.

Sverdlov, Ilya, transl., in Джесси Л. Байок. *Исландия эпохи викингов*. Corpus Books, Moscow, 2012.

Tucker, John, transl., *The Saga of the People of Vopnafjord*. In Viðar Hreinsson et al., eds. *The Complete Sagas of Icelanders*. Reykjavík: Leifur Eiríksson, 1997, pp. 313–34.

Secondary Literature:

Baldursdóttir, Sigríður, "Hugmyndaheimur Vopnfirðinga sögu: byggingarlag sagna frá Austfjörðum." *Gripla* 13, 2002, pp. 61–105.

Benediktsson, Jakob, "Vápnfirðinga saga." In *Kulturhistorisk Leksikon for Nordisk Middelalder fra Vikingetid til Reformationstid*, 2nd ed., Viborg: Rosenkilde og Bagge. Vol. 19, 1982. cols. 528–29.

Benediktsson, Jakob, *Landnámabók*, Íslenzk fornrit I. Reykjavík: Hið íslenzka fornritafélag, 1986.

Berger, Alan, "Lawyers in the Old Icelandic Family Sagas: Heroes, Villains, and Authors." *Saga-Book* 20, 1978–1979, pp. 70–79.

Binns, Alan, "The Story of Þorsteinn Uxafóts." *Saga-Book* 14, 1953–1957, pp. 36–60.

Byock, Jesse L., "Social Memory and the Sagas: The Case of *Egils saga*." *Scandinavian Studies* 76/3, 2004, pp. 299–316

Byock, Jesse L., *Viking Age Iceland*. London and New York: Penguin Books, 2001, Chapter 13, "Friendship, Blood Feud, and Power. The Saga of the People of Weapon's Fjord," pp. 233–51.

Byock, Jesse L., "Choices of Honor: Telling Saga Feud, *Tháttr*, and the Fundamental Oral Progression." *Oral Tradition* 10/1, 1995, pp. 166–80.

Byock, Jesse L., *Feud in the Icelandic Saga*. Berkeley and Los Angeles: University of California Press, 1982.

Byock, Jesse and Randall Gordon, eds., *The Tale of Thorstein Staff-Struck (Þorsteins þáttr stangarhǫggs): A New English Translation with Old Norse Text, Vocabulary and Notes*. Pacific Palisades, California: Jules William Press, 2022.

Cook, Robert, "Vápnfirðinga saga (The Saga of the People of Vápnafjǫrðr)." In *Medieval Scandinavia: An Encyclopedia*, ed. Paul Pulsiano and Kristen Wolf. New York: Garland Publishing, 1993, pp. 687–88.

Egilsdóttir, Ásdís, "Þættir: Einkenni og staða innan íslenskra miðaldabókmennta." Dissertation, University of Iceland, 1982.

Einarsdóttir, Ólafía, *Studier i kronologisk metode i tidlig islandsk historieskrivning*, Bibliotheca Historica Lundensis 13. Stockholm: Natur och kultur, 1964, pp. 293–326.

Fentress, James and Chris Wickham, *Social Memory*. Oxford: Blackwell Publishers, 1992.

Grágás. 1852. Ed. Vilhjálmur Finsen. Vol. I a-b *Grágás: Islændernes Lovbog i Fristatens Tid, udgivet efter det kongelige Bibliotheks Haandskrift*. Copenhagen: Det nordiske Literatur Samfund. *Grágás*.

Grágás. 1992. *Grágás. Lagasafn íslenska þjóðveldisins*. Ed. Gunnar Karlsson, Kristján Sveinsson, Mǫrður Árnason. 1992. Reykjavík: Mál og menning. For a partial translation in English: *Grágás*. 1980.

Harris, Joseph C., "Genre and Narrative Structure in Some Íslendinga Þættir." *Scandinavian Studies* Vol. 44, 1972, pp. 1–27.

Helgason, Jón, "Paris í Troja, Þorsteinn på Borg och Brodd-Helgi på Hof." In *Nordiska studier i filologi och lingvistik. Festskrift tillägnad Gösta Holm på 60-årsdagen den 8 juli 1976*; ed. Lars Svensson et al. Lund: Studentlitteratur, 1976, pp. 192–94.

Helgason, Jón, "Syv sagablade (AM 162 C fol, bl. 1–7)." *Opuscula* 5, Bibliotheca Arnamagnæana 31. Copenhagen: Munksgaard, 1975, pp. 1–97.

Heller, Rolf, "Droplaugarsona saga—Vápnfirðinga saga—Laxdæla saga." *Arkiv för nordisk filologi*, 78, 1963, pp. 140–69.

Heller, Rolf, "Studien zu Aufbau und Stil der Vápnfirðinga saga." *Arkiv för nordisk filologi* 78, 1963, pp. 170–89.

Heller, Rolf, "Über einige Anzeichen einer literarischen Beziehung zwischen der Knytlinga saga und der Vápnfirðinga saga." *Beiträge zur Geschichte der deutschen Sprache und Literatur* 90, 1968, pp. 300–304.

Jónsson, Guðni, *Annálar og Nafnaskrá*. Reykjavík: Íslendingasagnaútgáfan, 1948.

Kähler, G. and Dreher, M., "Vápnfirðinga saga." In *Kindlers Neues Literatur Lexikon*, ed. Rudolf Radler. Munich: Kindler. Vol. 19, 1992, pp. 719–20.

Kristjánsson, Jónas, "Íslendingadrápa and Oral Tradition." *Gripla* 1, 1975, pp. 76–91

Kristjánsson, Jónas, "Annálar og Íslendingasögur." *Gripla* 4, 1980, pp. 295–319.

Laws of Early Iceland: Grágás I. Trans. Andrew Dennis, Peter Foote and Richard Perkins. University of Manitoba Icelandic Studies 3. Winnipeg: University of Manitoba Press, 1980.

Nordal, Sigurður, ed., *Flateyjarbók*, 4 vols. Reykjavík: Flateyjarútgáfan, 1944–1945.

Ólason, Vésteinn, "Íslendingasögur." In *Medieval Scandinavia: An Encyclopedia*, ed. Paul Pulsiano and Kirsten Wolf. New York: Garland Publishing, 1993, pp. 333–36.

Ólason, Vésteinn, "Íslendingaþættir." *Tímarit Máls og menningar* 46/1, 1985, pp. 60–73.

Österberg, Eva, "Strategies of Silence: Milieu and Mentality in the Icelandic Sagas." In *Mentalities and Other Realities: Essays in Medieval and Early Modern Scandinavian History*, Lund Studies in International History 28. Lund: Lund University Press, 1991, pp. 9–30.

Schach, Paul, "Vápnfirðinga saga." In *Dictionary of the Middle Ages*, ed. Joseph Strayer et al. New York: Charles Scribner's Sons. Vol. 12, 1989, pp. 358–59.

Sigfússon, Björn, ed., *Ljósvetninga Saga*, Íslenzk fornrit X. Reykjavík: Hið íslenzka fornritafélag, 1940.

Sigfússon, Björn, "Full goðorð og forn og heimildir frá 12. öld." *Saga* 3, 1960–1963, pp. 48–75.

Simek, Rudolf and Hermann Pálsson, "Vápnfirðinga saga." In *Leksikon der Altnordischen Literatur*. Stuttgart: Kröner, 1987, pp. 378–79.

Stefánsson, Halldór, "Vopnafjörðr." In *Árbók 1968*. Reykjavík: Ferðafélag Íslands, 1968.

Sveitir og Jarðir í Múlaþingi, 1. bindi, Búnaðarsamband Austurlands, 1974.

Vigfússon, Guðbrandur, "Um nokkrar íslendingasögur." *Ný félagsrit* XXI. Kaupmannahöfn, 1861, pp. 118–27.

Vigfússon, Guðbrandur, "Um tímatal í Íslendinga sögum í fornöld." In *Safn til sögu Íslands og íslenzkra bókmenta að fornu og nýju*, Vol 1. Copenhagen: Hið Íslenzka bókmentafélag, 1856.

Vigfússon, Sigurður, "Ransókn í Austfirðingafjórðungi 1890." *Árbók Hins íslenzka fornleifafélags 1893*, pp. 28–60.

Walter, Ernst, "Studien zur Vápnfirðinga saga." *Saga: Untersuchungen zur Nordischen Literatur- und Sprachgeschichte* 1, ed. Walter Baetke. Halle: Niemeyer, 1956.

Þorsteinsson, Björn, *Íslenzka Þjóðveldið*. Reykjavík: Heimskringla, 1953.

FURTHER SUGGESTED READINGS

THE VIKING LANGUAGE SERIES

Modern introductions to Old Norse language, runes, and Icelandic sagas, with viking history and literature

Viking Language 1: Learn Old Norse, Runes and Icelandic Sagas (2nd Edition) is a new introduction to Old Norse, Icelandic sagas, and runes. Requires no previous language knowledge. Everything from beginner to advanced in one book: graded lessons, vocabulary, grammar exercises, pronunciation, and extensive maps. Includes sections on Viking history, literature, and myth. Innovative word-frequency method greatly speeds learning. Modern Icelandic has changed little from Old Norse and students are well on the way to mastering Modern Icelandic. **Free Answer Key** to the exercises in *Viking Language 1* on our website www.oldnorse.org

Viking Language 2: The Old Norse Reader is a treasure trove of Scandinavian lore. It offers a wide variety of Old Norse sources and runes and contains a large vocabulary, chapters on eddic and skaldic poetry, and a full reference grammar. (The latter, invaluable for learning to read sagas.) The reader also includes myths, legends, and runic inscriptions about Scandinavian gods, vikings, monster-slayers, dwarves, giants, warrior kings, and valkyries.

PRONOUNCIATION ALBUMS
for *Viking Language 1*

Two MP3 Albums, **Audio Lessons 1-8 and Audio Lessons 9-15,** teach the pronunciation of saga passages and runes in *Viking Language 1*. The pronunciation is a slightly archaic modern Icelandic as used in the saga and language courses at the University of Iceland. Both albums are available for download and purchase on our website www.oldnorse.org and on Amazon and iTunes.

For more information visit our website www.oldnorse.org

FURTHER MATERIALS FOR LEARNING OLD NORSE

Old Norse–Old Icelandic: Concise Introduction to the Language of the Sagas answers the need for a modern "primer" to teach the language of the sagas. The beginner quickly starts reading original passages from Icelandic sagas, myths, and sources about the Viking Age. Designed for quick learning on one's own or in class, the lessons supply all necessary grammar, exercises, and vocabulary.

Supplementary Exercises for Old Norse – Old Icelandic is a highly useful book of exercises that adds to the exercises in *Old Norse-Old Icelandic: Concise Introduction to the Language of the Sagas*. It provides additional grammar and vocabulary activities. Together, these two books make the sagas accessible for anyone learning Old Norse.

AUCH IN DEUTSCH ERHÄLTLICH
(*Viking Language 1* in German)

Altnordisch 1: Die Sprache der Wikinger, Runen und isländischen Sagas gliedert sich in fünfzehn inhaltlich aufeinander aufbauende Lektionen bestehend aus altnordischen Textpassagen, Runen, Grammatikbaukästen, Übungen, Karten. Das Buch enthält ein vollständiges Wörterverzeichnis, eine Kurzgrammatik sowie Hinweise zur (rekonstruierten) Aussprache. Available in bookstores and on amazon.de.

Jules Williams Press books are available on Amazon and for booksellers on Ingram ipage. www.oldnorse.org

THE ICELANDIC SAGA SERIES
New English dual-language translations with the original Old Norse text, vocabulary, introductions, maps, and notes

The Tale of Thorstein Staff Struck (Þorsteins þáttr stangarhǫggs) is a short saga set in Iceland's East Fjords during the 10ᵗʰ-century Viking Age. Thorstein, a peaceful young man, is forced to live with the humiliating nickname "staff struck." Even Thorstein's father, an old Viking, looks down on his son as a coward. But Thorstein is no coward. Waiting for the right moment to take revenge, Thorstein reclaims his good name in a way that brings honor both to him and his chieftain.

Saga of the People of Weapon's Fjord (Vápnfirðinga saga) is a classic Icelandic saga of feuding chieftains struggling for power and survival. Set during the Viking Age in Iceland's East Fjords, the saga recounts how a rich Norwegian merchant stirs the greed of the local Icelanders. Sons avenge fathers, while wives and mothers demand honor for their families. This new edition opens for the modern reader a lost world in the far North Atlantic.

COMING SOON

Egil's Bones: Icelandic Sagas, Blood Feud, and Viking Archaeology by Jesse Byock explores Viking Age Iceland: its origins, sagas, heroes, society, and archaeology. The book provides a comprehensive picture of an unusual North Atlantic community steeped in the lore of the past. You will explore the background of legendary heroes such as Sigurd the dragon slayer, whose saga influenced J.R.R. Tolkien and Richard Wagner. So also, consider the archaeological bones of the Viking warrior poet, Egil Skalla-Grimsson. Edited by Davide Zori, Björn Þráinn Þórðarson, and Ilya Sverdlov.

ADDITIONAL RESOURCES

Viking Age Iceland combines anthropology, archaeology, and history. It offers crucial insights into the Icelandic sagas and the inner workings of a feuding society. Unusual for Western Europe, Iceland had no king, no foreign policy, and no defense forces and shows intriguing proto-democratic tendencies. It should have been a utopia, yet its sagas are dominated by blood feud, killings, and the search for peace. In exploring the processes of conflict and peace-making this study has broad implications for the international study of feud and conflict.

Feud in the Icelandic Saga explores conflicts at the core of Iceland's sagas. Jesse Byock shows how the dominant concern of medieval society was the channeling of violence into accepted patterns of feud and the regulation of conflict. The sometimes conflicting demands of blood feud and honor are explored. This wide-ranging study also considers the narrative structure and oral background of the sagas and the role of these stories in a Viking heritage society in the far North Atlantic.